Tito Schipa

Tito Schipa

A biography by Tito Schipa, Jr.

with a critical appreciation by
Franco Serpa

translated by
Brian Williams
edited and revised by Samuel Chase with notes by Thomas G. Kaufman
chronology updated by
Thomas G. Kaufman

discography by
William Shaman *with* William R. Moran *and* Alan Kelly
compact disc prepared by
William Shaman *and* Peter Adamson

GREAT VOICES
3

BASKERVILLE
PUBLISHERS, INC.

Baskerville Publishers, Inc.
7616 LBJ Freeway, Suite 510, Dallas, TX 75251-1008

Library of Congress Cataloging-in-Publication Data

Schipa, Tito, Jr., 1946-
  [Tito Schipa. English]
    Tito Schipa : a biography / by Tito Schipa, Jr. ; with a critical appreciation by
Franco Serpa ; translated by Brian Williams ; edited and revised by Samuel Chase
with notes by Thomas G. Kaufman ; discography by William Shaman with William
B. Moran and Alan Kelly ; compact disc prepared by William Shaman and Peter
Adamson.
      p. cm. + 1 sound disc (digital ; 4 3/4 in.). --(Great voices ; 3)
  Translated from Italian.
  Discography: p.
  Includes bibliographical references (p.) and indexes.
  ISBN 1-880909-48-0
    1. Schipa, Tito, 1889-1965, 2. Tenors (Singers)--Italy--Biography. I. Title.
II. Series.
ML420.S354S3513 1996 <Phon Case>
782.1'092--dc20
[B]
                                              96-43574
                                              MN

Manufactured in the United States of America
First Printing, 1996

Selections on CD

Tito Schipa, Tenor
Great Voices, Volume 3

Original issues follow matrix numbers or, in the case of nos. 3-5, Pathé master cylinder numbers (in brackets). All selections are *commercial* recordings except no. 17, which is taken from an NBC broadcast air-check. Corresponding discography numbers for each item are given in brackets at the far right.

1. *Manon*, Act III: Ah! dispar vision [Ah! fuyez, douce image] (Massenet)
   722aj   Gram 052421   Milan, 10 Nov 1913   [1]

2. *La bohème*, Act I: Che gelida manina (Puccini)
   731aj   Gram 052422   Milan, 14 Nov 1913   [2]

3. *Rigoletto*, Act I: Questa o quella (Verdi)
   [86568]   Pathé 10242   Milan, 1916   [26]

4. *Tosca*, Act III: E non giungono ... Trionfal di nuova speme (Puccini)
   w. GIUSEPPINA BALDASSARE-TEDESCHI
   [86565]   Pathé 12554   Milan, 1916   [23]

5. *Falstaff*, Act II: Dal labbro il canto estasiato (Verdi)
   [68384]   Pathé 54060   New York, 1921   [48]

6. *Mignon*, Act III: Ah! non credevi tu [Elle ne croyait pas] (Thomas)
   C-30079-3   Victor 6465   14 May 1924   [72]

7. *Il barbiere di Siviglia*, Act I: Se il mio nome saper (Rossini)
   B-28050-5   Victor 965   22 Sep 1923   [68]

8. *Rigoletto*, Act I: È il sol dell'anima (Verdi) w. AMELITA GALLI-CURCI
   B-30909-2   Victor 3034   17 Sep 1924   [84]

9. *La traviata*, Act III: Parigi, o cara (Verdi) w. AMELITA GALLI-CURCI
   BVE-30908-8   Victor 3054   7 Sep 1928   [83]

10. *Martha*, Act III: M'apparì [Ach, so fromm] (Flotow)
    CVE-33939-2   Victor 6570   24 Nov 1925   [93]

11. *Werther*, Act III: Pourquoi me réveiller? (Massenet)
    BVE-33945-3   Victor 1187   25 Nov 1925   [97]

12. "I Shall Return" (Cross-Schipa)
    BVE-42938-4   Victor 1479   13 Feb 1930   [124]

13. *L'elisir d'amore*, Act I: Adina, credimi (Donizetti)
    BVE-47430-2   Victor 1362   6 Sep 1928   [130]

14. *Lakmé*, Act I: Fantaisie aux divins mensonges (Delibes)
    BVE-28494-10   Victor 1187   25 Nov 1925   [71]

15. *Don Pasquale*, Act I: Prender moglie! ... Due parole ancor di volo (Donizetti)
    w. ERNESTO BADINI
    2M 869-2/870-2HMV C.2521/2522Milan, Oct 1932   [188]

16. *Il Pirro e Demetrio*: Rugiadose, odorose, violette graziose ["Le violette"]
    (Alessandro Scarlatti)
    0BA 2911-2   HMV DA 5362   Milan, 7 Jan 1939   [266]

17. *Don Giovanni*, K. 527, Act II: Il mio tesoro (Mozart)
    Metropolitan Opera broadcast, New York City, 20 Jan 1934   [308]

18. "'Na sera 'è maggio" (Cioffi-Pisano)
         Durium A1.10638   Milan, circa Oct 1955   [295]

19. "Mu! Mu!" (de Angelis-R. Bellini)
    0M 1281-2   HMV DA 1323   Milan, 14 Mar 1933   [199]

20. *L'amico Fritz*, Act II: Suzel buon dì ... Tutto tace ["Cherry Duet"](Mascagni)
    w. MAFALDA FAVERO
    2BA 1700-2/1701-2   HMV DB 3067   Milan, Jan 1937   [232-233]

Studio orchestra probably conducted by Carlo Sabajno (1-2), studio orchestra/ conductor unknown (3-5); studio orchestra/Rosario Bourdon (6, 8-14); Members of La Scala Orchestra/Carlo Sabajno (15); studio orchestra/Dino Olivieri (16); Metropolitan Opera House Orchestra/Tullio Serafin (17); Orchestra Napoletana della Canzone/Mino Campanio (18); La Scala Orchestra/Alberto Semprini (19); and La Scala Orchestra/ Giuseppe Antonicelli (20). Tito Schipa, guitar, and unknown pianist (7).

All selections sung in Italian except nos. 11 and 14 (French), 12 (English), and 18 (Neapolitan), and at score pitch except the *Bohème* (2), *Martha* (10), and *Werther* (11) arias, which were transposed down a half-step by the singer.

Compiled by William Shaman and Peter Adamson

Contents

I

Mardi Gras, 1964

Fancy-dress parties are no longer in vogue. But a certain penchant for the theater leads me to organize one for my high-school class-mates.

It costs a lot to rent costumes. I decide to draw on an exclusive supply, a hidden treasure which has held all the fascination of a mystery for me ever since early childhood.

Every time I passed in front of that closet, I'd slow down, and two out of three times I'd be unable to resist opening it. The odor that greeted me from within was always my own personal version of Proust's little madeleine. I know now that it always will be. A mixture of old greasepaint, the heavy balsamic scent of indio, stage-powder, indefinable but unmistakable, and well-worn velvet and leather.

My schoolfriends are greeted by a warm waft of this odor when I open up the old doors of the closet for them. Eighteen-year-old boys and girls, after standing for a moment open-mouthed, immediately begin selecting their own character and chattering happily among themselves.

Suddenly an elderly gentleman emerges from his study with an inquiring look on his face, seeming a little irritated, for he has been disturbed. His eyebrows are slightly raised, his expression is

1

somewhat stormy, the profile of his face is rather sharper than usual. The white hair, unfashionably long, seems to the young-sters to be a relic of the nineteenth century, which squares with other little things they know about him, including the fact that he is an opera singer.

A pretty girl has put on the costume of Edgardo: no one in school has ever mentioned to her the fact that Edgardo is a lead-ing character in *Lucia di Lammermoor*.

Those black boots reaching halfway up the thigh make her look like something mid-way between the seventeenth century and Carnaby Street. But no one is aware of this yet, for the sixties have only recently begun. The old gentleman's hair is strictly un-fashionable—inconceivable as a glimpse of things to come.

His frowning gaze, with a touch of thyroid about it, rests for a moment, taking in the overall effect of this female musketeer. The girl is a little embarrassed, because the gaze which is being fixed on her is not precisely a paternal one.

"Lovely girl," says the man in a light voice, coming more from the head than the throat, and suddenly he gives her a smile. He could hardly have chosen a more obvious thing to say, but some-how, no one was expecting it. She turns as red as a hot coal while he goes on smiling at her. The others exchange glances, amused.

And suddenly, for the first time in my life, I feel the weight of time bearing down on me. I don't have a past yet, but that smile overburdened with memories has communicated the sense of the past to me as a form of possession.

Some days later, we are at the airport, he and I. At the far end of the glass corridor that looks out at the runways, we are waiting for the departure call. It is my father who is leaving, and leaving on his own: I've come with him to see him off.

I don't remember a word of the conversation. I'm not even sure that he spoke at all. I only remember a moment when I was standing beside him, and from there I noticed his absorbed ex-pression, looking towards the horizon as if America, which was awaiting him, was already there before his eyes.

"Well: 'bye then." I seem to remember that was all the greet-ing between us. Then that gray-suited man, a little portly in his bearing, made a dignified exit through the last embarkation gate of his incredible life.

I was well aware that it might be the last time I saw him, but I couldn't bring myself to believe in this as a concrete fact. His comings and goings had never had much impact on me; I was so used to them.

And in any case, in those months of 1964, his arrivals or departures were beginning to provoke ambivalent and uncertain reactions in me, because my recurring dream had already begun. That dream was that my father, even before his departure, had already returned. And what's more: that even though he was still alive, my father had in fact returned *despite his death*.

I have this recurring dream: my father has come back.

II

The uniqueness of Tito Schipa

My work of research and reconstruction on what is meant to be just a first step towards complete documentation of the life and work of a unique artist has been gaining in rhythm and regularity over the years. I was driven by the increasing number of questions I should have put to him and never did—questions which were no different from those everyone would like to ask other great artists of the past. I had this particular artist within arm's reach until a few years previously, but it never entered my head to get him to sit down in the living-room and subject him to a final and comprehensive interview!

I know now that in that mind and head there was the key to a lost secret: a priceless secret similar to the one which vanished into nothing with the disappearance of the great contrapuntal tradition of the sixteenth and seventeenth centuries. This secret certainly consisted in a supreme elegance of phrasing, which was capable of rendering every passage, even the most difficult, an amazing parenthesis of "musical conversation" (as it has been called by the great Italian musicologist Giorgio Gualerzi). It also consisted in the superior elegance of a stage presence; of being at one and the same time inside and outside the character, as in a perfect Stanislavskian dream. It involved something of his ability to hypnotize, almost to stun, the audience with a non-sound, a pause, a silence, a gesture. But above all, this secret consisted in an unequalled mode of utterance, natural and spontaneous in every detail; even sublime, since those moments when a composer entrusts his message to such a diabolically difficult "string" are even more charged with expressive effect.

Two simple words: "always effortless." (Sandro Cappelletti). However, to say this about a tenor is rather like saying about a marathon runner that he is "never panting," or about a boxer "never a bruise." It's a mark of uniqueness.

Given that technique is the cornerstone of any art, everything else in Tito Schipa, however extraordinary and unique, comes from (and with) this miraculous power.

There is also a further motive for curiosity, and a not unimportant one. This man was an innovator at every level; an artist who went decidedly against the tide in the way things were done in his day—against the fashions of his métier. He was the sole initiator of an approach which was almost obligatory in any other art, but virtually unknown in his—a "critical interpretative distance" (Franco Serpa). And yet despite this he managed to break down any resistance, winning a place very rapidly as a star of the first order, as a real living legend, and accumulating from his youth onwards what few other great innovators succeed in building up in a whole lifetime. Moreover he won consensus from the public and from critics alike, from fanatical opera buffs and refined aesthetes, from musical experts and fans in the gallery. They were all united in a single judgment, and it certainly came not only from the heart of the opera-going public but also from the head. This blending together of head and heart in unreserved acclamation is the other mark of Tito Schipa's uniqueness.

Shadows of my ancestors

The greatest difficulty in reconstructing the life of Tito Schipa comes from the fact that although it is his own son who is writing about him, the generation gap is one which would normally exist between a grandfather and grandson. In fact, at the time of my birth my father was 57 (and my mother 22!). But my father's father too had been quite late in his decision to bring a musician into the world, since he only succeeded on the fourth attempt when he was 51. It follows that direct evidence has tended to wear thin—to the point, reached some years ago, when it was no longer possible to rely on anyone to say anything completely credible about the childhood and adolescence of Tito Schipa.

This habit of the Schipas not to bring sons into the world until they were well on in years, thus slowing down the generational rhythm, was already well-established. With only a few rare exceptions, every generational interval lasted more than fifty years. The result is that if we go back five generations, to the days of Paolino Schipa, we are already back in the *seventeenth* century!

Further back, in the misty years before that century (where the parish registers of Lecce fade out), the date when a certain Albanian family crossed the sea remains lost in obscurity. They may well have been fleeing from the Turks, and they settled in the extreme point of the "heel of the Italian boot," contributing to the foundation of the unique linguistic and cultural "archipelago" of the triangle formed by Calabria, Lucania and Puglia, where the languages of origin—Greek and Albanian—have remained almost intact right down to our own times.

For convenience, when some kind of a crude census was being taken, someone may have called the family "gli Schipetari," or "Albanians," and then, for even greater brevity, "gli Schipa." In this way, they had baptized the family with a quite remarkable name, literally, "the Eagles"—because Albania is called "Schiperia" in its mother tongue, or in other words, the "land of the eagles." Schipetari in fact means "sons of the eagles."

The surname remained quite restricted, I would even say definitely rare. It would seem that only two branches remain, both originating from Lecce, but mysteriously unrelated to each other—or at least both unaware of each other since before the seventeenth century, for unknown reasons.

The historian Michelangelo Schipa (Lecce 1854-Naples 1939) belonged to the branch not strictly related to our family: he was the author of a famous work on Masaniello, and an expert on the Bourbon kingdom. Carlo Schipa told me that Tito and Michelangelo knew very well that they were not related, but by common accord they decided to allow it to be believed that they were. Thus each contributed to the other's fame.

Carlo Schipa (1900—1988) was the last of the Schipa children to be born. He emigrated to America when he was very young, and became one of the most closely-attached relatives of the great singer, and his financial manager, especially in the "California period." The audio-cassette that I recorded with him in Hollywood in 1982 is one of those in which I have preserved the voices of the last witnesses to an era.

Similar interviews are available in the family archives with the live voice of Gianna Pederzini (his closest artistic collaborator), with Ennio Neri (one of the librettists of Schipa's operetta, *La Principessa Liana)*, with Michele Verderamo, the last descendant of a Lecce family who were very fond of him, with Caterina Boratto, the actress who was one of Schipa's great loves, and with Luisa Merli, the housekeeper who served him faithfully for more than thirty years. Naturally, there is also the long interview that Maestro Vincenzo Bellezza recorded live with Schipa on behalf of RAI, towards the end of the fifties.

In addition, there is the patiently assembled collection of press clippings which his first wife put together between 1920 and 1937, and the very detailed diary of the second Signora Schipa, who was my mother. There are also long conversations held in Lecce and elsewhere, but these are impossible to document. In addition, there is a brief series of my father's letter-copies, dating back to the "Spanish period" of 1915—1919, and naturally there is the patient work of some of my friends who for quite a long time now have turned themselves into moles in the periodical and newspaper libraries.

There is a book written by Renzo D'Andrea, which provides interesting documents on Schipa's relations with Lecce, but completely leaves out the most important—i.e. the international—part of his career. And there is yet more: for instance about fifteen articles ascribed (though not with certainty) to Schipa himself, published in a theater magazine of the early forties and later edited into a small volume called "Tito Schipa confesses." A distinctly vacuous self-portrait emerges from this, designed almost certainly to satisfy a superficial public, as the cinema (and musical-comedy) public is assumed to be. This was a portrait of a "tenor" in the worst sense of the word, and a poor service to an artist who never ceased to assert:

"Be warned! I am NOT a tenor! What I am is a man who sings in the tenor voice!"

Lecce—a historical note

Lecce is a place of enchantment. It is a triumph of delicate architecture like arabesques in foam; a city which seems to be made out of powder, so that a gust of wind might blow it away from one moment to the next. Lecce tufa, which differs radically from its poor relation of the same name in central Italy, is a genuinely priceless material with its golden color, its velvety consistency, as of plaster, and its unusual property of preserving and distributing the heat in the winter and coolness in the summer, and it has become the hallmark—the material and metaphysical substance—of the town. In molding it as if it were clay, the chiselers of Lecce, an ancient race of specialized craftsmen who in the golden days of the baroque were even summoned overseas to work, have made doorways and façades and rosettes out of it which seem as if they are not and could not be made out of stone!

All around, as far as the eye can see, under a cloudless blue sky lie arid and stony plains, drystone walls and endless olive groves. Every now and then comes a surprise: a tiny village with a handful of inhabitants, built in the image of the mother city, but on a miniature scale. And further away—a little too far away, in fact—there lies a coastline which at certain points can rival many others in Italy that are much better known.

It *is* a little too far away, that sea. In the opinion of many historians, the lack of harbor facilities has had a strong effect on Lecce and its relations with the outside world, helping to enclose it in that cocoon of isolation to which the city eventually became almost pathologically attached. A friend with a family pedigree from Lecce used to say to me frequently: "We want to be left alone."

He said it with a smile, but he wasn't joking.

The most obvious sign of this difference of destinies in peoples living so close together could be heard in the language. We are a thousand miles away from the friendly open sing-song of the natives of Bari (the ancient Peucetians), or the sharp cadences of the Foggians (formerly the Dauni). In Lecce, which in ancient times was the home of the Messapi and Iapigi, a dialect of peculiar finesse is spoken, a sort of gentler version of Sicilian, rendered highly aristocratic by a special grace of utterance and tone. The men are soft-spoken and reserved; the women sweetly shrill, and very feminine. Peculiarities not found in any other part of the South are the mysterious "muting" of the "e," the sensuous softening of the "z," and the "ddh" group which replaces the normal Italian double "l," a real abnormality of pronunciation, with a dental-liquid character. The dialect also shows surprising closeness to Latin, if we observe that "they are"—"*illi sunt*" in Latin, is pronounced "*iddhi suntu*" in Leccese.

This discussion is not a digression. When one seeks to understand why Tito Schipa's voice is recognizable at the sound of the first syllable, and why he manages to infuse his characters with that note of sublime and dream-like nobility, one cannot ignore the fact that the singer is a genuine and typical son of "*Lecce gentile e beddha*"—gentle, beautiful Lecce.

That's how the Leccese are, then—attached to their own solitude even to a pathological degree. As citizens of the town which was first christened the "Athens" and then the "Florence" of the South, in the elegance of their dialect the people of the Salento reflect an aristocracy of soul which makes them exaggeratedly wary of any kind of involvement. This is not an overstated portrait. Basically, we are here in the only corner of the South where the word "Mafia" (and its grim correlatives) has had almost no connotation for centuries. From the time of the Romans, greedy for outlets to the sea, and therefore not very interested in Lecce, then under the progressive waves of invasions from the North, and later still under the hypnotic blanket of the Spanish dominion (the most appreciated because of its comfortable idleness)—and right up to the Risorgimento, which was tolerated rather than genuinely desired—these people have striven more than others to remain in their own shell, and have adopted a dreamy introspection, similar to that found in Sicily, but without the island's "death-wish." They have remained contemplative, smiling and madly enamored of music, especially singing.

Like a red thread weaving its way through the whole of this

story while remaining miraculously not a part of it, there is a touch of the irrational, the Bacchic, once again expressed mainly in music.

The multicolored ribbons of the *tarantate* with their white dresses and the strange ritual of their musical exorcism, provide the final touch to a truly exceptional people. The archetype of music as the unleashing of the instincts, and at the same time their tamer and healer, survives here even today. Here, the Bacchic dancers still appear every July, drunk and lascivious, on the road to Galatina. This is no joke: Dionysus isn't dead in the Salento, nor in the Terra d'Otranto or the Terre Aride or the Terre del Rimorso, or in Lupia, Lipia, Luppia, Lupio, Lispia, Licio, Lictia, Licea, Licia, Lecce, or whatever name you choose out of the legions that have been tried. Dionysus is not dead in these parts; indeed his dancing frenzy is secretly adored and feared. Thanks to a timeless tradition, music unleashes it, and for millennia it has also been music which soothes and heals.

It was in 1888, and in the very poor quarter of Le Scalze, that Lecce witnessed the birth of the greatest of all its musical healers.

III

(1888–1902)

A nocturnal peal

It isn't all that easy to find out who Tito's parents were and what they did. In the testimony of those who knew them (but they were already well on in years, and not inclined to storytelling), Grandfather Luigi and Grandmother Antonietta Vallone are sometimes an unemployed workman and a weaver, sometimes a postman and a simple housewife and then again a member of the Alpine regiment and follower of Garibaldi and later a customs officer (in his case) and a well-known model of piety and frequenter of the church of the Carmine (in hers). Some would even have it that they were manure collectors for small-time local farmers, a trade that in those days was far from being despised. Our hero himself once remarked laconically that he was born "in a carpenter's workshop." There is no historical evidence for this. But there are, of course, distinguished historical precedents....

It seems likely that *all* these varied attributions have some truth in them, and that the couple did their best to bring up their growing family by various jobs, some of them perhaps at the same time as others. If this is so, then we can recognize an Italy which was not all that different from the present.

But let's turn to the memorable night, one of the last in the year 1888, and listen to the account thatTito Schipa himself gives of it:

If my mother and my brother Umberto are to be believed, it seems that my story should begin, no less, some time before my actual birth: when the time to give birth arrived, at the first sign of labor pains, the relations in my part of the world used to strike some notes on the bells of a local church, to invite people to pray that the birth would be a happy one. My brother Umberto was entrusted with this task, and he managed to wake up the sacristan of the Carmine, but not to drag him out of bed, and even less to get him to climb up the belltower for the prescribed tocsin. So what was to be done? If the birth took place without the ritual peal, who knew what monster might be born? So up went Umberto himself, a little boy who was afraid of the dark, into the belfry to grab hold with both hands of the bellrope, and to heave it down with all his strength: Clang! Clang!–it seemed like Holy Saturday, and the whole city woke with a jump. Villains pillaging the Church? The Sacristan of the Carmine suddenly gone out of his mind? No, less–much less, in fact. Just another Schipa coming into the world.

All this clearly contradicts the well-established story that his birth took place in the last days of 1888, and was kept hidden until January 2nd, 1889, in order to gain a year's postponement of military service. A secret birth certainly doesn't accord very well with a nocturnal peal of bells! In any case, all the fuss was for nothing; when it came to the examination for military service, young Schipa was in fact first sent back for further tests and then exempted.

Whatever the truth may be, in those first days of January 1889, the registry official confirmed the birth of the seventh citizen of Lecce to see the light in 1889: "In the house situated in Vico dei Penzini at number 6, at 6.00 a.m., was born Schipa Raffaele Attilio Amedeo, of the male sex, to Luigi and Vallone Isabella" (commonly called Antonietta, however). Of the name "Tito" there is no trace at this stage.

A little fellow but a great ear

In fact, surely *two* great ears, if we can trust the photo which shows him in his elementary school class, a little urchin among other urchins. Between these two impressive flaps, a round head, ruthlessly cropped, probably to defend it against lice. As for the voice, once again we have to put our faith in oral tradition, which adds the portrait of an infant constantly in tears (in fact yelling day and night, to the delight of the neighbors), to the many ritual legends concerning the adolescence of a genius. The reason for this can't have been his character, which even at that stage must have been positive and amiable as it was throughout his life. It is much more likely to be found in an ailment which he himself called "constipation," but which according to the family was a nasty form of chronic enteritis, very common in those days among children in southern Italy. It seems to have attacked him viciously, in alliance with an exceptional appetite that can only have worsened matters. It wasn't all that easy to save him, this wailing waif with the round head, and he had more than one relapse into the illness.

The legend divides into two acts: in the first, the dominant event is the visit of an old man, unknown in the town. He prophesied to the mother, stressed by the constant vigil and the pain:

"Your cross? What are you saying? This child is going to be your fortune!"

The second act opens with the hungry infant's escape from the house: "No more donkey-milk!" (This form of cure was fashionable at the time, it seems). It reaches its climax in an inn, where some customers, quite unaware of what was up, bartered a plate of beans and cod, and a glass of wine in exchange for a song—maybe because he was already acquiring a little local reputation.

> Enough said! I don't know how, since I was both hungry and ill, but I managed to find the breath to sing. I sang one of my favorite childhood songs: "*Quante stelle ci sono in cielo, tanti baci io ti darìa...*"

"*Pasuli*" (local for beans) and cod, with chronic enteritis! And wine, as well... The morning after, the fever was gone, the pains were gone, and as far as we know, he never had another twinge until the diabetes which overtook him in his fifties. Was it the beans, perhaps? Or maybe the song. From what he himself says, at the end of the story:

> Singing is a prescription that should be introduced into the medical book as a remedy for extreme cases!

13

Naturally, he was no good in school

I say naturally, because all the elect are, at least according to their biographers. But in this case, the confession does come from the man himself:

> I soon showed that I was not excessively given to study...

However, in those days in Lecce in particular music seems to have had an importance and an esteem which is reserved today for physical education. Just like today's athletic coach, the music master of those days could grant reprieve to chosen students from the punishments inflicted by his colleagues. At least this is the rosy situation which emerges from the author's own account. In our case the specific subject was choral singing and the maestro was called Giovanni Albani. This obscure teacher was to leave unforgettable traces in the memory of his "miraculous urchin."

During one of the first lessons, in which the whole class was singing "*Ve la dipinge*" from *La sonnambula*, Albani raised his eyebrows, nodded to the choir to stop singing, and in the accepted way said: "You, with the big head....come here a moment..."

He asked Raffaele to sing on his own, and his surprise was turned into astonishment. He was the first person to feel this astonishment at what he had just heard; a multitude would follow.

The immediate outcome of this episode did not reflect much credit on my father, and I'm not sure why he always insisted on telling it at every possible opportunity. It seems that Albani used him from that moment onwards to pick out the children who were tone-deaf during the lessons. This role of *gauleiter* of the growlers hardly seems to be a very honorable one.

What was more encouraging was that Albani decided immediately to give him free private singing lessons, and even more so, the fact that he was given the role of soloist during a ceremony in honor of the teaching staff.

The audience was completely quiet as he sang his solo, and when he was done there was overwhelming applause from the three hundred other members of the choir, the authorities, and the public; this marked the first time young Raffaele Schipa attracted public notice. This is his own account, which begins with a transparent subterfuge concerning his age:

> It was July 1900, so I was not even ten years old, and it was the first time that I saw my name mentioned in the local papers–the excitement was unbearable! The *Provincia di Lecce* wrote: "A solo sung by the pupil Raffaele Schipa caught the attention of everyone more than anything else: a most attractive voice, true in tone, which showed his excellent approach to singing and which it will be desirable to cultivate in the future…"

We should add that the "Gazzetta delle Puglie" shows that he even got the date wrong, and quite notably so: the day of the ceremony had in fact been July 29th of the previous year. The atmosphere was spoiled by a minor row between the authorities and the local press. A final tribute to King Umberto, who had just been assassinated, had been added—without consultation—to the teachers' ceremony and the students' prize-giving. The press considered this an inappropriate mixture, which showed too much haste and a disrespect for high matters of state. This incident affecting his first public appearance in Lecce was oddly similar to the one which, by a stroke of irony, affected his last.

[The last appearance was that of January 1966, when the coffin, recently brought back from New York, lay in state in the church of Santa Croce so that his beloved city could say its last farewells. Because of his divorce, which had taken place in 1947, there were already problems about allowing the coffin to enter the church. Then the officiant, when he discovered that among the singers who had come from Bari to accompany the rite actually included women, tried to stop them from singing, making use of a rule which had applied before the Vatican Council. The choirmaster, hoping to get away with a fait accompli, *feigned obedience, but then called in the chorus to sing just the same. And the priest cut short the funeral service halfway through!]*

Anyway, on this great day of his childhood, the following are the exact words of the first song ever sung by Schipa on an official occasion: *"Dalla tomba mentre tace/ l'urlo querulo del vento/ grazie, grazie grideranno/ non è spento nostro amor."*

The music, naturally, was by Giovanni Albani. The following are the exact words of the first review he ever received from a critic, in the "Gazzetta": "...(there was) a solo by the youngster, Schipa, who proved to be a delightful surprise to everyone, because he has a wonderful tenor voice, and we would call the attention of those whose duty it is to do so, to encourage this young man, by offering him a place in a Musical Conservatory."

Two more years would pass before someone would take up this recommendation—at this stage "the youngster Schipa" was completely unknown to him. Meanwhile the youngster had earned himself a new suit, and this was presented to him by Countess Zecca. Even today we still hear mention of this family and of others much given to both generous support and sharp criticism of the arts in the city. They are patrons and protectors, whose role was soon to become decisive in helping a unique career to begin; however, we can hardly blame them for not having been in the right place at the right time to recognize the nascent genius. This was due to the fact that the genius himself had spent his free time up to that point creating havoc around the dusty streets of Lecce like all his schoolmates, probably barelegged and battling with countless hosts of flies. These are images of the poorest quarters of the Salento which I remember myself from the time of my first visits to the south in my early childhood. Imagine what it must have been like a hundred years ago!

However, when the golden light on the tufa stone fell at sunset on the town, finally free for a moment from the stifling hot wind, the sweat and the insects, a local band might parade past. This was the moment for Raffaele's eyes to light up, and for him to dash with all the strength his slender legs could muster toward the source of the sound. From that moment onwards, even if the world were falling apart, he would have followed the players anywhere, then stopped hesitantly in the corner of a piazza when the colored festoons of a bandstand were set up in the evening. In the cool calm of the evening, the concert was a perfect event.

[It may be that this was the moment when, following the acrobatic performance of a solo clarinet, he began to formulate in his listening mind the miracle which would later characterize his vocal offerings. These were times when a brilliant player on the clarinet enjoyed the same prestige as a top football player today. Sought-after, disputed-over among provincial capitals and various groups, the soloists of the band reached high levels of popu-

larity and payment, and they were welcomed with wild enthusiasm, only inferior to the champions of song themselves. Following the soundwaves from some local star or other, little Raffaele must have begun to note the exclusive excitement of perfect breath-control and dynamic variation, imperceptible but all-conditioning, and an attack that was rapier-sharp in lightness and intonation.]

What could the Zeccas, the Bernadinis, the D'Elìas, the Blasis imagine of all this? They were families devoted to patronage, but they certainly had no talent scouts infiltrating the bands of urchins, least of all those from the Scalze, among the poorest areas of the city. It was more the friends of the family, ordinary people, small artisans who realized that something was beginning. Some of them played a part by offering little Raffaele possibilities of work, which were by no means unwelcome to his family.

This is what we hear from the goldsmith Galasso, or the cardboard makers Guacci and Faraone, who were willing to take the boy on in their workshop. Papier-mâché together with baroque design, figs preserved with almonds, the wild tarantula dance (tarantella) and the brass bands, all are specialties of the Salento. Even though it was only a matter of making Christmas cribs, the little boy soon began to take an interest in design and representation.

Destiny never errs.

At ten, Raffaele had already finished his regular schooling. But at work as at school, he was an incorrigible truant, sometimes even wandering off from a visit to a neighboring village where he was supposed to be selling saints and shepherds.

His escapes always had one sole and constant objective: that of hurrying off to the singing rehearsals which took place in the city, especially at the Teatro Politeama. Regularly found out and punished, he would promise not to do it again, but in the tunes he could whistle to perfection, the number of lines he had memorized was growing daily.

Nor did he ignore the popular repertoire. And here too there was a glimpse of the future. Nicola Maldacea was a genial composer of pretty mediocre music, the *macchiette* which were much in fashion in those days. And these little vignettes were perfectly assimilated by the little monster with the astonishing musical memory. With the help of a *terzina*, a small guitar suited to his small hands, which his brother Umberto had lent him, he gave his first performances of music to small audiences of urchins in intervals between their games. The performances at the school concerts were Raffaele's first formal stage appearances, but since they had taken place before a sincere and demanding public, they were Tito Schipa's first personal successes.

Tito? Yes, because "Titu" is the name by which Raffaele was known to his friends and relations. Here as elsewhere in Italy, a nickname was often more suited to the image of its bearer, and better described him, than his baptismal name. In this instance it conveyed the impression of a "little chap" because that is what "titu" means in the Salentine dialect. Incidentally, it has nothing to do with the legendary bishop of Crete of the same name, canonized by the Church. However, the Church, specifically the Roman Catholic Church, is about to enter the story quite dramatically, and by way of a bishop, no less.

A gift of God

That a fine voice was indeed such a gift was the profound conviction of Don Gennaro Trama, a canon of the cathedral of Naples and fiscal supervisor of the Archidiocesan Curia. He was convinced of this issue to the point of dogma, and advocated it in such terms that there was some doubt as to whether his love of singing might not outstrip his love of the Lord. He soon proved that his two beliefs were in harmony and able to operate jointly on the grand scale, but in the meantime he was about to take the leading role in a case of ecclesiastical administration that can be described as unique, rather than just rare. This is the story.

The episcopal see of Lecce had been vacant since September 17th, 1901, when Monsignor Evangelista Di Milia had died. On December 17th "La Libertà," a Naples Catholic newspaper, published a short notice announcing the appointment of its fellow-Neapolitan, Gennaro Trama, to the post. There was nothing strange about this, except for the fact that in the recent Consistory held in Rome, the monsignor from Naples had already been nominated Bishop of Cafarnao! And in fact, on 20 December, Trama had an audience with Leo XIII, and it was as Bishop of Cafarnao that the

"Osservatore Romano" mentioned him to its readers. The next day, "La Libertà" faithfully copied the news and the title, but then twenty-four hours later, without explanation, reiterated the statement that Trama had in fact been appointed to Lecce. The stubbornness of the Neapolitan newspaper in persisting in this ambiguity seems odd. And even more odd is the fact that no correction came from the Holy See.

Things took on an even more peculiar flavor when, on December 22nd, in the Basilica of San Lorenzo in Damaso in Rome, Gennaro Trama was, unexpectedly, consecrated Bishop as "Episcopus Ecclesiae Lycien." Or in other words, Lecce.

The "mischief" of Modernism was in the air at the time, and the eternal thorny question of divorce, along with the specific issue of royal patronage of appointments to bishoprics. All this contributed to creating tensions with the Italian state, and every move was made with paralyzing caution. So this lightning change of mind by the Vatican over which see should be attributed to Mgr. Trama made it seem as if the Neapolitan journal, apparently so sure of itself, was managed by some band of prophetic spirits.

In fact, the matter was easily explained, but such a crack in ecclesiastical solidarity and its public relations management is, to say the least, surprising.

The reason for this disorderly debut of Trama in his pastorate in Lecce can be found in the dispute between the state and the church over episcopal appointments. The see of Lecce had been since 1876 one of the numerous ones (97 in all) which were subject to the right of approval and nomination on the part of the secular authorities. When the left came to power, the state made good use of this lever. The decision of the Vatican to appoint Trama to Lecce was genuine and dated from November 1901, but it had been observed that the time for completing the nomination was very short indeed, since the Consistory had been fixed for December 16th. Consequently, if they wished to get things done in time, it was necessary at all costs to avoid the long delays and obstructionism of the process of royal approval, so the bishop should be assigned nominally to a see which did not need ratification from the government: a "titular" see, in fact, as it was called. Cafarnao was chosen, but it was tacitly understood that "Cafarnao" really stood for Lecce. The conspiracy of silence on this issue had, however, to some extent been broken, and this had put "La Libertà" in a position to publish its clairvoyant scoop!

Logical explanations were pushed aside, however, and there was a prevailing notion that Trama had been "assigned" to Lecce before the Pope had decided to send him there. And since without Gennaro Trama, there might well have been no Tito Schipa, the aura of legend and predestination around this strange couple later acquired a certain reality, even for those who were well-informed.

On May 11th, 1902, Gennaro Trama arrived by train in Lecce, and immediately began an intense pastoral ministry, accompanied by official letters, visits and decrees. His first letter to the diocese opened with a reminder of the founder of the first Christian community in that area of Southern Italy, and by coincidence it happened to be "Titus Justus, the distinguished disciple of St. Paul." But the opera-lover was lurking, even then, in the background. A little further on, referring to the rationalist tendencies which were always threatening, he stated:

"In the created order there are secret movements, *melodious harmonies*, which the *ear* of human intelligence cannot perceive."

Also in defense of this soul which he saw as being endowed with sensitive ears, he immediately devoted his energies to the strenuous defense of the values of Gregorian chant, and this was one way of guaranteeing that there would always be music in the air.

Here, then, was a bishop with a thirst for music moving with a holy zeal for organization from one village of the province to another, while at exactly the same time a fourteen-year-old with a splendid—and as yet unbroken—voice also began moving around, from church to church in the surrounding area of Lecce. He had been constantly encouraged by Maestro Giuseppe D'Elìa to get as much practice as possible in sacred music. The meeting between the two star players in this legend was thus inevitable.

> While I was singing in a church in Lecce, Bishop Gennaro Trama heard me, and the next day he wrote to my parents asking them to bring me to the diocesan offices because he wanted to talk to them about me. He said that he had heard me sing and had appreciated my voice; he added that it would be a shame to waste it, by going on singing in churches without any kind of proper study, and thus lose that "gift which the good Lord had bestowed on me." If my

parents would allow it, he wanted to have me enter the Seminary, entirely at his expense, for he knew that my parents couldn't afford a penny.

There is one phrase in this passage of reminiscence which shows that in the meeting with Trama there was a *special form* of fortune. It appears here for the first time, and will crop up again and again, always at just the right moment. I refer to the words "it would be a shame to waste it." Such a voice, others had confined themselves to discovering and putting to immediate use (one could say exploiting) without any due care and attention. This awareness, that the study of singing consisted above all in *safeguarding* the voice, took root in Tito thanks to the recommendation of an enlightened prelate, and it was to grow stronger as a result of at least two other meetings. Eventually it would become established in the consciousness of the young prodigy, and would bear magnificent fruit many years later.

Tito's parents accepted, according to their own testimony, with great delight. His mother, in fact, perceived the will of God in the offer to Tito. And this contrasts somewhat with the picture that Tito paints elsewhere of her, as a woman who instinctively crossed herself every time the word "artist" was mentioned.

However, what is true beyond doubt in this memoir is above all that "they couldn't afford to spend a penny," and that as a result of Trama's proposal, they were able to remove at least one hungry mouth from their household.

Now I must duly report young Raffaele Schipa's entry into seminary, which everyone agrees took place, although there is not a shred of documentary evidence except for one single photograph which shows him in a seminarian's cassock, his face unbelievably pious, kneeling at the feet of a priest.

The novice found the excellent Maestro Albani in the seminary as well, along with a number of other well-disposed teachers and new friends. He also found other doors which were a lot harder to open than those of the papier-mâché workshop.

However, nothing seemed able to stop him from making, at all hours of the day and the evening, those escapes to the enchanted world of the stage. While the word began to circulate in the town more and more frequently: "Did you hear that boy's voice in the big service?," he would be saying over and over again to his dormitory-mates, "This new *Tosca* by Puccini! It's fantastic! But mind—don't let on that I told you!"

But his escapades were always found out, and cost him endless severe reprimands from his teachers, to his mother's despair. This didn't mean that he wasn't asked to sing on every possible occasion, and he won enthusiastic praise, sometimes even a few minutes after he'd been given a scolding. It reached the point at the end of a particularly brilliant performance on Christmas Eve, that he was awarded a prize dinner in which the first course was *maccheroni al burro!*

> I looked at it amazed, and didn't dare to begin; then I decided to ask, hesitantly:
> – Butter? On Christmas Eve?
> And Monsignor, smiling, said: Just eat, and be quiet!

In the not-too-distant future, there would be quite astonishing rewards, but this one, given the time and the place, was tantamount to an Oscar.

And in this way, the embryonic divo was gradually shaped in Lecce, and he perceived perfectly that those who seemed to be his patrons were in fact his slaves—slaves, that is, of the beauty that took mysterious form each time he opened his mouth to sing, without his even knowing how. However, he was well aware of his own power, especially because he had not yet found anyone in his path who was capable of inducing real respect and obedience from him.

He was to encounter such a person before long, but in the meantime he accepted little roles from visiting companies, getting himself a place in the children's chorus in *Carmen* (always the shortest in the row) or playing the famous, and very brief, role of the pestilent child who appears in the second act of *La Bohème* ("*Vo' la tromba, il cavallin...*"). It seemed to become a real little romanza when he sang it, so much so that it even provoked an audible murmur of appreciation from the public.

The pay was ten soldi per performance, but now many other, greater satisfactions there were! He wanted his brother to have a free seat in the theater. The manager objected. So he wouldn't sing. The chorusmaster intervened, under threat of losing the pillar of his children's section, and lo and behold, there was the three-foot-high divo, right under the nose of the ticket-seller, entering just as he wished and with whomever he wished, smirking with satisfaction.

[We will be reminded of this again, in the 1930s, when he put his own embargo on a visit to the United Kingdom in order to avoid having to subject his pet monkey, Toto, to quarantine. "No Toto? No Tito!" shouted the headlines of the English dailies. It was the same in Milan in 1949, when he rebelled against one of the first "updated" versions of an opera in the history of the art, and although the director had moved the period of "The Secret Marriage" forward by a few decades, the sixty-year-old Tito, in the role of Paolino, strode stubbornly onto the stage in his usual costume, that of the familiar "serving-man" of the Goldoni era.

"Imagine a servant worrying himself about fashion. Go and think about it, Mr. Director!"

The name of that "Mr. Director" was Giorgio Strehler, and it was probably the first and last time that he ever had to submit to anyone's dictates.]

However, this childhood development of a sense of absolute power was accompanied by a more unpredictable sensation, for we learn that the young artist began to ask himself: "Could it be that they love my voice more than me?"

This particular emotional insecurity was a leitmotif throughout his life, and very likely the secret of one of the most agonizing of all his interpretative chords...

IV

(1903–1908)

The Teacher

Squinzano is a little village just outside Lecce, famous for its wine. However, for the Schipas, this place was always synonymous with the Blasi family, who had been friends from Tito's earliest years, and were always ready with help and encouragement. The local chemist in Squinzano was a Blasi, Nicola by name, but known to his close friends as 'Cocco.' He was an amateur organist, and this led him to play a role in another of the basic steps on Tito's road to fame.

Bishop Trama had just dreamt up another scheme: he had decided that he wanted to hear the urchin-prodigy singing a "lamentation." God knows what hopes of Paradise he had managed to evoke from this combination of genre and interpretation: he had gone so far as to obtain a dispensation from the papal court, since such performances were strictly reserved to canons of the church. The day came for him to enjoy the results of his efforts, and it was Easter Day itself. Cocco Blasi was at the organ; Tito was standing very upright and proud at the balustrade of the organ loft, but given his tiny stature, he was inevitably invisible. Once again the great bishop had opened a door to Divine Providence, and Divine Providence was in the congregation that Sunday, bearing the name Alceste Gerunda.

About Gerunda, we know that the great Francesco Paolo Tosti

(1846-1916) in his voluntary exile in England often spoke of him with heartfelt nostalgia. And Tosti was not the type to indulge in maudlin sentimentality, despite the melancholy of his celebrated tunes. In the British court, where he had been made a baronet, he went around with a quite well-known practical joker, Mario Costa. It seems that their favorite trick was to make fun of the whole pompous environment by singing the famous songs in a Neapolitan dialect, very far from the original version, and stuffed with appalling obscenities; they relied, of course, on the fact that no one understood them. However, when he mentioned Gerunda, the singer and musicologist of Lecce, Tosti used to ask:

"Where is my dear old Alceste? What's he doing? No one has ever sung my songs the way he did!..."

We also know that Alceste belonged to the generation of 1847, and that he was a pupil of Mercadante, who also launched him on his singing career when Alceste wanted to confine himself to the piano. We know that he had a pair of moustaches which would have made even Francesco Crispi envious; that he taught in the state boarding school called the Palmieri, and then in the Vittorio Emanuele Girls' Academy. Finally he held the chair of music in the State Training College, also in Lecce. He opened a private school in his own house, and this was a real gathering place for the whole music-teaching world of the South. Finally, we know he died in 1917, and his last wish was to die listening to a voice singing.

On that Easter Day, Gerunda was there, under Cocco Blasi's organ loft, and the height of the balustrade in the choir certainly didn't mean that he didn't notice the little singer, whose voice must even then have shown that it was capable of overcoming any architectural barrier that happened to be in the way, with its natural timbre similar to that of an oboe.

[Among the episodes that old operagoers recount with an air of enchantment, almost as if they were unveiling an ancient mystery, is the story of the time that they decided—and they still talk about it in lowered tones, as if they wanted to recapture the rather daring sense of this long-ago decision—that they would move right up to the last row of seats in the auditorium of the Caracalla Baths in Rome, where the stage looks like a picture postcard.

—Let's hear what Schipa's little voice sounds like at this distance...

And then came the miracle: for that "little voice," soft and flowing like a band of silk, reached that back row, standing out cleanly above the chorus and the orchestra, and above all his colleagues, who were blissfully unaware of this "hi-fi" effect.]

In the Easter "Lamentation" at Lecce, we find the "special destiny" at work once again. In Alceste Gerunda, Tito not only found the ideal teacher, the maestro of all the maestri, but also the upholder of the golden rule already laid down by Bishop Trama: preservation, even before teaching.

Gerunda's first concern was to make sure that Tito never opened his mouth in public except under his tutelage, and that his dedication to his destiny should be complete, and even monastic. For this purpose he wanted him in his own private school. He convinced his parents and the bishop to give him carte blanche, and to let Tito give up the seminarian's cassock. This was a way of ensuring that the boy's vocal activities were entirely under his control, and that they were limited exclusively to voice training. Exercises, more exercises, and nothing but exercises—and woe betide him if he uttered a single note that was not strictly within the logic of the form; woe betide him if he allowed himself the voluptuous luxury of a phrase, an extemporaneous breath, an unguarded vowel. Tito remembered the nightmare of that threat every time his mind went back to his training under Gerunda:

– God help me if I made a mistake! Three years of vocal exercises, he would say... Then one day I slipped up....

Some of my friends begged me over and over again, so insistently that I ended up singing one single verse of "O sole mio," accompanying myself on the guitar. And I remained impervious to all demands for any more. But the next day, off I went at the usual time to the Maestro's house...he was waiting for me, as always, in his shirtsleeves, and with a pipe in his mouth...

– Where were you yesterday evening?
– At home.
– Doing what?
– What do you mean, doing what? I was sleeping..

The response was immediate: such a hard box on the ears that I felt as if I'd left half my face behind!

The seminary was left behind with few regrets. "*Puozzo fà 'o prèvete?*" (What would I be doing as a priest?) Tito would have asked himself in the words of a celebrated comic sketch of his favorite, Maldacea.

He spent five years in this way, years in which the student kept himself and helped his family by working as a trainee in a lawyer's office. But even here he never abandoned his musical vocation; he used to organize secret concerts with his boss's sister. The concerts featured the guitar, the clarinet and the mandolin, however; the voice was never to be heard. He had got the message. But he was allowed to play, and also to compose. Indeed, Gerunda, who showed a more and more inspired instinct, first set him in the way of musical creativity at the piano, by starting him off on the techniques of harmony and counterpoint. Tito was to call composition the "second passion of my life," and it was to bear its first fruits quite soon in the composition of a Mass, of strictly conventional character, which he was to carry with him everywhere he went in the world in the hope of having it performed. However, his creative genius would reveal itself later, in certain songs which were really worthy of the classical repertoire.

In the sixth year of his musical training, years that were as long and disciplined as those spent by the old contrapuntalists—and just as valuable—Gerunda prepared, finally, to "launch" the voice. He did so by insisting, with the maximum of caution, that he must only sing a pair of light pieces by Denza and, naturally, Tosti. However, something was wrong. Perhaps because it was too cramped by his long and severe training, like an engine which has been run in for too long, and too carefully, the vocal instrument of the young Schipa seemed to Gerunda's ears not to have enough "pull" on the emotional plane. Something was lacking. Motive was missing—not musical motif, but motivation. So the maestro invented an innocent little excuse to introduce into his lessons a subject that no one can actually teach: a sort of sentimental education. He thought he was just suggesting a passing experiment. But instead, he had opened a Pandora's box, which no one could even have imagined.

One day, Gerunda said to me: – You've never made love to a girl, have you?
– What, me? No! I replied.
– Well, what are you waiting for?

27

I didn't need telling twice. I latched on at once to one of my cousins whom I already fancied quite a lot, and who returned my affection enthusiastically.

And that's all. Not another word about this "cousin" in Tito Schipa's autobiography. It was just a bare mention, and yet it concerned one of the episodes which really altered his life, and which must have conditioned him, in the depths of his artistic and emotional existence. But there was at least one very good reason why he remained silent about it. For in the 1940's, when the brief autobiography was published, someone was still living in a certain convent who could not be allowed, for any reason in the world, to become involved in any matters of this world.

Emilia

This is a story that echoed for many years in the narrow streets of Lecce, passed down orally like a legend. After my father's death, I heard a number of different versions of it. Even in the family it isn't easy to get the main events straight. But what I lacked above all was the spectacular finale, without which the whole episode can't be weighed up in the full impact of its consequences. Some years later I managed to get a direct witness. Quite by chance, a friend enabled me to meet the only living brother of the heroine of the story. It was a strange and unlikely love story he told me.

When Tito mentioned a "cousin," he actually meant a cousin by adoption, a girl of his own age, the daughter of the first marriage of his uncle's wife. The family history is full of histories of second marriages with children from the first marriage still around. My great-grandmother had had two broods of children, the first bearing the name Colangelo and the second Schipa. However, these links were felt very intensely, so much so that Raffaele Colangelo, a half-cousin, was to be like a brother to Tito from the time of his infancy in the stuffy back-streets of Lecce right up to his last days amid the skyscrapers of New York, when Raffaele (by now called Ralph) was to be with him in his last hours.

Because of the heavy value bestowed on even the slightest family link, even if it were only nominal, the young Emilia Cesano, born in 1890, was considered to be a real cousin. The only faded pho-

28

tograph which has survived of her, at eighteen, was shown me by her brother with a trembling hand. Leaning against a marble column, a bunch of fake flowers at waist-level, it was like the ectoplasm of a fine-looking girl, a perfect Fair Maid of Lecce with her soft, subtle lines and the gentle irony of her expression. The rather nonchalant pose which the photographer has coaxed from her doesn't suit her, and one can see that she is uncomfortable with it. This slight air of malaise in her stance reveals something of the crazy destiny which awaited her, hastened by her one and only love.

The friendship between Tito and Emilia can't have been anything new at the time when Gerunda made his suggestion: go and make love! It would certainly not have reached that point between the two youngsters, given the time and the age; however, it was known in Lecce that a certain level of affection existed between the two, and the town smiled on it, that was all.

However, there were no more smiles when Tito received the edict from his maestro, and made the official choice of his partner known to the family circle. The character of the two young people was not such as to do things by halves, or in muted fashion. He was vibrant and passionate, and catastrophically apt to fall for feminine charm; she was delicate and faithful, but perhaps on edge from the constant effort of having to restrain her equally passionate nature so strictly. They were an impassioned but chaste couple, plagued by desire and self-denial, by contact and provocation. They wanted the world to know about their newly discovered, flaming affair.

But a violent reaction then followed on the part of her parents. Among Emilia's relations were the most famous confectioners of Lecce. And in that city, control over the production of sweets and pastries, marzipans and jellies, was no small matter, even in economic terms. Tito's parents, on the other hand, were poor in material terms, but full of pride—especially Luigi who seemed to be a man of few words, and those few very succinct and to the point. When he got to know that Emilia's family had publicly snubbed the poor relation and banned any contact, the countermeasures taken in the Schipa household were of the opposite kind, but they had the same effect (in essence, anyone who rejects us is unworthy of us). So far, everything was in the best tradition of

stories of this kind, including the logical reaction of the two forbidden lovers: to become even crazier about each other and devise
all kinds of tricks and subterfuges. Just as predictable, but altogether more grave, was the final turn of the screw on the part of
the Cesanos. They locked the girl up for part of the week in a
boarding school run by nuns, the Istituto Margherita.

But it was not very likely that fate would allow the matter to
be tied up so neatly.

Right opposite the Istituto Margherita, halfway down one of
the main streets of the old part of town, stands the massive bulk
of the Palazzo Guarini. In that extraordinary work of architectural genius, a kind of synthesis of the grandiose and delicate qualities of the building-style of Lecce, Joachim Murat had left his own
very individual signature when he was on his ill-fated sally through
southern Italy. He had in fact scratched it crudely on a mirror
with his diamond ring. This act of authority and vainglory immortalized on a mirror contributed to the charm of a place which
was already both enchanting and enchanted, full of shadowy historical scenes, ageless ivy, little balconies and great staircases. On
the top floor, where the windows become small and low-pitched,
the attics of the Guarini mansion and the Istituto Margherita practically meet. In the mild evenings Emilia had undoubtedly heard
echoes of the traditional chamber concerts given once a week in
the lower rooms of the Palazzo. It should not be difficult to guess
who had managed to get himself included with stubborn regularity in these weekly concerts!

Just a matter of a couple of songs, perhaps a pair of eighteenth
century Italian numbers of the lightest sort (so as not to break
Gerunda's rule). The usual old-style musical declarations of love;
the usual old-style promises. It was another way of earning a few
pence and getting his name—which was already becoming known—
talked about more widely. But above all it was the chance to make
good use of the interval by racing up the gloomy grand staircase
which led to the upper floors, and there hang out of the window of
one of the attic rooms. Just a few feet away, near but untouchable,
scarcely visible between the gables and the starry sky, Emilia was
waiting for him, pale and trembling. In the perfect stillness of the
night, far above the noises of the street, there followed new declarations, and new promises, whispered across the abyss.

The most frequently-repeated promise was to wait for each other, no matter how much time and how many sacrifices might be required. There was no other way for the young artist but to go north, to Milan, to seek his fortune, yet if she didn't want him to, he said he was ready to give up there and then. Emilia was almost offended at the suggestion; she answered that she could give no greater proof of her love than to urge him on towards fame and fortune. In return, she asked for the usual simple, impossible things: fidelity and sincerity. The promise would cost Tito nothing.

At this point, the story is interrupted by the least-known and most influential concert in Tito Schipa's life story.

Another Emilia

There was another Emilia in Tito's life. This was Emilia Bernardini Macor, the daughter of Carlo Macor, the engineer who was also a patriot who had been persecuted by the Austrians.

At the time that Tito was an adolescent, Emilia Bernardini was the undisputed power behind all the social activities of Lecce. She had the advantages of a journalist's column and upper-class birth, and she laid down the rules for the arts and for behavior. In short, she was a public relations genius.

When Tito's friends began to wonder what they could do to help the boy to take wing and leave the province, she was the one who put an end to all the dithering on the part of Gerunda and Blasi and D'Elìa, and suggested a concert. Not exactly a benefit concert of the kind she was constantly organizing, because this time the beneficiary (for once) would be the artist himself. With the take Tito would be able to buy a ticket for Milan.

The machine went into action, backed by a newspaper which was fully involved in the affair (having also taken on one of Tito's sisters, Elvira, as an employee at that time) and a small group of willing friends who sold tickets from door to door for three weeks. For their part, the representatives of the publishers Sonzogno and Ricordi made a contribution by waiving the payment of authors' copyright as an exceptional concession for that evening. But the big question-mark remained: would the people of Lecce turn out for an event which was not for a charity or some pious purpose, but for a well-known local scapegrace?

Gerunda, that old fox of show business, produced a program which was more of an ultimatum than a cast: apart from the participation of the two Addobbato sisters (a pianist and a harpist of some note, but sadly blind), there was also the pianist Alessio Fannaccone, another young talent seeking publicity, and standing out brashly on the bills there were also the names of the amateur tenor Oronzo Miglietta and baritone Oronzo Gasparri—both of them notable local attorneys, whose clientèle included the cream of the city. Who would have risked offending their family lawyers by not going to hear them sing? There was no doubt of a full house.

Finally, when everything was ready, the date of the concert was fixed for the 22nd of June. This was in 1908, and I was exactly seventeen-and-a-half years old.

Another "slip"—he was in fact eighteen. Memory of his part in earlier concerts had superimposed itself, in particular one which had been given in the Teatro Paisiello a few months earlier. The newspaper "Provincia di Lecce" contains a review of this concert in which the name "Tito" appears for the first time alongside the surname Schipa.

[This happened without his knowledge, and it came as a great surprise. The compositor of the newspaper, who was probably one of Tito's companions in his boyhood escapades, in haste to get the copy to the press and in the absence of competent proofreaders, wrote in good faith what he had always called him and heard him called: "Tito" Schipa. Tito must have been quite furious at finding himself in the diminutive even in the review of his début, but his anger didn't last. When they all met together to decide what should be done, under the guidance of Emilia Bernardini's keen sense of public relations, it was realized that in fact Tito sounded a lot better than Raffaele. And so it was decided that he should go on calling himself that. When the posters appeared on the walls of Lecce in June, the baptism of a new genius was only a short time away. But that fateful moment of distraction had already decided what the genius should be called. It was a name which had certain qualities—it sounded right and was

32

snappy—which shouldn't be underestimated in the events that followed. Among other things, a name was now added to the surname Schipa (which meant an eagle in Albanian as we have already mentioned), and that name, if derived from the Latin Titus meant a wild dove. Names are omens, as the Latin proverb says: the destiny written in that name was to soar high and fast. (Eighty-one years later, on the centenary of the birth of Tito, the US magazine "Opera News" was to caption its commemorative article: "Tito Schipa, the name is the voice.")]

The part of the program which concerned him, according to his own account, was limited to *"Una furtiva lagrima"* from Donizetti's *L'elisir d'amore*. It was a great success. But the real surprise came when the take was counted: five hundred and fifty lire! There was enough for the journey, and by making the sacrifice of traveling third class, there would be enough to hang on until his dreamed-of début in the North. In the meantime it would also suffice to enable him to continue his studies with a more influential maestro than Gerunda.

Six years of studying like a maniac in Lecce, and still not enough! He intended to spend that money because he was determined to gain greater technical mastery. Was it Gerunda who advised him to do this? Tito doesn't tell us, but he must really have felt the need, since he mentions having asked in all seriousness:

– But isn't there a *fourth* class that one can travel by?

On the station bench at the far end of the single track that led down to the heel of Italy, his mother's advice on life's problems must have been mingled with Gerunda's words of wisdom on his work. In his pocket, he had a hundred of the lire he had earned.

The rest was in a bank savings account in the name of his brother Umberto (soon to prove useful, but in a completely unforeseen way). Then came the affectionate farewells, the tears, the handkerchiefs, the crowd of well-wishers, including Emilia Bernardini.

But one figure was absent: Emilia Cesano was not able to be there.

Scene one of a life drama

Among the many ways of keeping in contact which the two young people had invented, despite the barriers imposed by their families, was the time-honored use of the go-between, the sympathetic friend, the bearer of written and oral messages, who had free access to both partners. In this case, in the days when Lecce at the turn of the century might have seemed just like Shakespeare's Verona, the favored go-between for Emilia and Tito was Vittoria, a mutual friend. By a combination of lucky chances she happened to live near the Istituto Margherita and could easily slip love-letters through the trellis of the convent. In folk memory, which still lives on in Lecce, Vittoria has taken on the character of a kind of Iago in skirts, engaged as she was in double and triple games which were destined to get out of control. The behavior of this girl towards the two lovers was in fact more than a little ambiguous. Was she in love with him? Envious of her? Or, indeed, as some insist, just the reverse? Whatever the case may be, Vittoria tainted the little services she performed as postman with personal venom. She dripped tiny drops of it into Emilia's ear. In the period while Tito was still in Lecce, she advised her to reconcile herself to her fate, to give up her hopes and dreams of some eternal idyll. Then, once he had gone North, she systematically undermined Emilia's faith in his constancy, in his willingness to wait and to come back. And once the echo of his first successes began to be heard, so that even the Cesano family began to soften their attitude, she whispered insistently:

"Now that he's making his fortune, when do you think you're going to see your Tito Schipa again?"

People who warn you over and over about possible dangers sometimes end by making them happen to prove themselves right.

During one of his last recitals in the north (legend has it that it was at Crema, but it's more likely that it was a performance of *Mignon* in Chioggia), while in his dressing room, Tito received a perfumed, passionate letter from an unknown admirer. Veiled promises and requests for a tête-à-tête were included. Without thinking twice about it he replied *"come tutti gli sventurati,"* as Manzoni puts it.

Not only that: he replied in writing, vying with the sender in intensity and double meanings. Then he awaited the confirmation, tingling with excitement. If he had known whose hand had sent that letter, and who was now turning over the pages of the reply, he would have been tingling with shame. Because, whether by chance or design, Vittoria, "the friend and letter-carrier," was in town at the time.

When she had achieved her treacherous aim, Vittoria hurried back to Lecce and thrust Tito's answer under the nose of poor Emilia.

Emilia at once retired into a devastating silence. A few days later, when Tito returned, she invited him to lunch in her own home. The young artist was sure he was to be fêted; instead, his astonished gaze was confronted with a dining room entirely lined with white paper—walls, ceilings and floor. Every piece of furniture and ornament had disappeared from these unique and immaculate surroundings. It was a hallucinating, daytime nightmare, in which the sacred whiteness of the ancient tarantic ghost emerges from the depths of antiquity to celebrate its rites of chastity and folly. There was no food, just the proclamation of the end of their love. Tito reminded her that they had promised to belong to each other. Emilia replied that her only lord and master was God. A few days later, she went to Naples, and there, deaf to the pleas of her parents and of Tito, she took the veil and enclosed herself in a convent. Tito's desperate vigils at the entry to the cloister were of no avail, nor were the repeated visits of his mother Antonietta, who had realized what a terrible trauma such an event might cause in the emotional life of her son. Nothing helped. Emilia Cesano no longer existed.

The woman who many years later emerged from the convent to dedicate her life to medicine (and most surprisingly to the cure of rabies), was no longer called Emilia, but Sister Pia. Day by day, despite her attempts to disguise the fact, she followed the career and the fortunes of Tito, but she did everything possible to avoid meeting him again.

She was to die in 1975, at Lauro near Naples, having survived her one fated love by more than ten years.

The affair became a legend in Lecce. But when I hear the story retold, with its blending of real life and hypothetical drama from an opera libretto, and its confusion of real events with those on the big stage, I seem closer to a deeper understanding of this man's character. People who saw and heard assert that this devastating episode brought Tito to within a few short steps of madness. It was a children's game with a tragic ending. The sense of guilt which was to follow him for the rest of his life was perhaps the hidden source of all his lies, his amorous extravagances, his stubborn, obsessive Don Juanism. But on the stage, it certainly gave that quality of nostalgia and regret, of dream-like elegy and unattainable satisfaction to his singing. Every woman in his life (and there were so many...), every female character in his performances, was—and at the same time never could be—his Emilia. When the family moved to Naples, from 1913 to 1920, the forced proximity to his cloistered love, the fact that he had to look out on the same mountain, the same sea, the same moon, without being able to see her or speak to her, perhaps contributed to making his Neapolitan song interpretations into the masterpieces they were, and to rendering the lover's lament of "*Tu ca nun chiagne*" with real tears of burning passion instead of the usual sobstuff for the tenor voice.

"What you really lack, is love!"

At a great distance in time, the diabolical Maestro Gerunda had nevertheless managed to have his way.

The real Bohème

> I was awaited in Milan. Not, of course, by the Milanese, but by my compatriots from Lecce. Three of my friends from my old home were there waiting for me. I was indispensable to enable them to form the perfect "Hunger Quartet."

Huge, noisy and ultra-modern. These are the adjectives which first came to Tito's mind when he wrote to describe his powerful impressions of the Lombard capital. We can certainly not imagine a more complete contrast when we think of the muffled silence of the city of tufa and palms from which he had been uprooted in a matter of hours.

His three friends were Filippo Biancofiore, who was studying as a baritone, Carlo De Marco and Aristotele Guido. The tiny colony of natives of Lecce immediately formed a tight bond, only occasionally broken by some ferocious row. This would usually be over the rotation for sleeping on the sofa, the only sleeping-place available in the tiny room which Tito and one of his companions shared in an area under the stairs. Perfect harmony reigned, on the other hand, over the survival strategy: they decided to seduce one well-off girl each; if possible the daughters of different kinds of foodstore owners—a baker, a grocer, a restaurateur. The quartet's agreed meeting place was the Trattoria della Rosa, in a vanished Via Soncino Merate (while Puccini's Café Momus really existed, no trace can be found of this Milan street).

Inviting a girl to lunch, even once a month, was enough to upset the whole budget, and a certain little ring passed back and forth monthly through the portals of the "Sacro Monte" (the pawnshop). When things got really bad they would eat bread and cheese hidden away in their closet under the stairs, and there would be no end of trouble if the landlady found out. Between one frugal mouthful and another Tito must have begun to dream on the grand scale, and not only about his career. In an interview in 1934 he said:

> I have a plan, or rather a wonderful dream that I want to make into a reality. I would like to found right here in Milan a great academy for Italian *bel canto* to which young singers from all over the world would come, attracted by the fame of great masters. And it would be the only institution of its kind in Italy. They would also learn to act properly there, and they would be provided with plenty of scholarships: in fact, why not one for every nation of the world?

When he talked about a "unique" institution it is clear that he was thinking about the unique character, at least for those days, of a multi-disciplinary school in which the art of acting was given equal status with that of singing. It was the complete, multiform man of the stage that was speaking: the man who was well aware of the importance of *maestri* even in the life of a maestro.

However, in the beginning the word was bread and cheese. This allowed him to save, and to procure for himself for six months the help of an

> intelligent and sensitive, top-quality musician and excellent teacher, whose school has produced many of the finest voices which the opera stage boasts today.

He was referring to the Venetian Emilio Piccoli, who had been the voice teacher of his friend Biancofiore in Milan. He had been introduced, but without getting more than a doubtful frown. It seems that Piccoli took on the responsibility more because of an instinctive sympathy for the youngster, so self-confident and elegant in his poverty, than because he saw any real chance of success. However, lessons began, and according to Tito they were based on a somewhat bizarre teaching method: sharp pinches on the leg at every wrong note.

> As a result of his teaching, my voice began to change, finally educating itself, and under his guidance I persevered in the all-out pursuit of perfection and preparation for the longed-for début in a stage opera.

This change in a voice which had already been brought to the highest standards of perfection by Alceste Gerunda, can probably be explained more by a further physiological development than by Piccoli's teaching. In fact, the very first records, which date from a few years after this period, still seem to have been made by a boy rather than a man of twenty-five. That prodigious instrument must have developed very slowly, and perhaps the secret of its longevity also lay in that fact. The process of "perfection," on the other hand, in the sense of the completion of his artistic personality and initiation into the basic rules of performance, does carry Piccoli's unmistakable signature.

This "pincher of geniuses" was not only a prestigious teacher; he was also a careful and accomplished manager. He soon became convinced that behind the apparent poverty of his vocal means, Tito was hiding a prodigious sensitivity and versatility. As a connoisseur of the classical testing-grounds, which from the time of Verdi and Puccini had all required passage through the great salons of Milan, he began showing off his pupil in the homes of the Campostellas, the Bentivoglios, the De Capitanis and Arzaghis. In these evenings it was easy to gain the approval which counted, and no less important, to get some providential sustenance out of the buffets! But everything was confined to a decent meal, some genuine applause and an occasional glance at a pretty woman. Then, back to the garret.

The daylight hours which were not given over to study were spent in the Galleria, Milan's great arcade. In those years all the hopes of the young in search of fortune, especially the novices of the opera, revolved around those few covered meters which run from Piazza Duomo to Piazza della Scala. These were the times, as Savinio puts it, when realistic melodrama was passing through its golden age. La Scala, the Dal Verme, the Carcano, the Lirico vied with each other to produce the latest works. Operas flourished in their brief season: *Manuele Menendez* by Filiasi,[1] *La nave rossa* by Sepilli,[2] a second *Cavalleria rusticana* by a certain Monleone,[3] the débuts of Zandonai and Alfano. Some new artist every evening. A musical aura enveloped the city and penetrated the thick blanket of mist. When the better weather caused the windows to open, exercises and gargles sounded from every room.

The "grigioni" lorded it in the Galleria: topcoats with half-belts, beaver-fur collars, bowler hats worn well to the back of the head...

In a photo of those days this is the exact portrait that we have of Tito Schipa. His beaver collar is pulled tightly up to his chin; he and the other southerners used to call it the "caracollo," and in the shadow of the bowler hat shading his eyes, he is wearing a mocking smile. This smile must have changed all at once into an ecstatic expression when none other than Giacomo Puccini himself strolled by, heading for the Cova *pâtisserie* where he took his morning cappuccino and *petit beurre*.

An infinite number of original composers were first tried out by Sonzogno or Ricordi. Lost legions of young singers languished at the doors of the agents, most of them untrustworthy if not

---

[1] *Manuel Menendez* by Lorenzo Filiasi had its premiere at the Teatro Lirico in Milan on May 15, 1904. It was highly successful, being widely performed both in and outside Italy.

[2] *La nave rossa* by Armando Sepilli was premiered at the Teatro Lirico on November 27, 1907, and was fairly successful.

[3] *Cavalleria rusticana* by Domenico Monleone (to the same libretto as Mascagni's opera) was first given in Amsterdam February 5, 1907. It was given in several other European cities under that title. The Italian premiere, in Turin on July 10, 1907, resulted in legal action by Sonzogno, the owners of the Mascagni score, and further productions in Italy were blocked. The work was eventually set to a totally different libretto and given in Florence.

downright criminal. Even a kind of amorous blackmail was possible. Tito explicitly says that the close associate of an intermediary asked him outright for sexual favors, gasping out "Nice, my little lad from Puglia!" To make matters worse, she was quite repulsive; quite beneath temptation, with the best will in the world.

"*Ce ssi' rracchia!*" ("What a hideous hag you are!") cried Tito in his dialect, and fled, slamming the door behind him.

A little while later, on the other hand, when his career had already begun, he frankly admits that he did give in. Indeed, he claims to have been cheated by not having realized that the equivalent of over half his fee was being "paid" to him in "embraces" by the agent's assistant. He believed he was paying a toll with this amorous adventure; in fact, however, he was getting paid in kind...

At the moment, however, he couldn't go on in this way. He needed to turn his back on it. Piccoli was called in to do whatever he could. Time was passing, there were the promises made back home, Emilia was waiting (alas)... there was the burning desire for the stage. And then there were some regrettable occurrences, like the time that a certain Vanda, a mezzo-soprano with high hopes and a commanding presence, had let it be known that what she wanted most in the world at that moment was a cool drink. It was a hot stuffy summer, and a bit of cool relief would have broken down such a lot of resistance... but when he hunted furiously in his pocket, he found nothing but a forlorn five-cent coin! That was the end of the story with Vanda.

A few weeks later, in order to overcome some other resistances, he found himself fumbling frantically in his pocket again. This time, however, a very different sum was involved: fifty lire! This was what the only impresario that Piccoli had been able to discover was demanding. He had been convinced after a lot of hard effort: in the *Traviata* which was being prepared for the Teatro Facchinetti in Vercelli, the role of Alfredo was to go to the young Schipa—oh, joyous day!—but he demanded that he should not get a penny less than the very substantial percentage he would have obtained from a better-known and more talked-about tenor. The lost percentage, he said, added up to fifty lire, and he wanted the whole sum from Tito. He managed to get part of it from Umberto, who scraped the barrel for what was left of the bank deposit, and sent every penny he could, crossing his fingers. The remaining sum was promised by Piccoli from his own pocket; in this way he proved his sincerity and the strength of his efforts, for by now he was completely won over.

The next day a train which was awaited more than any in the world left the gray skies of Milan's bohemian world, and headed west, between the great open skies and the rice-fields. Above Vercelli, a clearing away of the clouds was predicted.

V

(1909–1910)

Alfredo? A poor slip of a thing....

On February 4th, 1989, an enthusiastic group of scholars, surrounded by artists, opera-lovers and a large, attentive audience
(according to newspaper reports of the evening) gathered in the
Teatro Facchinetti in Vercelli to commemorate both the centenary
of Tito Schipa's birth and the eightieth anniversary of his début,
which took place in that same city, and at that same theater. The
whole building with its stage facilities had been substantially altered from what it had been a century earlier. The audience, silent
and rapt, listened to some sputtering, remote recordings, among
which was inevitably what little remains of the *Traviata* in which
Alfredo is sung by Schipa. The newspapers were thus able to lavish praise not only on the departed artist and the critics who spoke,
but also on a fine theater and a top-class audience. But if we read
over what the artist himself stated in an interview about his début,
it would seem that things were very different in the far-off days of
1909.

First there was the matter of the theater itself. It must have
been in a tragic condition, especially as far as the stage was concerned, for Tito described it as an "ignoble carcass." Then there
was his audience, the Vercellesi themselves. Although they experienced the original sound, without any of the background swish,

42

of those arias which a century ago would have hypnotized them, they made no bones about adding a great deal of background noise to the singing. It could be described as a crackling, since the origin of the nuisance was in fact a regular shower of chewed pumpkin seeds which poured down from the Gods and even found their way onto the stage.

> I would say that the Vercellesi knew perfectly well what they were doing, but it was always a mystery to me why they had come to the theater. Perhaps it was forbidden in those days to spit pumpkin-seeds out in the streets of Vercelli: anyway, I gather they no longer throw them at the singers today. And quite right they are: in those circumstances it would be better to use really fresh fruit and toma-toes. As for the seeds which attended my début, the shower got more intense at the end of each act; instead of applauding the audi-ence showed its satisfaction in this way, and the shower became a deluge. It was necessary to bow, to show appreciation, and at the same time somehow clean one's face with one's hands...

There wasn't much that the orchestra could do to combat this odd disturbance, since it was only made up of about twelve in-struments! Poor Verdi. And there was even less that the very green, shabby Alfredo could do, half-smothered in a costume that was much too large, rented from heaven knows where, and forced to sing not only under the threatening eye of the manager (to whom Piccoli had promised to supply that very evening the twenty lire still outstanding from the deal), but also under the weight of an outsize Violetta:

> At the famous "*Amami, Alfredo!*" I found myself overwhelmed by such a great wave of abundant fleshly charms that I felt a little like the delicate snowdrop under the advance of an avalanche... So much so that from the gallery, a daring voice, worried for my safety, ad-monished the singer: – *Ohè, fà nen mal, a cul pôr cit*!

"Mind you don't hurt the poor little thing!" The Vercelli audi-ence had immediately joined the public of Lecce in a spirit of ten-derness for this diminutive figure, who provoked similar descriptions at long distances apart ("cit" in their dialect being equivalent to "titu" in Leccese).

The performance continued, or rather rolled on with all its unexpected moments, typical of an arranged début but new to this particular beginner. However, he showed that he had an innate talent for getting out of awkward situations. In the payment scene, Tito fumbled in his pocket and realized with a shudder that the wardrobe-mistress hadn't put the bundle of banknotes there. How was Violetta to be "paid"? ("Was I supposed to sign a check?") Then, pursued by the orchestra, he had to decide. He pretended to take a coin from his pocket, drew close to his unfaithful lover, and pressed it into her hand.

The commentator from the gallery was not slow off the mark. "Well—*she* didn't cost you much!"

So the "poor little thing" brought his first performance to a close. The audience response was not all that enthusiastic at the beginning. His voice, like the rest of him, was still too small, even though it already had a stylistic perfection which was perhaps so superior that it could not be appreciated by an undiscerning public, nor by provincial critics. However, it was not really an unhappy début either; indeed, Tito later described it as excellent, but he backs his description with elements derived from his more mature years. He states in fact that the clearest proof of satisfaction was the succession of fierce criticisms and sarcasms he had to face in the Galleria once he had returned to Milan, from what even then was dubbed the "Academy of the Scissors."

[*The innate good taste of the young artist saw to it that he made no attempt to compensate for the lightness of his voice by any artificial means. But that lightness does account for his uncertain beginning, the obscure journeys, and the rapidly—and willingly forgotten—encounters with quite varied forms of disapproval, including those which were based on motives which had little to do with music and singing. In a* Mignon *at Chioggia, for instance, he was fired after three performances because of the whims of the primadonna, who wanted a different tenor as her partner—since he happened also to be her partner in real life! However great their disdain they could find no better excuse than to say that his voice was "too baritone for the part." We really reach the level of farce here. But one of his acquaintances was to say many years later that he had some trouble in saving him from the declared intention of throwing himself in the river.*]

The small-scale début of the small man in the theater of Vercelli ended with a small success. But on that night in Piedmont (escaping through the stage door with his affectionate Maestro Piccoli to avoid paying the manager the rest of the fee), a long flight to the misty regions began, of which we have only the slightest trace left, never amplified by the singer himself. He appeared in Romania, who knows how or when; he appeared in Sebenico immediately afterwards (nine lire per performance); then in Savona and Crema, and doubtless in many other places.[4] But there are no recollections, no anecdotes which would throw a little light; everything is wrapped in a fog of the memory similar to the fogs of northern Italy, and which probably has much the same function: to protect an over-delicate shoot from the over-violent light of the morning.

Another father

The protective veil which hides the memories of a difficult time from us is set aside for the first time in Trento. However, it is worth mentioning that his dismissal of this troubled period is important in portraying the man as he was offstage.

If we wanted to drag the psychoanalysts into this, we might mention an anxiety neurosis. In his obstinate refusal to make any mention of the problem; in his desire to convince both others and himself that the problem, whatever it was, simply did not exist; in creating an image for himself of life and humankind made up entirely of gentlemen and grand ladies, and loyal chivalrous relationships, he revealed a wild terror of falling back into the anxiety which must have shaken him so violently after the exaggerated reaction by Emilia.

However, once he had arrived at Trent, two episodes lodged firmly in his memory, with what seems almost a contrary obstinacy. Both of them concerned not work but women. We shall take a look first at the reasons why.

First of all, we have to shake off this all-enveloping mist by meeting up with the sun which had dispersed it. It was a sun with a little pointed beard, a pair of moustaches already turning gray, and a crusty sort of expression: the face of Giuseppe Borboni. A

---

[4] Many of the places have now been identified in the chronology.

well-known opera impresario, the father of a future bright star of
Italian drama (Paola), Giuseppe Borboni[5] had experienced all the
ups and downs of the operatic world. In particular, he maintained
a considerable network of touring venues in the provinces, and
the provinces represented the best in intimate contact between the
Opera and Italy. Paradoxically it was with the centralizing of
"events" in the big opera houses of the major cities and their social and cultural cachet that the tragic gap arose between Opera
and the masses who had demanded it, adored it and imposed it on
the whole world. But at the time of our story, everything was still
going along famously, and the provinces were the best sounding-
board and test of maturity that an artist could find, simply because that was where he met up with a public that counted,
understood and remembered.

Tito had met Borboni in Milan, still in the "stagnant waters"
of his uncertain launching. He had gone with his friend Biancofiore
to a theatrical agent, unsophisticated but very effective—a Sicilian by the name of Gaetano Cannella. Gifted with sharp insight,
Cannella had insisted on hearing Tito as well, and immediately
got him an appointment with Borboni, persuading him to return
specially from Trent, where the young tenor was performing in
those days. In Cannella's office, accompanied at the piano by
Piccoli, Tito sang a few passages from *The Barber of Seville*. Perhaps they included that very same *"Ecco ridente in cielo"* which
still leaves us amazed today at the minute precision of its agility,
at a display of coloratura which seems to come more from the
filigree work of a light soprano than from a male voice. We don't
know whether his excitement had allowed him to produce this
prodigy on that fateful afternoon. But it is certain that Borboni's
face remained quite impassive.

He got up and pronounced a timeless phrase, which every artist has heard and endured a thousand times: "Don't call me; I'll
call you."

But he did call him. Showing himself to be a man of great
experience, he demonstrated ten years in advance what was to be

---

[5]Giuseppe Borboni was one of many now-forgotten Italian impresarios. He toured Italy
and nearby countries almost continuously from at least 1908 to the early 1920s. Amelita
Galli-Curci toured with him briefly in 1909.

the attitude of the Americans: he realized that the youngster was superbly gifted, but he had doubts about the impact he would make on current taste, and he made everything depend on a début which would not be a matter of chance but careful planning. He suggested that at Trent there should be just one trial performance (but in the official records there is no trace at all of it!).

> – You'll only be paid travel and expenses, Cannella added, and if you're a success, which I'm sure you will be, you'll be engaged for three months, at a fee of four hundred lire a month, with the obligation of singing alternate days.

Tito speaks of "prospects of ease." He was to be content with this kind of cachet for the rest of his life. Singing alternate days was a kind of imposed burden which, he knew very well, would have scandalized Gerunda. But caution had to give way to necessity. So he descended on Trent, determined to risk all for all. That "ghostly" *Barber* organized under Borboni's auspices seems to have gone well. Borboni confirmed his undertaking and Tito leapt to the stars in delight.

However, still strongly determined to perfect his technique, the talented youngster hid behind the scenes, and when he was not actually onstage, he observed his colleagues, more experienced than he was, and learned a great deal from their interpretations. They are all mentioned in his memoirs, these colleagues of the early days: the tenor Giovanelli Gotti, the baritone Marcello Giorda, Gennaro Maria Curci (a painter in his spare time and the future husband of the soprano Amelita Galli, who was herself to partner Tito in the later years of his greatest splendor). Curci is described as an "absolute" bass, to distinguish him from the comic bass Carlo Rossi, on whom Tito developed an unforgettable artistic "crush." Throughout his life he considered him the best Don Pasquale he had ever met, and acknowledged that he had "borrowed" as much of his art as he could from him, hidden there in the wings. It may be from this apprenticeship under a true master of the comic in music that accounts for the delicate humor with which Tito was to embellish his unforgettable Nemorino.

Everything was supervised and organized by Borboni's talent for publicity. His link with the star being born extended far beyond those first three months. And it also extended far beyond the provinces.

In 1911, after a long tour which took in Pola and Zara and then Umbria and the Lazio, he prepared to descend on Rome on the occasion of the Universal Exhibition. Tito, who had seen Emilia Bernadini Macor as a sort of second mother, now presented Giuseppe Borboni to his friends and admirers as a second father. And Paola Borboni discovered an adoptive brother.

A lady in black

Possibly because in Trent things were beginning to head in the right direction, his memory too seems at this point to open up to recording little anecdotes, and the romantic fantasies of a passionate youth. And since there is no romanticism worth the name without a good deal of moonlight and a graveyard scene, the episode which carved itself into his memory was a strange nocturnal delirium made up of carriages and cypress trees, hoopoes and a mantle of snow under the rays of the moon,

> ...an episode which has always remained odd and incomprehensible to me. Among the many letters from admirers, I received one so strange that my curiosity was roused, and I thought I had better not throw it away.
>
> It offered me an appointment in a cemetery; I would recognize her at once because she would be wearing mourning and a black veil covering her face. The macabre character of this date fascinated me, and I kept it. I found her a little way from the entrance-gate: tall and slim in build, clothed in black, with the black veil: but this was very thick and long, so that it was quite impossible not only to see her but even to make out the outline of her face, which it hid completely. She spoke very little, as if she were keeping watch, and the timbre of her voice was almost funereal. She had wanted to meet me in person; she had done so, and that was enough. I begged her to lift the veil from her face, but she replied with such a categorical "no" that I didn't dare insist. I asked her if that was the only reason for the appointment, and she answered that it was, nor could she imagine what else I might have been expecting. She held out her hand and dismissed me with great charm. I asked if I might, as a remembrance of this strange encounter, give her a kiss: she

answered yes, on the forehead. I have never in my life bestowed such a meaningless, and indeed even repulsive, kiss on anyone. I kissed a thick black veil, and felt a shudder run up and down my spine.

On the way back, I let my fantasy run wild, to explain this strange and unnatural encounter, almost like something out of Shakespeare, but no kind of invention seemed capable of suggesting to me what might be the explanation–at least of that very thick black veil. Did it, perhaps, hide some kind of horrifying deformity? I recoiled in horror from such a thought!...

This version of the episode dates from 1943, and seems to reflect a sense of shame, a specific wish to underplay the incident, possibly so as not to hurt the sensibilities of his then companion: Caterina Boratto, who represented, after Emilia, the most painful love experience of his life. However, there are many other versions, each quite different from the others. Sometimes it was snowing, sometimes there was a moon; on occasions the mysterious lady arrives on foot, at other times in a black carriage drawn by four horses (also black). At times the dialogue is cold and suspicious, at others it is a love-scene composed only of words which seem almost to profit from this mysterious imposition of chastity. In the years to come, this ordinary tale was to become a virtual leitmotif of his memories, it would be featured by newspapers the world over, filling whole pages of dailies and magazines, and it would be embellished by drawings by famous artists and environmental details added by imaginative journalists. It would be repeated by him in America with a thoroughly European touch of class and mystery, and then taken up by his womenfolk as an example of his fanciful nature, over-prone to adventures. But above all, and this is the real reason for repeating it here, it would seem to have a basic importance for him, the explanation for which has always escaped me. But every reference to it made him tremble with genuine excitement.

Soon, there would be hundreds of women waiting outside the stage door. At his debut in Trieste, at the Teatro Fenice, he seems to have barely escaped from an amorous lynching. On that occasion, accompanied by a pair of Austrian policemen, and rescued by Borboni, who literally carried him away on his shoulders, he had to refuse any encounters on pain of risking his life. But no crowd of shouting women ever remained in his heart like that mysterious woman in black. Those who are best-informed have sought to identify her with someone very high in the royal court, so elevated, in fact, that they dared not reveal her name. But this was not what mattered to him. It seemed rather that the sign of success as he understood it and had always awaited it was indeed constituted in this way, with a measure of mystery and exaltation and also a certain touch of exhilarating frustration.

Onstage: final battles; first meetings

As I have already mentioned, it is difficult even for a professional chronicler to sort out the truth from all these vague remembrances, uncertain witnesses, and ephemeral seasons which leave no trace at all. Take for instance, the short season in Lecce when he returned for the first time in professional guise to his beloved native city. Tito doesn't blush at giving the date as 1913, while the accounts in the "Corriere delle Puglie" are indisputably dated 1910. Rather than just bad memory, what is involved here is once again that capricious whim that led him to take a few years off his age. However, he makes a mistake: he correctly identifies the impresario who organized the recitals as Piero Minciotti, and thus explicitly rules out the possibility that it could have happened in a period subsequent to Borboni, who would certainly not have given up his exclusive rights!

What matters, however, is that for the first time since he had left it for the unknown, accompanied by the good wishes of a city which half applauded him and half laughed up its sleeve, the young tenor got out of the train, passed through the clouds of steam, and made his way once again amongst the cactus plants, palms and the glowing tufa. It was the first of a countless series of returns, which were to punctuate his whole life, at intervals which were as regular as possible. He preferred the end of August, when Piazza Sant'Oronzo was full of luminous balloons floating towards the starry night sky, with the sound of the bands, and the many-colored lights of the decorations and the scent of coffee and cream-cakes. Every triumph registered in remote parts of the globe seemed only to serve to bring back its echo to his native city, to receive the only applause which really counted for him. He seemed only really to relax there, where he was finally home, finally at peace.

But his first return was certainly not peaceful. On April 3rd, 1910, the "Corriere delle Puglie" announced:

"Tomorrow evening, Sunday, we confirm that the part of Count Maurice of Saxony will be sung by our young fellow-citizen Tito Schipa, pupil of our Maestro Gerunda, who has won applause and admiration in other theaters." (It did not even need mentioning, in a province so devoted to the Opera, that the work in question was *Adriana Lecouvreur*.)

It seemed that everything was going along smoothly, but there was a parish-pump battle in the air, and the ranks were already drawn up; the idols were facing each other. One, obviously, was our hero, the deity of the Schipiani; the other was called Guglielmo Zanasi, and the Zanassians were numerous, and quite aggressive. They began by pulling the carpet out from under the feet of the young adversary, by denigrating him on the social plane:

– The son of a workman?, said someone, the son of a Lecce craftsman in the ranks of the artists? Never..

Incredibly enough, they seem to have prevailed. The impresario backed down. Gerunda stuck to his guns, and the two groups began to hurl insults at each other; there were even a few scuffles. Then, by great good luck, Zanasi was taken ill, and it isn't hard to guess who was signed up to substitute for him.

That evening, while the orchestra was tuning up, the Politeama of Lecce seemed like the Campo in Siena five minutes before the Palio begins.

I came onstage, not without a certain degree of panic, I must admit–and it was the first time after years on the stage that I'd felt it. I was greeted by fairly enthusiastic applause from the gallery; in the stalls, apart from a few of my admirers, there was complete silence. When the first moments of perplexity had passed, I began the delightful "*Bella tu sei*," and went on to the end of the duet with a sureness which surprised even myself; my voice, which was not all that great in volume, seemed on that evening to have redoubled in sound. The high notes came from me freely, clearly, and with a great finesse.

51

So it was, but without bellowing or vulgarity. And his adversaries were triumphant, since they were devotees of a kind of clamorous high-note singing which was unfortunately already becoming popular. Rumor spread round the city of a "mezzo-tenor" with a voice which was hardly good enough for operetta. The opera-lovers in the gallery took note of this and remained on guard, like their counterparts in Vercelli (in opera galleries, Italy had been united long before the days of Garibaldi).

Later that year, during a *Rigoletto*, their moment arrived. Their "soloist" barely waited till Tito began "*Questa o quella*," then, at the end of the aria, in the moment of silence which preceded the applause, the comment was shouted:

"Ahh: call that a voice?"

In the interval, two streams of opera-lovers, exasperated by days of tension and arguments, converged on the foyer from different directions: the Zanasiani from the stalls and the Schipiani from the cheaper seats. The atmosphere was explosive. The mocker had been identified. He was surrounded and thrust up against a wall, while all around a frantic ballet of shoving and invective went on. Terrified, the catcaller tried to change his phrase by adding an 'I':

"No! No! What I said was 'I call that a voice!'"

It didn't work. He received a black eye. The forces of order intervened, and the performance continued in an atmosphere of guerrilla warfare.

Once the show was over, with the most conflicting reactions imaginable, the squabble spilled over into the streets of the city. Like mobs of football hooligans, the factions sought each other out, followed one another and clashed in the warm night. Count Zecca, a member of an aristocratic family of opera-lovers, chose the wrong faction to side with on this occasion, and in the middle of Piazza Sant'Oronzo he was struck on the chin by a Schipa fan. He fell to the ground and someone planted a foot on his chest and flung a coin into his face as a sign of contempt. They still talk about it in Lecce....

Nor was this the end. A few days later, in order to avoid losing the support of his public, Zanasi decided to sing *Mignon*, despite his "indisposition." But predictably, the B-flat which he emitted in the second act proved to be a little *too* flat... In the seconds which followed, as he tried to compensate, he forced out a couple of sharps not intended by the composer, and then the brief wobble turned into a real bray of a false note.

It was immediately echoed from the gods by a merciless whistle. All hell broke loose. Tito was present, and it wouldn't have taken much for his fans to carry him shoulder-high on to the stage while the curtain was still open.

But we have to remember his style, and his real fear of confrontations. He rejected this easy form of success, went to the dressing room to apologize to Zanasi, then returned to the foyer and found himself at the center of the usual two bands of fanatics who were facing each other menacingly. He asked for the whistler to be pointed out to him, and the latter, grinning exultantly, admitted openly: "Sure, I was the one who whistled" and he found himself suddenly lying on the floor, not knowing what had hit him. In fact the straight right that had laid him out had not been thrown by some indistinguishable Schipa supporter this time, but by the maestro himself.

> I yelled at him: – You...are a rat!
> It was only later that I realized that he was one of my best friends!

The short season continued in a climate of civil war. Zanasi was taken ill again, and all the other tenors but Schipa also found themselves indisposed—understandably enough. The result was that there was a whole season of seemingly endless stand-in roles for Tito in Lecce, as we shall see. First of all he had to replace a Russian who was convinced he had found a universal panacea for the opera singer: boiled eggs! On the evening when, before a performance, he gobbled fifteen of them in a row, they had to carry him off in a coma, and Tito was forced to stand in for him, with little preparation. (This may be why he became a sworn enemy of cholesterol!)

He sang everything—and more than that, in the sense that he had to sing roles which were unsuited to him, and even roles he didn't know at all. He learned *Mefistofele* in three days, and while his musical ear never failed him by a sixteenth, when it came to the words, he had to resort to using his brother Umberto as a prompter. The outcome was not such as to resolve the dispute in his favor. Even Minciotti became involved in the rumpus: for Tito's debut in *Zazà* he had the great idea of saving expenses by using the same sets as he had already used for *Adriana Lecouvreur*. There was nearly a riot—and of course it was not a success. The press only spared Tito himself, and during the rest of the season they no longer denied the young artist a certain amount of praise. The tireless journalistic energies of Emilia Bernardini continued to work on his behalf. When the point of "suspended contract" performances was reached (the equivalent of today's non-subscription holders), the theaters were full to the doors, and the Zanasi fans found themselves with their backs to the wall. In the newspapers, favorable and more or less categorical judgments began to appear:

"We like the music; we like the execution: that's all that's needed."

A *Zazà* repeated in Tito's honor was reported as a distinct personal success. However, the newspaper reports didn't correspond yet with what the audiences were saying—not *all* the audiences, admittedly, but some. Even so, Tito was not making anything like a real income. He left Lecce with rather a sour taste in his mouth, and with the echo of an article which reflected Gerunda's *idée fixe* in his ears.

"All honor to young Schipa, but this does not exempt him from the need to go on studying with constant devotion, to perfect himself and develop a repertoire suited to his capacities."

Despite this, when people insisted in later years that Tito Schipa was whistled at in Lecce (and the Leccesi themselves were to repeat it frequently, in the constant severe self-criticism which is so typical of them), Tito always denied, very firmly, that this had ever happened.

A few months later, at the Teatro Mastroieni in Messina, Tito was far away from faces and voices—whether friendly or hostile—that were familiar; in fact, he was alone, as only a young artist without wealth or fame can be. There he met a young woman of his own age, who was in the same profession. She was the daughter of a stage director, and like Tito she had the theater in her blood. She was also young and attractive, and something of an individualist like Tito himself; she lived her characters to the fingertips, and allowed herself to be possessed by them, almost as if in a trance. They performed together in a *Traviata* which nobody from the audience is still alive to recall, which certainly no one was in a position to record, and which even Tito never referred to personally. It was a run of the mill performance, the names were not big, and the people of Messina had a great deal to think about (and would have a great deal more: the catastrophic earthquake was only two years away). They didn't pay much attention to the love duets written by a composer who seemed to be on the road to oblivion, sung by two excessively odd young singers. But the two singers were Tito Schipa and Claudia Muzio, and the earthquake victims who saw and heard that *Traviata* had something, at least, to be grateful for.

VI

(1911–1916)

Not yet a success

That tour of the South, in Tito's vague memory, is in fact the amalgam of various brief road trips which the records date between 1910 and 1912. The climax came in November in Palermo, where Tito (among other roles) sang *Antony* for the second time in his brief career, an opera by the maestro Riccardo Casalaina, who had died at twenty-six in the Messina earthquake, and whose work might be worth some research. The season, rather light-hearted in its performances, naturally included other more classical titles. The newspapers of the period report as follows:

"After the hasty execution of *La favorita* and of *Lucia*, the next production to be staged was *La sonnambula*... The tenor, Schipa, gave an excellent interpretation of the part of Elvino. It can be stated that the applause was due to the faithful interpretation of Schipa.... the chorus was fairly good, but the staging bad, and the orchestra poor. *Tosca* is now in rehearsal." ("Musica," November 10, 1912.)

With this same *Tosca*, the privileged spectators of the Teatro Biondo were getting a preview of an event which a few years later was to be hailed as a miracle. Tito was delving into the intimate character of the score, refining his stage presence by a confrontation with, among others, the Scarpia of Eugenio Giraldoni. In the scene of the *"alba vindice"* this fine baritone was the first to experience actual physical terror of the young and ferocious Leccese. Years after, the great Battistini would beg Sciarrone and Spoletta to keep a firm hold on that diabolical Cavaradossi. Tito's mother was present in the theater in Palermo, and after an over-realistic execution, she dashed out, crying out to her son to know whether he was badly hurt. In all the subsequent performances she was to pay a tip to the extras "so that they don't shoot for real." No one in the family seemed able to distinguish between stage fantasy and reality.

[At a distance of eternity from all this, in one of the last performances of his beloved Werther, *at the moment when he falls fatally injured with his shirt soaked with blood, he was to hear the desperate cry of a four-year-old boy from the proscenium stalls—his son, who was forbidden by the doctor to attend Massenet's masterpiece from that evening on, either in rehearsal or on the stage.]*

The climax of the period in which Tito was linked to Giuseppe Borboni coincides with his debut in the two major Italian cities. Rome came first—during the Universal Exhibition which was held to celebrate the fiftieth anniversary of national unity—where he appeared on the stage of the Teatro Quirino. As in many other theaters in the capital which are today converted to cinemas or devoted only to ordinary stage productions, this theater had a long and traditional opera season; in this case a summer one. Oddly enough, however, Tito's memoirs put more stress on colorful anecdotes than on a specific feeling of success. Perhaps the provinces had offered him more.

In fact, the Rome critics were not very warm: "In overall terms, and given the popular character of the season, we can say that we are satisfied"...

Tito only features in the list of names ("Musica," October 8, 1911). The Italy of the great cities did not evince the same enthusiasm as the provinces, and when speaking of opera, the word "provincial" has a meaning diametrically opposed to the one we normally give it. In this Roman non-triumph, or the Milanese one which followed, there may well have been some hidden reaction on Tito's part which led to his decision a few months later to start crossing continental and intercontinental frontiers.

In Rome, however, we do find him taking an interest in a young soprano, his regular partner Isabella De Frate, for whom he must have entertained some tender feelings. He also derived no end of amusement from the banditries of Borboni, who in order to pull in the crowds did not hesitate to engage (incredibly!) a young unknown named Lina Cavalleri and to pass her off, by means of an extremely deliberate "typographical error" on the program, for her ultra-famous namesake, who spelled her name -lieri instead of -lleri, and numbered her admirers in thousands! Naturally we also find Tito continuing to sing everything—or rather to sing all sorts of things completely out of keeping with his vocal stature.

By some miracle, his voice survived. But he would soon have to cling tightly to *Werther* (which he sang for the first time at this stage, amid general indifference), and to get rid of that impossible *Cavalleria rusticana*!

[And yet with what passion and tenderness this Turiddu sings the Siciliana—or indeed the toast—in the surviving recordings! This is the way to convey the feeling of feverish excitement and heavenly delight which overtakes one at the sight of a lover! Here Turiddu really is in his twenties, and with extraordinary vocal skill he manages to utter a cry of love which seems no more than a whisper. And those final sighs, those groans of passion, uttered with the same delicacy with which one breathes on a soap bubble! Only a southerner, innately possessed of an ancient Mediterranean sadness, or if you prefer, expert in murmuring sweet nothings under the windows of married women—only such a man could enter into a score which is unashamedly "passionate" and which for that reason had become the happy hunting-ground of so many ear-bashers!]

Milan had previously spoken to Tito in accents which had a strange ring of Lecce to them: those of his hungry young friends from his native city of a few years earlier. The Milan of the first contract, on the other hand, spoke to him now, in 1913, in accents which were unmistakably Roman—those of Oreste Poli, the manager of the Teatro Dal Verme. This was yet another of those second-rank debuts, for it was certainly not the Milan of La Scala and Toscanini. As often happens, it was only his return from an emigration which opened those doors and those hearts to him. The most important thing he received from Poli, in this brief period, consisted of a nickname (*sorcio moscarolo*—midget-mouse) and a good publicity slogan, typical of the man of the stage. Tito held it to be the best of praise, and was to present it for the rest of his life as a prestigious credential:

> One evening, after the second act of *Sonnambula*, Poli came to seek me out in my dressing-room, as he often did.
> – My dear midget-mouse, you have some grand enemies!
> – And who might they be?– I replied, alarmed – envious rivals?
> – Think again!
> – Some impresario?
> – No! The libretto-sellers, because when you sing, they don't sell a single copy!

So his perfect pronunciation and inimitable phrasing were already of note in these years. That "musical conversing," that diction which made him a "Florentine of the South," already impressed old theater buffs. But it wasn't enough to bring about a triumph. And it should be said that Tito himself wouldn't have been completely satisfied, either, if the success that he won had not been due purely to musical reasons. So he prepared to put himself to the test in that regard by seeking confirmation in foreign lands, where the music of his voice alone, independently of the perfection of his phrasing, would have to suffice.

Encore!

> My mother went on worrying, and sighing, thinking of the huge ocean that awaited me–maybe even to swallow me up!

Antonietta's apprehension was not completely unjustified: this first transatlantic crossing, undertaken in 1913, was to become an annual event until 1916, and would genuinely become dangerous, since a world war was to arise in the meantime. When this point was reached, maternal anxieties were to meet with a response from him too, as we shall see. For now, Tito embarked on the *Principessa Mafalda*, full of emotion and loaded with very heavy baggage, including a *Madama Butterfly* which had recently gone to press, which was soon to be added to the list of things that Gerunda would not have approved of. Apart from anything else, he looked absurd in a blond wig: nothing could have been further from an officer of the US Navy! However, this is how the South Americans first made his acquaintance. Fortunately, his opening in Buenos Aires was in *La sonnambula,* and this guaranteed a good start.

There are few better cases than this of something begun well ending exceptionally. The Teatro Colón, which welcomed him to its stage for the first time on June 16th, 1913, became his home base in the southern hemisphere. He established a harmonious relationship with the Argentines which was to last for fifty years, and a really intimate knowledge of the Spanish language which went far beyond mere conversation. He was to learn many languages with an offhand ease, and in fact could eventually sing in ten (eleven, if you consider Neapolitan, as he did, a language of its own). But Spanish became his real second stage language, and here lies the secret of his complete triumph in all the countries where Castilian is spoken.

As time goes on, the inaccuracies about time in his autobiography are reduced from years to merely months and days. For this first South American tour, the discrepancies are limited to about twenty days and one title (according to him the début took place on 25 May and the opera was *Mignon*). There is no confusion, on the other hand about the name of his prestigious partner: Maria Barrientos, whose fame helped to guide him right to the hearts of the Argentines. But there was also an antagonist, no less prestigious in standing. This was Giuseppe Anselmi,[6] also an idol of the galleries—and Tito's contract provided (just for a change) that he should stand in when the star was too exhausted.

It was a constant, obsessive source of comparisons: Anselmi, Anselmi—always Anselmi. The impresario Rendina,[7] the conductors Podesti[8] and Guarnieri,[9] were all agreed: surely you don't want

---

[6] Giuseppe Anselmi was one of the most important lyric tenors in the world between the turn of the century and 1918. He was particularly popular in Spain, Russia and Argentina, and recorded widely for Fonotipia.

[7] During the first third of the twentieth century there was an enormous amount of operatic activity in South America. There usually were two, and often three touring companies starting in Buenos Aires and then proceeding elsewhere, most often to the Argentine provinces, Uruguay, Brazil or Chile. The major theaters in Buenos Aires were the Colón, the Coliseo, and the Politeama. Several impresarios were involved, the most important

to take on Massenet's *Manon?* Nobody will ever sing it like Anselmi! Surely you don't want to try and outdo Anselmi in singing in Spanish? No, just learn *Les Pêcheurs de Perles,* which Anselmi doesn't want to do anyway. And in how long? Oh, a few hours will do—hurry. And he did learn it. But when he was ready to go on, the great rival decided that he would sing after all, and Tito proudly reflects:

– Well, I thought, Anselmi's beginning to be afraid of me. To stop me getting another success, he's decided to sing this one himself!

A bit like Zanasi in Lecce. But it was a rivalry which didn't last long. The bond of real physical affection which linked Anselmi to the Spanish public (especially the women) couldn't be undermined, and it reached such a degree that when he was on the point of death the great tenor from Catania even left his heart to "the women of Spain." And not just symbolically: the generous organ is still preserved in Madrid!

All this was schooling for Tito, however—a school of glamour and fascination. And the maestro himself must have sensed that in Tito he had found his real heir, for he actually passed on to him his costume from *Manon,* a wild fantasy of ivory-colored satin and hand-embroidered roses amid whorls of gold thread.

It was natural that the constant visits to South America, the improvement in his knowledge of Spanish—both the language and the spirit—the lessons learnt from Anselmi, and the comparison with the latter, should eventually result in a visit to Spain in order to come to terms with a myth—and to meet directly with one of the most passionate publics in the world. But before this, there was a matter to be settled with Italy, and with that nagging impression of a half-success which he had left behind in 1913.

We are at the moment of one of his returns from overseas.

of whom was Walter Mocchi. Sometimes the Mocchi companies sang at the Colón, at other times at the Coliseo. In 1913 Michele Rendina had the concession for the Colón while Walter Mocchi was at the Coliseo.

[8] Vittorio Podesti was a fairly important conductor. He had spent many years heading the very important Italian seasons at the Grande Salle du Conservatoire in St. Petersburg, which featured Caruso, Tamagno, Tetrazzini, Battistini, and many other great singers. He also conducted at the Metropolitan for three seasons (from 1909-1912).

[9] Arnaldo Guarnieri was another distinguished Italian conductor.

The year is 1914, and it is not Milan or Rome or even Palermo which can claim the honor of having consecrated Tito Schipa's fame in anticipation of the glory that was to come in Spain. It was in fact Naples, the capital of music understood as daily bread of the soul. And capital too, even now, of a "Kingdom of the Two Sicilies" in terms of art, which the political unity of Italy has never succeeded in obliterating from the hearts of the people of Lecce. And Tito was a Leccese, even excessively so, and like all his fellow-citizens, he had always regarded Naples as the Paris of the South, the center of attraction for all musical aspiration, the place where even a little song is a *romanza*. There is a theater there where one must sing if one wants to exist at all: the San Carlo! A cycle of predestination, begun at Naples with the mysterious appointment of Gennaro Trama as Bishop of Lecce, ended in Naples with the signature of Tito on a contract which also carried that of the impresario Laganà.

This was not all. In Naples, the conductor was Leopoldo Mugnone, a magnificent veteran, authoritative and authoritarian, a Neapolitan to his fingertips. At the rehearsals for Falstaff, he began like this:

> – Schipetiè! Look: it's not the Duke of Mantua we have here; it's Fen*tòn*: I'm not going to say any more to you; you seem to me to be intelligent enough to understand...

If Mugnone had known the Duke of Mantua as Tito interpreted him, a prodigy of finesse and elegance (we will come back to that when dealing with Chicago), he might well have spared him that advice. But the phrase serves to emphasize the extent to which the great maestro was as attentive to theatrical matters as he was to the merely musical. It was no coincidence that fourteen years earlier, Giacomo Puccini had wanted him to direct the world première of *Tosca*, the absolute outpost at that time of "theater in music." And it was now a Neapolitan *Tosca*, (after a *Falstaff* which won neither praise nor blame) which was to highlight the encounter between a composer, an interpreter and a director, all men of genius. January 3, 1914, was drawing near, but before discussing that production, we must deal with a vital matter in terms of opera—the "bis!"

The ancient Greeks, when they were particularly satisfied by something, cried "Autìs!" The Romans, on the other hand, handed down to us this three-letter word, the crown of thorns or of glory for any artist. The most famous *bis* of history was accorded to Domenico Cimarosa in 1792, when the Emperor Leopold II, at the end of the *Matrimonio segreto* demanded to hear the whole opera again. The fans of Caruso were no less demanding; in Rio de Janeiro in 1903 they made him sing *La donna è mobile* five times, and that remains a world record. In the times of the Wagnerian reformation, with the theater in darkness, the public solemnly well-behaved and the orchestra invisible, the "bis" had become decidedly out of favor, and then even severely prohibited. In Naples in 1914, under Leopoldo Mugnone, the innovative spirit was still raging, fostered above all by Toscanini. For this reason, no mention was even to be made of a "bis." Dourly, but paying Tito a great compliment at the same time, Mugnone maintained that "in any case, here in Naples they'd demand a bis even if you'd made a *pernacchio* (rude rasping noise or 'raspberry' [tr.]). Don't take any notice, for heaven's sake."

To this attitude of complete refusal must be added Tito's own personal determination, declared since the days of the Quirino, not to have anything to do with the claque. In Milan, soon afterwards, he was even to risk physical injury by forcefully rejecting the somewhat authoritarian demands of the leader of the claque. So Tito understood completely: there must be no mention, even, of a *bis*.

But then this *Tosca* came along.

As soon as he could allow himself to do so, Tito accepted Gerunda's advice of long ago, and in the course of a few years completely abandoned *Butterfly, Cavalleria* and *Tosca*—all fascinating material, but dangerous for his vocal organ. In this way he was to consign himself to a kind of miraculous vocal immortality, which would be the true basis of his immortality as an artist. However, even though this providential decision can only bring us pleasure in the end, part of us must still regret not having been able to hear in well-recorded form the miracle to which the accounts of the period and the early acoustical recordings only communicate with difficulty. In particular, the romanza from the third act of *Tosca*: "*E lucevan le stelle*" on the lips of Tito Schipa gained in a few days such force of impact on the Neapolitan listeners that the planned performances began to increase, then to multiply, in a crescendo of enthusiastic houses which culminated in the condemned Cavaradossi's aria as a bullfight culminates in the *coup de grâce*.

Some days before his debut, during the practices accompanied by the piano, Mugnone had appeared a little surprised (and also a little put out) by Tito's intention to obtain a long and unwritten pause of suspension halfway through the phrase *"disciogliea dai veli."* It served to allow him to utter the syllable "scio" exactly as he wanted.

"And the breath to finish the phrase off?"

"Don't worry, Maestro; I'll have enough!"

With the superior ear that he possessed, Mugnone must have noticed Tito's only slight defect of diction—which would remain with him to the end of his career, even though cleverly disguised. It only showed up when he was singing, and it affected this same group, "sci." When this sound was carrying a heavy emotional charge it tended to become simplified to "ssi," perhaps not to alter the character of the sound too greatly in a delicate passage. And yet it was precisely on that ultra-famous "scio" that Tito was about to win—unequivocally—the first laurels of his career.

There were repeated demands for a "bis"—obstinate and even violent (some years later Tito was to claim that the only time in his career that he heard the sound of a whistle was when he refused a "tris" in Spain!) In fact, because of frustration the applause often turned to whistles, and there was no avoiding it. But Mugnone was adamant; no "bis." Even at the cost of losing more time by refusing than granting it. Then came that crucial performance.

Tito approached the romance in a special state of grace. The images of dreamy sensuality followed each other in that irresistible sequence, and the public hung on them with bated breath. Then the phrase headed lightly towards a peak of sorrowful nostalgia, and that "di-*scio*-gliea" opened like a silk parachute, halting time for a moment in the consciousness of two thousand enchanted listeners.

The end came swiftly; the last notes died away. Silence...

A silence of many—too many—seconds. No premature yell, no throaty roar in the manner of a football crowd, but an inexplicable hypnotic state had captured the listeners, from which they could only free themselves with a sort of painful effort. When they did the first rustles of applause built rapidly to cries of *Bravo!* And naturally, the cries of *Bis!* (It would soon become the rule, the recurring enchantment of each performance, for decades: a "wish that there was no need to go home," which admirers recall with tears in their eyes.)

In the uproar Mugnone was strangely pensive. He stood gripping the rostrum, and said nothing. The first to realize that something was wrong were the stagehands behind the scenes, who were keeping their ears tuned. Mugnone, who up to that moment had been staring at Tito with a fixed expression, turned towards the audience, and with a gesture worthy of his baton, quieted the din. The silence of a tomb fell. Then he turned to face the stage, and with another, this time absolutely Neapolitan, gesture, he called Tito's attention, as if to say to him: "Listen here." Tito took a step forward, and the Maestro, in a confidential tone, yet one which the whole of the San Carlo could hear, said:

"*Schipetiè ... N'ata vota!*" ("Once more!")

History had already been made. But that was not all: he gestured with his thumb at the public behind him:

"*Ma no pe' cchisti.*" He tapped his chest and went on: "*Pe' mme!*" ("Not for them...for me!"}

This time it was Mugnone who won himself several seconds of stupefied silence. Then came the applause, the laughter, the shouts of approval. The clarinet silenced everyone, repeating its dreamy meditation and Tito gave his "bis." That evening, even if the world was as yet unaware of it, Tito Schipa was born, in all essential senses.

"All the same, in *Fedora* you're a real dog!"

This was the cold shower that Mugnone poured over Tito the next day, when he was still in the clouds over his triumph. And yet *Fedora* had gone very well. Why was the great man so savage? Because it was not just the artist which was great in him, but also the gentleman, loyal to certain unwritten but basic rules.

Naples was at that time the uncontested kingdom of a monarch in slow and irreversible decline: Fernando De Lucia. To sing *Fedora,* once his showpiece, and before his own public, was a real act of disrespect. It was of little importance that it was just another of many substitutions; it didn't matter that De Lucia himself really was ill. In practice it was a usurpation, and to make the indelicacy worse, undertaken at a time when the old divo had just undergone the humiliation of a very poor showing before his own favorite public. It was simply not the thing to do. And Mugnone didn't speak to Tito for weeks.

In this way, great encounters were had, great lessons learned. This time it was a course in style and behavior. Everything would be put to good effect, and splendidly. Proof of this is in a yellowing old score still preserved in our family, containing certain musical lyrics, where one can still read today a hand-written dedication:

"To the ideal artist and *gentleman*, Tito Schipa: these old and very insignificant notes are offered with affection and admiration by —Leopoldo Mugnone."

El Encantador

On April 16th, 1914, on the crest of the wave of his Neapolitan success, Tito's name appeared for the first time in the Teatro Costanzi in Rome, which was later to become the Rome Opera. In this *Don Pasquale* he met Rosina Storchio: a preview of the cast which we shall meet again before long at La Scala. Before he won new plaudits for himself in Milan, however, there was another excursion abroad: once again to South America, and once again to do *Tosca* and *Butterfly*. But he gave less and less performances of these because by now his ideal repertoire was beginning to take shape. There were also some unexpected novelties, such as *Le donne curiose* by Wolf-Ferrari, in Naples in March 1915, destined to win a small place in the chronicles.

Finally, in October of the same year, Tito arrived in Milan, to conclude his Italian campaign in the theater which in the future he would always mention with a touch of emotion. But before setting foot on the stage of La Scala, he still had to go through a "provincial" preparation in the city itself, so first came the Teatro Manzoni, and then, once more, the Dal Verme. In the latter he found himself face to face with a conductor with a penetrating gaze, an elegant and excitable character; and that *Traviata* which we still have fresh in our minds, with the duets with Muzio, was now transformed into a five-star performance with Schipa, Storchio—and Toscanini!

Traviata and *Falstaff*. This was the sole encounter with the great maestro. Their ways were to part at once at the artistic level, and long afterwards they would divide again, and even more seriously, when the gilded world of the primadonnas and heroes would fade away bitterly into a colorless and yet violent reality. But those days were far in the future. At this point the dream was growing and becoming more colorful from day to day, and it seemed constantly as if the best were yet to come.

In the specific instance of Milan and La Scala, the best was already at the door, and the proof was not long in coming. There *Prince Igor,* another anomaly in the Schipa repertoire, was the vehicle of his debut. Gino Marinuzzi conducted, another distinguished maestro, and one with whom, in contrast to Toscanini, he was to establish a long-lasting and profitable international relationship.

But the Milan public did not form its judgment on the basis of Borodin; it judged, when required, on Massenet. A performance of *Manon* with Alessandro Bonci still resounded in the memory of the Milanese audience. After the comparisons with Anselmi, this latest encounter with a myth was not expected, if the truth be told. But Bonci,

> having been unable to sing, as he was under contract to do, in *L'elisir d'amore*, wanted to sing in *Manon* instead. It was a great success, even considering the great reputation which Bonci possessed, but when I sang it, the success attained what could even be called alarming proportions!

"Alarming" is the right word: determined not to give in on his vow to have nothing to do with the claque, Tito had a violent encounter with its representatives, and even reached the point of paying them *not* to applaud him (twenty-five lire), denied them their free tickets, and received a very clear physical threat as a result. With no hesitation he went to police headquarters and brought charges on grounds of extortion!

> The newspapers, when they learned about the matter, approved.

As for the performance,

the famous romance, "*Chiudo gli occhi,*" was greeted with an ovation which it seemed would never end.

So for the moment, Italy was dealt with. Success had removed the bitter taste of winning it from his mouth. Now was the moment to give the lie to the old well-worn proverb: a prophet is not without honor, save in his own country... Old and well-worn, but still applicable.

Again he went abroad, and once more he reached South America, but this time on the way back he stopped off in Spain. If he had known what awaited him in that country, so similar to his own Salento in its refinement and its devotion to sweet things, he would have kissed the ground when he disembarked.

He made his debut in Barcelona, at the Teatro del Liceo. They allowed him to choose the opera himself, and he put all his eggs in one basket: *Manon.* He was warned that this was folly, and back came the name of the bogeyman, Anselmi. With regard to this delightful opera Tito found himself in a position similar to Puccini's when he wrote his own version of it. Nobody had believed that Puccini could surpass Massenet. And in fact he did not surpass him. He gave the work a completely different form, winning a triumph for himself which in no way detracted from the genius of his predecessor. Tito, although he didn't distance himself markedly from Anselmi's style, prepared to attain much the same result—i.e. to triumph equally, but on a different basis. Later on his perfection of phrasing and deepening understanding of the role would deliver the final blow. The opening *Manon* in Barcelona was a trial run. Tito and the Spanish took stock of each other, with a measure of circumspection.

When he was offered a role at the Real in Madrid, he put all his faith in the same strategy (although he must have accepted, even to sing *Manon,* with some difficulty, since the Real was the only theater in the world which intimidated him).

On the evening of the first night at the Real, when he was already in costume, a high-ranking official from the Bourbon court had approached him and announced that Alfonso XIII would be present in person at the performance.

At that moment I really was frightened. It was the first time that I
had had to sing before a monarch.

The result was a triumph, a whirl of success. Tito surged into
favor, breaking down whatever resistance was left in Spanish hearts.
For the whole of his life he would say that that evening of January
14, 1917, was the happiest of his career.

Some reviewers were still on the fence about the new tenor's
merit, however. The weekly "Blanco y Negro,"[10] 21 January 1917,
had this to say:

"Schipa has made his debut with *Manon,* and naturally he
was greeted with enthusiasm, confirming the good opinion which
had already been formed of him. He is a tenor with a sweet and
pleasing voice, who knows how to sing, and from whom great
results are expected. But he is not '*el divo*'—the famous divo who
draws the public and fills the theaters."

Tito was clearly piqued by that article, and by the word it
stressed:

The Teatro Real is a place where *divi* are consecrated. I had to
wager my whole career on the luck of one single card on that stage.

This critic was overcautious. He concludes by declaring the
imminent arrival of a tenor who, it is said, will be the heir of
Caruso.[11] He names no names. But as far as drawing publics and
filling theaters is concerned, he was going to have to rethink his
view of Tito Schipa. (And he did. A few years later the same review would be saying: "In our Teatro Real, Tito Schipa has inher-
ited the scepter of the great Commendatore, Giuseppe Anselmi.
Ah, if only all the romantic spiritual widows of Mr. Rudolph
Valentino had been able to enter a second fantasy marriage so
quickly!" ["Blanco y Negro," May 22, 1922.])

After his initial success in Madrid, profiting from his now nearly
perfect knowledge of the language, Tito began a work of slow,
methodical self-insertion into the consciousness of the Spanish

---

[10]*Blanco y Negro* was a weekly magazine issued in Madrid in conjunction with the
newspaper ABC, and subsequently became its weekly magazine section.

[11]This was Beniamino Gigli, who made his Madrid debut on March 17th and his Barcelona
debut on April 7th of that year.

public. He used all means. He often, and of his own free will, abandoned the formality of the operatic repertoire and came closer to everyday popular taste by interpreting *zarzuelas,* the local form of operetta. At a benefit performance for journalists, held in Madrid, they implored him to sing "Granadinas," taken from *Emigrantes* by Barreras. And they asked him to do it in Granadine costume—jerkin, cap and knee-breeches. He was a bit embarrassed, but discovered a piece of superior difficulty and beauty, which he immediately decided to record. He would preserve other selections—the most evocative of their kind—from the *zarzuelas,* and introduce them regularly into his concert repertoire. His genuine appreciation of the light repertoire, which came to be stressed more and more, would become a personal characteristic, the only one which was later to be attacked by his most severe critics. But when we listen to "Granadinas," in which the lace of Spanish mantillas and the filigree of the baroque of Lecce seem to interweave in a vocal embroidery of stunning finesse, we are once again delighted by his transgressions. There would be more drastic ones in the future, and these too were to be a source of pleasure.

When his appearances had become familiar in the world of song, he decided to set off again. On a steamboat returning from South America, he had met a very prolific and brilliant composer, José Padilla, who was close to him in age. Practically in front of his eyes, the musician had written "Princesita" for him, tailor-made for him to sing. Their common project bore excellent fruit within a few years. In particular, "Princesita" was an international success, and no less successful were "Violetera," "Valencia," and many others.

Stimulated by Padilla's presence, Schipa began trying his own hand as a composer. In this the extensive studies in pianoforte and composition which Gerunda had imposed on him as an accompaniment to his vocal education were to prove useful. He always said that composing was his second passion. And when he was still quite young, he had confirmed this in a way with the four-part Mass used as a final test in his contrapuntal training. A strict analysis of the work, however, would not satisfy a perfectionist.

He was much more at home in the lighter repertoire, where without doubt he had an outstanding gift for melody. But when it was a matter of composing music or words for the Spanish language, his ear seemed only to be able to function in tangos. Certainly they were very fine tangos, in surprisingly modern style. "Gaucho" or "Pampero" are enough in themselves to merit fame as a composer. The latter of these two pieces was composed with four hands in the company of an underestimated genius of songwriting, the Frenchman Richard Barthélemy, who at the moment of composition could switch to Spanish or Neapolitan indiscriminately.

While all this was going on, there was no falling-off in the triumphs on the operatic stage; indeed they increased. The mixture of popular appreciation, which now came near hysteria, and success in the more solemn world of the stage seemed to produce the conditions required for the auspicious words to be heard: "a *divo* is born." The newspapers invented slogans; they said the people were demanding "bread and... Schipa." Nicknames were invented; the most flattering as well as the most appropriate was the Spanish *"El Encantador"*—the Enchanter.

No one escaped the spell, men or women, plebs or patricians. At the end of a triumphant performance in the Real in Madrid, from the shadows of one of the proscenium boxes came a bouquet of flowers which landed on the boards with a slight thud. Tito searched among the petals and found a minute scroll. In the dressing room, he unraveled it and found two cufflinks decorated with pearls and diamonds, more resplendent than anything he had ever seen or dreamed of. Whose hand had thrown them? Reliable sources spoke very quietly of one of the great ladies of the royal family.

However, the bachelor-prodigy, now twenty-eight, was about to meet the first woman who would succeed in trapping him properly. She was a long way from being a lady of the court, nor could she allow herself to bestow a gift of that kind. In fact, just at that very moment, even her survival might have been in jeopardy. But destiny has its own ways, and in this case, the way led to Monte Carlo, where it had decided that her path should converge and unite with that of Giacomo Puccini.

VII

(1917 – 1919)

The Diabolical Mr. C.

In Tito's memoirs, the approach to Monte Carlo is like a little interval of total comedy inspired by a terror which few southern Italians escape completely—especially if they are involved in the world of entertainment—*la jella:* the jinx. This time the cause of the irritating but not mortal pestilence was a musician. Tito in fact called him a "maniac for music and singing." This is how he describes the unlucky event:

> Do you believe in jinxes? The real, black, unavoidable, unpreventable kind? Well, anyway, it was 1917. That's enough in itself (Seventeen is *the* unlucky number in Italian. *Tr.*) I was in Barcelona, and I had to travel to Madrid and Lisbon, where I had a series of performances in the Coliseu. And what happens? This fellow attaches himself to me... I won't mention his name, let's just call him Mr. C.: a 'cellist, a devotee of songs, and above all, an infallible bringer of bad luck.
>
> Together with me were Masini Pieralli, the bass, and my sister Elvira. As soon as Mr. C. appeared, I noticed that Masini Pieralli was performing a ritual all of his own making, with every gesture imaginable to ward off the evil eye... But my sister just said:
>
> – Oh, come on, it can't be true: don't give it a thought...
>
> And we started off by missing the train. Well, O.K. My sister insisted:

– Just a coincidence...

And the car which we took instead of the train first bumped into some poor devil of a mongrel hound, and then had a double puncture – two in one go!

– Tito, said my sister: don't get a fixation!

So, to avoid getting fixated, I thought I'd distract my mind by eating a nice, peppery sausage during a layover. And what happens? I get a terrific, violent attack of colic! And in the evening, at the performance, I'm forced to sing the whole opera in a state which you can easily imagine.

When we reached the frontier, where are the passports? You've guessed: left behind in Madrid. We had to postpone our transfer for two days.

Oh, Mr. C. was fine. He was really pleased with himself. My sister said:

– Well, things can't get any worse; let's relax – it's all over.

And that evening she herself took to her bed, with a high fever. Spanish flu. Finally she admitted:

– My God, it really must be true!

To cheer her up, I said:

– No, no, you were right; it's all just coincidence... Fixation!

And the next day, I took to my bed too...

At the end of all these tribulations; there was the opening of *La rondine*. I can't say that it went badly, but certainly in comparison with other works by Puccini...

Needless to say, Mr. C. hadn't left us alone for a moment, even during rehearsals.

– Oh God, what else has gone wrong? I thought, terrified.

But then I discovered that Puccini had cried with emotion because he was so pleased with the performance...

Tito always ended the account of this affair in this way, delighted, and as the years went on the story acquired extra details and effects. But apart from the laughs and the specter of possible credulity, which is somewhat alarming, there is one genuine source of fright in this story: the "Spanish 'flu" which in the next few months claimed thousands of victims all over Europe. It may seem a bit far-fetched to us to put down the sicknesses of both Tito and Elvira to this dread disease, but it is recorded with certainty that this was the case with Antoinette Michel d'Ogoy, known as Lillì, who was fighting against death in those days in a boardinghouse in Monte Carlo, not so far away from the places where Tito Schipa and Giacomo Puccini at the piano were putting the final touches to the new score.

It seemed in retrospect that destiny had brought Tito to Monte Carlo for the sole purpose of finding him a wife, since nothing connected with *La rondine* seems to be considered worth mentioning in his autobiography, except a rather tight-lipped correction:

> So it isn't true that Gigli was the creator of *La rondine*: I was the first to sing it and Gigli only sang it later in Italy.

But we do know that the outcome of the first night was not all that triumphant, and that of all Puccini's works, *La rondine* always trailed at the end of the list.[12] Maybe Mr. C. had struck again. However, Tito seized the opportunity to impress the great composer with the quality of his musicianship—and not only Puccini, but also other musicians who were present at that season in Monte Carlo. For instance, Umberto Benedetti, who at that time played first 'cello in the local orchestra.

Benedetti recalled that during the rehearsals for *Tosca*, he chanced to hear Tito, who was humming. But not humming the part of Cavaradossi: he was humming the 'cello part, with his mouth closed, and "with the precision and sensitivity of a great artist." He questioned him about this, and the reply was that it was natural for someone singing a leading role to know by heart the parts of the other artists and the leading orchestral ones as well.

That evening, in the performance, Benedetti spent all the time that he was not actually playing in listening to something that he was later to describe as "without precedent." It's no less astonishing a little later, on February 27th, 1925, to read an interview with Tito in the "Galesburg Illinois Mail" in which, apart from invaluable information on the technique of learning a role, we discover that Borboni may have been first to arrange the perfect match of Schipa and Werther:

> I have been asked to tell of the way in which I study a role. Suppose I take a part I love so well – that of Massenet's *Werther*. When first the impresario gave me the word that I was to be the poet/singer, I was delighted, for I realized the opportunities of the part. But I was

---

[12] *La rondine* was given much more often than the early *Edgar* and probably somewhat more often than *Le Villi*.

in no hurry to rush to the arias. There are so many singers who know their own arias and duets. They know nothing else! Ask them what the whole action is about, they look at you in a dumbfounded way... which explains why they sing and don't give the feeling of reality. Ah, no–when *Werther* was put in my hand, I went to the sources of information. I read again the Goethe work. I concentrated on it until I felt the poet's history, his point of view, his outlook on life, his way of doing things....his response and reaction to all ideas.

After I felt that I knew Werther intimately, I called my pianist to my home. I had him play the entire score to me, while I followed it carefully. This was done for several days, until the ensemble of the music was with me. This included the overtures and intermezzi, which for me are essential for my mind.

Then I began to study the words of the libretto. But I did not study them alone, nor did I start to sing them–no, no! I take the rhythmic values first. Not the melody, you understand, but merely the "swing," and the rhythmic values. This I do until it is well implanted in my brain. For I believe that no interruption is right which goes out of the square—I mean that the singer must remember that it is an opera, and must keep to the construction of the composer's framework. He cannot sing irrespective of the orchestration, or the rest of the cast; must know his rhythmic place.

Now comes the music. I went to the piano with the accompanist, and went over the role, singing in soft voice, until the melody was within my throat.

Mastering a role is not a difficult task, therefore, for me; two or three weeks' study generally is sufficient.

I would stress: this was 1925. Not the 1990s, with Placido Domingo who amazes us so greatly by his all-around musicianship and knowledge, but the twenties, with Tito Schipa who, with that phrase about "knowing one's place," had discovered the secret, and himself been the first to seize upon it. And the word "swing," too—we shall have more to say about that shortly. In the meantime, we must confine ourselves to imagining, each in his own way, the meeting between the young, freewheeling tenor at the beginning of his dizzy rise to fame, and the cabaret dancer and singer, who had moved to Monte Carlo after a series of professional disappointments in her native Paris. Unfortunately, no direct testimony to the circumstances and manner of this meeting survives.

Lillì

Antoinette Michel d'Ogoy flaunted her double surname with some pride, but not legitimately. She was the natural daughter of a nobleman whose family had always refused to recognize his union with a *petite bourgeoise*. When he died from falling off a horse, Antoinette's mother married, bringing as her dowry a not inconsiderable allowance left by her titled lover. This bequest enabled Antoinette to become independent as soon as she was of age.

Pretty, with the soft and generous curving lines of the feminine stereotype of that period, she had sandy hair and very attractive green eyes; it was easy enough for her to enter the world of the variety theater, but she never managed to make a name for herself there. In Monte Carlo she was for one of the last times throwing herself against a door which would never open. In compensation, she had one of the most unlikely encounters... but, as we have said, of this meeting, so important for Tito's private life and for hers, we know nothing. Elena, one of Tito and Antoinette's daughters, says she never heard her parents talk about their first meeting. Even less was anything ever said about it in my family, since the sad course of events had caused us to be seen as enemies of Elena's. Only one phrase from my father, slightly barbed, and possibly spoken to please my mother, has remained in my mind:

– Lucrezia Bori told me that that same Antoinette had been one of her brother's amours, but that now she was free...

Was it true? Did the great soprano act as a go-between in this important encounter which began as a bit of fun? The fact remains that when, two years later, in 1919, Tito returned for the third time to Monte Carlo (and again interpreted *La rondine* there), the little adventure had become something a good deal more serious, and matrimony was in the air. And in his biography, he never names Antoinette (who from now on will be Lillì for us) except from 1919 onwards, and then as his future wife. Because...this is the way a gentleman should behave.

The wedding would eventually take place, in North America,

almost as if to confirm the beginning of a new path in the life of the artist (and perhaps to remove him once and for all from the influence of the inauspicious Mr. C....?). But before the great leap to the U.S., the nightingale from Lecce flew round and round in concentric circles, just like one of the birds of annual migration before the great flight begins. And between 1917 and 1919, everything is centered on Monte Carlo. From there, the excursions continued, reaching their limits in Lisbon to the west and Rome to the east, and always with Spain as a first preference. It could even be said that in those years Tito's real fixed abode consisted of a couple of Spanish hotels. Even the repertoire was repetitious, and not yet free from those "dangerous" titles which were now, however, effectively reduced to *Tosca* alone. Now that he had felt Puccini's affectionate gaze resting on him, Tito found it even more difficult to say goodbye to the work.

There are also some entries in the chronology which were to remain isolated episodes in his career: two *zarzuelas—Jugar con fuego* by Barbieri and *La bruja* by Chapí, and *Manole*, an opera by Gunsbourg.

In these months, Tito's family moved from Lecce and settled in Naples, in an apartment near the Angiporto Galleria district. And in Naples, Tito improved his talent for comedy, which was to distinguish him on the stage as much as his talent for drama. He performed in obscure theaters, where, however, some memorable events took place.

> When I went to hear Scarpetta in Naples, I used to burst out so often into gusty, noisy laughter that I had frequently to leave the theater so as not to disturb other people. Scarpetta noticed this and when my shrill laughter was heard above the general hilarity of the audience, he stopped his performance, jumped the footlights and came into the darkened auditorium, saying: "How's it going, Schipa?"

In Naples, a meeting with Mascagni not only led to two very successful opera productions, but also to the formation of an unbeatable partnership for the card game, *scopone*. It was said of them that in an international tournament for players of this highly sophisticated game, they would be first choice to represent Italy and would surely win first prize. In the intervals between one match and another the great musical names from Lecce and Livorno would find time to attend the San Carlo, and there were memorable performances of *L'amico Fritz* and *Lodoletta*, with the composer conducting.

But the title which seems to possess a magic quality at this time appears, or rather reappears, in the bills for Lisbon on May 31, 1919: *Werther*.

A Werther unmoved!

It is genuinely difficult to convey in words the emotional impact which the name of Werther and that of Tito Schipa together provoke in those who were initiated into the mystery of this meeting up of a character with his ideal interpreter. I had myself been accustomed since childhood to think of these twinned names as a kind of hallmark of perfection, having been lulled by the enchantment of two romanzas, recorded on 78s. So many admirers had held forth on the subject, so many critics and colleagues. Yet when I actually found myself, by a series of lucky coincidences, confronted with the surviving record of the whole performance, I felt as if I'd been turned to stone. Far beyond any confirmation of the ecstatic phrases I'd been hearing all through the years, what struck me most forcibly was the sense of modernity conveyed by the battered grooves of that old recording.

And here is the real meaning of that word "swing" which seemed so anachronistic and even heretical on the lips of a giant of operatic melodrama. Here is that capacity to sing "on," i.e. carried along by, the rhythm as one sings "on" the breath, uttering the phrases with effortless lightness and at the same time keeping pace with a superior rhythm such as no metronome can ever produce, so akin to the transcendent beat of a great jazz musician. Here too is the diabolical ability to make use of all that skill, and then reenter with startling effect at the right moment into the traditional rules, and give the values intended by the composer to the melodic flight, the perfect harmony, the sigh of a pause—while bestowing a wholly new meaning on them. Above all, here is that gift for *not* doing, *not* forcing, *not* stressing, that "evocation by omission" of everything that others strove so hard to achieve by excess. And we have to remember too that the old recording technique could never capture the stage setting of that sound miracle, achieved more by absence than overload, or as the orientals would say, made from "nothingness."

How much we could learn about the genesis and growth of this masterpiece! But how sparing its artificer was of information and details. However, we do know that in that May performance in the Coliseu Dos Recrejos in Lisbon, something happened which laid a foundation-stone of this monument.

There Tito and Werther were meeting each other on the stage for the second time. This Portuguese performance of 1919 followed the Roman one of 1911, and between those two dates, the name of the love-crazed youth created by Goethe had not appeared on any poster coupled with the name of Schipa. A strange suspended interval.

And the legends have accumulated here, as usual; all of them intended to explain that surprising quality leap which Tito's interpretation had taken in the meantime. This pause, say the wise heads, cannot have been accidental. It must have been a pause for meditative and profound reflection. And here we find appearing in the writings of those who follow the myth (but also help to create it), in these years of the interval between the debut and the finished performance (spent in differing experiences not only of opera but also of theater in the broader and deeper sense) the shadowy figure of a French "maestro," an old and unidentifiable actor of the Comédie Française, to whom Tito is supposed to have turned for advice.

This shows that it has always seemed evident to everyone that when mention was made of Schipa-Werther, there was always "someone else" behind it. And it was also obvious to opera fans themselves, the most exclusive and sectarian of people. For they were ready to admit that such mastery could never have been cultivated solely in the soil of opera and its *divi*—good at the high notes, but pretty limited, poor dears, by their restricted interpretative horizons.

This grand old man of the stage is supposed to have lived in Paris, and Tito is believed to have gone there on pilgrimage, convincing him—not without encountering a certain reluctance—to give him acting lessons. As a basic text, the young tenor is supposed to have suggested not a classical tragedy, but an opera libretto. Metrically scanning *that* libretto in time with music only heard only in the imagination would have been a real exercise in interpretation, in which even the maestro himself must have found some elements of novelty.

At the end of this supposed apprenticeship, but actually in a complete reinterpretation of the role rather than a repetition, almost as if it were a new beginning, comes the Lisbon performance of *Werther.*

Werther was not exactly what could be called one of the great operatic favorites (nor has it ever become so, despite its beauty). It is true that the great and omnipresent Anselmi had made it his warhorse, but the opera did not even feature in the list of those that everyone knows by heart, stagehands included. If we add the fact that of all the many languages which Tito set about learning, Portuguese was never one, it seems clear why, before mounting the stage that evening, he felt the need to make an arrangement with a backstage assistant.

Experience had taught him that in the key scene of the third act, when Werther, abandoned by Charlotte, flings himself against the door she has just slammed in his face and beats on it in rage and desperation, there was a risk of getting too carried away. It might be that part of the set wasn't firmly fixed, and there could be a collapse; the pathos of the moment would give way to a scene of embarrassment. For this reason, Tito had begged a huge fellow who was working backstage to place himself as a counterweight behind the set, and to support it with all his strength. He had made him understand, more by gesture than word, that the moment to push should coincide with the first rap that he heard on that painted panel. This was Schipa the "director" already in the making, an artist who knew the limits of productions that had had no onstage trials, provisional in everything except the music.

The fact remains that the great hunk appeared to have understood, and the performance went ahead without hitches until the fateful entry of Werther to Charlotte's room. Here, in his usual interpretation, as soon as he was recognized by her, Tito would lean up against the doorpost as if he wanted to disappear into the wall in a sudden fit of hesitation, a rethinking or a sort of unexpected exhaustion. This was the position in which he uttered his first phrases, admitting his weakness, the obsession which had caused his return. Then he would move away from the wall, and coming forward with a newly-recovered assurance, would begin to sing what everyone was waiting for: "*Ah, pourquoi me reveiller?*," which marks the culmination of the opera. And he tried to do everything just this way that evening too, but at that very moment a light tug at his neck froze the blood in his veins. The tail of his wig had become fiendishly caught in the narrow space between the wall and the door; the black bow which tied it at the far end had slipped outside, and now formed an effective brake against all attempts to dislodge it. A couple of furtive tugs confirmed the worst: Tito knew there was nothing to be done.

Or rather, it would have been possible to sacrifice the strict demands of the stage for those of the music, and free himself from the wig, and go on singing indifferently. But Tito Schipa was convinced more than anyone else that opera was above all theater, and that theater, at least during a performance, must be safeguarded as much as, if not more than, the music. So he took his time and did not move. The requirements of the action did make it possible for Werther to remain a few moments longer in that troublesome position; there was a very short space of time to try to attract the attention of the huge oaf and get himself free of the diabolical door frame.

So Tito began to hammer with his finger on the wall. The man, only a few centimeters behind the scene, but divided by light years of incomprehension, and with only a very slight knowledge of the opera, at first didn't react at all, being convinced that the only signal for him would consist of loud knocks on the door. Then, however, he could hardly fail to notice Tito's desperate message. But he deduced that his moment had come and disastrously began to push. The result of this was that the offending tail was now well and truly wedged into the scenery.

Tito rapped more sharply, but the other only became more determined in his pushing. So the scene went forward, before the eyes of a Charlotte who was already terrified and a conductor who began almost unconsciously to slow down. But the music could not stop altogether, and the "Wallpaper Werther" was forced to act out the awaited recognition scene across the room without moving even a millimeter from the shadowy corner where he was transfixed. And thus he sang, listing with dreamy precision the spinet and all the other objects full of memories, without actually being able to see them. And he resigned himself to disaster, just hoping that he would be set free in time for the romanza, at least. But the stagehand didn't budge. The moment came for Werther to notice the books, and he had no alternative but to recognize them from afar, and now came the dreaded moment. He began: "*Traduire...*" and miraculously, gently and perhaps inspired by the genius of Massenet, the giant released his pressure and freed the prisoner. Tito just had time to move a mere three paces forward when the arpeggio from the orchestra signalled the beginning of his aria.

In the subliminal moment that followed before the first syllable, he glanced at the front row, expecting to see faces showing amusement, or at least compassion at his misfortune. But instead, his look met with glazed expressions, with eyes fixed in a kind of trance, which seemed to be looking beyond him in contemplation of a memory. Eyes misty with tears, mouths half-open. Later, in his dressing room, amid breathless compliments, friends and admirers full of emotion tried to express the inexpressible to him, asking how he had managed, in that introduction to the romanza, to have spellbound them in such a way.

Whether it was a synthesis worked out on the spot or something arrived at gradually over the years, there is no doubt that from that evening onwards there took root in him the unprecedented conviction, all bright and shining, of *not* doing, *not* adding anything, of leaving the route by which the spectator should be reached to the force of the impact of his own emotion. No interposing of a diaphragm, no hodgepodge of gesture and manner, no rusty scheme learnt at third hand together with vocalizations and anecdotes.

He was enlightened by the flash which had been lighting up music and painting and literature for some decades, and which a few years later was to bring light to the theater as well. In Duse, in Ricci and Benassi, it would give a twist to the very notion of being onstage, but in the specific context of opera it represented an unheard-of break with established tradition: the character could exist *in reality* on the stage, not "impersonated" by the actor but transformed into the pure and simple *existence* of the actor. On those dusty boards and against those backdrops, painted as in a puppet-theater, there was no need to feign anything, to act anything. There was no need to *act* at all, slaves of an inferiority complex towards the plays which had endured for centuries (and which had been transmuted, as so often happens, in a contemptuous attitude of superiority). Stanislavsky and his interpretative revolution broke through the backdrops and flats of the Opera just at the moment that Tito realized that Tito Schipa should not *seem to be* Werther, but that it was Werther that must *be Tito Schipa*.

From that day onward, an interpretation already consisting of subtleties barely hinted at was receiving final form in every performance, reaching truly astonishing levels of abstraction. The mere gesture of removing a hat, on the first exit (that blue tall hat in conical sections which was to become a fetish for the post-war public), came more and more to assume all the ritual quality and force of a spell, simply by virtue of a bold and unprecedented simplicity. And it was in a kind of hypnosis, a wicked, spell-casting sweetness, that the audience found itself as the blonde wig was slowly uncovered. At the first syllables: "*Allor, sta proprio qua il signor podestà*," the battle was already won, the enemy at his feet, the triumph taking place.

The death-scene, which lasts for a whole act, and which was one of the things which contributed to the age-old joke about singers who take an unconscionable time dying, not only became credible but almost seemed brief in his hands. And it was solved by letting the curtain go up on Werther already sprawled in an armchair, a pistol in his trailing hand, a red stain on his shirt. This red stain, throughout the whole act, would be the only thing in *Werther* which moved! A simple but perfect mechanism, constructed by Tito himself and applied by very slow degrees, emitted a slow flow of colored material which made the bloodstain expand inexorably before the eyes of the public, convinced by now that it was seeing things. Moreover, an absolute order had been given to his partner not to touch it, under any circumstances. He would sing the whole scene in that position, his head lolling against the back of the armchair. At the moment of death, a simple relaxing of position, and the body would be allowed to go wherever the free fall took it. In most cases it simply lapsed into immobility.

And that was the end.

If, during the performance, a moment of impulsiveness, of genuine expressive fury had left the audience and the critics open-mouthed, provoking comments about the great actor, the master of the stage, that too had happened as a result of the fact that the long connecting periods between one interpretative peak and another passed in a detached, superior bearing, in an extended calm which left everything to the instrument, the prodigy of sound.

Others like him, superior artists, realized that the Opera needed a renaissance in its notion of the singer-actor, and a few even succeeded in producing the miracle of a *complete spectacle*, since this is, or should be, the true essence of melodrama. These true geniuses of the stage were people like Claudia Muzio, Feodor Chaliapin, or Mary Garden, and much later on Maria Callas, Tito Gobbi, Italo Tajo and others. But in Tito Schipa this conquest was united to the miracle of an unsurpassed vocal quality, in itself enough to create a myth. The artist, even when transplanted into a colorless concert hall, would succeed, as we shall see, in utilizing all the secrets of his magic powers, even in the most complete immobility and lack of theatricality. There was in addition a personal fascination which could be discovered quite outside the theater and the concert hall, and which entered vigorously into life, to transform the everyday life of a man and those linked to him into a spectacle, often brilliant and sometimes tragic. With this explosive mixture in hand, the young aspirant from Lecce, by now on the brink of his apotheosis, was preparing to set the world on fire.

Waiting for peace to break out

Among the rare documents from this period, a small book made up entirely of thin sheets of letter-copies has come down to us. In this Tito preserved copies of every kind of correspondence. Unfortunately it only goes as far as 1919, but it provides interesting details on the last part of his Spanish period. For example, already on the first page, here are the standard demands which the artist was accustomed to make on his producers:

Dear Volpini and Zenatello, Barcelona:

The following is agreed between yourselves and me:

1 – that you will engage me at the Teatro Real in Madrid for a minimum of three guaranteed performances at 4000 pesetas each from 10 January 1919 until 25 (inc.) of the same month. The performances will be paid: the last on confirmation of the present by yourselves, which will be not later than 20 of next month; the other two will be advanced on the morning of each performance.

2 – that I undertake to sing at the aforesaid theater, in the position of principal tenor exclusively, the following works, at your choice: *Tosca*, *Manon* (M), *Werther*, *Fra' Diavolo*, *Rigoletto*, *Barbiere* and *Sonnambula*.

3 – that I will not sing in any concert or festival, even for benefit purposes, without your written permission.

4 – that in case of illness I will have the right to two days separately or consecutively.

5 – that I will not pay any mediations of any sort nor State or other tax (sic).

6 – that in advertisements where my name is featured, no other name shall appear in larger print than mine.

7 – that I will not sing more than three performances in one week, and never two consecutively.

8 – that I will grant you one performance gratis which will be the final performance that I give at the Real.

Faithfully, and with good wishes,

Tito Schipa,
Barcelona, 17.11.1918.

What a transformation! The unsophisticated young man from Lecce knew by this time exactly what he wanted and how to demand it. Who could have suspected that, on the contrary, his future career would be marked by the most incredible improvidence? However, apart from these matters of everyday business, at this time a dispute took place which had important repercussions. The correspondents in this extraordinary exchange of letters are two Milanese impresarios, Malco and Walter Mocchi, already mentioned,[13] who some time earlier, had arranged one of Tito's tours in South America, destined to reach its climax not at the Teatro Colón in Buenos Aires, as usual, but in the Teatro Coliseo. From the beginning of 1917, however, word was abroad that German

---

[13] See footnote 7, page 60-61. Mocchi was touring South America regularly from 1912 to the late 1920s. Tito Schipa sang for him for several seasons, including 1914 and 1919.

submarines were also attacking passenger ships, even if they belonged to neutral countries. This was what led to Tito's irrevocable decision: to the devil with contractual obligations—no sea-voyages until further notice. And even though the armistice was as good as signed when these letters were written, he still insisted:

> Wait until the peace is signed; I have the right to wait for this moment before deciding to cross the seas again.

The impresarios, to whose names we should add those of Lusardi, Bonetti and Chinelli, were all involved with each other in a complex game of intermediation and percentages. They opposed Tito's understandable instinct of self-preservation in every way, even insinuating that it was all a put-up job to obtain the Colón instead of the Coliseo. The tone of the correspondence must have become quite sharp, for on 25 November Tito wrote:

> A few words in reply to yours of the 17th inst. You tell me that I should refrain from being insolent to you? With all respect, my friend, I tell you you are wrong. And badly wrong. You should know that if you wish to enter combat with me, I am not one of those who give in easily! Nor am I to be intimidated! I have already stated that you have to do with a gentleman who is discussing his own rights, and who is not accustomed to dealing with Jesuitry–and it seems to me that you are pushing me somewhat too far!

> Yours truly, Tito Schipa.

Every device to avoid the Kaiser's torpedos is valid. Including a sudden increase in the financial demands, justified by the claim that "I am passing through my best phase." There is also, finally, a willingness to pay forfeits. It seems likely to me that the other party insisted. Eventually a judgment was reached, and the courts recognized the artist's right to preserve his own safety. From what we gather from the correspondence there was a compromise, with a postponement until the war was over.

And Tito complained that he had to leave his "beautiful, friendly Seville" because of this commitment of which he was now heartily sick, and set sail once again on the Spanish liner *Española*.

Towards a second homeland

Another name which appears frequently in his letter-copy book is Cleofonte Campanini, and it appears immediately, specifically on November 30, 1918. This makes it clear that the negotiations for a first approach to North America were already going on by that date, but not fully concluded as far as the second year of any eventual stay was concerned. The artist asked for fifteen thousand gold francs for eighteen performances (which were referred to as "functions" in this period), even though his fee at the Colón in Buenos Aires was, at that point, still eight thousand. We do not know what the other party offered. However the last page of the letter-copy book, undated but certainly later than May 4, 1919, is the copy of a quite enthusiastic telegram:

> WERTHER TREMENDOUS SUCCESS–STOP–HAVE CAMPANINI SEND ME URGENTLY THREE THOUSAND TWO HUNDRED FIFTY-TWO DOLLARS, COST OF JOURNEY RIO–NEW YORK. WILL WRITE. SCHIPA.

The *Werther* in question is presumably the one given in São Paulo do Brasile in October 1919, at the Teatro Municipal, conducted by Gino Marinuzzi. The latter was preparing, in turn, to journey to Chicago along with Tito.

But who was this 'Campanini' who invited two great artists to Chicago, and who was the woman who was his principal collaborator? For indeed, very little happened in the life of the young artist from Lecce which didn't have something to do with a woman, even if it was only in matters of organization.

Cleofonte Campanini was from Parma, and this meant that from the beginning he was a devotee of all things operatic. But to his natural birthright there was soon added a notable talent for music and conducting; so much so that he had mounted the rostrum of the Teatro Reinach in his native city when he was only twenty—though the results were not all that distinguished. This first lack of success must have rankled, since almost the whole of his life, which was subsequently crowned with much success, seems to have been aimed at one final gesture: to buy that theater for

87

himself, manage it, and initiate a competition for opera composers. In the course of his career, however, he had also enjoyed other considerable satisfactions, including the launching of masterpieces like *Adriana Lecouvreur* and *Madama Butterfly*. He made the latter into another of his great causes, in fact, and after its memorable opening failure in Turin he succeeded in directing not only its temporary flop in Milan but also its triumphant resurrection a year later in the Teatro Grande in Brescia. Apart from this, he was courageous in taking on new projects, very often putting himself personally at risk, always attentive to innovation, and present everywhere in the international scene, together with his wife, the soprano Eva Tetrazzini. He chose to spend his last years (when "his" Teatro Reinach had already passed by inheritance to his nephew Lohengrin) in Chicago, and it was there that he ended an enviable career as manager by finally launching one of the most successful interpretative careers of the century, that of Tito Schipa.

Assisting him in the management of the "Chicago Opera Association," as it was then known, which presented operas at the Chicago Auditorium, the biggest theater in Chicago, was another of those characters about whom it is a pity not to have a whole volume at our disposal.[14]

Mary Garden was a Scot by birth (born in Aberdeen, February 20, 1874), and after coming to the United States with her parents had lived with them in Hartford, Connecticut and Chicago before beginning a rather erratic career as a singer. She studied with Mrs. Robinson Duff before going to France for further study. There in 1900 she made her debut in *Louise* at the Opéra-Comique in Paris. In Paris she caught the eye of a chubby-faced gentleman named Claude Debussy, who exclaimed "But that is my Mélisande!" She created Mélisande at the Opéra-Comique in 1902.

By now Miss Mary Garden had found herself launched on an outstanding career, mainly based on the French operatic repertoire. She more or less went through a second naturalization, but when success made her feel ready for decisions affecting organiza-

---

[14]This was true at the time this book was written, however a book on Mary Garden by Michael Turnbull—*Mary Garden*—is scheduled to be published in the U.K. by Scolar, and will be published in the U.S. by Amadeus Press in the winter of 1996-97.

tion, she made it her first objective to introduce the American public to the recent repertoire of her second adoptive country.

Apart from these geographical details of her career, however, Mary Garden remains in the public and critical memory of the first half of this century as one of the most complete interpreters ever to have appeared on the operatic stage. In the words of one of her biographers, one who "performed with the body, the heart and the mind," a queen of diction who was known more for the perfection of her sung recitative than for the beauty of her voice. But for those who believe firmly that opera is above all theater, another phrase of that same M. Debussy will be familiar and reassuring: "The most beautiful of voices can turn itself into the unconscious enemy of the right expression of a character."

In preparing to add the roles of talent-scout and manager to her achievements, Mary Garden must have jumped with delight when, at some unknown time and place, but certainly in Europe immediately after the War, she met up with Tito Schipa. This time perhaps it was she who murmured to herself: "Here he is—the singer who can sing with mastery, and *even so* still be an ideal interpreter." Accordingly she talked up the engagement with Campanini, in whose theater in Chicago she was a leading light. (She would take the reins of its administration into her own hands in 1921.) One further reason for being sure of her choice was that same *Manon* with which Tito was gaining greater success at every performance. Mary, in her desire to spread the fame of Massenet on the other side of the Atlantic, could hardly have found a better representative. And from all the evidence, she had not yet even heard *Werther*, otherwise there seems to be no explanation for the substantial delay before this other masterpiece was performed in the USA. Or perhaps her sixth sense was even more finely honed than it seems, considering the unenthusiastic reception which the Americans subsequently gave to *Werther*.

But we are getting too far ahead of ourselves. To return to 1919:

In October Tito Schipa, after having revisited his faithful South America and recharged his batteries with the enthusiasm and recognition which was now a foregone conclusion, embarked on his first coastal voyage and traveled from Rio to New York, where a violent cultural shock awaited him in a matter of a few days, a decisive public reception in a matter of weeks, and a Justice of the Peace with a set of wedding rings in a few months.

VIII

(1920–1931)

Chicago: the golden decade

In that autumn of 1919, an immigrant arrived in America who differed greatly from the thousands of his poor fellow-country-men gathered at the famous barriers beneath the Statue of Liberty. New York welcomed the young man from Puglia and his female companion as first-class passengers, fully accoutred, bounding with vitality and ready to try anything. And everything about the U.S. seemed to Tito so distant and so different from his homeland— and yet at the same time so similar, in its adoration for music in particular, and above all for the Opera. Chicago, moreover, though already conquered by the artistic and organizational avant-garde of European opera, was also a very rich and complex melting-pot.

In these same months, the advance troops of four "armies" flooded into America: in the first case, the specialists in the long-established tradition of the Italian musical stage; secondly the soldiers of the most efficient and vicious criminal organization known to history; thirdly, the performers, would-be performers and technicians of the cinema, about to undergo its revolutionary move into sound, and lastly the devotees of jazz, rich in revolutionary potential, the real heir to the great rhythmic and harmonic upheaval that had begun at the end of the nineteenth century.

The exponents of jazz—of mixed blood, the offspring of an

astonishing union between European impressionism and African rhythm—were taking over the stage of the Vendôme Theater; those of opera had their castle in the theater of Cleofonte Campanini and Mary Garden; all around them cars raced about frenetically, with night-time shoot-outs, the flutter of greenbacks and blond heads, a merry-go-round with gangster-commandos dressed in chalk-striped suits—and the cinema was preparing to convert the whole of this Babel into a myth.

Naturally, Tito Schipa, ever-eager to involve himself in everything, would not be able to resist scattering his energies equally in all directions, for better and for worse. Within a few months, he would be involved with all four components of this new scene. However, his sense of duty did see to it that at least his first thought was for his debut. The chosen opera was *Rigoletto*, the conductor was again Marinuzzi, and his partners were Amelita Galli-Curci and Carlo Galeffi. The date was December 4, 1919.

If Campanini's intention was to put this thirty-year-old tenor with the somewhat odd reputation to the test immediately, the chosen opera was the best possible one. All the critics were now agreed on the voice; they praised its matchless grace, style and sensitivity. But all too often, one heard just a murmur of an adjective which was rarely pronounced too openly: "small..." So now it was a matter of seeing how the American public would react. It was certainly not a public like Italy's which had been spoiled for centuries by vocal histrionics and hysterical jostling for first place among the primadonnas and tenors. Nevertheless, it had for some time now been lined up in deferential homage to Enrico Caruso, to his semi-divine powers and his incandescent soaring range. Nothing yet suggested that the king of the stage, recently married and only just become the father of a baby daughter, had no more than a year to live. Even so, the search for a successor, although carefully concealed, was already in the air. Every new talent which arrived from Italy was quietly assessed and compared with the quasi-mythical Neapolitan. What chance did the pure silk thread and angelic delicacy of Tito Schipa have against the fiery sword of Enrico Caruso? This is what Campanini and Mary Garden wanted to know, before accepting the onerous conditions that the new arrival was demanding for any renewal of his contract.

What needed to be done was to give Tito the chance to appear in a role which would not expose his limitations right from the start, and would not brand him immediately with the image of a graceful but flimsy "light tenor." But at the same time it was necessary to show that his vocal capacities—prodigious but with some limitations—would not make a bad impression with the Duke of Mantua, an intractable and temperamental role, but would instead show him in a new light, and reveal an unexpected side of his talent. In short, there was a need to show that what were claimed to be Tito Schipa's limitations were in fact his strong points.

Mary Garden already knew that this was possible. Gino Marinuzzi had already spotted it and made it happen. Cleofonte Campanini knew something of it for himself, and in part he put his trust in the judgment of the other two, and crossed his fingers as he took his seat.

That performance was a definitive and conclusive success. The astonished opera-lovers of Chicago found themselves presented with a Duke who was all subtle irony and mocking elegance, even to the point of fragility, and yet prone to unexpected moments of proud arrogance and sudden biting fits of rage. It was not only the beginning of an American career, but also the beginning of a way of conceiving this role, which was to be a future inspiration for many others.

After the events of January 3, 1914 in Naples, and January 14, 1917 in Madrid, December 4, 1919, can be considered as the date that the career of Tito Schipa, as we know him, was finally consecrated. This is not so much because on that American winter evening he surpassed himself, as because all the components of a rich success converged.

The natural and already well-established enthusiasm of the public and the critics was combined with the attention of the most powerful media in the world, the most efficient show-business machine of the century, and last but not least, the recording industry. It is no coincidence that the renewal of his Chicago contract coincided, in the next year, with an emotionally highly-charged recording test for Victor ("Amarilli" by Caccini) and immediately after, with his first signature on a Victor recording contract.

For a few years more it would be a matter of entrusting the whole mystery and complexity of his interpretations to a kind of magic grinding machine. It was only in 1925 that electrical power would intervene to give a little more fidelity to the recordings. At that moment, the publicity machine was improving, and the financial rewards were increasing. But the technical side remained approximately what it was during the first hard-won recordings of 1913, made by Gramophone and Pathé. Tito often recalled those pioneering days in the recording studios with a smile; days when singing meant regulating the volume oneself by getting nearer to or further away from the funnel-shaped microphone, and the needle which was scratching the voice onto a glass plate:

> ...when experience wasn't enough, there was a sound-recording assistant who would take you by the hips and propel you forward or backward, according to the intensity of the sound!

Quite a humiliating routine for a prince of the stage, a wizard of vocal light and shade! Who knows whether his later instinctive rejection of recorded performances didn't derive directly from this initial shock? It led him to record many individual items on disk, but throughout his life to avoid—to our great loss—recording the complete operas which rendered him immortal.

A few days after the triumph of December 4th, 1919, Cleofonte Campanini died, ending his admirable life with a sensational success. His place was taken by Mary Garden, of whose financial management many bad things were later alleged, but who, even so, succeeded in maintaining the artistic level of the theater at the point to which Campanini had brought it.

Neither of the two results caused her any difficulty at all: neither scoring successes nor almost falling into bankruptcy. In both cases, she was ably abetted by the new star from Lecce, who for a start upped his own fee to $3000 a night—an unheard-of sum for that period, and if converted into modern figures, well above today's top salaries.

One anecdote from this period has become almost proverbial when talking about Tito Schipa, and it refers to this very sum, already exceptional in itself. It is said (and he himself often repeated it) that almost as a joke—and because of a habit contracted in Europe, when the exchange between the different currencies required a comparative estimate in gold at the moment of receipt of the fee—payment in the precious metal was also demanded in Chicago. And from that moment every evening, the three thousand dollars arrived in the form of gold plate encased in a casket.

I had said:
– In gold, mind; don't forget!– just to make fun of the financial
jargon. But they took me seriously!

It should also be remembered that the rhythm of his appearances, already quite demanding in terms of operas, was now rapidly increasing because of concerts, a form of performance in which Tito made rapid strides, and in which his fees were even more substantial. This led him to have nearly two hundred evenings booked during the year. He moved from the Chicago center (now called the Civic Opera Company) to the summer site in Ravinia; he offered the public a wealth of performances in which the names of divinities like Graciela Pareto, Rosina Storchio, Claudia Muzio and Amelita Galli-Curci were added to the by now very well-known name of Tito Schipa. Galli-Curci was a frequent partner in Chicago and on concert tours, perhaps because she had married a native of Lecce.

The *divo* for whom the Spanish press had clamored so noisily a few years ago (it seemed like a century!) was finally born. To the first enthusiastic wave of articles in the newspapers all over the country, was added the publicity output of the artist's own personal agency, Evans and Salter, who used ultra-modern promotional techniques, collecting the most significant comments and arranging them in elegant brochures accompanied by splendid photographs (from such firms as Lumière and Daguerre). Whole pages of the specialist press were also given over to the photos. Below is an early selection of American press cuttings in our possession, which appeared in various journals, and were distributed in the early years of his stay in the USA. What can be seen in them is not only the extent of his success, but also the notable refinement of the judgments, some of them surprising in their perspicacity.

"His voice, honeylike in its sweetness, and his vocalization, showed him the master musician. He is, without doubt, the best purely lyric tenor..." (Chicago Journal of Commerce, Nov. 22, 1921).

"His gift is a combination of lovely voice used with rare intelligence and refinement, lit with his young, enthusiastic temperament, ease, and grace of stage deportment..." (Chicago American,

Dec. 27, 1921).

"For the music of the old Italian repertory, I have never heard his superior and today know not his equal..." (Chicago Evening Post, Dec. 27, 1921).

The warmth of his reception elsewhere was often just as extreme.

"...We were treated to an unusual exhibition of pure Bel Canto singing, in which every tone was of velvet, perfectly controlled, warm, appealing and floating throughout the registers with zephyr-like ease. No more satisfying mezza-voice singing has ever been heard here..." (Colorado Springs Gazette, Nov. 23, 1922).

"His pure lyric voice was under absolute control and the velvety smoothness of it from phrase to phrase was of a perfection probably unsurpassed among tenors of the day..." (New Orleans Times-Picayune, Nov. 15, 1922).

What strikes one is the capacity to discern immediately and fully the real designer-label of Tito's artistic personality, as if in a few months the American critics had clearly perceived what Europe had been struggling to define for years.

Again: "These attributes, coupled with a fine personality, an absence of affected mannerisms, and a splendid stage-presence, stamp him as an artist who can always be counted upon to afford his listeners the keenest enjoyment" (another New Orleans item, Nov. 14, 1922).

The portrait emerging was already a good likeness of Tito Schipa, as he was then and as he would be in the future. Some American and Canadian journalists began preparing to proclaim the advent of the new Caruso in the days that followed, but it was more of a valued compliment than a truth. In reality, Tito Schipa was to all effects the "anti-Caruso." He was not a highly specialized super-athlete, but a complete and eclectic artist, whom the Americans, on the point of taking in the European operatic heritage in order to translate it into the language of the musical theater of Broadway, wanted to see on the stage, whether in Mozart or Verdi, Gershwin or Cole Porter.

[Half a century later, a somewhat badly briefed journalist, Anna Angelini, interviewed Luciano Pavarotti on his plans to interpret Werther. She asked him:

"Couldn't you do Werther? Tito Schipa created Werther, and he was a disaster physically."[15]
Incredible!
Pavarotti replied, frigidly: "Tito Schipa was the prince of gentle-men."]

Close-up

The major concern of the biographer, once this stage has been reached, is to avoid the risk of monotony. To record in written form the successes of Tito Schipa in America, and by extension in the world at large, we would find ourselves faced with a line which stretches out, rapidly reaches its peak, and then runs, constant and uniform, for twenty years and more. The reports of the victories always read in much the same way, similar to those which he himself inserted into his autobiography in these first months in America: I came, I sang, I conquered. At concerts there were never less than 15 or 16 encores, in front of enthusiastic audiences the majority of which were formed by local spectators, but the hard core of which always consisted of delighted groups of Italians of various generations, now alerted to the new phenomenon all over the world, and ready to enjoy a post-Caruso era consisting of new waves of exhilarating melody. For Tito's opening in San Francisco a record was smashed: the excess of spectators (that is, over 9000!) had to be accommodated not on the stage—which was something that had happened before—but behind the backdrops, where they could hear without seeing a thing. But they were hearing Tito Schipa and Claudia Muzio!

It can be said with certainty that another of the characteristics of Schipa was the exceptional uniformity of his renderings. Fanatical attention to his vocal organ, and a thousand extremely punctilious precautions, made him a safe bet for the impresarios, protected from any oscillations in the level of performance. For instance, the twenty-four hours which he would spend without

---

[15] It is well known that Tito Schipa did not create Werther, except possibly in a few of the cities where he sang it. The creator of the role (Vienna, 1892) was Ernest van Dyck.

uttering a sound before any performance have become legendary. Nothing—not even a simple "Ciao." It was only one of the precautions which he reserved for himself, and which made him a hygiene fanatic before his time, determined about ideas and doctrines which were in their turn ahead of their era. On the other hand, none of the typical fixations and tics of the tenor found any echo in him.

There was no warmup before a performance. He arrived at the theater already wrapped in his protective cocoon, composed of absolute silence; he made up, dressed, went onstage, opened his mouth, and sang. And there was the voice, all ready, immediately available, complete with all its characteristic features.

There were no precautions based on the dangers that sex was thought to pose for the voice. His genuine second talent never had to be subjected to any restriction, as the women who had longterm relationships with him—and became long-suffering victims—could readily attest.

There was no red meat, ever. Only chicken and fish. No red wine. No strong liquor, and of course, no smoking. All this without even the least letup or exception.

However, in compensation, he did take a great deal of coffee (like Verdi), had an excessive sweet tooth, and had an enormous faith in medicines: weaknesses, however, which would make themselves felt mainly in later years.

He used to say, with regard to his being almost a vegetarian, that in these years in Chicago, when he mentioned this instinctive habit to a doctor, the latter replied: "Keep it to yourself, for heaven's sake. If the public finds out, we'll all be out of a job."

He was also a great devotee of every new technical development which affected entertainment. Despite his refusal to get too involved with recording (due to the conviction that record-buyers would never bother to go and hear him in the flesh!), he avidly collected every type of sound-reproduction equipment. He was a radio buff, and soon took part in newspaper advertising for radios. He was literally crazy about the cinema. Secretly he always regretted, believe it or not, that he had not realized his potential in his film career. And what little acting he did, he did well. But even just as a spectator, he was capable of watching as many as three projections a day, going from one movie-theater to another wrapped in his scarf, his face hidden by the brim of his Homburg. However, for some odd reason, he was never very enthusiastic about television.

He was completely fascinated by jazz, and especially by the sound of the saxophone; he was struck by its similarity to the human voice. His greatest ambition, in the first decade of his life in America, was to compose an opera based on the sound and harmonies of black music. He stated this to the newspapers, which took up the unlikely story for months; he also put the project into practice, at least in the early stages, asking a very prolific young songwriter of the period, who was also an orchestral conductor and owner of a broadcasting station (the twenty-four year old Ted Fiorito), for guidance in this strange undertaking. And even though the project was beached, to be transformed later on into the sketch of a traditional-style operetta, Tito remained fascinated throughout his life with exotic rhythms, and with the notion of "swing."

If we listen to him singing a South American classic such as "O Manicero," the "swing" is clear and conscious in his singing; he is a long way from being a slave of the downbeat and traditional accents. Personally, when I listen to the rapid flight which is his "*Son'io*" in the second act of *Werther*, I've always caught my breath. That lightness and phrasing have their roots elsewhere, not in the operatic tradition. The man who was fifteen years ahead of George Gershwin in his project for a jazz opera, was well aware of it.

To complete the portrait of a personality which was anything but limited to his own field, there was the ardent passion for pure exhibitions of bravura, for dynamic performance.

He was almost completely uninterested in what is expressed statically, and not related to a physically present public, capable of taking part. For this reason he was fairly indifferent to figurative art, to poetry and to some extent even to literature. But he was a relentless frequenter of concert-halls, ballets, theater performances and, with great enthusiasm, of circuses—and of the cinema, of course. The way in which an acrobat or even an athlete in a race developed his or her performance would have him glued to his seat, and caused him to repeat, ecstatically, the exclamation that most frequently came to his lips:

"*Che bellezza!*" ("What beauty!")

This, in small matters, was the man who within a few months of his triumphal arrival in the USA was already able to provide himself and his wife with the ultimate in luxury, success and fame. The man in whom all the newspapers of America were beginning to take a consuming interest, not only at the professional level, but also in every aspect of his private and personal life.

Splendor and folly

The world of the cinema soon had its conditioning effect on the life of the Schipas, even in their habits and lifestyle. In the USA it was already the era of Beverly Hills and its legendary houses. The ascent of the family (which on August 15, 1923 was augmented by the birth of his first daughter, Elena) was rapid. From a first very showy residence in Florida, at Daytona Beach, they decided on California, where they purchased their first "Italian-style villa" at Santa Monica, on the coast near Los Angeles.

But the desire to live a few paces away from the celluloid myths of Hollywood was strong, and when an Italian put his house in Beverly Hills up for sale, at the junction between Alpine Drive and the fateful Sunset Boulevard, Tito signed a check for an astronomic amount and bought it, counting on matching the costs with the sale of his previous property. But

> ...alas! not even...a week later there was the famous Wall Street crash; even the much vaunted property market came to a full stop, and...

—and he went ahead, confirming a dangerous tendency: wild expenditure, never backed by adequate reserves, but only by the constant flow of cash from his work. Certainly, with an income like that, Tito Schipa hardly even noticed the collapse which was bringing America to its knees, and he continued his series of ill-judged expenditures. But his disastrous economic adventures deserve a section on their own: his incapacity to embark on any business transaction which was not already on the way down to net loss; his deliberate, maniacal habit of buying at a hundred and reselling at ten; his tendency to entrust his most delicate interests to the least suitable hands, openly inviting crooks and cheats to take advantage of him.

He had already left behind a few catastrophes in Italy, where he had tried to build a property for himself not far from Lecce: this was an enormous parcel of land which was resold in great haste and fury at one twentieth of its real value. Then there was the house built on the road to Cavallino, again on the edge of Lecce, in the Liberty style, and somewhat eccentric (in the form of a lyre!): this appeared in and disappeared from his account books in a matter of months. Near Rome, he got himself mixed up in a large-scale poultry farm, investing a million in the land alone, and devising great schemes for the sale of eggs. Then, when they told him that the "hens"—which were in fact neutered—weren't laying, he felt he had been swindled, and sold it off at top speed for the price which just about matched the cost of the legal deeds.

For his family, and for his brothers and sisters, Elvira, Umberto and Carmen, who had moved to Rome in 1923, he bought a dream of an apartment block on the Lungotevere Arnaldo da Brescia (a very prestigious modern riverside area). This was only the first of a series of complete apartment-blocks which he purchased in the capital, and which subsequently vanished into the void.

He threw himself into a project for the building of a skyscraper in the center of Milan, with a commercial center and cinema attached. The front pages had a field day; the project designs spread around everywhere. The anticipated expenditure was in hundreds of millions (in the high-value lire of those days, of course). How much would be needed to get the project off the ground? How much would he fork out personally? We do not know the answers, but the project collapsed into nothing, leaving behind a hole in which an oil-magnate might have drowned. Tito Schipa hardly noticed. He couldn't. With his equivalent of sixty to seventy million lire a night (in gold, naturally), and with two hundred nights a year, he could laugh in the face of anyone who advised caution—first and foremost Lillì, who began to realize that all was not going smoothly in her husband's life, and rightly decided to build up for herself a personal reserve of fur coats and valuables, thus contributing to making the family treasury similar to a bank's.

Meanwhile, the years rolled on; in 1929, on June 1st, Liana

was born. While Elena's baptism had been sensational enough, (with Titta Ruffo as godfather and Amelita Galli-Curci as godmother), Liana's was to set all the newspapers of America talking. It was Mary Pickford who presented the baby at the font, accompanied by Douglas Fairbanks.

Tito's entire supply of affection was, somewhat unpredictably, lavished on this serious and introverted little girl, so different from her self-confident and communicative sister, Elena. He was to put her at the center of his attention, falling in love with her completely, and he would even go so far as to dedicate that famous operetta project to her, with the title *La Principessa Liana*. But the child would always hide away from the clamor and lights of the entertainment world, showing her predilection for medicine, even from childhood. Elena, on the other hand, needed no bidding, and in fact when the operetta had its debut, she actually played a role as a ballerina.

The press hurled itself voraciously on these baptisms and buying-and-selling operations, and social events in general. The development of photography as part of the newspapers went hand in hand with that of Schipa as a fixture in every edition. Photos in stage costume, however, are only a small part, in comparison with the accounts of what automobile Schipa had bought now, and why; what radio receiver he used, what razor he preferred, and even what cigarettes (*sic*) he preferred to smoke. His passion for jazz and the cinema was a subject of discussion; his amorous adventures, both before his marriage and indeed during it, filled whole pages. The famous story of the woman in black became the dream-fantasy of every young girl in America. One of his fans managed to kiss him in a surprise assault in a big store, before the eyes of Lillì, who reacted by giving her a slap in the face; this confirmed his reputation as an all-round Italian, and hers as a vigorous, uninhibited woman with a healthy measure of aggression. The scene of the slap in the face was reproduced by newspaper illustrators of the country, with full-page drawings.

Then came the honors. Tito collected awards—first the Spanish royal order, then the Italian ones. He became a Cavaliere, a Grand Officer, and he received the Order of San Maurizio. France awarded him the *Légion d'honneur* (1931). But he was not above accepting the title of Honorary Captain of the New York and San

Francisco Police, so that the press could christen him, then and there, "the greatest magician in the police force." There was also a rumor that he was a freemason; this was never confirmed. Then there was a rumor that he had asked for American citizenship: once again it was not confirmed, and indeed he gave an interview in favor of a proposed law of the Italian kingdom which would make it obligatory for Italian artists to spend an annual period of at least two months in their own country.

There were also rumors that he was a fascist. And these he did not deny. But the Americans at that time still looked benevolently on the amusing rustic comedy that was being enacted in Italy, and when they photographed Tito listening to the radio which the Duce had sent him, they titled the picture "Mussolini's radio." The caption was good-natured, and declarations like the following:

> Mussolini is making Italy into a livable country. I see no reason why I shouldn't agree with that!

were fully accepted.

American fathers took their children to the theater with no reservations, but not so much to hear him sing as to point to an example of "how to get on"! Nothing surprising in that, since in the list of best-paid artists in America (and hence in the world) his name featured in the first twenty out of all categories. He was so rich that he could allow himself the privilege in 1931 of refusing the part of Napoleon in a film (probably so as not to provoke unwelcome comparisons on the subject of height!), even though this meant quite cavalierly rejecting an offer of 500,000 dollars!

Meanwhile a certain Ramòn Schipa was traveling around America signing blank checks and claiming to be his brother. He was not very well informed, because Tito's "official" brother in America was in fact called Carlo, the last-born of the Lecce family; at that time he was around thirty and had been transported across the Atlantic by his famous relation in the hope that he might win the competition for succession to Rudolph Valentino. In fact Carlo was not a bad actor, and his face was more than ordinarily pleasing. But to be called Schipa didn't mean automatic access to glory and gold.

With tremendous help from Tito, the younger Schipa managed to make it as far as a leading role in a good film with Mary

Pickford (*Little Annie Rooney*, in 1925), but from then onward he only got a series of walk-on parts, until a wise decision led him to start a successful agency for extras in Hollywood, a place with which he could no longer bear to part company.

These are only a few examples of the atmosphere of glamour and popularity which surrounded the Schipas in their first period in Chicago.

These were times when the ships in which he traveled for his periodic returns to Italy found their tickets becoming the subject of unrestricted bargaining at the mere news that he would be on board. There was always a risk of a delayed departure at the ports in which the ships called; often they did not leave until Tito had bestowed an unscheduled concert on the inhabitants of the place or the passengers of another ship. There were those who deprived themselves of personal possessions to reward him as best they could; with a precious gold watch, for instance, and there was trouble for everyone if he didn't accept, for there would be no departure!

It shouldn't be thought, however, that this brilliant social life caused our protagonist to deviate one inch from his cult of efficiency and the constant perfecting of his art. Right in the middle of this first period of sparkling activity, listen to the tone of one article chosen at random from among those bearing the date 1924.

"What a voice is Schipa's!... Reflects all life... When Schipa sings, the unexpected, the unhoped-for takes place. The things you are accustomed to seeing in a recital hall seem to disappear... Whether it emerges from the hidden soul of things to enrapture the listeners and carry them through the wonders of the celestial spheres; whether it comes from the flowers or the luminous pupils of children at play: whether it reflects the gentle tints of dawn or the passionate colors of sunset...the only thing that any imagination might fathom is that it is the iridescent, fascinating flow of human soul and intellect combined..." (Kansas City Journal, Oct. 29, 1924).

The world of the critics and the cognoscenti would not allow itself to be swayed by social glitter. It was recognized that the man had a fascination and a verve which was completely unknown to his fellow vocalists, and so he was forgiven his constant excursions into other fields of action. He was forgiven the cinema, for instance, and the fact that he was constantly being photographed dressed as an Indian or a cowboy; he was forgiven for grabbing the megaphone from De Mille in order to sing into it (and also for dreaming up a tempting scheme, once again ahead of its time, to make a film-opera of *Werther* or *Manon*). He was forgiven his jazz (also because he moved rapidly from words to deeds, and occasionally directed a Big Band—with some success, too); he was forgiven, as we shall see, a dubious contact with the world of organized crime. He was even forgiven for not being the talent scout he imagined himself to be: in 1926 he brought a sixteen-year-old boy, a certain Nicola Cafario, from Europe, swearing that he was a tenor of astonishing promise. Great photographs, big articles...and no results.

Everything was forgiven him, because wide-ranging interests never caused him to deviate from the brilliant path of his operatic career. Indeed, he had become a champion of the Opera. For instance in 1930, again on the leading pages of the newspapers of America, he engaged in a fierce debate with Amelita Galli-Curci on the vitality of operatic melodrama, which she declared was in eclipse.

And, of course, he was forgiven his women. So many of them, and always more. His references to the "burning" letters which he received from someone in the highest ranks of European royalty, such as to cause alarm in a whole cabinet of ministers, sent the housewives of America into raptures, and Her Mysterious Highness was only one of many star-struck women who burst into his dressing room in the intervals of performances, threatening suicide if they were not immediately satisfied.

However, all were tales of one-night stands, which never affected the outward stability of his relations with Lillì, but which were the gossip of all the city. The press gave him yet another nickname—"the Valentino of the Opera." It had its effect on his career, often in a positive sense: at a benefit concert for a Louisville Women's Club, on November 4th, 1924, the newspaper caption read: "Enthusiasm for Schipa has been transformed into a kind of furore."

Lillì, too, continued to forgive him, but a bit too often, by this stage. She pretended nothing was wrong, and it was still possible for her to carry on, but she needed a little help. A glass of cognac, here and there. It reminded her of her home country, and helped her forget so many small humiliations.

The ex-dancer, who had by now abandoned all hope of personal success, and become a mere shadow to her husband in his triumphs, took refuge more and more in her affection for little Elena and Liana.

But the two delightful children remained two, while the glasses of cognac increased in number. Among all the successful shows and honors, the coin flipped every now and then and showed its reverse side.

Incidents

The yellowing articles which tell the story of the Schipa era during the first years in America seem to come in waves. An undercurrent of photographs, identical for each event, is taken up from time to time by all the agencies and published in the same way by all the journals. Thus we find pages and pages of a certain model of portable radio, with the delighted, singing owner standing next to it. He and Tom Mix are portrayed fighting a pistol duel. Again, we find him with his hands raised as he is searched on entering a political demonstration, and here are a hundred ecstatic articles celebrating the fact that the pedestrian Tito Schipa has been fined for passing a red light!

And then, finally, at some date around January 1923, we find the far from reassuring news that a certain opera star has been blackmailed by gangsters for $50,000!

This happened while a brilliantly successful *Traviata* was in progress, with the inseparable Galli-Curci, and conducted by Giorgio Polacco.

"Schipa is in great form," reported the "Chicago Post": "the role fits him like a glove." An unlucky analogy since the papers in the days that followed were to suggest the image of another hand, and of a worrisome color. The letter that Tito had received, in fact, was signed (we might say) by none other than the Black Hand!

"Tenor in Danger!" proclaimed the "New York Journal," and the Chicago press, the first to check up on the facts, naturally, specified the outrageous sum that had been demanded of Tito under the threat that he would be "killed like a dog." The day after, the "Chicago Herald" published a photograph of the macabre message. It arrived in a pink envelope, was postmarked Chicago, was addressed to Toto (*sic*) Schipa, Congress Hotel, City, and was written in a non-American hand, in an uncertain Italian, presumably by a fellow-countryman who was not very comfortable with a pen. We can only reproduce the text from the English translation, published by all the newspapers of the USA:

"We need desperately $50,000 to help our friends. Not more than three days are given you to raise that amount of money and if you refuse the direct calamity will you befall.

"You must realize that we have an organization that at any time any place can kill you. Don't think that by leaving Chicago you will be safe, as our activities are worldwide."

The newspaper refers to Tito as being somewhat "short of breath" at the moment that he burst into the police station. It seems that his words were:

"Fifty thousand dollars? Where am I supposed to find that?"

The inspector, perhaps with a conspiratorial smile, seems to have calmed his fears; there was no need to cry ruin at once, and anyway nobody would have believed him. He could relax: letters of this kind had also been reaching other members of the Chicago Opera in recent days, and none of them seemed to have a follow-up.

The press, however, had not talked about any of these—and certainly not made such a splash of them. The fear was that, even if it was just a joke, the idea which was now being so widely publicized might be adopted by someone who would take it seriously. Tragically, the prediction was to be fulfilled, though at a long distance of time from this event: a tenor of a certain fame, and a friend of Tito's, named Vito Bascone, was in fact killed by the rackets in 1926. The investigators and the press had no hesitation at all in connecting the two incidents.

Evidently, Tito must have tried to make contact with the top ranks of the terrible criminal organization of Chicago. Perhaps he was sustained by the conviction that his own Italian identity and his success, or even his charm, would have had some sort of effect on the original Italian chromosomes of those merciless hotheads. The fact remains that a second envelope without sender's name and address arrived at the Schipa residence. No threats, this time: in fact a gift. But in that offer of excuses, in that declaration of friendship, there were implications that called into question the actual circles which the restless singer had been frequenting. The matter would crop up again some years later, in more tragic and painful circumstances. Meanwhile, a ring with a diamond worthy of a maharajah lay shimmering in Lillì's expert and careful hands. Inscribed on the inside, like an engagement ring, was a simple "signature" consisting of just two letters: "Al."

Even his professional life showed signs of anxiety at this stage, possibly as a result of a growing malaise in the life of the family. As his partner in his first public dispute with a conductor Tito chose the most prestigious of his colleagues of that time, Claudia Muzio. The personalities of the two future myths created sparks offstage as well as on. In 1924, there was a direct clash with the conductor, Giorgio Polacco, who considered that he had been insulted by Claudia in front of the orchestra during rehearsals, and then disregarded by Tito over an encore of "M'apparì" snatched during a *Martha* in the face of all the usual strict prohibitions.

A great rumpus ensued, during which the Muzio-Schipa partnership threatened resignation. It goes without saying who won the contest. Here is the account of the episode from his biography: as usual self-indulgent and self-justifying.

> I exited immediately via the wings, as the scene requires, hoping to cool off the enthusiasm, but no, the cries, hand-clapping and calls continued... there was a threat that the show might not be able to go on. The maestro, after three fruitless attempts to resume, had crossed his arms and was waiting patiently, but he gave a nod which I didn't really understand. I replied with another nod, which was meant to say: Right–let's do it again!
>
> He then made a gesture which seemed to say: – Impossible!
>
> And then the unexpected happened: the whole orchestra, without waiting for a sign from the conductor, replayed the introduction to the romanza...

There were health problems, too. Another flurry of articles dated May 1925, tells us that on the 15th Tito Schipa had an operation. An actual operation of plastic surgery is mentioned, aimed at reshaping his nose and taking away a fragment of bone which had been displaced by an accident some years earlier. No further detail is given about this accident. But it is stated, though on what authority it is not clear, that the operation would improve the singer's upper range.

As for Tito himself, he says that the decision to submit to the surgery came from a troublesome tendency to sneeze, which often overtook him onstage, sometimes even in the midst of an aria. A few days later there was no more mention of it. Signs of the operation cannot have been noticeable, since a photograph shows him to us taking part in an Easter ceremony in the open air, before an incredible crowd which has gathered to hear him. It is an impressive picture. And the caption mentions fifty thousand people!

My idea of happiness? These are the things that bring it to me: singing, my home, my wife and the children, then sport, and especially baseball... Every night before I go onstage I receive a telegram from my wife, which brings me hope and courage. After the performance, I wire to her about how the performance has gone and how many encores there were... In the car with her mother, little Elena recently asked her: – Where's daddy?

And the answer was: – This evening he's singing at Saint Louis to earn some money for his little girl.

A little while later, Elena saw a calf in a field. The mother was near it, and had a bell round its neck, which tinkled.

– She's making money for her little girl too! Elena said, surmising that, like her father, the cow too was a musician.

This was how Tito Schipa portrayed himself to the press in those days. There is an obvious attempt to revive the image of the family, which had been shaken by the first serious problems with Lillì. But there was also a good deal of real desire for peace and security, and perhaps also the genuine hope that all would turn out for the best, and that both her self-destructive tendencies and his own incorrigible philandering would pass without a trace, like the mysterious operation on his nose.

Hope often turns into a prayer. A most uncustomary statement dates from this period:

For me, music is prayer. When I sing, I pray with my head held high.

IX

(1932–1936)

Almost thirteen years passed in this way, at a frantic pace. The farewell concert in Chicago took place on October 31, 1932, and even though the contract with the Metropolitan in New York was already drawn up, his adopted city said goodbye to him not only without rancor, but with unbounded affection. Eugene Stinson, in the "Chicago News" on November 1, 1932, honored him with these words:

"(Mr. Schipa's) singing has been more use to me than simply to provide a consoling and indeed indispensable verification of what without him I should merely have *hoped* to find both possible and true... It is where we end. We cannot go beyond Mr. Schipa."

Chicago continued, periodically, to claim Schipa as its own, but even so it was the end of an era, of a legendary period which had seen great social events on the one hand, and on the other, artistic triumphs which can only be remembered with a tremor of excitement. What was daily fare in the opera theaters of Chicago in the winter, Ravinia in the summer, and occasionally throughout the rest of the Americas, one is unlikely to see these days even once in a year. The list of the female partners who sang with Tito Schipa in these years, evening by evening, is the Almanach de Gotha of twentieth-century bel canto: Galli-Curci, Raisa, Macbeth,

Storchio, Besanzoni, Muzio, Pareto, Mason, Sabanieeva, Bori, De Hidalgo, Salvi, Novotna, Pagliughi, Saraceni, Cigna, Sayão, Glade, Pons, Carosio—and these are not the only prestigious names one could list.

Schipa had two partners who would pass into the history of song with their names intimately associated with his: Gianna Pederzini had not yet appeared; he would not sing with her until 1934. But on December 8, 1925, in the Chicago Auditorium, he stood side by side for the first time with that delightful creature Toti Dal Monte, whose voice suited his perfectly: delicate and spirited, magisterial and discreet. In duets these two nightingales came together intimately in a harmony based on mutual respect. Equally rich in knowledge and musicianship, they were at their best when a composer wanted two voices to become one on the double stave. Their face-to-face duets, where they never got in each other's way, but observed pauses and intervals in perfect, single-voiced unison, still seem to me to be the most glowing example I know of the professionalism and modesty, the sacrifice of individuality in favor of an overall result, which distinguishes the perfect artist.

Tito and Toti, another destiny in two names. Until they were both well on in years, naming one to the other meant seeing a light in the eyes which was not just a simple memory of a stage companion, but the regret for an essential complement, almost a part of oneself.

A decisive choice

The Metropolitan and Beniamino Gigli had come to blows in the first months of 1932 for financial reasons. The manager of that great theater, Giulio Gatti-Casazza, encouraged in his anti-crisis measures by the whole Board of Directors and the sponsors, had found himself forced to drastically reduce the fees paid to his stars. Gigli, backed by his colleague Clarence Whitehill, had claimed a gigantic sum, and in the end resigned. In the subsequent May, a huge wave of articles began to fill the pages of all the national newspapers. The news was of the signing of Schipa in New York as the Metropolitan's permanent leading tenor.

It is in this year 1932, when Schipa established his primacy on the American stage, that we can find the answer to a longstanding question: why did the name of Gigli have far more effect on the public imagination in Italy, where even today he is remembered more often and more widely than in the USA? In view of the historic events which ended by putting two such friendly nations as Italy and the USA into opposite camps, Schipa, aggressive, a modernist, chose the latter (even if he wasn't able to do so completely and wholeheartedly, as we shall see), while Gigli, a fervent Catholic and a sentimentalist, set out to consolidate his reputation in the mother country, and to do so by making very popular choices of both songs and films.

But before passing on to Schipa's New York period, we should take a look at some of the contacts with Italy and with Europe which preceded his "American option." The European nations which Schipa never pardoned for a certain initial indifference were France, Germany and, particularly, Britain.

Tito, accompanied at the piano by the ever-faithful Federico Longas, made his London debut in May of 1927 at the Queen's Hall, and met with a great success among the public, which called the performance to a close with the usual flurry of encores. But the critics of those days, for some reason, provided the only instances of "less than full marks" in this artist's golden period.

None of the reviewers fails to mention the "enthusiastic state" to which the singer had brought the audience. But they also seem to be of one mind in considering his vocal gifts in relative terms, and in not finding any real reason to get carried away. It is incredible how such a musically refined nation (even though by no means in the musical lead in those times, as if it were suspended between Purcell and the Beatles) completely failed to see the point of the art of Tito Schipa.

These reviewers got bogged down in disquisitions about the poverty of his lower register; they made comparisons with other tenors who in fact were not destined to become historic figures, and who could not be compared in vocal terms—singers such as Marshall,[16] Hayes[17] and Ansseau:[18] they kept coming back to ba-

---

[16]Charles Marshall was actually an American tenor who also sang in Italy as Carlo Marziali. He was the leading dramatic tenor of the Chicago company for a number of years. He made a few records.

nal questions such as "who has the best voice?" that were more appropriate to people in a poorly attended theater than to those who had once been the enlightened patrons of a Haydn.

What was the root cause of this? Was it perhaps just an evening when he wasn't on his best form? It seems unlikely, Certainly things began badly right from Tito's arrival on the shores of the kingdom a year earlier. The English, an animal-loving people more than any other, had nevertheless caused a major pet-related problem for Schipa, which should in fact have made them feel more affection for the man who liked to joke about himself, though not in any pejorative sense, as a "dog."

Tito's love for animals was a dominant theme of his life. Wherever he lived his house was always crowded with little beasts of various types—monkeys, birds, cats—until the final point was reached in his "Piedmontese" period, in the fifties, when his home was virtually transformed into a branch of the Togni Circus.

However, in March of 1926, the Customs and Excise Officers of Her Britannic Majesty dared to put Tito's pet monkey, a type of marmoset, into quarantine; as we know, its name was Toto. I also mentioned the "No Toto? No Tito!" slogan by which the newspaper headlines summed up the battle of wills between the artist and the authorities. Tito threatened not to sing without his faithful mascot, then took advantage of the journalistic uproar to suggest to British authorities that in any case, he needed a monkey to go onstage. (Was he even unfaithful to Toto, then?) Anyway, the English didn't need asking twice: to the consternation of the doorman of the singer's residence, more than a hundred aspiring mascots were delivered within a few days: all of them chattering, excitable, noisy creatures with four hands. Fittingly the first photographs of 1932, at the time of the signing of the Metropolitan contract, show him with his little friend perched on his shoulder; both of them seem to be saying: "It's better in America!"

Toto was eventually freed from quarantine, but an enduring sullenness persisted between Tito and Great Britain. Is it too much

---

[17]Roland Hayes was an African-American tenor who had concertized all over Europe and given a command performance for King George of England.

[18]Fernand Ansseau was an important Belgian tenor who sang in Chicago from 1923 to 1928. He made numerous important recordings for HMV.

to assume that this may have been a cause? It is certainly true that one of the most glaring anomalies in Schipa's career is precisely the fact that he never appeared at Covent Garden, nor sang in *any* opera in England.

Another fundamental reason for Tito's periodic moves to Europe in the years before the signing of the contract with the Metropolitan, was the spring season which he designed and organized in 1926 for his own native city. The signing had been preceded by a series of euphoric letters from Schipa in Chicago to Amedeo and Gaetano Greco, the two owners of the Teatro Politeama in Lecce. There were discussions of income tax, boxes reserved for the authorities, plants for the stage—all very managerial. The intent was to stage a *Barber* in Lecce, and a *Lucia*, in which he would naturally sing, as well as a performance of *L'amore dei tre re* by Italo Montemezzi. This plan was an absolute first for that area of Italy, and an unusual piece of foresight for a more or less amateur artistic director like Tito Schipa.

The project went smoothly, but it cost a fortune. All the money came out of Tito Schipa's pocket, and the returns were minimal. His willingness to spend the money is understandable if we remember his constant desire to impress the people of his own city, as if to compensate a fear that they would take no notice of him without a showy display of his successes. Thus, to the straightforward financing of the season were added the princely expenses of refurbishing the whole Politeama theater, which was brought up to international standards: an orchestra pit was created, the stalls raked, the stage-equipment and ceiling improved, a gallery added, dressing rooms built for the extras, along with a hundred other modifications. New seating was even brought from Milan, as were some of the skilled workers and technicians. The artists, moreover, had to be "di cartello," and in fact names of the caliber of Riccardo Stracciari can be found in the cast. The whole venture was to culminate in a special gala performance in which, at the end of *Lucia di Lammermoor*, the Vice-Secretary of the National Fascist Party, Achille Starace, who came from the Lecce area and was a personal friend, would confer the order of the Crown of Italy on Tito.

In an atmosphere of wild excitement, all went as planned. Lecce enjoyed what was probably the most brilliant artistic season of its history, considering that the newspaper accounts appeared regularly in the next few weeks in all the American papers, as if it had been a great event in Paris or New York. The Italian media did not lag behind, and provided some exemplary accounts of the evening in the fascist style: floods of rhetoric, but also the description of an evening during which the Lecce audience must have been brought to a white-hot fervor. To the splendors of *Lucia*, performed as only Schipa knew how to perform it, were added the ardent, nationalistic touches of the uniforms, the decorations, the forceful utterances of Starace: ("I kiss you: and in my kiss you must feel..." etc., etc.) Tito's mother was embraced at the front of the stage, and finally, with Starace joining in, there were choruses of patriotic hymns.

The cost of this gratification—a million lire in the money of those days—was dispersed entirely from the pocket of Tito Schipa. But at the root of all this effort, of this imperial gift to his own city, there was a gesture of profound affection towards his father. The American papers wrote that the whole venture originated in Tito's wish to offer the aged Luigi Schipa (born in 1839), the possibility of enjoying good music in Lecce, since the state of his health didn't allow him to travel. Few were aware of the sad premonition that had come to Tito that evening—except perhaps his father, who embraced his son, saying: "I don't think we'll ever see each other again."

Meanwhile, however, the one-time shoeless ragamuffin had brought to a close a cycle that had begun thirty years earlier by dedicating the whole season to his father, and thus offering the old customs officer of Vicolo dei Pensini a homage straight out of a fairy tale.

This type of involvement with the fascist régime might seem to contradict what was said earlier, and suggest that Tito Schipa was adored by the Italians even more than Beniamino Gigli. But even though Gabriele D'Annunzio wrote him letters of admiration which began with the words "Gloriosissima Voce," Tito could not remain constant in his flirtation with imperial Italy. To the oft-repeated pressures from the Duce to have him more often, or even permanently, in Italy, Tito replied with a series of virtual desertions, which were played up in the newspapers, as always. And Mussolini even found himself ridiculed in the American press because of the shameless escapes of his favorite tenor. This account is evidence that the genius from Lecce knew how to play his cards well, and he was able to barter his participation in patriotic benefit-events for the right to be the only Italian who could do what he liked with impunity. For example, in 1936 he received a special recognition on the part of the régime for the very exhausting series of concerts by which he had gathered the funds needed to build the monument to the Italian sailor in the harbor at Brindisi. This time, in one stroke, he was able to silence Il Duce and also to present his region of origin with another not inconsiderable offering. Then in 1932, the year of his final transfer to New York, he was wise enough to balance his departure with the event in Milan which remains one of the most important of his whole career: a *Barber of Seville* at La Scala where Schipa shared the stage with Dal Monte-Franci-Baccaloni-Chaliapin. This was the so-called "Barbierone," an event not easily matched in all of operatic history.

To settle the matter of where his heart belonged while he was going back and forth between America and Italy we must take into account the way the American public and press made him aware of their nostalgia for him when he was in Italy, as if they were a whole nation of the lovelorn, while Tito's nostalgia for Italy might have been confined only to Lecce, where his roots were. If so, a period in 1926 and 1927 may have been decisive in shaping the singer's loyalties and sense of belonging.

On December 12th, 1926, while Tito was preparing to appear on the stage of the Auditorium in Chicago for one of those run-of-the-mill, too-frequent performances of *Martha*, a telegram reached Lillì in her Los Angeles residence. She read it, but did not have the courage to do anything about it; she passed it to the agency, Evans and Salter, who decided not to make the contents public until the performance was over. As he left the stage amid the continuing applause, Tito learned of the death of his father. Bursting into uncontrollable tears, he fled to his dressing room.

Less than a year later, on November 9, 1927, the spiritual father of his adolescence, Bishop Gennaro Trama, also died. The American press wrote of him as a grand patron. With less public notice, but no less anguish for Tito, Emilia Bernardini Macor, the woman who had supported him in his most difficult period and become his "second mother," had also died in the previous September; thus, in a matter of eleven months Lecce, and with it the whole of Italy, was in Tito's eyes stripped of its most important subjects of gratitude, affection and nostalgia. The call of America no longer had any real competition. It is significant that at precisely this point in his autobiography Tito indulged in exaggerated praise of Italy and its theaters. One gets the impression that during this period he felt the need to find absolution for the decision to become an American.

But before he established himself in New York he made one more important return to Italy—for the debut of the well-known operetta that he'd been working on for almost seven years, passing through the stages of jazz opera, folk operetta, and so on. It was initially called *Mimì*. After a few try-outs in America, which met with a fairly positive reception from the press, it opened at the Teatro Adriano in Rome on June 22, 1929. The final title was *La Principessa Liana*. The title role was played on this occasion by Nanda Primavera, but it passed in future stage productions and broadcasts to Iris Adami Corradetti, and then to the ever-surprising Gianna Pederzini. The libretto, somewhat short of genius, is based on a fairly predictable story of a young girl, star of a circus, and is packed with the usual disguises, recognition-scenes and apotheoses. However, it was the work of an author, Alcide Santoro, who had the great merit (in Tito's eyes) of being from Lecce, and that was enough. True, the co-author, Ennio Neri, was a writer of some fame. Even so, the result was quite disappointing.

The music was a good deal better, and confirmed that Tito Schipa as a composer had a very pleasing gift for melody, which ensured a big success with the audience (25 calls). The press was somewhat reserved—except for the Puglia newspapers, naturally, which gave it rave reviews. It was difficult for critics to swallow something composed by Schipa which contained foxtrots and barcaroles. But the tango "El Gaucho," which at a certain point of the performance Tito sang from the conductor's podium (this was the role which he had kept for himself), was enough to determine the success of the whole performance.

Once again, an act of homage lay at the bottom of it all. It seems that in his life there were two basic desires, to seduce, and to gratify. In *La Principessa* it was the little adored Liana who was treated as a princess, and not only in the title of the work. But Tito's descendants would all seem to be entitled to princely rank since in those days circles of illustrious admirers, led by the most prestigious families in the capital, referred to him by a very flattering nickname, with provocative undertones—"the Emperor."

New York

On November 23, 1932, the Metropolitan was celebrating a fine series of anniversaries which coincided: the fiftieth year of its foundation, the twenty-fifth under the direction of Gatti-Casazza, and the centenary of *L'elisir d'amore*, a performance of which began the season. Needless to say, the cast had to be memorable, and indeed it was: Ezio Pinza, Giuseppe De Luca, Edita Fleischer and Tito Schipa sang under the baton of Tullio Serafin. Donizetti was well-honored, and so was New York.

To tell the truth, the reviews of the first night were not all that brilliant, however. One reviewer actually found Tito guilty of a tendency to sing "crescendo" (sic). But after triumphant performances of *Lucia* and *Don Giovanni*, New York was finally conquered, and the newspapers returned to full-page appraisals of the "successor of Caruso."

Here too are plenty of photographs and articles with sensational subject-matter: he had not even arrived in New York when newspapers and magazines were full of images of him stretched out on a hospital bed, in striped pajamas and in the act of singing. Incredible but true: he had just undergone another operation in the ear-nose-and-throat area. This time he had had his tonsils removed by a certain Dr. Kellogg who boasted of having performed the same operation on Lily Pons, with impressive results in the extension of her range. Tito declared with comfortable self-assurance that he hoped, once out of hospital, to find a high-flying E-flat in his throat! And the newspapers published graphic illustrations, even musical staves, to explain the situation to the uninitiated. He also said that he was willing to go to President Roosevelt to make a speech on behalf of the opera theaters concerning subsidies. Perhaps he was beginning to share Gigli's feelings about the fees paid to artists in New York! He also took part in benefit concerts and demonstrations against Prohibition!

During one of his later returns to the city, a full-page headline summed up the spirit of those days: "Schipa invades New York again!" His picture also appears frequently alongside that of Toscanini, who was concluding the first stage of his collaboration with the New York Philharmonic Symphony Society at the time. However, the two artists never appear in the same photo, nor are there any traces of a meeting between them. Their opposing attitudes towards the situation in Italy must already have affected their relations, and blocked the way to any collaboration (which might have yielded who knows what results).

In a review of a concert in Minneapolis on December 12, 1933, the reviewer shows traces of reservation—probably the usual misunderstanding about his "lack of a great voice." Someone could always be found ready to swear that opera must be reduced to the flexing of vocal muscle. And this reviewer accused Schipa of "wishing to keep too much in reserve." It is a tired argument given a fresh façade. A few days later the press columns went back to the chorus of "enchanting," and "sublime" and "incomparable," but there was a difference. These headlines were no longer about him.

Lucrezia Bori, Claudia Muzio and Lily Pons took the lion's share of attention, and in general the attention of the column writers seemed to focus on the female characters. Schipa is taken for granted. Tito Schipa was in fact by this time obliged to turn out a top performance every time; it was considered a given. He only managed to win extra comment for an occasional hoarse utterance. One Philadelphia newspaper was dazzling in its discrepancy, with headlines proclaiming "Schipa disppoints in *Traviata*," while the article consists of the usual paeans of praise. The only reservation, right at the end, is a negative judgment on the artist's excessive participation in the glittering social world. Perhaps a moment of editorial distraction caused such a disparaging headline.

In this golden monotony articles dealing with other subjects are the most interesting, particularly those which allow the reader a glance at Schipa's opinions on vocal manner and technique. Although his teaching could have been of incalculable value, he always kept quiet on the subject until the last part of his career. A statement like the following, from "Corriere D'America," can therefore be viewed as unique rather than merely rare:

> In Italy there is an infinite number of young people who possess splendid voices, and there are many teachers. The unfortunate thing is that there is no study, or at least very little... The little that they have learned they forget, and when no longer guided by their teachers they acquire faults and get gradually worse and worse... In modern music there is the so-called "declamatory" element, which in my view is a useless accumulation of one word on top of another. While previously, in a vocal melody the overall meaning of the words was expressed in synthesis, and the missing words were suggested, because the ear didn't always catch them, or because they were only hinted at, now one word is piled on another, and (I repeat) uselessly, because as soon as the voice begins to rise to the high register, there is no singer, however good, who manages to pronounce clearly... In the higher registers the singer, in order to be able to emit true and pleasing sounds, resorts to "special" vocal techniques which allow him to avoid distinguishing the syllables: in other words he seeks to eliminate the contractions of the words in his throat, and contents himself with vocalization. It's an unavoidable mechanical necessity... In modern music the vocal chords are treated like any other instrument, but while with the latter one can get the sound one wants by mechanical means, this certainly isn't true of the human vocal chords.

Thus he completely ignores the fact that one of the most formidable peculiarities of his own art was in fact the capacity to express himself with crystal clarity even in the medium-high register, making a mockery of that "unavoidable mechanical necessity." And once again, he does not give even a hint as to how it is achieved.

The film star

In the interviews which Tito gave to newspapers from around the world from his house in Hollywood, he repeats obsessively that he has great hopes of a future as a film actor, and that this is what he wants to do when he "grows up." In a man who had reached the highest possible peak in his own field, the desire to act in films seems to persist like an adolescent dream. Perhaps the secret of his artistic longevity lay here, and in fact it was a recurrent saying by his second wife, who was close to him in the last years of his life: "At seventy, he still seemed to be waiting for his début."

Strangely enough, although he was a great devourer of films (he would view as many as three in a day), he hated the incidental music and never ceased to insist on its uselessness.

After his first experience of 1929, in which he appeared in a few shorts for Paramount singing songs and arias (*"M'appari,"* *"Princesita,"* *"Una furtiva lagrima,"* *"Chi se ne scorda cchiù"* and "I Shall Return"), 1932 brought the great opportunity to take part in a full-length film. The idea came from Mario Bonnard, an actor who had recently moved to directing with excellent results. The title of the film was *I Sing For You Alone*, (The Italian title being *"Tre uomini in frac,"* or *"Three Men in Tails"*) and the cast was outstanding. In the roles of an accomplished but very shy singer and his two slippery managers were Tito Schipa, and the two De Filippo brothers, Peppino and Eduardo. The female lead was played by Milly.

The general opinion is that this film is the best of Tito's career, together with the more famous—and triumphantly successful—*Vivere!*. And in fact it is a comic gem, of a kind from which Tito would later distance himself in order to play more conventional melodic and sentimental roles. Unfortunately, the Italian version of the film seems to be lost, and the same is true for three out of the five short films produced by Samuel Goldwyn in 1929.

Three Men in Tails was a definite success. Five years were to pass, however, before another cinema part was offered to him. This time the production was by Appia, and the director was Guido Brignone, an excellent craftsman, whose films' formal elegance was comparable to that of American light comedies. Tito accepted enthusiastically. But the man who arrived in Italy to honor his engagement was very different from the one who accepted it, no longer firmly bound to the United States, but a survivor of events which had put his life in question.

"Let them go!"

From the first months of 1935 Tito had been stating in his American interviews that European work prospects were beginning to interest him again, and that in any case he considered that the fees he was being paid in New York were inadequate. Somewhat later, then, we find him repeating the claims made by Gigli, who had gone to Europe for similar reasons, and whom he had in effect replaced.

But such figures! He said that after the $3000 per performance in Chicago, he had already become used to the $7000 (!) paid in San Francisco and other major cities. New York had reduced his Chicago per performance salary by a third. He decided to leave New York when a further reduction of 10% was announced. Unlike Gigli, however, he let his anger spill over, causing an incident.

Giovanni Martinelli, his great colleague, who was also on the Metropolitan's payroll, publicly accused Tito Schipa of disloyalty to the theater which had carried him to stardom. Lucrezia Bori, unusually bitter after years of compromise both on the stage and in life, stated succinctly: "Oh well, there are other tenors in America..." and Helen Dunning, columnist of the "San Francisco News," after recalling the similar attitudes of Lauri-Volpi and Muzio, completed Bori's unfinished phrase with the headline which was to become proverbial in those months:

"Let them go!"

Tito had made a grave mistake. Not so much because he gave rise to a wide debate on the possibilities of an all-American opera theater, but because this disdainful and somewhat ungrateful slap in the face coincided disastrously with the worsening of relations between the USA and Italy.

Before long the memory of the artist's desertion would be mingled with that of his many pro-Mussolini statements, and the result would be a poisonous cocktail.

Even so, in his mid-forties, with his artistic career in full swing, he was still sailing in the calm seas of guaranteed triumphs; it seemed impossible for him to go wrong. He enjoyed a kind of comprehensive insurance, because, remembering the teachings of Gerunda and the warnings of Mugnone, he had restricted his repertoire to a handful of works no one could imagine without him. The leveling out of critical praise probably had its origins in this superb monotony. His performances never induced a shiver in anticipation of the unprecedented, of risks about to be taken. But it was the price to pay in return for a regularity in standard of performance which no other singer had ever offered, or would ever again offer, to his public.

This, then, was his collection of gems, as he himself presented it to the press: *Elisir d'amore, Mignon, Don Pasquale, Traviata, Lucia di Lammermoor, L'amico Fritz, Marcella,*[19] *Werther.* These were not all the operas in his restricted repertoire, but they were the ones which he said he felt were most his own. There were, however, two anomalies.

Werther in America—a failure

First of all, there was *Werther.* The European performances of years before had already linked Schipa's name indissolubly with that of the melancholy young hero created by Goethe. But despite the fact that Tito's U.S. career had now lasted fifteen years, the work had not yet appeared on the billboards of Chicago, New York, or any other U.S. theater.[20]

However strange it may seem, discrepancies of this kind were frequent in the USA, where the choice of operatic repertoire on the part of artistic directors was often dictated by commercial criteria just as rigid as those of Broadway, or sometimes by odd snobbery towards certain composers or works. One example is *Martha,* considered for years an opera of the "lower repertoire"; Tito Schipa personally battled for its inclusion among standard offerings. Similarly, there had been a long period of reluctance to accept Massenet's *Werther* possibly due to the none-too-enthusiastic opinion of critics whose reservations at the first American performance later proved to be irreversible.

That crucial first performance took place on November 22, 1935, in San Francisco, and was preceded by a low-key press campaign. No reference was made to Tito Schipa's clashes with the

---

[19] Although Giordano's *Marcella* is included in this list, it was not a part of Schipa's regular repertory. He only sang it on two occasions, both in Naples: 1914 and 1938.

[20] As in note 16, Tito Schipa actually did not create Werther in the United States, although he probably did so in San Francisco. The U.S. premiere took place in Chicago on March 29, 1894; it was also given in New York and New Orleans later that year. However, it was certainly not a repertory opera in the United States, although it was fairly common in other countries.

Metropolitan. More than anything else there were expressions of pleasure that Tito Schipa was finally going to tackle something which was new to North America. It was no coincidence that after this innovative performance his critical reviews demonstrated a resurgence in enthusiasm, and his name once again hit the headlines.

It was a freewheeling Tito Schipa who undertook this absolute première—a singer used to realizing his ambition and satisfying the demands of his talent in its many facets. Even though he had just returned from a journey to Italy during which his mother died—or possibly just because of this—he made an effort to give his Californian performances an atmosphere of more gaiety and glamour than usual, if that were possible. Under the new exclusive management of Harry A. Cahill, the rehearsals for *Werther* alternated with jazz concerts conducted by Tito, and all kinds of shows—including parodies and sketches for which he wrote words and music—in which he also involved his famous partners. He also organized an audition for his operetta. He seemed to want to make himself dizzy in celebration as a kind of atonement for his breach with the Met. We find him repeatedly asserting that his personal relationship with Gatti-Casazza was not even minimally affected by what had happened.

As for Massenet's masterpiece, he took over the direction (or what we call direction today), and would have conducted the orchestra as well, except that ubiquity was not among his innumerable talents. Certainly the testimony of Gianna Pederzini and other partners agrees in stating that in that opera, conductors were completely subordinate to Schipa's conception, his tempi and his balances.

The conductor on that November evening was Gaetano Merola, and his leading lady was Coe Glade. The performance was not outstanding either in cohesion or organization. The reviewer in the "San Francisco Chronicle" states that *Werther* is far short of a masterpiece; it seems rather to be an opéra comique, which does everything it can to turn into a grand opera without succeeding. He also mentions the fact that one could not avoid a certain irritation at hearing Schipa sing his part in Italian while everyone else onstage was singing in French. The reviewer then goes on to compare Massenet's opera with his more famous *Manon*, and judges it inferior in comparison. He accuses the composer of being an "incomplete Puccini," and even apologizes to Halévy for having previously stated that *La juive* was the worst opera of the season. Then, however, comes the usual praise for the protagonist, augmented by the acknowledgment that it was he who really carried the whole opera along.

The "Call Bulletin" wrote, "The audience was cold with everyone except Schipa and Glade. But Schipa's heavenly voice transcends the role."

In the weeks that followed half-pages were once again devoted to Schipa, his family, his work, and his myth. In the brilliant atmosphere of California, the troubles of New York seemed to have been forgotten. And yet it seems likely that this *Werther*, which Tito had kept like an ace up his sleeve, which was supposed to signal his renewal and relaunch him in the USA, was a resounding failure. One may ask to what extent Tito's imminent break with the USA could have been due to this disappointment, but it is also likely that the rejection influenced his perfection of this role, in which he reached his expressive peak much later.

Whatever the case may be, the San Francisco *Werther* was limited to one performance, the only one which had been given or would be given by him in North America. It was the prelude to Schipa's gradual disappearance from American opera theaters. From then until the end of his long career, his opera appearances there could be counted on two hands. He would appear almost exclusively in concerts. Fifteen years after his arrival in Chicago, Schipa's plans for the future were redirected to Europe and South America.

Returning to the list of his favorite operas, the other peculiarity is a notable absence: *L'Arlesiana*. But the adventure which was to link his name to this almost unknown work still lay in the future. An unpredictable chain of events led him to create a new masterpiece when nobody would have expected it and *live* the key phrase of the main aria: "il dolce sembiante"—that surge of emotions, of devastated tenderness, of infinite nostalgia which does not become part of an artist's identity by mere chance. It was life which prepared the ground for it, with yet another great romance.

Caterina

As the reels began to spin in the making of *Vivere!*, Tito Schipa appeared more unstable in his affinities than he ever had before. His national identity wavered, halfway between the suffocating embrace of the Duce on the one hand and the complications of America on the other. His family life was also precarious, with Lillì already a tragic slave to alcohol, and obsessed with jealousy. Alas, his voice too was showing the first, almost imperceptible signs of wavering. At forty-eight, however, this was normal enough; indeed, the decline of that extraordinary larynx was hugely delayed in comparison with the norm. The slight darkening in timbre, the hardly noticeable increase in the vibrato (always of a perfect regularity, however), the decided avoidance of the highest notes appeared in him ten years later than in most voices. Moreover his artistic maturity had led to such results that we might have the overall impression of a still-ascending curve. Nevertheless, it is quite touching, in the play of coincidence, that the first American article to talk explicitly about his vocal decline appeared right on the morrow of his first concert in the New York Town Hall, the scene, in the future, of his farewell concert. But that was still twenty-five years away, and Tito still had many cards to play.

Word had gone around Italian film circles that the director Guido Brignone was looking for a girl who could sing for his film with Tito Schipa. Singing ability was a strange requirement, considering that the part did not involve a musical number! However, the search went on all over Italy, and reached Turin, where just then a magnificent talent was living and studying. She was the daughter of a clever entrepreneur who had died young, and she had grown up with a very old-fashioned set of values and standards—almost Bourbon in character, as she herself said. Her name was Caterina Boratto, and at the moment when the representatives of the celluloid world contacted her, she had just finished her studies in pianoforte and singing, gaining high honors. One of her companions in musical studies, who was also destined to be famous, Fernanda Pivano, an expert in American literature, remembers her as an excellent instrumentalist and "as beautiful as an apparition."

"Fate put me in the road to meet up with 'la Boratto' in the first months of 1967. I was a young assistant director in one of Lina Wertmuller's films, and Caterina was still, as always, that same 'apparition.' So she seemed to me one morning when she arrived, contracted for a special appearance, while we were shooting some sequences in the Rome Hilton.

"I arrived on the set early, as the subs have to, and I immediately noticed something strange in the air. Stagehands and electricians were giving me furtive glances, half-spoken phrases were being muttered. Later the director and actors also arrived, and the ceremony of smiles and glances continued. Of course, I didn't understand at once. I was still a novice in the cinema world and I was quite unaware that stories like that of Caterina Boratto and Tito Schipa have a permanent place in the legends of the cinema, and are passed down from father to son together with the jargon and technical expertise and the hierarchy.

"That morning there was to be a sort of symbolic meeting, even if by way of a substitute, between the two principals in a great love of the past, and when I finally met up with Caterina, having taken her lines over to her, I turned and saw the whole troupe standing in a semicircle around the spot where we were shaking hands. Those universally similar smiles, from the lowest stagehand to the producer in person, gave the impression of having been waiting for thirty years on the lips of Rome's 'cinema people.'

"An instinctive friendship grew up at once between Caterina and me, but a natural tendency on her part not to open up too much, to hide the signs of a none-too-easy past delayed the moment of a complete retelling of the story for many years—in fact, until 1983, when armed with a tape recorder I decided to call at her house and put her gently up against the wall: I wanted to know everything.

"Surprisingly, she didn't need any coaxing. It was as if I'd divined that the right moment had come, or entered some secret corridor. She talked, spontaneously, for almost four hours. It was a fine sunny afternoon. From the luminous window of her apartment, the lights of Monte Parioli were reflected in her astonishing eyes, fixed on some distant point; a couple of times they filled with tears. And I learned, listening to a story which had once been 'on everybody's lips,' something that truly nobody else knew."

The very blonde Caterina who came to audition for Guido Brignone in 1936 was a good deal less than twenty years old, even though because of her above-average height, her Nordic complexion and a certain innate severity in her exceptionally beautiful face, she seemed older than her years. Once a certain reluctance on her mother's part had been overcome, and with strong backing by a producer who was a family friend, she agreed to present herself to the director of the film. She would, if chosen, play the daughter of the world-famous lead.

The audition consisted of two short scenes with Nino Besozzi, and for Caterina they were particularly successful. The reel was then watched by Brignone and Tito Schipa. However, the latter immediately chilled the director's enthusiasm, handing out a negative judgment with an intolerant air: he couldn't understand how Brignone could think of starring him against a "Viking" who was a hand taller than himself—"more like a sister of Brigitte Helm than the daughter of a Leccese."

In reality, however, Tito had thought to himself from the first glimpse: "This is Charlotte." And because in Caterina's heart Tito had always seemed not just to be the interpreter of *Werther*, but rather Werther in person, the dice of fate were already loaded from that first moment. Yet nothing happened for some time.

Initially there was a fierce battle of wills between the director and the star over the acceptance of the ethereal girl from Turin. Commendably, Brignone prevailed. And it could not have been easy, in that era, to get the better of a star of Tito Schipa's caliber. The movie was a fantastic success, the public flocked to the theaters. Right after the first private viewings in Paris and New York the critics heralded the long-awaited arrival of a tenor who was neither "overweight nor sickly-sweet"; a shrewd actor and a singer with a voice which was once again perfect (the film was made with a live sound-track of both the dialogues and songs). *Vivere!* immediately outshone other films of its class, and added to its triumph not only by winning popularity abroad, but also by launching two songs at once: "*Vivere!*" and "*Torna piccina,*" which earned money for the already well-known composer Cesare Andrea Bixio, and put Tito Schipa back right at the top of the charts. The "little one" (piccina) in question was of course Caterina, who for a few months longer continued to find herself treated like a real daughter by the man she admired most in the world. But his own feelings were heading in quite another direction, and when Brignone brought the two protagonists back together in an attempt to repeat the success of *Vivere!* Tito found that his life was made much easier by the fact that in the new film this lovely girl was not to play his daughter but his young lover.

This, however, was not popular with the public, who—when they did not find the familiar ingredients of the previous film—disappointed the hopes of the producers. *Chi è più felice di me?* had no success in the box-office, but it did have a very deep effect on the life of Tito Schipa, who halfway through the shooting made his declaration to the young girl from Turin:

"Shyly, embarrassed like a student," Caterina recalled, explaining that she had always felt ashamed to tell the history of this love-affair, which had stolen her heart for seven long years during her youth. The reticence came from the total improbability of such events, from the terms of the relationship, from its dramatic and painful ending... and from the mutual and unlikely "pact" which more than anything was what made the story different. For with angry insistence and stubbornness, and without ever allowing any doubt or uncertainty, the two leading actors in this drama (which was an epic story in its day) always swore that they had never allowed their relationship to pass beyond a very deeply-felt Platonic friendship. Tito's recurrent cry, right to the end, was: "I never laid a finger on her!"

Naturally, no one was willing to believe this.

And yet, if we look more closely at this romantic story between the "Emperor" and the austere Nordic beauty, it may yet be that this absurd claim does make some sense; there could have been a logical factor that gave the story a special sting for a man on the threshold of his fifties. In other words, this discreet "touch me not" might be concealing the cause of the fierce blows which followed later. But the first years of their love give us little help in understanding their relationship. To get the whole story we have to move to the forties, when Schipa began forming yet another identity and career for himself in Europe.

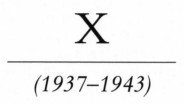

X

(1937–1943)

A Public Danger

Since the early twenties, the Schipa family and their immediate relations had been living in Rome. The first residence acquired by Tito for his parents was an imposing building on the riverside Lungotevere Arnaldo da Brescia. He continued to buy them houses of various types over the years in several different districts: Parioli, the quarter built by the architect Coppedè, San Giovanni, the Salaria, Prati, the Flaminia, and also Fregene on the coast north of the city, where he wanted to build a theater for himself alongside a princely villa. Properties in the name of Schipa also began to sprout like mushrooms all over other parts of Italy: in Alba, in Latina, in Romagna. The most impressive one, in this period, was the one at Castelvetro near Modena, where the great tenor's property included not only the house, but also several cheese-factories whose production of Parmesan would in itself have paid for his whole career. But of course this new manifestation of his prosperity didn't last. Instead, the usual crooked administrator appeared, punctually, out of nowhere. His sudden adoption of a princely lifestyle aroused the curiosity of the police, and sparked satirical newspaper articles. But we might say that for Tito this was just an everyday affair!

The disputes in America and the opportunity to devote himself to the cinema led him to settle, towards the end of the thirties, in one of the houses on Monte Parioli, the smartest quarter of Rome. And of course he still had his two Hollywood villas, administered by Carlo for the time being.

In Rome, during his search for staff to look after Lillì, who needed more and more help, someone turned up who was to play an important role in the Schipa family. She was called Luisa Merli, and she was an energetic Florentine girl who had been brought up in an orphanage. She had been in service with a family in Messina for some years, and through mutual acquaintances she was introduced into the Schipa household in 1937. From then onward, through more than fifty years of faithful service, she was to be a vital help to Lillì and to the future second family, and thanks to the trust she had won would be an assiduous and constant witness of all the events in the family's life.

Tito only stayed for a few months in the luxurious residence in Parioli. In the days of *Vivere!* Caterina Boratto was often a guest at dinner, and she established friendly relations with Tito's wife and daughters. Then, in the period of *Chi è più felice di me?* the relations between Tito and Caterina came to be public knowledge, and Lillì certainly could not have remained ignorant of this. By the end of the decade, Tito was no longer sleeping at home, though this did not imply that he was living with Caterina, of course. But by separating their living-places, the husband and wife were in fact acknowledging a separation which had been a fact for a long time. They kept up appearances with daily meetings, usually at lunchtime.

The great tenor had resumed his place in the society pages by playing the part of a carefree, sport-loving bachelor. He carried his fifty years lightly and went to parties all over Rome. There was no secret about his relations with the lively and very young daughter of a famous family of producers, Bruna S. (and a number of other splendid women, which makes his alleged pact of chastity with Caterina in anticipation of a hypothetical wedding more probable).

He had another passion, too: fine cars. But the passion was not balanced by expertise in driving. He caused many accidents, about one a week, until he eventually hit an unfortunate pedestrian, causing him a serious leg fracture. Schipa was practically forbidden to drive after that. Actually, he decided on his own, perhaps shocked by the event, to give up driving from then on. Cartoonists from the Italian papers had a field day with this ultra-musical pedestrian-stopper, who presented a real danger to the public. In fact, one of his films, *Chi è più felice di me?*, starts off with a famous singer knocking down a child, and it presented him on screen at the wheel of his terrifying cream-colored Packard.

Fifty years under his belt. One thinks automatically of physical decline, of an artist surviving on the basis of fame already acquired, of taking every advantage of his reputation and success. But nothing of the sort happened—in fact, things were quite different.

In these years, with more frequent appearances in the Italian theaters, Tito Schipa deepened and strengthened his relationship with the public of his own country. Italians could finally follow him in regular summer and winter seasons, get to know his repertoire in depth, enjoy his extraordinary consistency in performance. And this increased interest was matched by the artist's own complete maturing, for in these years he perfected the definition of his characters, mastering their subtleties beyond any previous limits. In fact subtleties now came to the forefront to complete his interpretations with a retouching here, a little chiaroscuro there.

In *Werther* he could go no further in perfecting the singing or exploring the character, but now he wove a web of enchantment over the audience with mere pauses, gestures and glances. Edgardo in *Lucia* had long been raised to a Mozartian role in nobility and severity, but now great surprises were in store for those who only remembered a "light" voice, and in the moments of overwhelming passion, he overrode the choral scenes with an aggressiveness, polish and volume which were quite unexpected. To Nemorino, he brought the linear simplicity of the recitative to compete with the melody by subtlety of diction, sophisticated humor and sweet-and-sour sentiments.

In 1936 Schipa had his first and only encounter with the Verona Arena, and it was precisely as a fragile, forty-seven-year-old Nemorino that he conquered that overpowering space. But there are no time-limits for legends. The story circulated of a "light voice" which nevertheless carried over the orchestra and the chorus to be heard right at the far edges of that huge stone amphitheater, and resounded as clear as an oboe among the tables of the cafés in Piazza Bra.

The great Magda Olivero, who sang with Tito in a *Marcella* that she found unforgettable, found a phrase of his particularly memorable:

> Words are small. The vowels are formed on the lips. They fall from the lips, and it is the breath that makes them fly.

It seems like an answer from one of the Sibyls, but if Magda Olivero says that this truly enlightened her, the oracle must surely have been harboring a basic secret.

As for Tito Schipa's Federico, in 1936, he was just being born.

The *"dolce sembiante"*

In the Rome exhibition of an enthusiastic private collector, Antonio Margiotta, a score for piano and voice of the *"Lamento di Federico"* is on display. It carries two handwritten inscriptions with different dates:

"The most beautiful aria!, Beniamino Gigli, 1941."

"I agree wholeheartedly with my esteemed colleague!, Tito Schipa, 1950."

Thus the two greatest living exponents of the music agreed in their judgment of it. But another prestigious name completed the ideal jury which conferred on Francesco Cilea the title of the greatest musical poet among Puccini's successors: that of Enrico Caruso, who had succeeded in making *L'Arlesiana* a triumph on its opening night in 1897. It is in this delicate and evocative opera that the only genuine parallel between Schipa and Caruso exists; in everything else they were exact opposites. Only this story provides them with common ground; the story of a folly of love and a tragic fall from a haystack.

Tito had recorded Federico's sweet rapture of love on disk as early as 1916, and then again in 1927, but he only decided to interpret the complete role on April 11th, 1936, in the exclusive setting of La Scala, with the omnipresent Gianna Pederzini at his side along with Margherita Carosio and Mario Basiola.

The critics were enthusiastic, though not ecstatic, about the opera and its composer. But they reserved their highest praise for the protagonist. "Corriere della Sera" wrote:

"The storm of applause which greeted his stupendous rendering of the aria '*Anch'io vorrei*' also confirmed, if there was any need for confirmation, the unchanging adoration of the public for this magnificent singer, who in certain circumstances specially suited to his vocal qualities, is enough in himself to raise the fortunes of a performance."

But La Scala wasn't enough for Tito. He wanted to impress Milan in every way possible, so a few weeks later, on May 1st, he presented his own operetta at the Teatro Lirico. The lead was sung by Gianna Pederzini, who made up in this way for having been indisposed the first night of *L'Arlesiana*. Tito conducted the orchestra, and as usual, halfway through the performance he brought the house down by singing "El Gaucho." The newspapers were unreserved in their praise, and "Corriere" spoke of an "overwhelming success."

This was the way in which Tito reacted to the unprecedented "dull thud" of *Werther* in the USA—by creating a completely new character when he was nearly fifty. Not only that: by inscribing the name of Federico in letters of gold in the gallery of his characters, he also brought about the revival of a score which, after the death of Caruso, had run the risk of undeserved oblivion. For whatever reason, and it may have seemed like a deliberate retaliation to Tito, this opera was never again made available on the stage in the USA. Indeed, its novelty strengthened his new bond with the Italian public. Cilea himself expressed his gratitude, sometimes in impassioned terms.

The angelic features of Caterina had been slowly superimposed on that "*dolce sembiante*" (sweet likeness) about whom Federico was sadly rambling. According to a personal statement by Tito, we know that from a certain moment he could not sing that aria without imagining the face of his beloved. But the mixture of different genres (the key to this man's whole existence), the indefinite limits between the new and the antique, tradition and curiosity, were brewing a new storm: the "*dolce sembiante*" of Caterina was not confined exclusively to the imagination of Tito-Federico, but had also been splendidly captured on film by Otello Martelli, the director of photography in *Vivere!*, and in that form it crossed the ocean and wound up in the studios of Metro Goldwyn Mayer. Here Louis B. Mayer, one of the most formidable and decisive of all tycoons in the history of the cinema, was spellbound for a moment at the initial closeup of Caterina, with her blond hair and black domino. Then he hammered on the table and ordered that this dream of a girl should be brought to him—at once. He wanted to include her in the array of new recruits who were to be seen around his studio, unknown young ladies with names like Lana Turner and Judy Garland. It was an offer which nobody could even dream of refusing, least of all Caterina, who must have imagined that she was about to enjoy the same fortune that had befallen Hedy Lamarr.

It was Tito, however, who showed the greatest enthusiasm. The prospect of resuming work in California on the wave of a cinema success must have seemed to him yet another incredible twist in his already magic existence, an unhoped-for opportunity for *revenge*! And they packed their bags: Tito Schipa headed for his villa in Beverly Hills and Caterina Boratto for an apartment that MGM had arranged. Following the couple, as on the day of their first meeting, was Caterina's mother. In a previous trip to Paris and Germany, her presence had already complicated the lives of the two celebrated lovers. It seemed as if she wanted to personally witness and guarantee the chastity of their affair. Caterina, in her memoirs, says:

"I could not have allowed myself either to be or to appear to be the lover of anyone. It was not my style. I would belong to the man who would marry me." In support of this version of events, it was during these months that Tito asked Lillì for a divorce.

In California Caterina's life was anything but restful. Her day was regularly divided into studies of English, singing and acting, all in MGM courses, with a seven-year contract and a stipend of 150 dollars a week. Tito resumed his North American activity, limiting it exclusively to concerts. Caterina was still awaiting her first suitable role, but all Hollywood was predicting marvels for her. And the role arrived. It was to be a major part in *The Woman*, with Joan Crawford. What more could be asked? Various prospects opened up: success for her, the resumption of smooth relations in America for him, and above all, the chance to realize their dream of matrimony.

But there is always a price to be paid, and Benito Mussolini was no ordinary creditor. When he presented his bill, in fact, he caused a crisis not just for a couple of lovers, but for a whole planet. Italy declared itself the ally of Nazi Germany.

Caterina was called urgently to the manager's office. The civilities and compliments for her progress in English were rapid and formal. The essential questions came quickly, and were direct and unambiguous:

"You're Italian?" Caterina reflected for a moment on the advice that her manager had given her, that she should declare Swiss nationality. But a certain natural malaise at ambiguities did not allow her to try such evasions. She said yes. "Are you a fascist?" No one in her family had ever had any connection with politics, nor with dissent or opposition. She did not say no.

The conversation came to a rapid end: "We're sorry, but in that case, we would prefer to give the chance to someone else."

A few weeks later, when another opportunity for work came up, the proposal that was put to her was again to deny her Italian nationality publicly and then take part in a propaganda film.

What should she do? To whom could she go for advice? Not to her mother, who in the meantime had returned to Turin, full of anxiety about the fate of her son, who was a soldier in the front line. Not to Elvira, Tito's sister, who was living in Beverly Hills at the time, but like a fish out of water. And not to Tito himself, who in those months had increased his activities in South America and Australia, and was at that moment performing in some corner of Oceania, adding the language of the aborigines to the many he already sang in! Caterina was alone with her dilemma, and her thoughts too went to her brother, Filiberto, who was an officer with the royal army in Albania. Setting aside all caution, she refused to compromise.

Every American opening was immediately closed both to Caterina and to Tito, whose presence on the American scene had seemed about to reach a new intensity. In 1939, in fact, he had just appeared again in Chicago and then in San Francisco in his magisterial interpretations of *Manon* and *Lucia di Lammermoor*. But during the flight to San Francisco he had met with two emissaries of fate who dealt him a formidable blow. His difficult work situation was aggravated by an economic disaster brought on by his almost pathological openness to anyone who crossed his path.

This time it was a young couple, distinctive in appearance and habits, who introduced themselves to Tito on the plane, saying that they were financial advisors. They followed him to San Francisco, kept him company for weeks, bought him magnificent dinners, and persuaded him to invest in phantom oil companies.

It was an out-and-out fraud. They reduced him practically to penury. Every bit of cash which was not solidly tied down in property was whisked away in a trice.

Caterina recalls with emotion the tormented request that he was forced to make to her: could she possibly return to him, temporarily, the jewels he had given her? For a southern gentleman, accustomed to generosity, to lavish patronage and display, imagine the effect of such a step! But this was the state to which he had been reduced, and Caterina returned to him, with a good grace, the diamond bracelet as wide as a garter (one out of many gifts bestowed without a second thought in one of his expansive moments). She was more concerned about his falling into a dangerous depressive crisis than about losing her jewelry.

It was not the first episode of the kind, nor was it to be the last. His concert income still enabled him to get out of the mess and he returned to Italy in great haste.

A real tragedy

While the world war was raging, Tito Schipa retired to his own country. His performances became more and more restricted, and only took place on home territory. The divorce proceedings with Lillì were drawn out, and affairs in general went on at a slower pace.

During these years the talent-scout in him resurfaced. In his unconditional love for Caterina (it really was a passionate love), Tito became convinced that she had the artistic talent to be a singer. He encouraged her to study further and persuaded her to appear before the public with him, putting pressure on impresarios to give their backing to this strange couple.

The idea may seem risky from many points of view, but the public accepted it. The echo of *Vivere!* was still strong all over the country, and Caterina sang pleasantly enough, in the graceful voice of a light soprano. For these reasons Tito easily aroused great curiosity in the public and a remarkable respect from the critics. In any case, their performing partnership would hardly have seemed more than an American-style caprice if a series of events had not combined to bring their relationship to a dramatic conclusion.

This dramatic denouement came about on September 8, 1943, the inevitable consequence of an unwanted war and a nation which was not of one heart and mind. But no one could have foreseen the breach that would separate Tito and Caterina at one stroke and condemn them to live alone and apart, as if groping in the dark.

Thanks to Tito's infallible instinct for anything to do with the stage, the concert with Caterina was working, and working well. The happiness of this joint success was the last positive moment the two lovers were able to enjoy. All over Italy terrible news was spreading: the Germans, in reprisal for Badoglio's proclamation of Italian neutrality, were shooting hundreds of Italian officers, many of them in Cephalonia, where the Acqui Division was stationed. Among the officers in the Acqui Division was Lieutenant Filiberto Boratto, Caterina's twenty-three-year-old brother.

The way in which Caterina learned what happened in Cephalonia seemed to have come from the script of a sensational film.

During a concert with Tito in the Milan area Caterina was approached by an unknown girl who informed her, pale and trembling, that a soldier had returned from the Albanian front. Wounded and near death, this soldier had vital news for her. Caterina felt herself grow cold with fear; she did not even have the courage to go meet him. Another of her brothers hurried to Lecco,[21] where he found a man in desperate straits, who had somehow managed to escape from the shooting. He told how he had remained for a day and a night beneath a heap of bodies, wounded but conscious. A woman had saved him during the night, and got him onto a merchant ship leaving for Genoa. From there he was hoisted onto a train and he had arrived at Lecco in an appalling

---

[21] Lecce is in the deep south of Italy, while Lecco, a city with a similar name, is in Lombardy.

state: his stomach sewn together in improvised fashion with metal thread. He hardly had time to say that he had brought the last message of Filiberto Boratto to his sister, uttered moments before the rifles of the SS had fired, before he, too, died.

The veil fell at once from the eyes of the young film star. Her existence was transformed into a nightmare. Neither she, nor her mother, nor her brothers were ever to recover from this trauma. The reality of an absurd war, and of the madness which had dragged Italy to ruin, was brought home to her in the fate of the brother whom she adored. Every aspect of her everyday life changed in meaning and value. She immediately reevaluated her commitment to perform for the Germans and the fascist "repubblichini" in northern Italy. She decided that she would do nothing for the assassins of her brother, least of all sing. But in this irrevocable decision, she met up with resistance from the person she least desired as an adversary, Tito Schipa, who was iron-willed in his determination to perform the concerts that were scheduled, and stubbornly attached to an idea which did not suit the times—the superiority of the artist over matters of politics.

I can state with conviction that Tito Schipa was no fascist, even though he might have been accused of being one. It could be said, certainly, that he was a fervent monarchist, led to misunderstand gravely, as indeed many Italians were, the real nature of events. But he was not a fascist. Let this be stated by someone who knew him well, who was close to him and had the chance to converse with him often in the accusatory tones which only eighteen-year-olds are capable of using with their unlucky parents. It is true that in 1936, on the occasion of a performance of *Lucia* at La Scala, and before the bemused eyes of the spectators, he did give a box with no less than *seven kilograms* of gold ingots to his native land, which was demanding gold for its bizarre imperial adventures. It is also true that as a result he was seriously booed by trade unionists during a tour in Mexico in the same year, provoking a great scandal in the press. But Tito Schipa was not a fascist. It is also true that in the same year, during a tour in Australia, he reacted angrily to a ruling prohibiting the discussion of Italian politics by saluting the public with his arm raised: even so, he was not a fascist. He was not a fascist for the same reasons that later on he was not a communist (even though he was vociferously accused of being one!).

To be something in politics presupposes some connection with reality, some relationship with others. But this is not a given with stars. Tito Schipa was a star as much as anyone could be—a divo, a divinity. Anyone who dealt with him often was aware of his incapacity for entertaining any kind of systematic conviction. He could not create a scheme of critical thought about the reality surrounding him, or about the great questions and dramas of human coexistence, even though onstage he was, as Franco Serpa rightly states, much more lucid and critical than his colleagues: "a singer from the neck up in the midst of singers from the neck down." So this distance of his was another of his great mysteries and gifts. But it did not save him from the impact of the postwar world; indeed it increased the war's traumatic effect on him. He was even more vulnerable because he had succeeded in harmonizing the extremely unreal, fairy-tale dimension of the divo with a far more showy and dynamic appearance in "life as it is lived" than that of his colleagues, which was often quite limited. But this apparent "presence" of his should not deceive us, nor lead us to believe that he had a different idea of reality from that of any primadonna (no term better renders the catastrophic inconsistency of these legendary singers).

None of us, I believe, can say what passes through the mind of a creature who knows this kind of success, this sensation of omnipotence, of a world ready to do his bidding after a wave of his hand or the least soft sound of his voice. How can we expect from such atypical creatures, in the grip of a hallucinating dream which is more real than reality to them, any kind of coherence, any analysis, any consistency? This man, veteran of a dream career, an existence lived like a game in which he had held all the cards: what could he ever understand of the Italy which was about to be born, made up of ruthless self-analysis, Byzantine distinctions, merciless counter-positions, an incomprehensible political jargon, and above all a complete dismantling and reconstruction of its own artistic traditions?

Tito found the first emissary of this unknown Italy, an Italy about to take shape before his eyes like the enigmatic apparition of a violent foe, where he would have least expected it: in the most beautiful, transparent and taciturn young woman for whom, at fifty, he had nurtured an almost adolescent passion.

Initially he succeeded in getting his own way, compelling Caterina to respect certain contracts which had already been signed, but the situation became more and more full of anguish. Gianna Pederzini, who often accompanied the couple on this tour, tells of rigorously separate bedrooms (though according to Tito and Caterina they had always been so), and constant quarrels; violent shouting which went on through the whole night, reducing them both to exhaustion, decline and, inevitably, affecting their work. Gianna even went so far as to intervene, attacking them, dividing them, telling them they belonged in a nursing home—trying every way imaginable to wake them from their joint nightmare. But it was all useless. The situation came to a crisis in a period of a few weeks. In the first weeks of 1944, suddenly, without warning anyone, Caterina vanished into thin air.

A little while later it was learnt that she had returned secretly to Turin and sought refuge with one of the friends of her adolescence, the engineer Armando Ceratto. As if to stress her intention of cancelling out the past, in the following June she married him. Thus she was lost to Tito and all Italians until the day in which (it seemed to be a century later) Federico Fellini woke her from her long regenerative sleep and brought her back to the screen in *Giulietta degli spiriti.*

Alone

Having reached these years, the so-called "autobiography" of Tito Schipa is interrupted.

Before taking his leave, he states that he has passed his fiftieth year; that the events he has recounted so far should therefore be broadly delineated by what he has said about himself. But you would find it hard to discover a single reference to these facts, and not even once did he cite the name of Caterina in those pages. Instead, a number of unexciting and superficial events are dwelt upon, so that he is constantly made to appear completely superior to questions of sex. Every episode ends with a fatherly pat on the cheek of the eighteen-year-old *bimbas* who tempt him, cleverly but in vain. The southern gentleman, who would perhaps rather have killed himself than involve the name of a lady in public, once again gets the better of the figure of entertainment and the businessman. If we add that not even one single date corresponds to the truth, we can only repeat the invitation which we issued at the outset, to ignore these pallid and useless pages, probably invented by an unscrupulous journalist, while the man himself was distracted by a great crisis.

For a real crisis it undoubtedly was, in that winter of 1943-44, when after a desperate attempt to intercept Caterina on her flight, Tito found himself sitting on a hotel bed holding the furs and jewels which she, with her usual correctness, had left when she fled. These are the only months in the life of Tito Schipa in which we cannot identify even the trace of a relationship, a secure friendship, a point of reference. The real tears which he had always shed when singing the "Lament of Federico," and the sensual "Malìa" by Tosti, must have acquired genuine bitterness in this period.

Here there is another small gap in the documents which tell us about his private affairs. The autobiography, as we mentioned, has been concluded. And so too has the patient work of Lillì, who until 1937 (no coincidence that this was the year in which Caterina appeared) had continued to gather and catalogue every piece of printed paper concerning her husband. The state of her health, among other things, made it impossible to continue doing this, and in any case her relations with Tito had worsened recently because of the war, during which Lillì had made no secret of her anti-German feelings, and had even had a taste of prison, along with the faithful Luisa.

In a year the next of Tito's amours, the very young Diana, would begin a lovesick and punctilious diary, but during this period there is nothing to fill in the gaps in what was written about the great singer. During this winter of discontent, with Italy torn apart, Diana was still in the mind of God.

There was no lack of work for Tito, but La Scala was missing. The reopening of the best-loved of all Italian opera houses was anxiously awaited, with no inkling of the surprise that was to accompany it.

There was no lack, either—once again—of high fees to console him. For this reason, not even the latest financial setbacks or the customary frauds practiced by his collaborators succeeded in making him more attentive to the passage of time. Indeed, the memory was still fresh of a season in Portugal side by side with his eternal rival, Beniamino Gigli, since a new historic contest had arisen between them, this time for the title of "world's highest-paid tenor." The newspaper headlines read:

"Schipa and Gigli: a million an evening!"—and this was 1942! The illusion that everything would always go well for him financially was taking dangerous root.

Even his great second passion, the cinema, continued to flatter him with frequent parts. But here the results were not up to the standard of the films of Brignone and Bonnard. Some films, like a ghostly *Vivere ancora*, are still lost in the swamps of third feature distribution. And some were never to come out at all.

It was precisely to take part in a film (which would never see the light of the screen) that Tito Schipa was called about halfway through 1944. So off he went to the studios in the Giudecca in Venice, and to an encounter which in the mind of a fifty-five-year-old disappointed in love should have been the most unlikely and unhoped-for event possible. In spite of the innate optimism which characterized his whole life, undoubtedly protected by a star which never faded, it is hard to imagine that Tito would have expected a new love so soon after the last one. It is even more difficult to imagine that he would have expected to find it in the arms of a twenty-year-old. As with the demigods, his divine element did not exempt him from the necessary passage of the years, but it was decreed (and what a satisfying consolation it was) that the tiresome problems of age should be compensated by another eternal youth: that of his latest companions.

XI

(1944–1945)

A chapter apart

There is a kind of invisible frontier which must exist around Piacenza, or towards Novara if one is arriving from that direction; it also depends on the day and the mood, or indeed on the weather, because it is undoubtedly a kind of suspended grayness, and you can never be sure whether it is mist or smoke which tells you that you have crossed the boundary. I'm tempted to say that I was born here, that this is my native country, but in fact that isn't the case.

There is a similar frontier too somewhere near Ostuni, beyond Bari, but the similarity between the two is something only I can see. Here it's hot, and the countryside melts under the blinding sun; the houses seem to be made of chalk, and the horizon is a fine edge of bluish water. As soon as you cross this other frontier, you are making your way through an infinite web of those low drystone walls and olive trees, and those trulli, and more olives again and more trulli, and stone walls, and trulli and trulli and trulli, until the repetitiveness almost lulls you into a trance, and when you wake with a start, after an hour or a day, there you are in Lecce.

But I wasn't born here, either. In fact I was born in Lisbon.

144

Perfect familiarity with these two wonderful corners of Italy, however—including an ear for their dialects (so different from each other), and a natural intimacy with their two populations (so similar in some ways)—are the product of an encounter between a fifty-five year old tenor born in Lecce, of Albanian origin, and a twenty-year-old girl born in the district of Cuneo, of gypsy origin. The Salento and the Langhe have always coexisted in me, and I often fail to distinguish between the dry, slim figures of some aged contemporaries of Cesare Pavese, who seem to have been born with their caps on their heads, and their equivalents from the area of Otranto, where that same leanness, that sharp profile and that dignified, almost offended, silence, are found in equal measure at a distance of a thousand kilometers, and divided by a genetic abyss. The strip of land ideally uniting Lecce and Gallipoli, the birthplaces respectively of my paternal grandfather and grandmother, has already been mentioned. Now our story takes us to the other zone, the far confines of which are marked by Montezemolo, the gateway to the Langhe, and the city of Genoa. This is where the events that led to the appearance of your narrator on the scene took place, and for this reason it can only be a chapter apart, in which I apologize for playing the leading role!

Teresa Jolanda Borgna was born in 1924 in Cardellini, a subdistrict of the kind only found in the Langhe, composed of two houses, and when I say two, I mean literally two. Not a shadow of a church, a school or a shop; two houses, a woodshed, and around them woods, woods and valleys as far as the eye can see. On the summit opposite—only in the summer, and fog permitting—one can make out two houses, or occasionally three, of the nearest hamlet. To find any kind of organized life, in those days, one had to travel at least an hour, in sun, snow or wind, and of course on foot. For this reason Teresa would have referred to herself as a "*montanara*"—a mountain girl.

A very special sort of *montanara*, however, and of outstanding beauty. Already when she was a child, she stood out conspicuously from her parents, though they were fine-looking folk, and her two sisters and one brother, who were all very pleasing in appearance. And when the family moved to Genoa in 1939, to the popular quarter of Bolzaneto, Teresa's beauty had everybody talking.

At sixteen she was working in the soap department of the Mira

Lanza company, but her thoughts were fixed elsewhere. While her workmates gave each other kissing lessons in anticipation of the fairy prince who would come and take them away from their shifts in the factory, Teresa was dreaming about the cinema. This was her passion as well as her relaxation and her "boyfriend." All the time which she didn't spend at work or at home, she devoted to the movie theater in her district. And there she learned to adore an artist who, in her eyes at that moment, was above all a marvelous interpreter of musical films. The fact that he was an opera singer was, for the time being at least, irrelevant. Seeing him in *Vivere!* was like a lightning-flash from a clear sky for her. His name was Tito Schipa, and everyone at home and in the factory teased her for constantly repeating his name.

It was natural that the first boy whom Teresa condescended to notice was a Genoese who was interested in film production, and who introduced her into the circle of talented young people in San Giorgio films. Then he did all he could to get her the right contacts in the film world. Of course, all this was concealed from her father, an ex-carabiniere who worked in the tram-depot of Pontedecimo. To him her associations were anything but a joke. Things weren't all that easy; there were obstacles and pitfalls of every kind to overcome—not least that same father, fiercely opposed to any kind of artistic extravagance. But when the time came for the right audition, and when the audition realized her daydreams with a real written contract, Teresa in effect ran away from home, and went off to Venice armed with a brand new name, Diana Prandi. A part was waiting for her at the Giudecca—a role that couldn't be called secondary in a film called *L'ultimo sogno*.

In itself this was another of those films without a future, at least in professional terms. But the consequences for the life of this young working girl from Piedmont were quite far-reaching.

Between takes Diana heard that *Rosalba* was being shot in a nearby studio, and that the protagonist was her "very own" Tito Schipa. She hardly had time to get over the surprise when someone organized a meeting for her, and this meeting led to a dinner-invitation. For the moment it was just a general affair among members of the two casts. But after a first expert glance, the great tenor made no bones about it:

"Bring that tall girl over here..."

He could only be referring to her, more than a head taller than all her colleagues. And consequently, a good deal taller than he was, too. But this did not put Tito Schipa off; he'd never seen his five feet, six inches as a drawback. Both Lillì and Caterina had been able to look down on him, and now once again he was contemplating his favorite proportions!

The dinner was over, and in the space of a moment in her dreams, Diana received another invitation. But this time it was for a tête-à-tête. On the waters of a lagoon which was made for the role of accomplice to great loves, Diana heard from the lips which she had admired more than any in the world the story of an unhappy love for an apparition by the name of Caterina, of the desperate state of a marriage with a French soubrette, of the loneliness of a famous tenor in these last months. Tito hid nothing, nor did he demand anything. And with equal honesty and determination, she offered herself up to this unforeseen turn of events, bound hand and foot for the sacrifice.

Fifty-six years against twenty; travels with him where she was introduced as his secretary; subterfuges, clandestine moves, unavoidable sarcasms from friends and acquaintances—none of it mattered. From personal experience, I can assure the reader that what grew out of that encounter was a real love affair.

Fortunello in armor

Now the two great cinema-lovers had met, united in the face of their thousand differences by a mutual passion. In movie terms we go to the next scene with a fade-out and fade in: the starlit lagoon of Venice begins to dissolve, and instead we are on a local road in some corner of the Republic of Salò.

It's cold, there is mist; the headlights of an old-fashioned methane-powered automobile penetrate the twilight in an austere black and white scene. The form which can be made out inside, wrapped in an enormous shawl and completely masked by the Homburg drawn right down to his nose, is that of the great tenor. He is ranting, adding his exclamations to the asthmatic grunts of the engine. He is not, we can see, very pleased with this vehicle. It is too slow, wheezing as if to protest its methane propellant and weighed down by the two brutally unaesthetic cylinders attached to the rear trunk. He is going to arrive late for the concert. A panoramic shot now: there is also something on one of the mudguards. In fact, some*one*. A kind of figurehead, a female form. With one hand she clings to the hood, with the other she shields her eyes against the wind and the heavy dew, striving to make out anything in the twilight ahead of her. The wind ruffles her hair, and brings a shine to her eyes. If we draw a little closer, we will recognize the former soap-maker from Mira Lanza, now promoted to in-house leading lady functioning as a windbreak.

This was how they have been traveling around northern Italy for some weeks, Tito Schipa and his new, very young, companion—hurrying from one place to another between sweeps, bombardments and ambushes. Or coming upon roadblocks exactly like the one which now stops them fifty yards in front of a huge fire which is lighting up the hills and the woods.

What's happened? There has been an air attack on a German military convoy: yes, in fact the very one which passed them only twenty minutes ago. "Dear God," thinks Tito, "We have to be grateful to the gas-cylinders which slowed us down. It might have been us down there!"

The Commander of the German division comes up and demands to see their documents. Tito Schipa raises his hat; this is enough to call the attention of the officer, who apologizes elegantly, and with a gesture, gives the car free passage. The driver doesn't need telling twice, and makes off with all speed. Too much speed, in fact: a young soldier on guard with his rifle, already stunned by the inferno which had broken out a little earlier, has not seen the officer's signal. He assumes the car's occupants are trying to make a break, and doesn't think twice: he fires on them.

The scene comes to a standstill. Nothing moves. The officer is speechless with rage; the soldier is like a block of stone, and from the car there is no sign of life. The camera moves forward, following the officer who cautiously advances towards the car. Inside they are all paralyzed. Then the great tenor, terrified, turns his head slowly and looks at the rear window. Exactly at the height of his head, the two much-abused gas cylinders have intercepted and obstructed two bullets aimed with fatal accuracy at the back of his neck. There is the proof, two holes the size of walnuts.

While the officer tears the poor young soldier to shreds, pointing the barrel of his Luger right at his throat, Tito Schipa rushes to his defense and probably saves his life.

A pair of friends traveling with Tito and the young Diana ask each other whether it is possible to have better luck than this. They have been traveling with him for two months—months of bombs falling a few feet away or failing to explode, air attacks avoided because of a flat tire, or even, as in this case, bullet-stopping gas-cylinders which even manage unaccountably not to explode in the process. To the nickname of "Fortunello," which has already been circulating for months, they now add the adjective "armor-plated."

From one adventure to another, on stages of every kind, from that of the Donizetti in Bergamo to the oratory of some unknown chapel, to the officers' mess of who knows what garrison, Tito Schipa sings almost every evening. And every evening his exceptionally beautiful lover, behind him in years but more sensitive to danger than he is, kneels before him before he goes onstage and begs him not to repeat "that phrase."

"What phrase?" he asks, distracted.

"What you say at the end of *"Torna a Surriento...*""

"Ah, yes," he concedes, "but that's just said for effect. It doesn't mean a thing, only the public like it a lot. It just means a bit of extra applause; what do you think could happen...?"

"They might shoot you," she says (and she's dead right).

"Oh, nonsense!" he concludes (a famous stock phrase of his), and he takes a step nearer the piano, smoothing down the best-fitting tailcoat in the whole history of opera.

He sings for half an hour, and then gives encores for forty minutes. Everything is fine. But one of the encores, the one Diana is mortally afraid of, is *"Torna a Surriento."* As long as he limits himself to amusing the audience by telling them that it is not, as many think, a song dedicated to a woman, but rather to a mayor who has resigned from office, all is still fine. But when he comes to spell out the title, Diana crosses her fingers and bites her lip. Inexorably, that world-famous voice, subtle and sharp, fills the theater:

"I'm going to sing '*Torna a Surriento*' for you" ...pause... "and we *will* return!" He's done it again. He's quite incorrigible, and quite unaware. He has such bravado. And even for an armor-plated Fortunello, this is too much.

We should keep clearly in mind this unequivocal picture of Tito Schipa openly siding with factions from the part of Italy where he had gone to live and work the better to understand why certain public perceptions of him that will be presented later in this book were unjust and ludicrous.

Engaged

The family of proud working people which welcomed Tito Schipa in the first days of 1945 to a modest apartment in the Teglia district was a microcosm of the Genoa which was spreading around them: half traditionally sensitive to musical and singing matters (Genoa is a sort of Naples of the North, where a song can open every door to you), and half firmly rooted in its working-class culture. In the encounter with the great artist a kind of ambiguity was possible. On the one hand, there was a real waking dream, while on the other hand there were certain preconceptions about the man, who was too exposed in the political sense. These problems, however, vanished away like snow in the sunshine when they met him for the first time.

As always, those meeting up with him found themselves completely disarmed after a few moments by his openness, friendliness and sense of humor. In this case he was able to conquer an ex-carabiniere from Cuneo serving in the tramway department! As for Gino and Katy and Maria, the younger siblings of Diana, the party celebrating the arrival of the living legend in flesh and blood on their own doorstep had begun a month earlier and is still going on today! The same went for the city, which after some initial suspicions welcomed Tito among its honorary citizens. It even went so far as to celebrate him in the popular verses which were chanted to Genoa and to its women: if Schipa had chosen one of them for himself, they must necessarily be the most beautiful of all!

Se o grande Schipa o se gh'è sposou
veu di che in gio belle on no 'ha attrovou!

His name was part of many popular sayings in those days. Alberto Rabagliati, in one of his songs which listed all the greats of jazz, concluded:

Tutto questo Tito Schipa non lo fa!

This "light," popular personality, rather than the unconquered interpreter of the opera houses, was the one that Diana's excited brothers and sisters were suddenly faced with in their home on an April morning. He arrived in a Fiat with which Cesare Valletta had presented him personally to replace the fateful methane-gas vehicle. It was a real family inspection, even if the idea of a refusal was inconceivable. Perhaps within himself the taciturn paterfamilias Giovanni, and the inexhaustible "mamma" Giuseppina may have been wondering whether that strange alliance would survive the years and the deepening of the age gap which divided them, but in the darkness of the Teatro Grattacielo, during a *Werther* to which the whole family had been invited and placed in seats of honor, all resistance was bound to collapse.

In that time, Diana began to keep her diary, which instead of a record of solemn and official events more closely resembled school exercise books full of simple and attentive observations. (Throughout her life she would remain simple and attentive and yet profound.)

The fixed point of his peregrinations in the North, then under siege, was Bergamo, where Tito lived temporarily with his new companion and several friends from Rome. The hotel was the Moderno, and his reception had been normal and respectful before April 25, 1945. But the son of the owner was a partisan; now spirits were heating up, and the Schipa clan was literally thrown out. Tito (on this occasion even less prepared than Nemorino), found himself out on the street wondering about the meaning of the word that was on everyone's lips: "Liberation."

He took refuge in a little boardinghouse near the station, where as early as May 9th he sat at the piano in the drawing-room, and sang a few songs for "Our English friends," as Diana referred to them. War, death and destruction were already behind and forgotten for Tito Schipa.

However, the group of partisans whom he encountered one

morning at the street corner were by no means so ready to forget. They recognized him at once, and served him with an arrest warrant. By his proverbial good fortune, an English officer happened to be passing in the same narrow little street at that moment: perhaps he was one of the beneficiaries of the previous evening's concert. He was escorting a German officer who was his prisoner. That crossroads in Bergamo instantly became symbolic of the thousand roads that had been interwoven to form his career. At the sight of the great artist the German officer stood at attention. The English officer too stood at attention, for he was from a music-loving family. The partisans looked dour when the Englishman pointed out that without an arrest warrant that was officially sanctioned, they had no right to arrest anyone.

"There IS a warrant: I've seen it in Milan!" one of the boys said.

"Go and get it, then," replied the phlegmatic English officer. They reached a compromise: Tito Schipa would pass the night in the police station, available in case the arrest warrant should be confirmed. This was the biggest concession that the English officer could manage to get out of them.

Prison. And it was not to be the last time. Some time later, he was to find himself virtually under house arrest on his estate at Castelvetro, and there again he was looked after by a little patrol of English soldiers who had the task of protecting him from death threats. Now, on a rough board in the police station in Bergamo, and then in the barracks for another two nights, playing *scopone* with the guards and other vigilantes, Diana's fiancé did perhaps feel a certain shiver of fear—and it was about time, too.

I say "perhaps," because who knows really? Maybe Fortunello was convinced that once again life would not have the bad taste to prove too realistic. Yes, indeed, his fellow-Leccean and bosom friend Achille Starace had been shot, in a preceding scene; and that other fellow, the Great Dictator whom he had often amused himself by making fun of, had been overthrown by the massed chorus and the extras; and Lillì, his French Donna Elvira, together with their two much-loved daughters, was singing her contemptuous arias over his new amorous adventure. But this time, it was simply that the curtain was a little late coming down on the last act of the tragedy. Just stay calm: sooner or later we'll reach the chorus of reconciliation at the end, and all will be well. And everyone—fascist bosses and partisans, dictators and Hollywood producers, fatal blondes and fiery brunettes, thieving secretaries, monkeys, Princess Liana—would all be there, lined up holding hands, as always smiling at the ovation from the audience, while the bouquets showered down. And then, everyone off to dinner...

And that was just how it was... The arrest warrant never arrived, and no more was seen of those lads with the strange scarves around their necks. On July 15th Tito Schipa gave a concert for the Committee of National Liberation! Everything seemed to have turned into a soap bubble. Off with the motley, and on to pocket the fee? Not quite: this time it would be a bit harder than usual.

After the war

His activities after the war centered around his estate in Castelvetro, a kind of feudal holding purchased in the hope that it would serve as a love nest for him and Caterina after their marriage. An article in a local paper referred officially to the "political clarification" which had taken place between the great opera star and the representatives of liberated Italy. But everything didn't become easier from then on; far from it. In a constant attempt to put the good faith of the ambiguous singer to the test, and with a clear intention of profiting from his need for expiation, representatives of various walks of life passed in and out of the estate gates, a real free port in the midst of the Milanese lowlands.

There were representatives of the CNL on the hunt for free concerts, clergymen in search of sung masses, English officers who wanted Schipa and Co. in their club, treating him almost like a saloon-bar singer. Then he sang for the wounded, at the invitation of the Red Cross, where the scenes of bandages, stretchers and orderlies were straight out of Hemingway. He slept in the house of a partisan charged with guarding him and avoiding nasty surprises from certain recalcitrant elements, and he rose early, to deal with the constant pilgrimage of *vigili* looking for a bit of refreshment on their round, military units needing to connect up an electric cable, inventors with a new patent for an accordion, needing financial help, and then the rest: associations, clubs, charities, all in search of song, and song and more song.

In exchange for all this, there were a few grains of advantage to be had. Mostly implicit promises to contribute to his redemption in the public eye; at other times, as at Solignano, the honorary presidency of the town band! And he accepted, and waited. He waited for the arrival of a sign from some higher authority, from those who would reroute the paths he had taken in the past— in fact, only a few months ago—though they seemed to belong to a dream of a hundred years earlier.

It was Livio D., his Bolognese secretary, who looked after his affairs. He was certainly no saint, but he was determined, for his own sake, too, to reopen the doors of the major theaters to his prestigious employer. Not even a mention of La Scala. The bombs had not spared it, and now an attempt was being made to get it back on its feet. He would have to settle accounts with Milan, which had lived directly through the Resistance. But in Rome, things should be easier. Rome was the same old city it had always been, a crucible of trends, factions and differing interests. No one needed to tread too carefully there.

On the evening of August 3, 1945, in Livio's house, they were waiting for a reply. But it was already late, maybe news would come tomorrow. His friend invited him to stay. What happened that night between Tito and Diana is recorded, in rather uncertain handwriting, in her diary—an occasion of no small importance for the writer of these lines!

Rome did accept. In what was still called, at that stage, the Royal Opera House. Tito Schipa returned to the stage for the umpteenth time, at fifty-seven years of age. Not for a return season, or for revived activity based on the fame of a name which had already become immortal: it can never be stressed enough that the final triumph of Schipa, the real consolidation of his legend, at least in Italy, belongs to these very years. With his incredible vocal longevity, Tito transformed the myth of the magic singer of the twenties and thirties into the amazingly solid master-interpreter of the late forties. And it was perhaps these months that added the final touch to his myth. I know people—aristocrats, elderly opera-lovers, ordinary professional people, solitary pensioners—whose eyes fill with tears merely at the memory of those days in October and November of 1945 when in less than a month it was possible to hear—in the same city, from the same seat, with the same season ticket—Tito Schipa engaged (and performing with fervor, given his desire for a new start) in productions of *Elisir d'amore, Lucia di Lammermoor, L'Arlesiana, Il barbiere di Siviglia, Don Pasquale, Werther,* and *Don Giovanni.* It was as if in forty days the best of everything that Schipa had given in thirty years to the lovers of theater in music was on offer. I know people who didn't miss a single opening night, and who then went to all the other performances too, and some who were so stubbornly infatuated that they even came to all the rehearsals as well.

After Rome, which was the first major Italian scene to reopen its doors to him, the chance of an international revival followed. The city which offered this possibility was Lisbon. The stay in the land of Fado (but also of Salazar) promised to be quite long; four months were planned, with movements to other cities besides the capital. For Diana it was to be the first long period away from the family. Later on, in May, a tiring tour in Spain and France was in the works, and then a reappearance in America, both North and South. This meant being left alone in Lisbon. For someone who had never traveled a mile beyond the frontier at Ventimiglia, the prospect was a nightmare. At her insistence Tito had made a pact with her: motherhood or no, never a day apart. The time would come when he would need to cling desperately to this "clause," but at the moment she was the one who was insisting on it, in view of that May of uncertainty.

Before leaving, there was only just time to take part in a filmed biography of Donizetti, *Cavaliere del Sogno* (Knight of Dreams). The set was in Bergamo, and there, while Tito was playing the traditional games of *scopone* with the technicians of the cast, constant telegrams reached him from San Marino. The case of Lillì's divorce had in fact come before the court there and was waiting to be "delibata," or transcribed for Italy when it was all completed. This was the final extension of a case initiated long ago for the sake of a love-dream with a statuesque blonde. Now it had arrived just in time to regularize his own position with an impassioned brunette. So much the better.

Portugal gave Tito a triumphal welcome in 1946, and reserved queenly treatment for his young companion. Her "irregular" position was not allowed to weigh against her at all. Indeed, the likelihood of a Schipa born in Portugal sent admirers and journalists into ecstasy, quite unaware of Diana's misgivings about it. On February 6th, a great gala evening was held in his honor. The packed Teatro Coliseu witnessed a bizarre miscellany: one act of *Werther*, one of *Manon*, and one of *Elisir*. It was a triumph, made more so by the débacle of Giacomo Lauri-Volpi, who on the first night was pitilessly booed for one ordinary missed note.

Tito never derived the slightest comfort from the misfortunes of his colleagues, maintaining the by now traditional attitude of loyalty and detachment that takes us back a lifetime, to the battles in Lecce between Schipians and Zanasians. The sentiment was generously reciprocated by all the greats, who never ventured a judgment of him that was less than respectful. Gigli first of them all, followed by Lauri-Volpi himself, who always carried his respect in the palm of his hand. The only momentary incident of misunderstanding was yet to occur, involving, quite innocently, however, Ferruccio Tagliavini. But it was a matter of small account, even though in a very unpleasant context.

As for "off" notes, for some time an annoying phenomenon affecting his larynx had been manifesting itself: in Diana's words, "his voice could disappear from one moment to another, completely and without the slightest forewarning, like a light bulb which suddenly goes out. And there was nothing to be done other than to wait for the equally unpredictable moment when it would come back." There was the risk that, if it occurred more frequently, this problem could also spoil some important performance for him. In fact the misfortunes of others were going to visit him in turn in only three weeks, when in Spain that "light bulb" was going to go out for him onstage.

A letter from his sister tells us that in Rome the polemics concerning Schipa's sympathies with Mussolini continued, but it all seemed far away in Lisbon. Reviews in Portugal improved every day, and ahead there was a period of travel which would seem interminable at times, especially to Diana.

At this point a curiosity arises which is highly embarrassing to me, but since it was repeated again and again on the lips of the great Schipa himself, I have no choice but to recount it.

When Diana was near to giving birth, she had increased her visits to the chapel of Estoril, which was very close to the hotel, even though she had never been especially religious. She felt impelled above all to appeal for some kind of "superior" intervention which would help her through this dreaded situation—being left alone when Tito departed. She had no idea what solution to ask for, but she did ask for a solution; kneeling in the deserted chapel, with her veil of black lace over her splendid brown hair, seriously troubled, she must have moved someone important if it is true that a phrase resounded among the empty pews, as clearly spoken as an actor's lines. Naturally the voice spoke perfect Italian, and said:

"Don't worry: your son will be born on April 18th."

Diana looked all round her, then searched in all the niches and little chapels, but there was nobody. Nobody other than the statue of St. Anthony, from which the voice had come. Well, it was certainly true that St. Anthony, though Portuguese, was at least Italian by adoption; however, that pronunciation and those clear words were too much, even for a miracle.

Diana returned to the hotel, and told the story to the great tenor himself. Her reward was a shrill burst of laughter to her face, and then an evening of merciless teasing. The day after, she also talked to her doctor, who said that, with all respect due to Sant' Antonio, births after eight months were very rare, and anyway, it seemed to him highly unlikely. There was no doubt that the new Schipa would be born in May, or perhaps even later. A question of mathematics.

Diana didn't say a word, but she felt strangely relieved.

On the evening of April 17th the Schipas were dining in the company of friends and colleagues, among them Franco Alfano and Maestro Angelo Questa. They were eating *orecchiette alla leccese*, prepared by Tito Schipa in person, who from time to time didn't mind putting his hand to the stove. Diana hadn't said a word about the small pains which had been afflicting her since the morning; she was just strangely relaxed and smiling. Then, during a toast, the smile faded a little, her expression was momentarily astonished, and in a flash she was lying under the table, having fainted. There was a mad dash to the Mongiardino Clinic, a sleepless night, and at 1:20 p.m. on the next day, Tito Schipa was reborn, in the form of a baby weighing nearly 8 pounds: yet another enthusiastic fan and an impassioned biographer.

XII

(1946–1947)

Back on the world stage

A few days before becoming a father for the third time (the third time *officially* at least), Tito had given a small private concert in the residence of the American ambassador in Lisbon. In so doing he was able to take small steps that would prepare his return to the USA. The granting of visas to him and his new family ended the ill-concealed fear that the rigid rejection of Schipa on the part of certain important Italian institutions, such as the Teatro alla Scala, would also have spread to America. Tito Schipa, together with Gianna Pederzini, Kirsten Flagstad, Pierisa Giri and others, did in fact appear on the unwritten list of artists who were "undesirable" to the new management of the great Milan theater, recently restored and reopened. The accusation was predictable, but disproportionate: collaboration with the fallen dictatorship.

Once again, Schipa found himself in opposition to the great conductor Toscanini. The aftermath of an ignoble civil war robbed Italy (among other things) of the possibility of such a desirable reunion, the resumption of a collaboration which was still limited to the single, proto-historic event of 1915. The great singer had already raised to proverbial level, and had repeated countless times, the phrase of the protagonist of *Adriana Lecouvreur*: "*Maledetta politica!*" But politics also had its own "*matte bizzarrie*" (the phrase in *Gianni Schicchi)*—as Tito was to find to his own cost.

In the European tour which preceded his great leap towards America, in 1946, the great tenor did find himself unexpectedly aligned in one matter, at least in ideal terms, with the great conductor. It was on the occasion of a *Don Pasquale* in the Sarah Bernhardt Theater in Paris, organized by the new impresario Léon Leonidoff. Tito went through a tremendous crisis of consciencebefore going on stage. The cession to France of Briga and Tenda, which had happened as a result of the peace treaty with Italy, infuriated Tito Schipa in exactly the same way as it infuriated Arturo Toscanini. The maestro had refused to conduct a concert for that reason. Tito was also about to walk out of the performance, but Diana persuaded him patiently "not to start all over again."

It was a small sign that times were a-changing, and of how soon the Italians would rediscover how to live with each other, ingeniously, in the midst of their thousand and one differences.

In the meantime, however, as we follow Tito away from the shores of the Atlantic and back again to Italy, we find the reviews worsening as the mother country draws nearer, with its inexhaustible squabbles. It may well be that for some time, wherever he found himself spending more than a week, he enthusiastically let it be known that he intended to settle permanently, but now the Italian newspapers accused him of wanting to become Portuguese. And it may be because during a *Werther* in Madrid, the famous "light bulb" in his throat once again went out, and left him without a glimmer of voice in front of a crowded theater (though he performed a kind of miracle, inventing a "different" but sufficient vocal line for himself, by virtue of heaven knows what secret of experience and technique). In any case, the audiences were frequently lukewarm, and the odd article-writer showed only too much readiness to rip his ear off, as with a dying bull. In fact, on a train journey to Brussels, Diana saw him take part in an unprecedented and embarrassing scene. He seized the attention of a couple of young traveling-companions and *claimed* their recognition, and *suggested* that they should ask for his autograph. This was a completely unheard-of attitude for a man who had always had to defend himself from an excess of fame.

In this distressing recourse to the "You don't know who you're talking to" formula, we seem to hear the first creaking, the first concession to the insecurity which sooner or later was bound to make itself felt (he was fifty-seven).

Sailing from Cadiz on July 12th, 1946, the unorthodox Schipa family headed for Brazil. The impresario of this tour was Alejandro Schujer. Diana's first experiences of these somewhat peculiar journeys were quite different from what she had expected. First, however, she had to exercise patience during the usual unforeseen stops, this time in Cape Verde, where he gave a benefit concert for a group of Italians who had been trapped there by the sinking of their ship during the war.

Diana also had to get used to the permanent zoo which followed and preceded Tito wherever he went. She had not yet had time to take in the phantasmagoria of the lights and smells of the Bay of Rio de Janeiro, when she found, wrapped round her neck, a coral snake, the gift of a friend from the city. Diana supposed that this was a friendly folk gesture which it would be possible to shake off as soon as possible, but in reality this sinuous, highly colored creature, its poisonous fangs removed, was to become one of the most affectionate domestic animals of the Schipa household for years and years to come.

Finally the girl from Piedmont had to learn to deal with a charming but hugely inconvenient custom: the veritable assault which the enthusiastic South American public launched on Tito at every corner. Europe was truly a long way away. Although it was a concerts-only tour, less exciting than those that took in the theaters, the police were constantly mobilized to protect him from being literally torn to pieces. For reasons of security it was decided that their newborn should always be left in the hotel, out of the range of a crowd which might even have considered him a valuable souvenir to take home!

Just for a change (so the Italian papers were right after all, Tito Schipa *did* want to change nationality!), he went back to his old refrain:

"It's so beautiful! Why don't we settle here?" and he even contemplated taking on the direction of the São Paulo Opera House. Then he decided to broaden his Brazilian fan-club by presenting himself as a composer as well, and he organized a performance of his mass for a quartet of male voices—the mass he had composed as a test-piece for his exams in musical studies in Lecce. The newspapers announced it as an absolute world première, though this was in fact not the case. He had already had it performed in Lecce in August 1920, at the time of his religious wedding ceremony with Lillì.

The performance took place this time in the Church of Our Lady of Peace, near São Paulo, and although it was a moderate success (more for his own solos than for the ensemble), this was not really the important event which was to take place within these sacred walls. For that, there was to be a delay of a couple more weeks.

At that time, Schipa junior was preparing to utter his first word. Normally, this would have been "*mamma*," but the normal was hardly the rule in this family, and so the infant, affected by the enthusiasm of the Brazilian fans, and showing a tendency which would mark him throughout his life, began speaking with the word "*papà*."

Meanwhile, the *papà* in question went frequently to hear Carlo Buti, who performed in a nightclub in Rio, and declared that *this* was the greatest singer who ever existed, that *this* was the finest voice which he had ever heard, and that if he had had that voice he would have performed prodigies which would have wiped out the whole history of bel canto in one note. Brazilian theater magazines seized on the fact, and created scenarios in which Schipa and Buti (rather than Schipa and Gigli) were seen as the rivals at the peak of the pyramid.

On September 14th, 1946, a telegram arrived from Italy announcing the completion of the divorce proceedings between Tito Schipa and Antoinette Michel d'Ogoy. The conditions dictated by his ex-wife were now in force: in exchange for a new life and a legal name for the little bastard born in Lisbon, Tito Schipa gave up to his previous family everything he possessed in Italy, property and movables, with no rights of access, with the sole exception of his estate in Modena. From this moment, the Schipa patrimony in Italy, hard to assess in modern terms but more appropriate to an industrial mogul than to an artist, changed proprietor, and it would be impossible to trace, for in the future the first family showed no evidence at all of this enormous wealth. In fact, the only thing left to Schipa was his estate in Modena and his two

California villas, and after going through the religious marriage ceremony in the chapel of Our Lady of Peace, the two newlyweds decided on California.

This wedding is rather an obscure matter, however. It is hard to puzzle out how it could have been permitted, since the religious marriage solemnized by Bishop Trama in 1920 in Lecce could not be dissolved by a civil divorce!

During this journey in South America (and others which were to follow soon after), Diana was to discover the sensations of the opening kick-off in mid-field, when Tito started off the matches amid the deafening bedlam of the stadiums of Maracanà or Boca. She also experienced the dizzying sensation of visits to lost villages in the Andes, on board clattering, rolling little trains, along tracks which crept along the edge of bottomless precipices: she even arrived on muleback at some places where concerts were to be performed, and flew in tiny aircraft zigzagging among the Andean peaks, in the hands of the most daredevil pilots in the whole world, or in that two-engine plane of the 1930s which in constant free flight between air pockets and appalling turbulence, transported her on the thirty-hour journey between Rio de Janeiro and New York. At the end of this flight, with her stomach churning and her heart offered up as a votive oblation to the by-now intimate and sympathetic St. Anthony, the former factory-girl from Bolzaneto swore that she would never fly again. And, up to the time of this writing, she never did!

As for him: "What nonsense! Rubbish!" But he ended up changing his habits, protesting the while.

A bad press

Tito Schipa's life continued to run along, amid the amazed expressions of a Cinderella from Cuneo who in a matter of a few months had found herself hurled from the modest, austere surroundings of Teglia in the suburbs of Genoa, to that of a first lady of the world of opera; amid amazing sums both being received and—more often—being disbursed: luxury, the shouts of enthusiasm and triumph, restlessness, and great cities whose appearance and rhythm of life were unimaginable to her.

A show of imperial dimensions at Radio City was her first encounter with New York. She attended with her husband, also in the role of a spectator on this occasion, while the negotiations between Albert Morini, his new agent for the American area, and the impresarios of various American opera-houses were proceeding feverishly. While waiting for the first engagement, the Schipas moved to the house of Ralph Oggiano, a very sophisticated Italo-American photographer. He was a fervent admirer of Tito, and took advantage of having him as a guest for a few weeks to take a couple of portraits of his young wife. They are the most beautiful that she ever had taken of her. Looking at these images, I wonder whether the Italian cinema didn't lose out on something when the elderly but fascinating tenor carried her off.

It goes without saying that from the first utterances of his friends and relations in New York, Tito came to realize that his position as an "Italian who chose the wrong side" was not going to be easy, even in North America. There were those who claimed to have put in a good word for him, otherwise it would have been unthinkable. Tito Schipa, returning to the USA! The atmosphere was very tense.

Tito gave the first American concert of the postwar period in Hartford, Connecticut, at the Capitol Theater on October 20, 1946; the evening found the protagonist in sparkling form, but behind the scenes a coterie of managers, friends, relations and supporters all had their fingers crossed. However, it was a great success. The murmurs of gossip never overcame the enthusiasm of the applause for a moment. But the applause was limited each time now to about ten minutes, while counter-publicity had the advantage of being able to carry on full time.

When the performance was to be given before a student audience, as at Saginaw and Boston, the auditorium was packed with plain-clothes agents, and two bodyguards escorted the singer from the moment he left his bed in the hotel to the piano, and back again. The only city which welcomed him like a prodigal son and spared him even the slightest sign of resentment was "his own" Chicago.

The tension, as can be imagined, found an outlet in his throat, troubling him with an irritating catarrh which stayed with him for weeks. And the first dissension with his wife also appeared at this point. She made the mistake of not disguising the anxiety caused by the heavy attentions of certain "friends,"and by the rumors of "sexual perversion," which according to some people must have been at the bottom of a love-story between a sixty-year-old and a girl of twenty. Quarrels arose, and Tito went off for the first time without Diana. He sang in Florida and the reason for the great success that he obtained there should perhaps be sought in the telegram begging for pardon which reached him a moment before he went onstage.

November 14th marked another "return," this time to the opera stage in the USA. First, a *Barber of Seville* planned for Philadelphia threatened cancellation because Tito Schipa was not registered in the Union (he was never to get away from this kind of problem: in his career as a singer who gained huge fortunes from his voice, there is not the minimum trace of *a single* contribution towards social security!). However, thanks to an intervention by Morini, everything was resolved.

A few days later, to the even greater astonishment of his young and inexperienced companion, they left for Hollywood. The two princely villas were waiting to give the final touch to the incredible adventure which had befallen Teresa Borgna, stage name Diana Prandi, and now Diana Schipa.

Not even twenty-four hours had passed before an exciting rumor was doing the rounds of the Beverly Hills residences: Tito Schipa had returned, fine: but more important, he had returned in the company of a new flame, about which the least that was known was that she had a masterly hand in preparing *spaghetti al pesto*. Since all the world is a village, the waiting list to come and sample the fare in the Schipa household grew longer every day, and names such as Mary Pickford, Greer Garson, Wallace Beery, Charles Laughton, Gregory Peck all joined the queue meekly: the last-named didn't even disdain a timid flirtation with the cook, in between one take and another of *The Paradine Case*.

On January 2nd, 1947, they celebrated both his birthday and his name-day (not the feast of St. Raphael, but that of St. Titus, Bishop, which at that time, before Vatican II, still fell on January 4th). The event would be of no importance in itself, were it not for the fact that we learn with amazement how many years he declared himself to have lived: Fifty-ONE! And Diana believed him. Naive she may have been, but she would have had a great deal of difficulty in finding the genuine date of birth of Tito Schipa from his passports. There was not a single one which hadn't been patiently blanked out and "readjusted" in ink. The time would come when the constant unreliability of his documents would provoke the (false) allegation that Tito Schipa had had an authorization from Mussolini in person to alter his date of birth even in the records of the official registry!

He began to show signs of a certain nervousness, and Diana found it impossible to understand why. A brief tour in Canada had gone as smoothly as oil. So what was he worrying about? On January 17th, during a concert on Victoria Island, the irritation which was plaguing him caused him to mistake an open trapdoor for the entrance to the understage. Only a miracle saved him from a fall of about 20 feet. Thoughts turned instinctively to the absurd way in which Italian stunt-man Mario Riva had died (by the same kind of error), and a shiver ran down his spine.

Finally, after a night of insistent pleading, Diana got him to come out with what was galling him. The issue was this: Morini was pestering him with a constant and highly unpleasant problem. It seems that a famous anchorman of American radio, Walter Winchell, had been dedicating himself heart and soul, from the day that Tito Schipa had set foot on American soil, to remorseless attacks on "the Duce's tenor." He was instigating troublemakers to take action, he boycotted the concerts and their organizers, and accused anyone who was involved directly or indirectly with Tito Schipa of being guilty of anti-Americanism.

It was no joking matter. Only a few years later, the name of Walter Winchell would be transmuted, by the Hollywood and Broadway intelligentsia, into a quintessential symbol of all that was absurd in McCarthyism. A whole series of gags in satirical films and comedies would make use of him as the perfect butt for their humor. But at the moment the game was completely in the hands of those who, with the same furious vehemence with which they were soon to give to the hunt for the so-called "Reds under the bed" at home, were now staining the name of alleged ex-fascists from abroad with infamy.

As a consequence of the appearance of this sworn enemy, things which had seemed to be easing off in the last few weeks once again took on troublesome aspects. Among other things, the attention to detail—often intimate and secret detail—with which Winchell packed his philippics, led to a suspicion that his information was coming directly from Lillì! This is one aspect of the unhealthy atmosphere which was also reflected in the words recorded by Diana in her diary: "I would just like to disappear with my child and live like a beast in his den, provided I could just have tranquility..."

It was equally stressful to find that rooms which had been booked in hotels were "not available"—not by accident, clearly, but by design. Or to see a concert at a military academy canceled, with the clear aim of protecting the young cadets from the dire implications of his presence. And then there was the circulation of rumors which constantly accused him of antisemitism.

The latter could prove to be a fatal matter in American society, and Tito was well aware of it. So he hastened to promote and sign a circular on artistic matters in favor of a Jewish organization. He brought out and polished up one of his favorite sayings for the occasion:

> And aren't we all Jews, anyway? If it wasn't for a few drops of water from John the Baptist...

He had never made any secret of a likely Jewish descent in his family, on his mother's side; in fact he spoke of it with a certain satisfied pride, and when the Nazis, in their macabre racist rigmarole, demanded that he declare in writing that he did not belong to the Jewish race, he reacted with disdain and genuine sarcasm:

> Do you want to know whether my grandmother was a Jewess or how well I can sing?

However, this wasn't enough for the bloodhound Walter Winchell, who continued with his weekly attacks, to the point that a group of lawyers suggested that Tito should resort to the most prestigious Italo-American journal, "Il Progresso," in the hope that its support would help him rebuild his image.

Meanwhile another concert was called off, scheduled for Tampa, and this time he broke into a flood of tears. Nor was he consoled by the three performances of *Barbiere* in Miami. Like a disappointed child, he declared: "I don't like the opera; it's never satisfied me." He complained about being badly paid. He accused Morini of fishing in troubled waters in order to reduce his fee. He talked about his wish to open a school for singers—virtually a plan for a step backwards.

The public reaction was strange and inconsistent. Wildly enthusiastic triumphs alternated with frigid and half-full theaters. The much-awaited concert at Carnegie Hall, on which so many hopes were pinned, was certainly full of people in the auditorium, but was also the scene of furious demonstrations outside, so that protective cordons of mounted guards and roadblocks had to be set up around the prestigious concert hall.

Eventually, Winchell reached the highest possible level of vilification: he no longer limited himself to inveighing with icy regularity against the individual whom he already considered Danger Number One to American Civilization (he managed to forget how much Tito Schipa and the genuine, great America had given each other in the past), but he reached the point of ending his broadcasts by advertising the next anti-Schipa attack, which would go on air at approximately such-and-such time, or appear in the press in such-and-such an edition of this or that newspaper. "Keep tuned in!"

Winchell announced that on March 11th there would be a particularly appetizing article. And there it was, right on time. Among the repeated attacks, there was one unusual, quite positive parenthesis: this was a full-length portrait of Lillì Michel, seen as a splendid martyr. Tito's ex-wife was depicted as the first of the victims of a monstrous Tito Schipa, a satyr and a reactionary. Back came the suspicion of an improbable collusion between Lillì and Winchell; back came the blind rage, and even Diana now fed the flames by reproaching him for the regular sums of money he sent his daughter Liana, who was in fact completely innocent in all this.

And just at this moment, certain old acquaintances made their surprise reappearance.

During the interval of a *Barber of Seville* in Orlando, with Tito Schipa in the costume of Lindoro—that is, Count Almaviva in disguise, in breeches, with a hairnet on his head—received a visit from two genuine desperados. They introduced themselves with great affability and courtesy, but their clothes and accents left no room for a shadow of doubt: of all possible types of Italo-Americans, these were two of the worst. An ancient peace-treaty signed in the early twenties between the rising star and the Chicago gangs must have been clearly on show somewhere for someone to have thought of reviving it at this precise moment. The proposal was quite clear:

"The words of a certain Walter Winchell are spreading around, and doing a lot of harm," said one of the two sweetly smiling figures. And beneath the nose of Lindoro he opened his hand. "But here, dear *commendatore*, there's something which can do a lot more harm, and which runs a good deal faster than any journalist can flee...

Under Tito's horrified eyes there appeared, shining and menacing, a bullet.

[But where are we? What year is it? Didn't these things happen in remote times past, when broad-brimmed hats and loose-fitting suits were worn?... When women were fairies outlined in eye-shadow, and the world was a collage of fabled realms and empires? Today, an overwhelming catastrophe has shattered the planet; people are talking a new and incomprehensible tongue, the great dream factories are collapsing all round, rusty and useless; and here we are suddenly faced with a revival not of the best of what used to be, not the ecstatic enchantment and the unmatched success, but the disgusting violence of a reality which truly he deserved to be spared.

When was it that he had to pay fifty lire to sing? A millennium earlier? And yet only a few weeks earlier he had been forced to fork out of his own pocket 7000 dollars (seven thousand!) as a guarantee to Morini over the outcome of his tour, because of the risk of a series of cancellations. And how many centuries earlier had that letter from a supposed admirer arrived in his dressing room, to which he had replied for a joke, and everything had ended in a bitter tragedy?

Wasn't the persistent, painful sense of guilt that he had been carrying around all his life enough? And yet here, even in this absurd present of 1947, here was his former companion, conspiring and crafty; here was Lillì reproaching him in the press of half the world for traitorous and vulgar behavior: he, who from the depths of the Italian South knew every subtle shade of the art of comportment to a lady, and who had bequeathed her, when he left her life, quite simply everything that he had! What can you ask of a man: more than everything?

And even Diana, now, taking so seriously those third-rate stories of the long distant past: grand ladies seen or not seen once, who every now and then reappeared to claim some kind of damages, a contribution towards who knows what operation...

It seemed impossible this time to get away from all this with the usual absolution; the usual debt-cancellation of an incomparable mezza-voce, the masterly and unprecedented interpretation given to a two-hundred-year-old musical phrase. This time it wasn't possible to say in his local dialect, smiling, as he so often did, to those who asked him the secret of his art:

"Ieu? Culla filatura, me nd'essu!" ("Me? With this fine little strand, I just manage it!")]

By good fortune, Schipa answered those "gentlemanly" compatriots of his with a short but emphatic no. And fortunately, they didn't persist. But as soon as he returned to Los Angeles, Tito rushed off to see the Italian Consul, Profili, to unload all his bitterness and terror, and to ask him whether Tito Schipa really was considered, in his beloved America, a public enemy.

Profili uttered a few placatory phrases, then went for a look at the security reports. Against the name of Raffaele Schipa, known as Tito, he found only one document, telling the story of his problems with Adelaide, a Portuguese nurse who had reported him for not having paid her her full wages at the time he left Lisbon. There was no record of any other charge in any office which had to do with security, neither in the USA nor in the offices of the Italian consulates.

As an immediate consequence of the appeal to the authorities, on April 5th in New York an article appeared strongly attacking Walter Winchell. But this was only a first, uncertain clearing of the skies. Other concerts were canceled, and his reaction was always the same: each time he burst into bitter tears, showing that his state of nerves was anything but steady.

Diana, furious but impotent, wrote in her diary "If Mr. Truman spoke Italian, I'd go and have a few words with him myself!"

Then, as in Italy in the days immediately after the war, Tito resumed benefit concerts, in a constant search to free himself from accusations of which he was hardly even aware. He sang for the wounded soldiers in Pasadena, and for artists in retirement in Quebec. Canada repaid him for this evening with a triumphal success, with the public and the critics in agreement.

When he returned to the USA, he had the great surprise of reading something in his defense on the front page of a Detroit newspaper:

"How," asked the writer of the article, "could the husband of so fervent an anti-fascist as Madame Antoinette Michel truly be a fascist?" Lillì, once again.

This time it was Diana who went into a rage, crazy with jealousy.

Whichever way one looked, there seemed to be headaches for him. A furious anonymous letter-writer also joined the fray. He insinuated that Schipa's new wife had a past which was anything but pure, and that the little Titino was in fact not the son of the great tenor, but of an SS Officer!

At this point, the Schipa family had had enough of the USA. The opportunity for a new tour was more welcome than ever before. He was to return to South America, which, uninhibited and chaotic as it might be, was at least completely enamored of him.

On the ship on which they traveled there was also the great director Rouben Mamoulian. Curiously the two greats of the cinema and the opera had never met, nor did they know anything of each other. The introductions were quite extraordinary:

"I am the director of *Dr. Jekyll and Mr. Hyde*," says one.

"I am the star of *Vivere!*" says the other... and he wasn't joking!

The telegram

In South America too he was only planning to give concerts. The results were certainly exhilarating, as always. No country in the world demonstrated (and still does demonstrate even today) such an untarnished devotion to Tito Schipa as Argentina. But the singer who sang in Spanish as if it were his native tongue was not spared some barbs (though only from official sources, not at all from the

170

public) even here.

Diana learned that he was not considered capable of sustaining a complete opera any longer! Indignant, she herself took over the role of manager and went off to see the management of the Teatro Colón. A crowning absurdity: this happened to be the one single place where, on this tour, Tito had not been asked to sing. It seemed that the example of La Scala was dangerously infecting the great opera houses of the world. And in fact, a courteous but firm refusal was all that Diana got in her attempt to set herself up as a manager. Not even at a benefit concert, proposed to numerous stars of *bel canto*, did Tito Schipa's name appear on the program.

The fears and the paranoia began all over again. It seemed to the isolated, gloom-ridden couple that they could see mocking grins on the faces of Gigli, Tagliavini, even the ultra-faithful Gianna Pederzini.

Meanwhile, news from North America didn't get any better. Now Winchell turned his radio and journalistic inquisition on to the alleged nullity of their marriage (and in the strictly religious sense, of course, he wasn't wrong).

Lillì sent from Rome to say that she was claiming that the figures (already enough to make one shudder) demanded for the divorce should be referred to pre-war values of the lira! If any court were to uphold her claim, it would be the final coup de grâce for the already shaky fortunes of Tito. And Diana noted that she seemed to perceive for the first time, in the man who was Singing Incarnate, a kind of "disaffection for singing."

> "I have an idea. Why don't we settle here in Chile? We could revive those old cinema studios, and make them work in the American style!"

As often happens the moment of crisis had set in motion remedies which risked turning out to be worse than the evil itself.

What was needed urgently to prevent some misguided adventure, a final breakdown? Only one thing: a telegram from La Scala, a swift little telegram which would make him feel wanted on the only stage in the world which had really bewitched the great bewitcher; the only stage which had really enchanted the Encantador. And that telegram, thank God, did arrive. It arrived on July 11th, 1947, and signaled the beginning of another revival, the slow, weary return to a life that was genuinely worth living.

What with one mishap and another, with crossings and cabotage, Tito had now touched almost every country of the world. In each of them where at least some minimal tradition existed, he had sung, and had sung everywhere—from the nightclub to the opera-stage—gaining from his reviewers undisputed recognition as the most-traveled operatic star, bar none.

When his career was summed up, only a very few countries were to remain outside the network of his journeys: among these, though, to his great regret, were both China and Japan.

In this autumn of 1947, Chile, Peru, Brazil and Argentina said farewell to Tito Schipa, who set sail for Europe on September 28th. On arrival here, the indefatigable traveler circled round before arriving in Italy, and flung himself into a crowded round of concerts and operas in France, Belgium, Holland, Norway and Sweden (where he added a new language to his collection of sung languages).

Finally he embarked on his regeneration in Milan with an *Elisir d'amore* on the 27th of December in a year he was never to forget.

What we have thrown away

The fact that the orchestra of La Scala showed a tendency to go its own way that evening; the fact that the audience at the premiere was enthusiastic while the second-night audience was rather cold; the fact that Tito was not in his best form: all this became insignificant in relation to his great sigh of relief at being "back home" again.

Then, during the third performance, he received an embarrassing complimentary call from the son of Achille Starace. Terrified, he received him with a show of coldness.

The performance was broadcast on the radio. It was 1948, and recording techniques were beginning to emerge from the experimental stage, and already to make it possible to get better than merely acceptable results, even though a lot of hard work was required. This was where the inexcusable, protracted series of outrages against the history and documentation of bel canto singing by the Italian radio corporation begins: this performance was not recorded. Neither were numerous other interpretations by Tito Schipa which the adjective *legendary* is hardly adequate to define. Or if any of these performances were recorded, vandals subsequently wiped them out. There are no words to describe the superficiality and ignorance of those semi-literate employees who, in these years, thoughtlessly threw into the trash can sublime performances by some of the greatest musical artists of history. Moreover, the growing denunciations of the corruption of our museums, the thousand accusations against those whose role is to preserve the artistic patrimony of Italy, seem for some reason to limit themselves exclusively to the treasures of figurative art. No serious research has been done, apart from that by heroic private collectors, to find out whether something may, just by chance, have survived. Music, the eternal Cinderella of the world's least musical nation, continues to take the depressing little that it can get from its position of neglect.

In January 1948 Tito Schipa moved to Rome to take part in a private projection of his film *Rosalba*, to be received in private audience by Pius XII, and to perform once again at what was formerly the Costanzi Theater, and is now the Opera, in *Elisir* and *Werther*. By the grace of God, on the following February 3rd, when the RAI broadcast the latest version of the Schipa-Massenet masterpiece, and Diana was recording in her diary a success at the Rome Opera House "I can't even describe," a worthy chemist of Trieste was listening in his own city armed with a mechanical apparatus for making vinyl disk records. On this rickety gadget, which carved clumsy furrows on ultra-fragile discs, filling the room with fine black shreds, Dr. Riccardo Gmeiner recorded and consigned to posterity, unique in the whole world, a witness to the complete role of *Werther* as Tito Schipa interpreted it. Many years later, he was to consign it reluctantly to me, almost kneeling in supplication at his feet; thus today it can be heard on a modern disk. Certainly it has been mutilated by the countless private hearings in that Trieste pharmacy; certainly it doesn't enjoy the international distribution of a rock disk, but it is one of the most luminous and moving evidences of what could happen on a golden evening in the times when Italy was still in possession of its most symbolic art; when a composer in a state of grace, his greatest interpreter and a knowledgeable and expert public came together for an expressive culmination.

The echo of recent polemics was fading away, but a few tail-ends remained. In a brief chat with Umberto Terracini[22] the great artist asked for some advice, and the great politician advised him to put the threats and acrimony and spite behind him. Italy, at the time of pacification, had very different problems to deal with from those of concern about the sympathies of an opera singer for the operetta Italy of the fascist years. The talk ended with an embrace between the two great but very different men, both of them with great bitternesses in their past to be forgotten, but both with a great future ahead, each in his own field.

Yes, indeed: a future. While fifty-nine-year-old Tito Schipa, still able to please, still willing to do so, began to accumulate successes once more as if nothing had happened, we are bound to think of these as the last flickers in an already long career, imagining that his advanced years would prove to be as brief as they would be intense. And yet the end of the great curve of his artistic life lay not five or even ten years in the future, but fourteen.

Fourteen years, for a singer of today, sometimes represents an entire career.

---

[22]A respected Italian leftist politician. (Tr.)

XIII

(1948–1963)

A family zoo

On February 28th, 1948, Tito Schipa and his wife were guests for lunch of the great baritone Mariano Stabile. After being informed about the future projects of the indefatigable tenor, Stabile told them how happy he was not to have to travel any more to make a living. It isn't clear how much mischief there was behind this remark, but the couple took it to heart somewhat. Evidently it was a sore point. Tito had often expressed his wish to live a less vagabond life, but the travels, instead of diminishing, had increased, and the tour that would take him to England, France and Spain a few weeks later, in April and May, was certainly the first series of concerts in which a number of constant and inexorable disappointments has to be recorded.

One unpleasant omen followed another; the Schipas were first present at a bullfight in which two toreadors were killed. Then a doctor consulted on the spur of the moment gave the opinion that Tito's vocal troubles were related to a dangerous heart condition (never again encountered): finally, there appeared in plain terms in the Madrid newspapers (the same ones which had discovered, launched and consecrated the myth of the first years of Schipa in 1915), the insinuation that "Tito Schipa is finished."

"It's all because of those powders he's taking to slim," wrote

Diana. And in fact the signs of age were beginning to blur his elegant lines, and to gray his hair rapidly.

To round out this gloomy period, on March 17th the news came from Rome of the death of Lillì. He felt sincere sorrow for the loss of the woman who had shared the golden years of his existence, and couldn't help the awareness that if he had waited a few months longer to complete that useless divorce, his entire Italian patrimony would still have been in his possession. It was another of fate's mockeries.

With the departure of Lillì, Tito's first family disintegrated rapidly. Elena, the elder daughter, married the heir of a rich Roman high-class family, the Straziotas, and went with her husband to live permanently in Venezuela. Liana, on the other hand, went off in turn to the USA, following an American officer whom she had only recently married. Her surname was thus changed to Nebel. Following her personal choice of profession, Tito's beloved "principessa" specialized in cancer research, and was to die in Los Angeles at the beginning of the seventies, the victim of that same illness which she had helped to combat on the front lines.

The relations between the two Schipa families had been limited to a single, fruitless attempt at *rapprochement*, a few months earlier in Rome. Although Lillì showed herself to be gentle and protective towards her ex-husband's new son, relations, not so much between Diana and her, but between Diana and Liana, proved impossible. Both Lillì and Elena were always agreed in identifying Caterina Boratto rather than the young girl from Piedmont as the prime cause of the deterioration of the first marriage. But Liana (and perhaps she was right) saw in Diana the real irreparable turning point in her father's choice, and she reacted with the anger of an injured beast.

The disappointing series of concerts ended with his first appearance on Dutch soil. In the Tivoli in Utrecht, the public applauded wildly, even stamping their feet, and in that bacchanal the first serious instance of vocal difficulty was forgotten. When they returned to Italy, the young wife took advantage of his recovered good spirits, took him by the hand, and for the first time imposed on him her notion of what their life should be like.

Even though precipitated all at once into the social whirl, Diana had not forgotten her Piedmontese roots, and she dreamed of setting up home with her two Titos as near as possible to her birth-place. A certain sum of money, set aside with great difficulty from that last world tour, was invested in Genoa in purchasing some apartments in which Tito's new in-laws were established, and a new country residence in Piedmont was bought for Tito and Diana. The first serious economic difficulties, however, were making them-selves felt. Diana had to sell a fur coat and even play the lottery in the hope of helping out the transaction!

However, the money scraped together also served to permit a few further extravagances, which Tito could never do without. For instance, the purchase of another Packard, that showy Ameri-can car which for a few months carved an unlikely path amid the mists of the Alessandria area. In fact, it was in Ovada that the Schipas settled temporarily. But after a few months they opted for a farmhouse at Pasturana, not far from Novi Ligure.

It was a simple rural house with farm buildings and stables attached, and an extensive vineyard, as well as thirty hectares of woodland, cornfields, and a little stream. In order to purchase it, the property in Modena had to be sold.

The new property was certainly not a bargain; indeed there was something of the usual folly about it. Just the marble flooring of the house in Castelvetro was worth as much as the whole prop-erty of Pasturana: but Tito needed cash. Thus the solid house on the banks of the Rio Riasco, two kilometers from the nearest vil-lage (of 700 inhabitants!) became the last of the many country houses held in the name of Tito Schipa, and was soon his refuge during the last interval of serenity in his long life. But at that mo-ment, there wasn't even time to do a little restoration work, be-cause they had to leave again immediately. In the house which they had just bought, which did not even have electricity yet, or any basic comforts, Tito's brother-in-law, Gino Riccio, the wid-ower of his sister Carmen, and Elvira, the last of his sisters still living, were installed.

Then they were off to Paris, to Rome (where in a *Lucia* in the Baths of Caracalla he once again stunned the public by soaring above everyone with that slender thread of voice, and then letting loose the storm of vehemence typical of a dramatic tenor in the accusation scene), and to Naples, where the motor-vessel Saturnia was waiting to carry them off once again to America.

On the quay, left like an orphan by the death of Lillì, to whom she had become attached almost as a mother, was Luisa Merli, the child-nurse, who had now joined them to look after little Tito Junior. In that small figure of the tiny woman, born in 1909, with her long plait and her severely professional white nylon blouse, it is hard to imagine a future basic member of the family, and the longest-surviving witness to the life of Tito Schipa.

A strange seed

The tour which began in those days was one of unprecedented intensity for an artist of Tito's years. Glancing through the chronology of his performances, the reader is struck with the fact that apart from a couple of brief Italian interludes, two whole years were spent in constant pilgrimage all over the world. From the USA to Venezuela, from South Africa to Australia, from Hungary to Egypt, the operas and concerts show no sign of a let-up at any point.

In the last New York interlude, during an *Aida* in a Brooklyn theater to which the impresario Salmaggi had invited him as guest of honor, the public divided into two factions. One saluted him with wild enthusiasm, the other, once again, flung the accusation of fascism at him, and hissed him angrily. The police intervened. The crazy rumor began to spread that the instigator was none other than Ferruccio Tagliavini! Tito was the first to laugh this to scorn, but this return of bitternesses which he had believed were long since buried hurt him profoundly.

In those days he had (once again) put in motion his application for US citizenship. Carlo kept advising him to settle his son and Diana in Los Angeles definitively, and to go off on his tours without them (advice which Diana claims was deplorably self-interested). The situation was saved, on the part of the over-desirable little wife, by a very strong crisis of nostalgia. A dream took her back to the carefree evenings in the dance-halls of the Langhe. This was enough to put an end to the Schipas' ideas of Americanization, and it decided the destiny of his second and last family. Tito let the application for naturalization lapse, and much time would pass before he decided to set foot in the States again.

As so often in his life, however, professional upset found reflection in upsets in his health (perhaps this was the reason why he remained a model of glowing health for such a long time!). In this instance, a medical diagnosis registered the beginnings of diabetes.

"The sweetness disease," he commented, ironically.

Indeed, to see the world through less sugary lenses might not have done him all that much harm. At this point they were living in Beverly Hills, but at Christmas they couldn't rent a Santa Claus outfit because 13 dollars was too much for the Schipa family, "reduced to poverty by Mr. Winchell." In fact, the annual returns for the year were depressing, made worse by the fact that for the first time Tito Schipa had accepted a singing job on a percentage basis.

His voice was by now equally divided between days of splendid form, of the kind which recalled his performances of ten years earlier, and others of total *débacle*. There was no way of predicting. Half the international audiences who heard him in these years listened enraptured, while the other half had to resign themselves to sympathizing. Only a day and a few kilometers apart, comments about "Tito Schipa reborn," and "Tito Schipa now quite out of the running," were to be heard. The same contrast was to be found in the papers. But on March 2nd, 1949, in the midst of a crisis which showed no signs of ending, a new event took place which was to have a basic significance, even though no one seems to have noticed it for some time: Tito Schipa, the nostalgic man of the Right, crossed the Hungarian frontier and set foot in Eastern Europe for the first time since the great restructuring of Yalta.

As a representative of Italy, a country more and more diffident towards the east European states, Tito Schipa found himself faced with a public which was more powerfully stimulated by its growing cultural isolation, and was already on the way to becoming one of the best audiences in his world. The welcome was delirious; it almost became unbearable. Diana, who by now had witnessed successes in every part of the world, wrote:

"Now I know I've never been present before at a real triumph."

But the one who was looking around, observing attentively as a spectator, astonishing himself and putting all sorts of questions to himself, was Tito. A strange seed had been sown, and before long it would yield even more unlikely fruit.

While the father was definitely used to the grind or touring, the son could not keep up with those rhythms and those distances, and when they went back for the first time to northern Italy, he was entrusted to Luisa and added to the small group of relations living permanently at Pasturana. Diana, on the other hand, was always required to follow Tito, even now that her original thinking had been reversed, and she would have preferred to devote herself full-time to her son. But Tito wouldn't budge, and demanded respect for the "Lisbon Clause," which had committed them never to split up for any reason.

[These are the days in which I grope my way with some difficulty out of the mists of unconsciousness. The first images my memory offers bear a likeness to the foggy hills of this corner of Italy, where Tito Schipa had gathered a few of his relatives, his son and an ill-defined number of animals of all types.

With a view to a near-at-hand retirement and to days which would finally be calm, my father had wanted to create the family-cum-zoo of which he had always dreamed. His sister Elvira, severe and taciturn head of the tribe; Gino, his brother-in-law who was a Neapolitan submarine commander, and the administrator of the family firm; Luisa, the Florentine orphan who had become the governess and was a substitute mother for me; Elisa, the distant great-aunt who was now 94, collector of walking-sticks and narrator of ancient tales about Lecce—and then in addition the Ravazzanos, husband and wife, sharecroppers, with their five children, who lived in the farm buildings next door to the villa itself—these made up the human material.

On the zoological side, it's more difficult to keep track. The already abundant farm livestock—hens, geese, ducks, oxen, bees, cows, bulls, horses, donkeys and pigs—were joined by the pets, and I still feel a lump in my throat when I recall the unforgettable heads of the pack, which was always growing—a succession of dogs, some of them of great age and fidelity, like Dogie and Blitz; a host of cats—Pippo and Panzuta come to mind—and then the more eccentric categories like guinea pigs, parrots and squirrels, down to the rarest specimens like our old friend the coral snake of Brazilian origin, and even a pair of lions, Pasha and Moira. Yes, lions, and in complete freedom. No wonder the postman asked for the mailbox to be moved a kilometer away from the house!

I couldn't go on the voyages, and I couldn't be present at my father's performances. The last time I'd been there when Werther killed himself, I'd ended up with a fever for three days...

In the sitting room there was an old Steinway piano, all gilded corners, from some forgotten salon of old America. This was to become my first toy, together with the typewriter in my father's study, which was the most deserted room in the house, since Tito Schipa's tours lasted for eleven months of the year. The big record-rack full of seventy-eights served to keep him present in my life, at least in an aural sense.

The rest is all dazzling summer sun, two meters of snow in the winter, the younger daughter of the sharecropper, Agostina, and an unlimited, pure and providential contact with nature.]

"I'm not old!"

"I'm not old: just look at me!" Tito Schipa seemed to be saying to his young wife as he dashed madly round the world, often for fees which barely covered the expenses.

The name of Caterina Boratto still made him wince, and just to speak of her could ruin a recital. But with something of gallantry and something of vindictiveness, he repeated to Diana every time he could, and especially in public: "If only I could have met you first!" Perhaps he hadn't actually taken into account the fact that this would almost have meant meeting a very small girl!

The ups and downs, now almost balancing each other out, continued for several years of exhausting coming and going, lit up here and there by variegated episodes: one of the most significant was the meeting with Strehler for a performance of *Il matrimonio segreto* in March 1949, which ended with almost complete incomprehension between two worlds, eras and cultures.

There was a farcical happening in Lebanon in the following November, when he was not allowed to land because "these musicians find work in a cabaret and then never leave." An unexpected and pleasant event was his return to composing.

I would stress again that some of the songs written by Tito Schipa in the various stages of his career really deserve better fortune. "El Gaucho," the splendid, mischievous tango included in his operetta, or "Fiammata," "Surriento" and "Manolita" would be enough in themselves to make a name for him as a composer.

But it was just at this time, in the early fifties, amid all his psychological and material difficulties, that Tito came across a very famous poem by Salvatore Di Giacomo, "*Pianefforte 'e notte*," and when he put it to music it turned out to be a piece that was not unworthy to stand with the great Neapolitan songs of the late nineteenth century. He also recorded it, with a Milanese record company, but like so many other things in his life, the operation was a mess: completely unprepared from the standpoint of publishing and promotion. This recording, which might have relieved some of the financial pressures of the moment, was to remain for decades in a forgotten corner before seeing the light of day again, posthumously, in the form of a compact disc in the 1990s.

Meanwhile, the "Tenuta Orto," the house in Pasturana, had been modernized and provided with comforts by a new financial effort. One of the two villas in California was put up for sale, and this helped with the purchase of some other apartments in Genoa. There was also a venture with a bar in the Ligurian capital: a clumsy attempt at an entrepreneurial adventure which never produced any results.

However, whether the initiatives were successful or doomed to failure; whether the management was brilliant or unbelievable, it was always his relations, his secretaries and his administrators who solidly backed the attempt to keep them going, never Tito Schipa who, in defiance of his sixty years went on accepting engagement after engagement, adding new touches to his international image without ever giving himself a day's rest.

During one of the frequent visits to South America, Diana was introduced to a splendid twenty-year-old brunette, a classical ballet dancer of a very high standard and daughter of one of Tito's old friends. The two girls soon got to know each other well. The young Argentinean girl was called Manon. She was invited to Pasturana, and during her stay there the friendship between her and Diana developed into a kind of sisterly relationship. Even her meeting with the still very young Tito junior was like a meeting of brother and sister. But nothing happens by chance. After a few weeks spent wondering about something strangely familiar in Manon's features, Diana was candidly told that the ballerina from

Buenos Aires was in fact Tito's natural daughter.

Being Tito Schipa's wife meant being ready for anything. Diana accepted this new circumstance with a surprising mental adaptability; I found a new sister, and my mother a genuine friend. Meanwhile Tito was getting ready to leave again, and Diana once more followed him, asking herself what else she still had left to discover on this world tour.

By this time only the Far East was not included in the list of satisfied publics. Eventually not even Diana could take any more. One day in 1950, she dug her heels in and refused to follow him on his Nth tour of South America. She wanted to stay at least once for a period a bit longer than a week in the place where her son was living.

In the form of a bundle of passionate letters written from every capital in Latin America a final testimony has survived to the vulnerability of the sentiments of this man. We are talking about a man who was a winner throughout his life, and never wanted to notice the fact; a man who at sixty was still writing fiery lines, who was crying real tears of sick jealousy for no reason at all, a slave to his love and his nostalgia. He was Werther to his fingertips, and above all a victim of an "abandonment complex" which takes us back inevitably to the trauma of his adolescence, to Emilia, and to that journey to the North from which he seemed never to have returned, such was the anguish of what he found when he did return.

São Paulo do Brasile, 8 November 1950

My adored Diana and Titino,

The sadness goes on; I can't find any peace while I'm alone and so far from you!

I don't know how I'm going to sing tomorrow evening; perhaps I'll sing with more real sentiment, more nostalgia, more emotion; but one thing I do know is that the unhappiness will go on without a break until the day I see you again. And when you, my lovely Diana, said to me: if you let me stay with Titino, if you go off on your own I'll love you all the more, didn't you realize that what you said was a contradiction? In fact, how can anyone say to someone they love: if you leave me I'll love you all the more?

Oh God!, how much I miss you Diana, my own! It is the first

and last time I'll ever travel without you! I'm going crazy. I could never have imagined that I'd suffer so much!

And then, of course:

> I tell you: if there really is a country where we will settle, that country just has to be Brazil! Just with a song-school I'd make... (etc.)

In January 1952, when he returned from one of these solitary tours, Tito found waiting for him a mountain of telegrams from the USA. Engagements? No—condolences! Word had gone around that he had died.

In fact, there *was* a mild outbreak of measles in the house. They laughed at the coincidence for a few days. As a good southerner, Tito was certain that episodes of this kind prolonged life...

Mingled with these telegrams, however, were a few visiting cards. They came from a certain Giovanbattista R., a native of Lecce who had moved to Genoa, and had been seeking insistently to meet him for several months. To introduce oneself to Tito Schipa as a fellow-citizen was effectively like a blank check. No limits: every request met with a response.

If he had only confined himself to a simple request for money, this latest in the line of con men. But no. In Police Headquarters in Genoa (as it turned out, though too late for action) there was a complete filing-cabinet dedicated to his frauds. Only a few days earlier he had hoodwinked about twenty families by erecting wooden scaffolding and selling phantom apartments allegedly under construction; then he vanished. The police of the whole of northern Italy were hunting for him, in vain. If they had looked for him in the Schipa household, they might have saved a host of troubles, because it was there that he was perfecting his latest masterpiece.

By playing on Tito Schipa's passion for songs, and on his more than justified aspirations as a composer, "R" convinced him immediately to relieve himself of the earnings from his latest tour by investing them in a publishing firm. Diana, who was already wary of every new face that appeared, looked daggers at him, scenting something rotten. Not wanting to have her working against him, and hoping to flatter the young wife who was Genoese by adoption, he suggested that the new firm should be called "Editrice La Lanterna" (the symbol of Genoa)—and that did the trick!

From the very outset, the publishing firm proved to be a disaster. Though it did print a few of Tito's best songs, the rest was all just filler-material, haphazardly put together from works by fictitious composers, with the sole aim of gaining copyrights with more or less genuine effectiveness: the whole thing for the benefit of the many-sided imagination of Giovanbattista R., who although he claimed to be an "Accountant/constructional entrepreneur" by profession (a somewhat bizarre title in any case), was also a musician.

However, as soon as the police appeared on the scene, Giovanbattista ended up in prison, and Tito Schipa was able to clear up his own position easily enough. But he had to bid a sad farewell to all the money invested.

The fraud shouldn't have mattered all that much, or at least it was certainly a great deal less serious than some of the historic swindles of which Tito had been victim. But there was a troublesome element this time, which consisted in the fact that the new venture didn't go down at the first fence. "La Lanterna" did indeed go into temporary eclipse, but it was to come back to life a few years later, like a pitiless monster, to strike the cruelest blow of all at the ingenuous tenor; the one from which he would never recover.

Tito's activity became more and more frenetic. At sixty-three and sixty-four years of age his calendar was more crowded that it had been in his earlier days. It sometimes led him to sing every evening for weeks in a row, even if the earnings of a single evening of the golden era were not matched by months of work at this time. Even the locations were a somewhat mixed bag. There was no pattern of continuity between the most prestigious theaters in Italy and the suburban cinemas, where he found himself giving more and more benefit concerts. And he was now more in need of benefit himself than others were.

Frontiers continued not to count as far as he was concerned, and he was constantly abroad. But once more it was in the East, during a brief turn in Yugoslavia, that he received his greatest accolade: "More than a success," Diana wrote, "a revolution!"

Naturally every kind of proposal was accepted, both for operas and concerts. The only complaint was that the great theaters seemed to be showing less and less interest. And it was just when he was making his greatest effort to win a return to some of the most prestigious stages that destiny ruled that he would have to leave the stage for ever.

It happened in Milan on September 21, 1955. Renato Carosone was appearing in a local night-spot, and the great tenor had a real weakness for this artist. As he was going down the stairs to the underground location, Tito put a foot wrong, slipped, and tumbled down several stairs. When he tried to get up, an agonizing stab of pain prevented him. It seemed not to be anything of great importance, and in fact Tito went on for a while honoring his engagements. But the pain got worse, and a thorough examination, carried out far too late, revealed that he had torn his meniscal disc. If it had been dealt with in time, it could have been cured by a month's rest. Now the movement of the joint was permanently damaged.

In practical terms there was nothing more than a slight uncertainty in movement, but for such an absolute perfectionist as Tito always was on the stage, that inability to move as he wished led him to take a drastic decision, taken without even a moment of reflection or apparent regret: the opera stage was to be abandoned for good. From then onward, he would only accept concert engagements.

While younger and infinitely more nimble colleagues than he continued to appear onstage despite whatever physical handicaps they had to overcome, the greatest of the actor-tenors retired completely from the theater rather than offer his public even a suggestion of something less than they expected.

A year of forced inactivity followed for Tito, passed between irritating bouts of treatment to correct the initial operation. Apart from the psychological implications, this was certainly not what the family finances needed. Moreover, the feeling that he ought to be giving his son a less wild sort of life, i.e., contact with human beings rather than lions, led him to consider a move to Rome.

The second and last villa in Beverly Hills was sold. Diana begged him at least not to sell Pasturana, his last important property, the last remaining fragment of an enormous patrimony which had long since been dispersed to the four winds. In a typical move, he pretended to accept the advice. Then he locked himself in the bathroom and signed the deed of sale. When Diana finally read it, she could hardly believe her eyes; a property bought for thirteen million lire in 1949, and restored at a cost of thirty-eight million, was sold off in 1955 for only eleven million. The former factory-girl from Bolzaneto collapsed into a chair, her mind flooded with confused memories.

She recalled the hundreds of times she had begged him not to sell for ten what he had bought for thirty. She thought of the one and only film made together with him, *I misteri di Venezia*, which would never appear on the screen, and of the fee which had never been paid; indeed, Tito had had to provide for paying some of the creditors of the production out of his own pocket. She thought of the objects which had been sold, forgotten about, lost and stolen, first and foremost the diamond bracelet as wide as a knee-bandage belonging to Caterina Boratto, and left behind in a moment of distraction on a hotel bed. She asked herself how it was possible that—absolutely without her knowledge—everything that had only recently been bought in Genoa had been sold off; she asked herself how it was possible that almost every secretary, every business manager, every collaborator of any kind had ended his term of office by running off with pockets full of money. She tried to imagine where the worthy Livio D. might be now—the one who, after paying millions and millions of small accounts of all types with Tito's money had disappeared with the rest, and had even taken a court action to recover what he claimed to have spent out of his own pocket. She would have loved to know why, after having financed the amiable Mr. Enzo C.'s project for supplying coffee-dispensers in trains—to the tune of several million lire—the travelers were still obliged to buy their coffee from mobile vendors. She asked herself what else could possibly happen, what other twists of fortune, merited or otherwise, were going to crop up to spoil the move to the capital.

In October 1955 the move took place; the mood of the moment was fairly relaxed and optimistic. It seemed in fact that the possibility of opening a song-school in Rome was not just a Utopia. Someone suggested requesting sponsoring and contributions from the highest authorities of the state, in the conviction that they would be unable to refuse. So what other troubles could lie ahead?

It didn't take long to find out: the fine apartment near Ponte Milvio, the last Italian residence of Tito Schipa, proved to be burdened with a heavy mortgage. For years and years it was a story of pay, pay, and pay again. It had been purchased through yet another of those "friends" and fellow citizens, acting as intermediary.

Yet another Leccese. Diana recalled her first journey to the dreamy Terra d'Otranto, undertaken a few years earlier in the company of her ageing husband who was as emotional as a child about it all. He had introduced her to his city, and like everyone else she had been astonished by its beauty. She had soaked up the baroque, the music, the sun and the folklore, amid illuminations, air-balloons, bands and effigies of Saint Oronzo, seated next to Tito at the table in the Caffè della Borsa where everyone came to pay tribute to him like a sort of deity. And she had met the Leccesi.

No half-measures with them. Some of the noblest, most dedicated, well-loved, reverential and trusting characters in Tito's life were people from Lecce. They showed an unconditional and disinterested affection for him which was in fact passed down from father to son, and which is found even today in the words and actions of young Leccesi who have never even met Tito Schipa. But on the other hand, a high percentage of the many twisted relationships and ill-omened encounters of his life and career were provided by his fellow-townsmen. Perhaps this was the price the great artist of the Salentino had to pay for having been in his day something which was unique rather than rare in the adolescence of a genius, a prophet in his own country.

Moscow, Moscow...

No sooner had he settled in Rome than Tito enjoyed a pleasing resurgence of popularity, due certainly to the easy accessibility of the TV studios. He received two invitations to *Musichiere*, presented then by the hugely popular Mario Riva, and then was asked to take part in the broadcasts of professor Alessandro Cutolo, which had a massive following. He won the silver mask for his career, and took part, limping but still sprightly, in countless high society events with the same people and in the same places as were about to be immortalized in *La dolce vita*. The Rome of the Via Veneto, which engulfed everyone and everything in a round of nightly parties, welcomed the beautiful Diana, now thirty, to its inner circle, and she played her new role to perfection.

During the days, they went ahead with moves aimed at getting the President of the Republic to give them premises and his blessing for a school of singing which would have the seal of official approval, a kind of "parallel chair" of music to those of the academies. Certainly, a recent period spent in Budapest as the visiting holder of such a chair at a senior high school (again a high honor received in eastern Europe) could only work in favor of the initiative. It is true that in November 1960 Diana had to call a press conference to reassure the authorities, who were worried by that "transfer" behind the iron curtain, and to explain the purely artistic motives for it; however, the trip was given little importance and the application for the school in Italy went ahead.

As so often happens in procedures of this kind in Italy, the final go-ahead never arrives, but neither does the final refusal, so one goes on from day to day, with a phone call here, a dinner there, cheered by the fact that, as it has every year, the invitation to the Quirinal Palace for the Anniversary of the Republic duly arrived.

In the first months of 1957, however, another invitation arrived, equally tempting, equally prestigious, and moreover with an entirely new flavor: Tito Schipa was officially invited to head the jury of the Singing Competition at the Moscow Youth Festival in August. It went without saying that the hoary wanderer, far from being tired of travel, enthusiastically accepted and left for distant Russia.

The train journey seemed endless, but finally it deposited him and his wife and his brother-in-law Gino in the land of the Communists. There they immediately made friends with the sweet, cordial and highly professional spy who had been ordered to dog their steps, and they threw themselves into the arms of a public which seemed to have been waiting for nothing else since the days of the Revolution.

[What enchanted him above all, and created the illusion of being in a time-lock, was the fact that his fame and myth had survived the passing of the decades there. In the rest of the world,

the young were beginning to raise their eyebrows inquiringly when the name of Tito Schipa was mentioned. Who was that? The age of operatic melodrama had been dismissed and sent into retirement by the outbreak of the rock revolution. The scepter of vocal glory, and the representation of young dreams, belonged to Elvis Presley, and all the rest was dust.]

It was true—beyond the Iron Curtain the theaters were full of twenty-year-olds who never seemed to have heard of the generation gap. Twenty years wiped out in one blow. Singing amid public enthusiasm... making records... running away from assaults from admirers similar to those of the great days in South America. And since he could not export a useless currency, he played at being rich again, commuting everything into furs for Diana, bearskins, silver, vodka, kilos of caviar, and a priceless camera for his brother-in-law. Gino accepted it delightedly, convinced as he had always been that every object touched by Fortunello brought a bold stroke of fortune to others. When he got back to Genoa he bartered this camera for some other object, which in turn he traded for something else, and although starting from nothing, he displayed an uncommon talent for business. Within a few years he was to find himself at the head of one of the most flourishing firms in the city.

How did the trouble begin? Who set the reaction in motion? Who lit the fuse? One of those Leccesi of the better type, a giant of a fellow who was always a dear friend of the family, and who was also a secret service agent, describes it in this way:

– On his return from Russia Tito began to accept invitations to the Soviet embassy. The first time he received thanks and congratulations, and this was understandable. And even a second occasion could be allowed to pass. But then there was a third and fourth time... and I said to him: Tito, don't go, take my advice, because in the Villa Abamalek there's *them*, and outside there's *us*, camouflaged and fully equipped, and we listen to everything they say, and for quite a while now we've had to listen to you, too... Someone may decide to take it the wrong way...
– Oh, rubbish, nonsense! he said.

Old Ritornello uttered this in a nervous tone, though, all from the head.]

But on the next June 2nd, the invitation from the Quirinale didn't arrive. And the replies about the song school became more and more evasive. The telephone began behaving strangely, with clicks and dings as if it had a life of its own. And in the dusty cupboards of a secret room, in some barracks or some ministry, a dossier labeled Tito Schipa began gradually to get thicker.

From that day onwards, anything which had to do with Italian institutions was closed to him. The Vatican behaved in the same way. It was a question, it seemed, of dealing with a notorious propagandist for atheistic and materialistic notions—by his own admission a personal friend of Bulganin. In its great charity the Church even went so far, through the agency of the Bishop of Lecce, as banning him from singing in church for Sant' Oronzo.

Tito Schipa, banned from singing in Lecce! What would that generous soul Monsignor Gennaro Trama have thought of such a thing?

This man, then, who was remembered as having been a fervent fascist sympathizer, and had made a tremendous effort to regain the esteem of a suspicious Italy, then found himself, at the same time, registered as a noted communist sympathizer, and gained the nickname of "the Pontecorvo of Opera." No one ever seems to have compared the two accusations.

If "opposite extremism" had been a current concept, Raffaele Attilio Amedeo Schipa would have established another world record in his life by representing both of them at one and the same time.

However, not even this latest tragi-comic misadventure discouraged him, nor did it persuade him to renege on his decision to end the long span of his career in his native land. An assured income had vanished in smoke, his relations with Diana were inevitably cooling, and the signs of age were getting the better of his seemingly indestructible juvenility. And yet none of it mattered. With the help of a friend, Maestro De Tommaso, he had begun to realize his dream of a song school in some rented premises in the Via Flaminia. Nothing could halt him.

Lessons in the school alternated with private ones given at home. He made no bones about appearing anywhere he was requested, indifferent to the patronizing smiles of those who found him onstage in a modest revue or singing in a church during Sunday service. He stubbornly rebelled against the onset of age, giving credence to doctors from every field, and charlatans of every description. My memories of those years are crowded not only with the usual vast numbers of animals, but with strange figures who arrived at the house sometimes with dozens of huge flasks full of yellowish liquid, surely some miraculous serum for long life and sexual energy!

"You know, he's preparing for his début," Diana repeated with a smile which still managed to have a little tenderness in it.

He was seventy, and still nothing could stop him. Or rather, only one thing could have done: a blow struck at the sole point, the sole value from which he never deviated, his own natural banner, his *plume blanche:* a blow at his gentlemanliness.

The blow fell, and hit hard.

Exile

Wizards with elixirs of eternal youth, scroungers of every type, stubbornly refusing to acknowledge that there was nothing left to scrounge; young girl pupils who suddenly became much more assiduous; barbers who came to make home calls and were then transformed into raconteurs of endless funny stories, with their pockets full of saucy photographs; fourth-rate tricksters who, since there was not so much available now as in the past, contented themselves with purloining a photograph or a record; Neapolitan wonder-workers, stars of the silent film era, secret agents, mythomaniacs of every shape and form, collectors pleading for a relic: everything served, everything combined to keep the heady rhythm of life at a high pace, even while his financial woes were weighing heavily.

The last thing that was needed at this juncture was a simple, consistent, mediocre crook, ordinary but capable.

Mr. Antonio L. stepped forward in the guise of a music publisher (once again!), and convinced Tito to bring La Lanterna—that trademark which had almost been mercifully forgotten—out of obscurity once more. All he needed was the prestigious name of Schipa; the rest would look after itself. Nothing to worry about; all Tito would have to do would be to pocket the earnings.

Already pressed by serious problems as to whether he could afford both lunch and dinner, the star of the opera accepted with his usual blind optimism, and was already dreaming of recovery and recoupment. The other man put together an office with a desk and two chairs, and then proposed to Tito that, since going around to sign contracts and bills might prove inconvenient, he himself should be authorized to use a stamp with the singer's prestigious signature. And so he began his "publishing" activities.

The previous experience had run aground in Genoa as a result of the maladroit attempts of Tito's partner to defraud the Society of Authors. Now, in Rome, the new collaborator dedicated heart and soul to a far more ignoble trick, which had only just been touched on in Genoa: defrauding young writers. Flashing Tito Schipa's name all over Italy in front of the eyes of thousands of young would-be songwriters, he advertised a competition for certain song lyrics which, if they were successful, would be set to music by the great tenor, and presented in every major song festival in the country. He asked every author for a down payment of twenty-five thousand lire, repayable in the case of non-classification.

Of course, all the songs were "winning entries." Mr. Antonio L. spent a few sous on printing, and a few weeks later his office in Rome began to fill with piles of sheets containing hundreds and hundreds of dreadful songs. The musical scores—a bunch of notes put together any old way—were all boldly signed Tito Schipa. Each author received his copy, and for a while sat waiting at home for news of his glorious success.

Quite apart from the dire quality of the music, it should have been evident to anyone that Tito Schipa could never have provided for putting this sea of texts to music even if he had been as fast and prolific as Donizetti. Furthermore, how and when could he have done it, seeing that in that period he had actually returned to North America? The USA had in fact sent to say that a tour by the elderly tenor would be welcomed with interest. The project was that of a long series of farewell concerts, divided up over a period of many months. Tito had not even finished reading the letter of engagement before he was off on a flight to New York.

He pulled it off once again. For some time he had gathered that in moments of difficulty, it was sufficient to resort to "Farewell Concerts" to obtain engagements everywhere. The first farewell concert in fact dated from 1949! And it still worked!

On October 3rd, 1962, New York Town Hall welcomed Tito Schipa for the first of his (final) farewell concerts in America. The polemics were now consigned to the remote past. An emotional and attentive audience waited for him, filling the concert hall to the point that—for yet one more occasion in his career—they had to resort to extra seating right up to the stage. Some impressions of the evening can be gathered from the press reports:

Harold C. Schonberg (New York Times): "The Town Hall was sold out, yesterday evening, and the seats flowed onto the stage... Cheers, yells and a standing ovation were the order of the evening"; Francis D. Perkins (Herald Tribune): "At seventy, his voice is still a source of exceptional pleasure"; Douglas Watt (Daily News): "The Italian tenor's voice is pure, warm and exciting...with widely appreciative admirers of all ages, he created a near Bedlam"; Harriet Johnson (New York Post): "The audience hailed his smooth bel canto and his special ability to bend a phrase spontaneously enough to make it seem carried by a breeze"; Miles Kastendieck (Journal-American): "They cheered and bravoed his remarkably clear enunciation, his meaningful turn of phrase, and the mellow presence of an Italian style of singing which grows rarer every year"; Louis Biancolli (World Telegram and Sun): "Whatever he sang, he was absolute master of his medium, a supreme artist with a hypnotic hold on the audience. He was like a King who had come out of retirement and found himself monarch of all he surveyed."

This is what America's severest critics said about a tenor who at more than seventy years of age could keep faith with the formula that had served him so well: "sing the way you speak." So easy to say...

While Tito was holding his last concert in California, and repeating his success there, in Rome, Mr. Antonio L. was occupied in his own way with celebrating the memory of the major vocal artist of this century. For greater security, apart from the rubber stamp, he had also issued a certain number of blank "autographs." As always, Diana had advised Tito not to sign anything, but he, with one foot already on the plane, had begged her, for the umpteenth time in their marriage, to "be a better sport."

194

In the summer of 1963, Tito returned to Italy, convinced that he would find echoes of his recent American triumphs there. Instead, he found a host of furious authors, now certain that they had been tricked. Mr. Antonio L. had flown the nest, and naturally both the victims of the deceit and the police had a lot of questions to ask of the unprepared tenor.

He even found it useless to proclaim his own good faith. His departure for America was seen not as a final embassy for the arts across the water, but as a flight which showed his guilt. He was charged with fraud, and declared bankrupt for fifty million lire, in the values of those days. Authorities, important friends and politicians all turned a deaf ear.

"Well, after all, he is a fascist," thought one.

"Well, after all he is a communist," thought another.

"This is what a man deserves when he marries a wife who is too pretty at a certain age," was what a minority certainly thought, repeating the finale of his *Don Pasquale*. And, why not:

"This is what you can expect if you have had seventy years of charmed existence, and have enjoyed one of the most legendary success stories, with the most exclusive fortune and honors. In life, these things are weighed on scales."

This time, he really did need to leave, for reasons other than artistic ones. Viareggio, not paying a lot of attention, was the place which heard the last performance in Italy by its greatest *tenore di grazia*, on a summer's day in 1963, at the Gran Caffè Margherita, where he gave a spontaneous concert accompanied by a small orchestra, and in the company of the soprano Vittoria Chiericati, his last true partner. The concert contained an *"Una furtiva lagrima"* sung to perfection, and it is recorded.

He was now seventy-five, and he was forced to leave once again, in order to avoid spending the last days of his life in jail. This time, it was exile.

During his last tour in America he had met a tall, blond girl— a "distant cousin," he said. A strange surname for a cousin to someone from Lecce: Haslett. However, we wanted to believe him; after all we had four grandparents, eight great-grandparents, sixteen great-great-grandparents, and so on. So it's undeniable that if we went back far enough, say twenty generations, we were all related.

Anyway, Diana believed it. Or rather let's say: she had no time to ask herself whether she believed it or not. While her impossible husband took refuge in his "cousin's" house in the suburbs of New York, and kept the wolf from the door with a few singing lessons, Diana fought like a tiger to redeem his name and save him from bankruptcy and dishonor.

Completely alone, without a penny, and without help, the former factory girl from Mira Lanza in Bolzaneto found herself flung back into far worse conditions than those from which her extraordinary marriage had rescued her. If she didn't lose her mind thinking about this incredible adventure it was only because she used all her energies in making appeals, picketing courts, demanding clarifications, searching for witnesses. When she had reached the end of her tether, there came the providential arrest and full confession of Mr. Antonio L., which completely exonerated Tito Schipa from all responsibility. From this to the clearing of his name in court proceedings was only a brief step.

[Diana only had the strength left to thank the one person who had stayed close to her during this nightmare, Attorney Tito Manlio Gazzoni, who was always among the few loyal friends. Then, completely exhausted, and realizing that Tito was not going to come back, that the financial situation was desperate and that no one could afford a ticket to the USA, she retired quietly to the friendly mists of her own North Italy, beginning her life all over again from zero, and adapting herself to the humblest kind of work. There, thanks to a meeting with Franco Cannonero, a providential companion who supported her and looked after her, she slowly succeeded in rebuilding a serene life for herself once more.

Teresa Borgna, you deserve a medal.]

XIV

(1964–1965)

Finale

Diana had returned to her native Piedmont, where she was work-ing in order to pay for her son's education. In the big house in Rome, in addition to Tito Jr. and innumerable dogs, Luisa Merli had remained behind; once a simple housemaid, she had been adopted by our family and transformed into an overall supervisor and administrator. With Elena in Caracas, Liana in Los Angeles, Manon in Buenos Aires and the ageing patriarch himself in New York, we had some claim to have become the most scattered fam-ily in the world.

In Forest Hills, Tito had opened a small private voice-training school. His "cousin," and her mother Priscilla, were his collabo-rators, and he was their guest. Young Miss Haslett was twenty-six at the time; she was studying voice, and on top of that, she was called Diana.

The two women were enterprising and sincere in their aim of creating a strong appeal by using his name (in New York not a great deal is needed if there is something substantial to back it up), but they were soon forced to face up to a stern reality: Tito Schipa was and always had been a great maestro—perhaps in tech-nical terms the greatest maestro of all—but he was absolutely not a teacher. Possibly it was because he had been familiar for so long

197

with a perfect vocal instrument that he now took it for granted, or possibly because a very peculiar physiology contributed to his own style (one of the ear, nose and throat specialists who examined him was astonished at the sight of his larynx, formed in such a way that the vocal cords were visible to the naked eye!). Whatever the reason, the greatest producer of sounds was quite unable to communicate to a pupil the first thing about how the sounds were produced!

Even during his earlier stint as a teacher in Rome, the majority of his students were bewildered after only a few lessons; they were usually dissatisfied, and decided to end their relation with him. It certainly didn't help that in the midst of his lessons he tended to drift off to a faraway place in his mind or imagination—possibly reminded by the notes of the piano of some long-past memory or some improbable comparison.

The magic formula which he loved to repeat to everyone consisted of a famous refrain:

"But it's so easy! You sing just the way you speak!"

He thought he was passing on a basic notion, something that was definitive, and simplicity itself in practice. He was like the great pianist who proclaimed: "Easy! Playing the piano just consists of pressing the right key with the right finger at the right moment!"

The pianist was joking. Tito, unfortunately, wasn't.

What his pupils could have learned from him could be deduced from his behavior, and even today could be learned from listening to his records. Unfortunately, it didn't consist of a vocal technique, which would remain an impenetrable mystery. But some of his words about the "essence" of a singer are probably quite valuable—advice that in today's world is all too often not given or ignored.

To those singers who dedicate themselves to the concert platform, I recommend that they never make any gestures. Gesticulating during individual pieces is in the worst possible taste, and not only that–it irritates the listener. I would suggest that the concert artiste should stand with one hand clasping the other, or holding a small book (preferably in black leather) which will in fact prevent him or her from moving the hands or gesticulating. At the same time it may serve to remind him of the occasional word, like a prompter.

The concert artiste should express what he is singing with his sentiments, with his heart, even with his facial expressions: never with
the hands and even less with the arms.

A short time before his final return to the USA, when he took
refuge for the last time in what—despite all the polemics—he still
considered his second homeland, he had paid a visit to Lecce. Perhaps he was looking for the traces of a lost world there, the secret
of certain singing-lessons which had echoed three quarters of a
century earlier from the studio of Alceste Gerunda, the teacher
par excellence.

And as if he were hunting for roots even further back, he had
also gone to Albania, singing for the first time in the land of his
ancestors. Shqipe, the Albanian eagle; Titus, a Latin name for a
wild dove. Nightingale, the predictable nickname which they had
given him. And indeed, even the Archangel Raphael had wings, of
course. "We've managed to create an aviary," he used to say with
a laugh.

From his home city, reminders of the distant climate, its lights
and its scents, came back to him every now and then. The relations of Ralph Colangelo, the (real) cousin whom he had redis-
covered in New York, used to smuggle foods with inimitable flavors
into the USA, and he even brought to the Haslett table his adored
roasted figs with crunchy almonds, the finest example of Salentine
skill in combining the sweet and the sour.

He could never resist this enchantment—or any other for that
matter. Diana and Priscilla, who in some ways exercised a kind of
affectionate control and régime over the elderly maestro which
came a little near to unlawful restraint (so that the Italian Diana
began to suspect some form of enslavement) were in other ways
over-indulgent, allowing him to satisfy many of his dangerous
weaknesses for sweet things. What with American apple pie and
figs from Lecce, the diabetes certainly didn't get any better. But
the younger Haslett told me:

"How could anyone resist him, when he used to plead with
those eyes: 'Please, just one more little bit?'"

A well-known collector of vocal recordings, Ed Rosen, lived a
few minutes by car from the Hasletts. For fifty dollars, he was
allowed to record certain songs which Tito Schipa had never put

on disk during his career. This is the most moving testimony to have survived: there is nothing left in these melodies except pure technique and unspoiled sentiment. But pure technique and genuine sentiment are the roots of the bel canto singing of this man. And the evidence is there for us to find, in this diaphanous witness, as in the last testament of a man who is dying but is still perfectly lucid.

The last piece, clearly chosen deliberately, was Puccini's "Hymn to Diana." But which Diana did he have in mind?

On November 30th, 1965, the sweet sickness that was invading his bloodstream finally brought him down. Without a sound, he collapsed to the floor, unconscious, and was rushed to Wickersham Hospital.

The notice of the sudden worsening of his condition struck Lecce like a bombshell as the City Council sat for its regular daily business. The usual noisy skirmishes between ideologues and parties were hushed, and a stunned silence took its place. Someone remembered that for years now there had been a scheme in Schipa's native city to make up for what had always been denied to its greatest citizen by Rome. In the musical high school which he had founded, and which bears his name, it seemed right to offer him a last refuge, an alternative to exile. But the proposal had been lost in the labyrinth of everyday business, and it was already too late to find out what had happened to it and revive it, so that it should have preferential treatment. They debated what to do.

From far-away Venezuela, Elena, the only one of his children to do so, rang New York. She spoke with a father whom she hadn't seen for fifteen years. The firm, slightly penetrating voice which she had once known was reduced to a light, uncertain thread. He reassured her: he'd be all right, as always. Not a word about all the adversities of recent times: the quarrels, the misunderstandings, the poverty. Only one admission—almost a surrender, for an optimist like him: "I'm lonely."

Meanwhile, things were happening in Lecce. An emergency motion was passed; something that would not leave them completely unprepared when their greatest son died. The document went for signature; there were no objections, and no speeches. However, against the workings of fate, sudden haste is almost the same as eternal slowness.

December 16, 1965. Tito's heart was unable to withstand the spread of the diabetes. A cardio-circulatory collapse ended his life at 7:15 in the evening, at the age of almost seventy-seven years; far away from his family, forgotten by many, and even poorer than that little half-clad ragamuffin whose singing first bewitched the Scalze quarter of Lecce and went on to captivate the whole world.

The doctor who drew up the death certificate, an Italo-American, described the deceased as a "war veteran." What could this final oddity mean? Was the doctor very distracted, or was he perhaps more than usually perceptive?

Before God

I hope he burst into the Creator's office with the same uninhibited zeal with which he used to burst into my room while I was studying, demanding to know whether I could give him a decent reply, or was in some way responsible:

"Titino! But can you tell me: if this God exists, why doesn't he show himself?

I didn't know how to answer this one. It was a matter of refined polemics between two divinities. Then he added, as if to excuse himself for such arrogance:

"Because, you know, I honestly believe that *something* exists... It wouldn't be called Jehovah, or Buddha, but maybe it's...oh well, I don't know...a chair...but *something* must exist!"

That uncertainty never took the shape of any other object. Always a chair.

I've often thought that his coupling of a simple chair with the idea of the divinity may have derived from an innate devotion to the seating in the theater, where the only God he worshipped all through his life used to sit.

I hope, too, that he never had to ask himself again, like the child a century ago:

"Could it be that they loved my voice more than me?"

Two things I can say with absolute sincerity and certainty of Tito Schipa, my father: the first is that I have never, never heard anyone sing like him; the second is that from a certain moment in his life, he no longer knew how to say no.

One of these things brought him the most enviable existence imaginable; the other, to some extent, ruined it for him.

XV

A recurring dream

I have a dream which keeps coming back: my father has returned.

After a very long absence, as when I was a small child and he came home from one of his long tours, there he was, smiling and affectionate as ever, but changed—older and more tired. And in the dream, just as it used to be when I was a little boy, when I see that he's back I have mixed feelings of pleasure and anxiety.

He has been gone just long enough to make it necessary for me to readjust to his presence, and to get over a slight feeling of alienation. In a corner of my mind, I'm aware of being a bit surprised at the fact that he isn't dead yet. In fact, yes, I realize that during his absence I have prepared myself for the idea; I have accepted the notion of his death. But I can't make out whether this sensation is part of my present dream and arises out of my awareness of the fact that he really is dead, or whether it already existed in my childhood.

However much I try to separate dream from reality, I realize that my father was already a memory, a myth inside me when I was a boy. Seeing him return in flesh and blood was always like an exhausting, magical, tormented resurrection rite.

In this way, now as then, his actual death continues to be something for which I was always prepared: a distressing event but not

203

a traumatic one, ambivalent, but completely irrelevant when compared to his profound presence.

I believe that it is like that for anyone who loves an artist and is something of a son to him in spirit. An artist, especially the artist whom you love, doesn't die. Death makes no sense in this dimension: every poet has always known that. To think of the mortal remains of Shakespeare or Mozart gives all of us the impression of a joke in bad taste. What does that empty husk, that collapsed puppet, have to do with the sea of emotions, the living word and the eternal solace of his work? The mystery of death is revealed in all its absurdity when the one who dies is a genius.

A similar and equally inscrutable mystery is the real nature of what art inspires in us. Every artist has his incomprehensible game of prestige, his perfect somersault, at the end of which you find yourself asking: "But what exactly happened: how did he do it?"

In the case of Tito Schipa, the matter is even more sealed away, and difficult to put into words. You may have listened to him over and over again during your lifetime; when you are a long way away from the record-player, your thoughts go back to the fact that that fine gentleman from Lecce was not Caruso, certainly, nor Gigli nor Giacomo Lauri-Volpi, nor even Frank Sinatra or Louis Armstrong or Carlos Gardel or Carlo Buti or Elvis Presley or Bob Dylan or Rod Stewart. None of those, in fact, who had in their vocal chords an instrument of highly personal character and great command, and who have become the top names in their particular way of singing. And then you wonder why, when listening to Tito Schipa, everything else seemed to you suddenly to fall into a reduced dimension—that is to say, in a very noble but restricted field, into the relative: something minimal against something absolute.

You return to the record-player, asking yourself, for the thousandth time, whether you haven't been exaggerating a little. And for the thousandth time, as that voice with its perfect pronunciation reaches out, as the incredible tension of the melodic pattern is felt, as the capacity of being present and whispering even in the most abstract and unnatural registers becomes apparent—all the old fascination returns.

One of the other great mysteries of the history of the theater comes to mind: you think of Hamlet, of that brooding youth about whom one is never sure whether he is a fool or whether he plays at being one; that half-man who doesn't have the stature of a Lear, the fascination of a Iago, the villainy of a Richard or the passion of a Romeo. And yet, every time you extract him from the page, there he is again, the uncontested greatest of all, the protagonist who is a class unto himself, the Number One. Once again you ask yourself why. And you conclude that for some reason, the titanic strength of Hamlet lies specifically in his not being one of those particular, great characters, but in being, foolishly and conclusively, man. Man and nothing else, with an ordinary man's story, sometimes passionate, sometimes rather wretched and tormented, sometimes absurd, but nevertheless profound because of the very fact of being alive, of being man. Thus the genius of Shakespeare, applied to an ordinary kind of man, has created a matchless masterpiece.

Tito Schipa applied the enormous range of a vocal art to the voice of an ordinary man, an art which was interpretative and creative, without equal in the story of singing.

For those of us who belong to the area between the Mediterranean and the forests of Central Europe, the area where great music was born and reached its peak; for those of us who have mysteriously repudiated the centuries-old tradition of narration in music which rendered us great in the eyes of the world; for those of us who must nevertheless have, hidden away somewhere in our chromosomes, the receptors of the great Melos; for us, *this* is the way of singing which more than any other must represent the release of the emotions, the reawakening of Dionysus, the enchantment before the ancient song of humanity.

Before that spinning disc, each time, once again, we realize that with Tito Schipa we are not merely listening to a great singer, but to what we know should be for us the voice of humanity itself singing. We are listening, simply, to the miracle of the voice. Our own voice.

XVI

Thanks

I would like to express warm thanks not only to those who have cooperated in producing this volume, but also to the individuals who in the career of Tito Schipa, in his life, and consequently also in mine to some extent, proved to be invaluable, effective, affectionate and positive.

In the first place, thanks go to Lecce, the city which gave birth to Tito Schipa. Today, Lecce remembers its "nightingale" at every corner. A huge piazza is dedicated to him, at the foot of the monumental castle known as Charles V's; a bust stands in the park, and a room of the city club. The Musical Conservatory, one of the most admired in Italy, is named after him; it is attended by hundreds of students from every region, a natural offspring of the musical high school which Schipa himself sought to create. A stone in the foyer of the Politeama Greek Theater recalls the love of his fellow citizens for "his sublime art."

The Association of the Friends of Opera is also dedicated to Tito Schipa. This is a circle of private benefactors who periodically organize an international singing competition bearing his name. The same name also appears on the banner of the city's band, and on the nameplates of schools, cinemas and bars in numerous neighboring villages, such as Gallipoli, Muro, Ostuni and many others.

Special thanks to the Administrative Council of the Province of Lecce. And to the many faithful friends of my father who reside in the city: the Angilla, Baldassare, Barbano, Candido, Giangrande, Greco, Ingrosso, Vitale, Massari, Mantovano, Mazzotta and Zaccaria families. I would like to mention even more, and be sure of not leaving out anyone. The same goes for his friends of the most difficult times in every part of the world: the Besios, Cametti-Aspris, Calabreses, Casavolas, Donatis, Donatos, Frascatores, Gaetanis, Gazzonis, Landras, Mac Branwins, Morgantinis, Nicolosis, Quattrociocchi-Brancas, Russos, Scorsonis, Sinimbergis, Vasellis and Verderamos, and all those whom, because of the age-difference between myself and my father, I never had the chance to meet.

Thanks to the Alecce family, and especially to Francesca, for having revealed to me the great nobility which resides in complete and disinterested admiration.

I would also like to mention the enthusiastic collectors specializing in the name of Schipa, the true preservers and transmitters of his art: Luciano Angione in Milan, Antonio Margiotta in Rome, Carlo Bino in Utrecht, Andrew N. Morra in New York, and others who must certainly exist but whom I have not yet had a chance to get to know.

For some of the notions about Puglia and its history, I thank Rina Durante, an indispensable voice when the Salentino is under discussion, and Professor Angela Pensato.

Thanks to the Vicariate of Lecce for its collaboration in genealogical research.

Thanks to Carolina Marconi for her research in the archives, to Ida Pieruccetti and Pia Santilli for their personal contribution in memories and documents.

Special thanks to the "Quotidiano di Lecce" and its editorial staff for their untiring work in representing and defending the name of Tito Schipa. And together with them, I owe a debt of gratitude to newspapers and journals all over Italy, to the radio and the television, the private and public bodies—it would be impossible to name all of them—who contributed to the centenary of Tito Schipa's birth in 1989.

In particular, heartfelt thanks to Radio Uno, the division of

RAI which has done more than any other for Tito Schipa, producing and repeating several times, among other things, the important radio production "*L'Usignolo di Lecce,*" to which credit goes to Elio Molinari and Ennio Ceccarini, as well as to Nanà Mavaracchio, Franca Boldrini, Ernestina Fava and Piero Boerio for their valuable technical contribution.

Thanks also to the directors of the Cineteca of the Experimental Cinema Center for the research into and recovery of many films in which Tito Schipa acted.

Finally thanks to the illustrious scholars who have collaborated in this book, enriching it greatly; the appearance of their names alongside my own does me much honor.

Tito Schipa: Singer from the Neck Up

Franco Serpa

I believe that Tito Schipa was one of the most significant interpreters of the musical taste of the twentieth century. No-one can deny that he was a great and original singer—no-one denied it in his own day, at a time when the public was staunchly partisan towards one or the other of the four great tenors—Schipa, Pertile, Gigli and Lauri-Volpi. But I believe Schipa was unique in knowing how to express the sense of crisis, of detachment coupled with intimate nostalgia, which characterize twentieth century responses to romantic sentiments.

What we term "twentieth century culture" does not begin with the opening of the century. For about a decade the conviction of continuity with the nineteenth century survived and was given energy by artists and audiences of operatic melodrama. In other fields changes were taking place more and more rapidly—in the way life was viewed, in the rules which governed the arts—but in the world of opera most artists and spectators had convinced themselves that the new tendency towards *verismo* was simply the modern aspect of romantic sensibility.

On the contrary! Verism was really the expression of a detachment, a malaise and a loss of ideas and styles, even though it may not have been recognized as such at the time. This existential and aesthetic unawareness—or call it innocence—explains the element of neurosis, of excess and anguish and languor in the interpretation of twentieth century Italian operatic melodrama. I do not wish to imply by this that there were no singers of the first rank, especially among the tenors. It was just that with the spirit of the twentieth century, the crisis of opera had begun—or rather the crisis of operatic melodrama, which gradually ceased to be the current mode of musical production. It was a form that could no longer express the mood of the times. The attempt to make the past real to the present by presenting it in up-to-date terms, which was the goal of operatic melodrama, became a problem of analysis and exegesis and evocation, or in other words, interpretation in its most profound and most difficult sense. The position of the interpreter should have been (but often was not) one of distance from the work, with instinctive perceptions of its dramatic quality replaced by formal and stylistic competence. The understanding of form and style had to be expressed with rigor and even with a kind of nostalgia for lost vitality. Such were the qualities required in the twentieth century for "classic" interpretation, which is the conservative aspect of modernity, and which in fact permits the only possible relationship with the nineteenth.

But what has all this to do with the art of Tito Schipa? The relationship lies in the basic character of Schipa's interpretation. Right from the beginning of his career, and with even greater determination as time went on, the dominant trend towards verism which was then in vogue for opera singers was completely alien to him. Even in the first years of his career, from 1910 to the outbreak of the first World War, the young Schipa did not make use of melodramatic conventions—neither the long-established ones of highly mannered vocalism (still to be heard in nineteenth century singers such as Battistini, De Lucia, Bonci, etc.), nor the more modern ones of declamation and pathos. Like John McCormack and Richard Tauber, who were also similar to him in other matters of outlook, Schipa was a unique and quite solitary interpreter, both in serious and popular music, because of his innate qualities of form, and above all because of his astonishing evocative and allusive capacity, with its balance between spontaneity and technique, emotion and introspection, nostalgia and irony. I do not mean by this that Schipa was anti-romantic by taste or upbringing: I mean rather that while certainly a great singer, he was not a

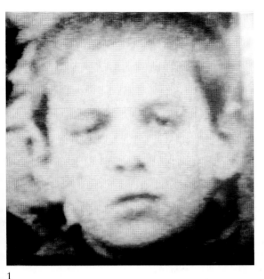

1

2

1. Schipa at age 12.

2. As a seminarian in Lecce.

3. Bishop Gennaro Trama, Schipa's patron.

3

4

4. With mother and pet Loris.

5. As a struggling student in Milan.

5

6

7

8

6. Emilia Cesano while engaged to Schipa.

7. Emilia Bernardini Macor, journalist and maecenas of Lecce.

8. The singing teacher Alceste Gerunda.

9

9. Antoinette Michel, known as "Lillì," Schipa's first wife.

10. With Elena, first daughter by Lillì.

11. Schipa about the time he met Lillì.

12. With second daughter, Liana.

10

12

11

13

13. Metropolitan Opera publicity photo.

14. Rehearsing *La rondine* with Dalla Rizza in Monte Carlo, 1917.

14

15

16

15. Publicity photo dedicated to Edith McCormick, wife of Harold F. McCormick. Both were important benefactors of the Chicago Opera.

16. Schipa with accompanist/pilot, on a flight from Havana to Florida to keep a concert engagement.

17. Tito with Toto.

17

18

18. With second family, parents-in-law, farmers and nurse Luisa (in white) at the villa in Pasturana, early 1950s.

19. Teresa Borgna (in art, Diana Prandi), Schipa's future second wife, at the time of their first meeting.

20. With second wife Diana, guests/prisoners in the villa of Castelvetro (Modena) with an English officer.

19

20

21

22

21. Schipa's second family in the 1950s.

22. Conducting the radio broadcast of his operetta
La Principessa Liana.

23

23. The magic closet of costumes.

24. Singing teacher in the school on Via Flaminia in Rome, early 1960s.

25. Having fun (with Ferruccio Tagliavini).

24

25

26. Jury duty in Moscow (1st Youth Festival).

27. Bon vivant.

28. Backstage with Toti Dal Monte in the 1950s.

26

27

28

Tito Schipa as Don Ottavio
in *Don Giovanni*

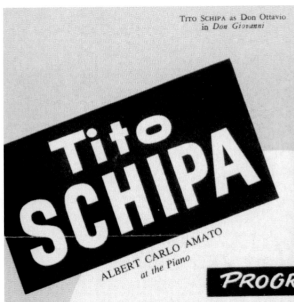

ALBERT CARLO AMATO
at the Piano

PROGRAM

I

Ave Maria — Schubert
La Serenata — Schubert

II

Le Violette — Scarlatti
Where'er You Walk "Semele" — Handel

III

Una Furtiva Lagrima
"L'Elisir D'Amore" — Donizetti

Gerchero Lontano Terra
"Don Pasquale" — Donizetti

M'Appari "Marta" — Flotow

— INTERMISSION —

IV

A Granada — Palacios
Desesperadamente — Ruiz
'I Te Vurria Vasa' — Di Capua

V

Marechiare — Tosti
Chi Se Nne Scorda Cchiu — Barthelemy

Angel Records

Tour Direction:
NATIONAL MUSIC THEATRE, Inc.
126 West 23rd Street
New York 11, N. Y.

FAREWELL CONCERT

WEDNESDAY OCTOBER 3 at 8:30 P. M.
TOWN HALL
123 WEST 43RD STREET · N.Y.C.
ORCH. $6.00, 5.00, · LOGE $6.00 · BALC. $4.00, 3.00
ON SALE: TOWN HALL BOX OFFICE · PHONE JU 2-4536 AND
NATIONAL MUSIC THEATRE, INC. 126 W. 23RD ST., N.Y. 11 N.Y. CH 3-0387

29. Programs of farewell concerts.

30

30. At the time of farewell concert in New York with Diana Haslett (far left).

31. Last photo taken in Italy; residence on Via Cassia in Rome.

31

32. Typical publicity photo at the height of his career.

33. Piazza Sant'Oronzo in Lecce the day of Schipa's funeral.

32

33

34. In *Fra Diavolo*.

35. Gerald in *Lakmé*.

36. Alfredo in *Traviata*.

34

36

35

37

37. In *Zazà* at the time of his Lecce debut.

38. As Cavaradossi in *Tosca* at the time of his Naples debut.

39, 40. As the Duke of Mantua in *Rigoletto*.

41. (l. to r.) Ezio Pinza as Sparafucile, Eva Gruninger as Maddalena and Tito Schipa as the Duke in *Rigoletto*. San Francisco Opera, 1935.

42. As the Duke in *Rigoletto*. San Francisco Opera, 1935.

43. As Don Ottavio in *Don Giovanni*.

44

44, 45. Don Ottavio in
Don Giovanni at the
Metropolitan Opera.

45

46. Edgardo in *Lucia di Lammermoor*. La Scala, 1935-36 season.

47. As Fenton in *Falstaff*.

To Bella

Bill Park

most sincerely

as Fenton

in "FALSTAFF"

by Verdi

Tito Slippa

Roma 1901

49

48. With Toti Dal Monte in *Don Pasquale* at La Scala.

49. As Nemorino in *L'elisir d'amore*.

PI34-7

50. As Nemorino in *L'elisir d'amore*.

51. Left - Helen Jepson and Tito Schipa (Lady Harriet and Lionel); Right - Coe Glade and Henri Shefoff (Nancy and Plunkett). *Martha*, San Francisco Opera, 1935.

TEATRO ALLA SCALA - STAGIONE LIRICA ANNO XV
GIANNA PEDERZINI-TITO SCHIPA
IN "MIGNON"

52. As Wilhelm Meister in *Mignon* with Gianna Pederzini.

53. As Des Grieux in *Manon*, with Bidú Sayão in the title role, about to go onstage for Act III. San Francisco Opera, 1939.

54

54. As Des Grieux in *Manon*.

55. As Wilhelm Meister in *Mignon* at La Scala.

55

56. Tito Schipa as Count Almaviva and Josephine Tumminia as Rosina in
Il barbiere di Siviglia. San Francisco Opera, 1935.

57. Baccaloni, Franci, Chaliapin, Dal Monte, and Schipa in *Il barbiere di Siviglia* at La Scala.

58. Schipa as Count Almaviva and Richard Bonelli as Figaro with choristers of the San Francisco Opera in *Il barbiere di Siviglia*, 1935.

59. The earliest picture of Schipa in the title role of Massenet's *Werther*.

60. In the title role of Massenet's *Werther*. San Francisco Opera, 1935.

61. Schipa in the title role and Coe Glade as Charlotte in *Werther*. San Francisco, 1935.

62. Onstage as Werther. San Francisco Opera, 1935.

63. In the title role of *Werther* with Coe Glade as Charlotte (holding his arm) and Anna Young as Sophie. San Francisco Opera, 1935.

64. Werther dying.

65. Last *Werther* in Rome.

"That voice of his. all velvet and gold. is one of the wonders of the world today"

Chicago Tribune, October 24th, 1927

SCHIPA

FROM COAST TO COAST—CRITICS UNANIMOUS

NEW YORK

It was a dramatic occasion when Tito Schipa stepped onto the stage at Carnegie Hall last night to sing in recital before the adoring crowd that packed the house and stage. The hall was filled intermittently with exquisite song and thunderous applause.

—*Evening Post, Nov. 22, 1927.*

CHICAGO

SCHIPA—One is justified in capitalizing this name. After his performance of yesterday afternoon at the Auditorium where he has won his spurs behind the footlights, one is again conquered by the matchless charm of this God-given voice, wedded as it is to the rare musical intelligence, the sense of fitness, the grace and dignity, the inescapable lyricism of Schipa's art.

—*Evening American, Oct. 24, 1927.*

LOS ANGELES

When he lilts forth a folk song of Italy or Spain, it seems that blue skies and lakes and moonlight and romance have existed from time immemorial solely to transmute themselves into sound and pour forth from the Schipa throat. His interpretations of the masterpieces of reflective literature are thoughtful, musicianly and engrossing. In the spontaneous growths from the music of the people, however, he is the fulfillment of destiny.

—*Examiner, Jan. 23, 1928.*

BOSTON

Inherently a voice of lyric timbre, it can nevertheless summon ardors after the manner of the most full-voiced tenors. No less it spins out the lightest of high tones that merely float as a breath upon the air. Whether the tone be light or full, quality is never sacrificed. Tone is always beautiful. Indeed, Mr. Schipa, by his voice alone, is one of those singers who make tenors the most popular of all popular idols.

—*Transcript, Nov. 28, 1927*

Season 1928-1929 Now Booking

Management:

Evans ＆ Salter

Victor Records   527 Fifth Avenue, New York   Mason & Hamlin Piano

66. Sample of full-page publicity in "The Musical Digest" (1928).

"theatrical" singer (and in this too he resembled McCormack, and even more, Tauber). Although he had considerable stage resources at certain moments, his exceptional qualities lay above all in meditative and elegiac expression—in other words, in the experience of the immediate and explicit crisis of sentiment.

So the story of the encounter between Caruso and Schipa has great symbolic value. Dorothy Caruso, wife of the great Enrico, recounts in her memoirs that he had an opportunity to hear his young colleague in New York in 1920, in a concert at the Lexington Theater (this was the year in which Schipa began his period with the Chicago Opera, which lasted for ten years). After a couple of pieces Caruso said to his wife: "It's all right. We go home now," and left the theater. The reaction would seem to be one of irritation masked by patronization. In 1920, as the recordings demonstrate, Schipa had reached the mature point of his style, which made its mark in a totally different way from Caruso's. The latter must have understood and appreciated very little (and in fact the pronouncement by Lauri-Volpi in his *Voci parallele* is almost equally dismissive, although he does allow Schipa some substantial recognition). Caruso was a singer "from the neck down," and the greatest of his era; here he was faced with the greatest of the tenors "from the neck up."

Here I am making use of the picturesque if rather brutal definition current among theater critics in those years to point to the contrast between actors of a late romantic tendency and those of a rationalist vein. The performing style of the latter was analytical and controlled, and the primary factor in it was the firmness of the voice and the semantic precision of every word. In the theater this was the new style of critcal rationalism, for which the feelings of everyday life and the emotions of the scene must never be superimposed or confused (in these years Ruggero Ruggeri performed in this way, for instance). In contrast, the acting of actors "from the neck down" was energetic and passionate, sometimes even frenetic because the scene did become confused with life, and the identification even reached out to embrace the spectators, who must suffer and weep (as could happen in the performances of Zacconi, Eleanora Duse, Lyda Borelli and Alexander Moissi).

In fact this counterposing of the two theatrical characters had already been noted by Artistotle, when he compared the *euphyeis*—

dramatists who were balanced and limpidly clear—with the *manikoì*, the obsessed and exalted (In *Poetics* 1455, a.32; for a reference to human characteristics in general, see the *Rhetoric* 1390, b.29, where Aristotle defines the one, the *manikòs*, as a degeneration of the other). It is thus right from its origins that dramatic art lives and prospers in the encounter between these two opposing attitudes: but there have been few epochs when the opposition was as dynamic as in the theater of the first years of our century. And yet in these same years, little of this kind was happening in the world of musical melodrama, where only the *manikoì* operated. And with a lineup of greats which included Caruso, Chaliapin, Titta Ruffo, the "singer from the neck down" won hands down (there is no time here to discuss how it was that Chaliapin reached the maximum of poignancy and exaltation on the stage, while still theorizing about the detachment and control of the interpreter). Was it a question of repertoire? This certainly played a role, because of the prevalence of veristic operas, and because the few nineteenth century melodramas, notably those of Verdi, and also *Mefistofele*, *La Gioconda* and *Carmen* were often performed with a taste for the passionate and the magniloquent.

But we should listen to the toast song from *Cavalleria rusticana* as recorded by Tito Schipa in 1913. It is of no importance that this is not one of his most significant recordings, nor that he had not yet perfected his style. But in comparison with the emphasis and the brashness customary at that time, Schipa gives a completely different kind of interpretation, which constitutes a kind of idealization of the village festival. I would stress again, his was not an anti-sentimental reinterpretation of melodrama, but it was already a rethinking of the strong sentiments which were becoming outmoded.

Certainly the originality of Schipa lies within a specific tradition, which was that of the romantic "tenore di grazia," the *amoroso*. And the role predetermined, to some degree, the manner and tone of the interpretation.

We know litle of the *tenori di grazia* of an earlier generation, the greatest of whom were Angelo Masini, Juliàn Gayarre and, in some ways, Roberto Stagno. We have sufficiently precise information about their personalities, which we can obtain from documents and reportage, but we must be cautious in judging the specific characters of their voices and their interpretations (also because their repertoire was different from that of the light-lyrical tenors of the next age).We are on surer ground with the vocal qualities and musical taste which came into their own with the great Italian tenors of the last decade of the nineteenth century and the first fifteen years of our own: Fernando De Lucia, Alessandro Bonci, Giuseppe Anselmi and some lesser names. The basis of their taste (especially De Lucia, who sang in Gounod's *Romeo and Juliet*, *The Pearl Fishers* and *Werther*, and Anselmi) must have been the modern one of the *opéra lyrique*, which requires elegance and skill in subtleties. But their vocal quality no longer has a definite orientation, and fluctuates between studied and subtle expression and warmer naturalistic singing. More generally, there is a variation between good taste and gallery-pleasing effects (which could turn into the false bravura typical of verism at its worst, or unmusical slovenliness).

Nothing of all this is to be found in Schipa.His most immediate predecessor, who shows some signs of the same elegiac and dreamlike style, Fernando De Lucia, is still halfway between the old and the new. But Schipa's interpretative taste is completely modern, based as it is on an infallible knowledge of form, and on a magical capacity to evoke what is past and what is distant.

In the first years of his career, Schipa's repertoire was also the mixed one of the lyric tenor of those days, who alternated between lightweight roles and more demanding ones. But it is significant that even in the first ten years of his activity, from 1910 to 1920, Schipa did not tackle the characters of Romantic heroism, and he was very diffident towards the ruling *verismo* style. Already, after three or four years of his career, he turned his back on many operas which were popular at the time. Sometimes this happened suddenly, as in the case of *Fedora*, which he sang in Naples in 1913, and then never again.

Certainly, the limitations of his voice, which was weak in the middle range and short in the highest area, made him cautious to a degree. But the fundamental reason for his artistic creed lay in the fact that he was a *euphyès* in a world in which the *manikoi* prevailed. In order to make a name for himself, he would have to bring his talent to the strictest level of perfection; in other words he would have to make it a stylistic category of its own. And for this reason, he is the only reflective artist among the eminently communicative—i.e. explicit, passionate, enthralling—tenors of his time. This goes not only for the dramatic tenors, but also for the lyric ones, first among them the great Gigli himself. So marked was Schipa's position as a man apart that one basic element of the success of any exhibition of the tenor voice, the sense of effort, the exciting tension of the psyche and the voice, is almost entirely lacking. It is not that his artistry was "disembodied and geometrical," as Leopardi said of insensitive and mannered artists; it is simply that in singing he is a "classic artist," and the classic quality is the one from which a substantial part of modern art has sprung: the informed awareness of the past and the need for order and harmony in the present. It is an aesthetic mode which exhbits a profound existential melancholy, and which imposes on itself the discrete form of every sentiment.

In order to understand this, the first level of analysis relating to the "vocal recitation" of Schipa is already a useful guide. In him, the pleasure of a beautiful melody or the emotion involved in singing it never prevails over the words, and never strains them. In whatever language Schipa is singing, the listener never misses a syllable. But the moment his tongue touches on a word expressing distance or memory or regret or amorous contemplation, the word is lit up, and the song takes wing. There are endless examples of this, and anyone who is familiar with Schipa's recordings can quote his favorite example. "*Un di felice, eterea, mi balenaste innante*" sung by Schipa is like the image of a marvelous epiphany. In his singing there is nothing indistinct, and nothing betrays the logic of the musical and verbal phrase. And yet in the secret trembling of those words and in their suprising vocal evocation, an astonishing enrichment takes place in the internal semantic and phonic relations (the vocal color of *innante* does not convey any indicative objectivity in Schipa's singing; instead it is a fact of his interior awareness, an emotional foretaste of *tremante*, more significant than the actual rhyme).

Another eloquent example, but this time aimed at attaining a different dynamic of expression, is the case of "*Umane e fragili qui cose sono,*" in the duet between the Duke and Gilda in *Rigoletto*. The seducer is seduced by his own emotion, and the thought of human frailty, and then, by contrast, the unfamiliar pity wakens in the libertine a vehement outburst of emotion: "Su, dunque, amiamoci, donna celeste," which Schipa sings with genuine passion. In the approach to *"Cielo e mar"* in *La Gioconda,* there is no sensuality, as there is in the singing of Caruso and that of Gigli (where the sensuality is one of fine sound for its own sake, not actually demanded by the meaning). Instead there is an elegaic amazement at the beauty of the night and the heavens, with an intense but restrained anxiety.

Another equally persuasive component of Schipa's vocal taste is the truly "anti-tenorish" delicacy of the assertive and commanding elements of his style. Certainly the amorous and anti-heroic characters which he preferred to represent need a tender and caressing mode of expression, but none of the tenors before and after Schipa knew as well as he did how to sing those gentle exhortations and offerings of love: *"Prendi,* l'anel *di dono,"* "Addio, Mignon, fa cor! Non lagrimar,"* and even the exaggerated *"Ah, dispar, vision."* This was partly due to the fact that the expressive intention was maintained by a superior technique.

What Schipa presented, then, was not just a vocal and interpretative manner at the peak of a certain tradition. It was also, and even more, the expression of intimate energies of sensitivity and character. What came naturally to Schipa, from the native tradition of Mediterranean popular music, was the impulse to sing in order to reveal bitter disquiet, the anxiety of solitude in the night or in the southern world. We need only hear the stunning execution which Schipa produced of the rumba of the Manicero, who is the seller of *mani,* peanuts, and we are at once seized by the effect of a voice which is singing to itself in a little lane or a piazza full of echoes. And generally speaking, every Italian or Latin-American song in Schipa's interpretation merits analysis, because his songs always have the stylization and the evocative capacity which the rumba had in those years when performed by Fred Astaire. But Schipa's elegance, for reasons I have mentioned, has its roots in far more ancient and natural soil.

Turning to the cultural matter of his work, the prime factor was certainly the French lyricism of the late romantic period (which was also an essential component of the classicism of the nineteenth century). These sentiments and their specific style were assimilated by Schipa from the characters of lovers in the *opéra lyrique*, as he lived out their personalities as William Meister in *Mignon* and as Des Grieux. These were the characters on which the major and best part of his career was based. In Schipa's interpretation, there is no trace of the languor and sentimental mannerism which creep into the substance of the music, and often into the interpretations which are given of it. The fact is that through his instinct, his ancestral memory and his intelligence, Schipa was able to perceive the wellsprings of this elegiac world (classical culture, up as far as Goethe, naturally), and in some way to reveal these sources in the purity of song, thanks to that instinctive classical bent which I have already mentioned.

Perhaps I could mention one personal experience which was an unexpected demonstration for me of the singular profundity of Schipa's art. The poetry of a great modern poet, Antonio Machado, both erudite and popular, innocent and reflective like no one else in our century, brought back to mind a day, out of the blue; a musical emotion, certainly, but in a rather uncertain way which I could not at first pin down. I was reading:

> *Palacio, buen amigo,*
> *? està la primavera*
> *vistiendo ya las ramas de los chopos*
> *del rio y los caminos? En la estepa*
> *del alto Duero, Primavera tarda,*
> *¡pero es tan bela y dulce quando llega!*

I had already heard such a sovereign grace in a voice; such an intense sentiment of expectancy, such an immediate sense of the melancholy of nature.

> *Pourquoi me réveiller, o souffle du printemps*
> *Sur mon front je sens tes caresses.....*

Did Messrs. Blau, Millet and Hartman know that in *Berrathon*, the last poem of Ossian, these are not the poetic thoughts of a man but a flower? Did Massenet know? And finally, did Schipa know? I think it is unlikely. And yet the sublime ingenuousness, the immediate brotherhood of man with the spirit of nature, the primaeval inspiration which the young Goethe believed he had found in the "ancient bard," was there, by some extraordinary evocation, firm and unadorned, in the voice of the modern singer.

Chronology

1909

VERCELLI — TEATRO FACCHINETTI
Feb 4   La traviata   L. Simeoli s.

SEBENICO — TEATRO MAZZOLENI
Apr 12   La traviata   M. Comida s. L. Silvetti b.

SAVONA — TEATRO CHIABRERA
May   La traviata

CREMA (CARNEVALE) — TEATRO SOCIALE
Dec 26?   Adriana Lecouvreur   M. Tensini-Peretti s. T. Forlano ms. G. Puliti b.
                               A. Sigismondo cond.

1910

CREMA (CARNEVALE) — TEATRO SOCIALE
Jan 8?   Zazà   M. Tensini-Peretti s. G. Puliti b.

LECCE — POLITEAMA GRECO
Apr 3   Adriana Lecouvreur   G. Bucceri cond.
Apr   Mignon
May 1   Zazà   M. Tensini-Peretti s. L. Montesanto b.
                               G. Bucceri cond.
May   Mefistofele

MESSINA — TEATRO MASTROIENI
July 9   La traviata (8 perf.) C. Muzio s. F. Biancofiori b. A. Sigismondo cond.
July 24   Rigoletto (7)   C. Muzio s. A. Oliva/F. Biancofiori b.
                                 A. Sigismondo cond.

BOZZOLO — TEATRO COMUNALE
Aug   Faust

CHIOGGIA — TEATRO GARIBALDI
Sep 29   Mignon (7)   A. Rizzini s. A. Cassani s. T. Montico bs.
                               C. Cavalieri cond.

LECCE (CARNEVALE) — POLITEAMA GRECO
Dec 26   Rigoletto   . . Boriani s. M. Longari ms. G. Viggiani b.
                               . .Vaccari bs. G. Marrone cond.

217

1911

CREMA — TEATRO SOCIALE
Jan 18	Rigoletto	L. Simeoli *s.*
		. . Rossi de Castelnuovo/P. Favaron *b.* . . Rossini
		bs. A. Sigismondo *cond.*
Feb 4	La bohème	I. Kramer *s.* L. Simeoli *s.* P. Favaron *b.*
		A. Sigismondo *cond.*
Feb	Rigoletto	L. Simeoli *s.* P. Favaron *b.* . . Vaccari *bs.*

POLA — TEATRO CISCUTTI
Mar 15	Il barbiere di Siviglia	M. Beltramo *s.* S. Canali *b.* G. Beltramo *bs.*
		G. Rubino *cond.*

ZARA (ZADAR) — TEATRO VERDI
Mar 25	Il barbiere di Siviglia	M. Beltramo *s.* S. Canali *b.* G. Beltramo *bs.*
		G. Rubino *cond.*

ANCONA — TEATRO VITTORIO EMANUELE
Mar 30	Il barbiere di Siviglia	M. Beltramo *s.* S. Canali *b.* G. Beltramo *bs.*
		C. Rossi *bs.* G. Rubino *cond.*

TERNI — POLITEAMA TERNANO
Apr 15	Il barbiere di Siviglia	L. Simeoli *s.* S. Canali *b.* A. Rizzo *bs.* C. Rossi *bs.*
		G. Rubino *cond.*
Apr 20	Don Pasquale	L. Simeoli *s.* S. Canali *b.* C. Rossi *bs.*
		G. Rubino *cond.*
Apr 26	Il maestro di cappella	A. Ballarin *ms.* C. Rossi *bs.* G. Rubino *cond.*

SPOLETO — TEATRO NUOVO
May 3	Il barbiere di Siviglia	L. Simeoli *s.* S. Canali *b.* A. Rizzo *bs.* C. Rossi *bs.*
		G. Rubino *cond.*
May 6?	Don Pasquale	L. Simeoli/I. Murray *s.* S. Canali *b.* C. Rossi *bs.*
		G. Rubino *cond.*
May	Il maestro di cappella	

GUBBIO — TEATRO COMUNALE
May 12	Don Pasquale
May	Il barbiere di Siviglia
May	Il maestro di cappella

PRATO — TEATRO METASTASIO
May	Don Pasquale (4)	L. Simeoli *s.* M. Bonanno *b.* C. Rossi *bs.*
		G. Rubino *cond.*

ROME — TEATRO QUIRINO
July 2	Don Pasquale (8)	I. De Frate/M. Gelcich *s.* A. Bellucci/V. Giorda *b.*
		C. Rossi *bs.* G. Rubino *cond.*
July 17	Werther (2)	B. Nelson *ms.* M. Passermann *s.* R. De Ferran *b.*
		G. Rubino *cond.*
July 25	Zazà (14)	L. Cavalleri *s.* R. De Ferran/V. Giorda *b.*
		G. Rubino *cond.*
Aug 14	Fedora (1)	B. Nelson *ms.* M. Passermann *s.* A. Laffi *b.*
		G. Rubino *cond.*
Sep 1	La sonnambula (11)	I. De Frate *s.* G. M. Curci *bs.* G. Rubino *cond.*

Sep 29	Cavalleria rusticana (20)	C. Rubini/A. Baldieri/V. Regi *s*. R. Caldani *b*. G. Rubino *cond*.
Oct 4	Il maestro di capella (2)	A. Ballarin *ms*. C. Rossi *bs*. G. Rubino *cond*.

CATANIA — TEATRO SANGIORGI

Nov 6	Don Pasquale	E. Bianchi *s*. V. Giorda *b*. C. Rossi *bs*. R. Bianchi *cond*.
Nov 8	La sonnambula	I. De Frate *s*. G. M. Curci *bs*. R. Bianchi *cond*.
Nov 9	La traviata	L. Simeoli/L. Cassandro *s*. /G. Giovenco *ms*. V. Bellabarba *b*. R. Bianchi/G. Torrisi *cond*.
Nov 21	Fra Diavolo	I. De Frate *s*. A. Ballarin *ms*. L. Bianchi *t*. V. Giorda/A. Paolini *b*. L. Ferraioli *bs*. C. Rossi *bs*.

PALERMO — TEATRO BIONDO

Dec 2	La sonnambula	I. De Frate/L. Cassandro *s*. G. M. Curci *bs*. R. Bianchi *cond*.
Dec 5	La traviata	L. Simeoli/L. Cassandro *s*. V. Bellabarba/M. Stabile *b*. R. Bianchi *cond*.
Dec 13	Rigoletto	I. De Frate *s*. A. Ballarin *ms*. . . Pavani/M. Stabile *b*. G. M. Curci *bs*. R. Bianchi *cond*.
Dec 20	Fra Diavolo	I. De Frate *s*. A. Ballarin *ms*. L. Bianchi *t*. V. Giorda *b*. L. Ferraioli *bs*. C. Rossi *bs*. R. Bianchi *cond*.
Dec 27	Cavalleria rusticana	L. Cassandro *s*. A. Ballarin *ms*. V. Bellabarba *b*. R. Bianchi *cond*.

1912

TRENT — TEATRO SOCIALE

Jan 3	La sonnambula (5)	I. De Frate *s*. G. M. Curci *bs*. R. Bianchi *cond*.
Jan 6	La traviata (6)	N. Garelli/L. Cassandro *s*. S. Canali *b*. R. Bianchi *cond*.
Jan 13	Fedora (4)	N. Garelli *s*. A. Ballarin *ms*. S. Canali *b*. R. Bianchi *cond*.

BORGO VALSUGANA — TEATRO SOCIALE

Jan 22	La traviata (1)	N. Garelli *s*. S. Canali *b*. R. Bianchi *cond*.

TRENT — TEATRO SOCIALE

Jan 28	Cavalleria rusticana (6)	L. Cassandro *s*. A. Ballarin *ms*. S. Canali *b*. R. Bianchi *cond*.
Feb 1	Il maestro di cappella (1)	A. Ballarin *ms*. C. Rossi *bs*. R. Bianchi *cond*.

MEZZOLOMBARDO — TEATRO COMUNALE

Feb 2	La sonnambula (1)	I. De Frate *s*. G. M. Curci *bs*. R. Bianchi *cond*.

TRENT — TEATRO SOCIALE

Feb 7	La bohème (5)	N. Garelli *s*. L. Cassandro *s*. V. Giorda *b*. S. Canali *b*. G. M. Curci *bs*. R. Bianchi *cond*.

PARMA — TEATRO REINACH

Apr 6	Don Pasquale	I. De Frate *s*. V. Giorda *b*. G. De Bernardi/C. Rossi *bs*. R. Bianchi *cond*.
Apr 8	Il barbiere di Siviglia	I. De Frate *s*. S. Canali *b*. G. M. Curci *bs*. G. De Bernardi *bs*. R. Bianchi *cond*.
Apr 14	Antony (4)	M. Baldi *s*. S. Canali *b*. R. Bianchi *cond*.

TRIESTE — TEATRO FENICE

May 8	La sonnambula (5)	I. De Frate/M. Bevignani s. G. M. Curci/A. Cucini bs. R. Bianchi cond.
May 9	Don Pasquale (3)	I. De Frate/M. Donatello s. V. Giorda b. C. Rossi bs. R. Bianchi cond.
May 10	Il barbiere di Siviglia (1)	I. De Frate s. V. Giorda b. G. M. Curci bs. C. Rossi bs. R. Bianchi cond.
May 14	La traviata (4)	M. Baldi s. A. Martellato b. R. Bianchi cond.
May 21	Antony (2)	M. Baldi s. A. Martellato b. R. Bianchi cond.
May 25	Lucia di Lammermoor (3)	I. De Frate s. A. Martellato b. G. M. Curci bs. R. Bianchi cond.
May 31	Cavalleria rusticana (5)	M. Baldi s. A. Ballarin ms. A. Martellato b. R. Bianchi cond.

CAPODISTRIA — TEATRO SOCIALE

June 10	La sonnambula (1)	I. De Frate s. G. M. Curci bs. R. Bianchi cond.
June 11	Don Pasquale (1)	I. De Frate s. V. Giorda b. C. Rossi bs. R. Bianchi cond.

TRIESTE — TEATRO FENICE

June 16	Fra Diavolo (1)	I. De Frate s. A. Ballarin ms. V. Giorda b. G. M. Curci bs. C. Rossi bs. R. Bianchi cond.
Aug 31	La favorita (6)	A. Beinat ms. G. Parigi b. C. Melocchi bs. R. Bianchi cond.
Sep 6	La traviata (5)	T. Enenkel s. G. Parigi b. R. Bianchi cond.

UDINE — TEATRO MINERVA

Sep 22	Don Pasquale (2)	M. Donatello s. V. Giorda b. C. Rossi bs. R. Bianchi cond.
Sep 23	La favorita (3)	A. Beinat ms. G. Parigi b. C. Melocchi bs. R. Bianchi cond.
Sep 27	La traviata (3)	T. Enenkel s. G. Parigi b. R. Bianchi cond.

BOLOGNA — TEATRO DUSE

Oct 2	La sonnambula (4)	I. De Frate s. C. Melocchi bs. R. Bianchi cond.
Oct 5	La traviata (5)	T. Enenkel s. G. Parigi b. R. Bianchi cond.
Oct 14	La favorita (1)	T. Massucci ms. G. Parigi b. C. Melocchi bs. R. Bianchi cond.

BOLOGNA — TEATRO VERDI

Oct 19	La traviata (1)	T. Enenkel s. G. Parigi b. R. Bianchi cond.
Oct 20	La favorita (2)	T. Massucci ms. G. Parigi b. C. Melocchi bs. R. Bianchi cond.

CATANIA — TEATRO SANGIORGI

Oct 24	La favorita	T. Massucci ms./L. Micucci s. G. Parigi b. A. Cucini bs. A. Fossati cond.

PALERMO — TEATRO BIONDO

Nov 1	La favorita	L. Micucci s. R. Meroni b. C. Melocchi bs. R. Bianchi cond.
Nov 6	La sonnambula	I. De Frate s. C. Melocchi/A. Cucini bs. R. Bianchi cond.
Nov 8	Tosca	L. D'Arsago s. E. Giraldoni b. R. Bianchi cond.
Nov 18	Antony	M. Baldi s. R. Meroni b. R. Bianchi cond.

MILAN — TEATRO DAL VERME
Dec 28   La traviata (14)   E. Allegri/R. Chollet s. A. Passuello/A. Capovia b.
                                      G. Radini Tedeschi cond.

1913

MILAN — TEATRO DAL VERME (continued)
Jan 11   Tosca (11)   J. Gozategui s. A. Passuello b.
                                     G. Radini Tedeschi cond.

BUENOS AIRES — TEATRO COLÓN
June 16   La sonnambula (1)   M. Barrientos s. A. Brondi bs. V. Podesti cond.
June 19   Mignon (4)   L. Berlendi s. M. Barrientos s. P. Ludikar bs.
                                     A. Guarnieri cond.

July 10   La traviata (4)   M. Barrientos s. R. Stracciari b.
                                     A. Guarnieri/V. Podesti cond.

ROSARIO — TEATRO DE LA OPERA
Aug 31   La sonnambula   M. Barrientos s. A. Brondi bs.

MILAN — TEATRO DAL VERME
Oct 16   La sonnambula (8)   A. Galli-Curci s. C. Scattola bs. E. Panizza cond.
Oct 29   La traviata (8)   G. Finzi Magrini s. A. Passuello b.
                                     E. Panizza cond.

Nov 20   Rigoletto (8)   M. Crosa s. I. Zizolfi/L. Mengaldo ms.
                                     D. Viglione Borghese b. V. Bettoni/B. Rimediotti bs.
                                     E. Panizza cond.

NAPLES — TEATRO SAN CARLO
Dec 26   Falstaff (9)   C. Carpi Toschi s. I. M. Ferraris s. T. Di Angelo ms.
                                     E. Bruno ms. M. Sammarco/E. Badini b.
                                     E. E. Badini b./R. Tegani b. G. Berenzone bs.
                                     L. Mugnone cond.

1914

NAPLES — TEATRO SAN CARLO (continued)
Jan 3   Tosca (21)   E. Magliulo/E. Cervi Caroli/G. Tess s.
                                     A. De Lieto Sammartino/B. Bellincioni Stagno/E.
                                     Korwin s. R. Tegani b. L. Mugnone/A. Morelli cond.
Feb 2   Fedora (3)   G. Tess s. /ms. M. Donatello s. R. Tegani b.
                                     A. Morelli cond.
Mar 26   Madama Butterfly (2)   B. Bellincioni Stagno s. R. Tegani b.
                                     A. Morelli cond.
Apr 3   Marcella (4)   A. Fitziu s. R. Tegani b. A. Morelli cond.

ROME — TEATRO COSTANZI
Apr 16   Don Pasquale (2)   R. Storchio s. G. De Luca b. G. Kaschmann b.
                                     E. Vitale cond.

BUENOS AIRES — TEATRO COLISEO
May 16   La traviata   R. Storchio s. M. Sammarco b. E. Vitale cond.
May 18   Il barbiere di Siviglia E. De Hidalgo s. M. Sammarco b. G. Cirino bs.
                                     G. Schottler bs. E. Vitale cond.

May 28	La bohème	G. Dalla Rizza *s.* A. Caterini *s.* E. Caronna *b.* T. Dentale *bs.* G. Cirino *bs.* E. Vitale *cond.*
May 29	Don Pasquale	R. Storchio *s.* G. Danise *b.* G. Schottler *bs.* E. Vitale *cond.*
June 1	Madama Butterfly	R. Storchio *s.* E. Caronna *b.* E. Vitale *cond.*
June 10	Tosca	M. De Lerma *s.* M. Sammarco *b.* E. Vitale *cond.*
June 19	Manon	R. Storchio *s.* E. Caronna *b.* G. Cirino *bs.* E. Vitale *cond.*

ROSARIO — TEATRO DE LA OPERA

June 21	Il barbiere di Siviglia	E. De Hidalgo *s.* M. Sammarco *b.* G. Cirino *bs.* G. Schottler *bs.* E. Vitale *cond.*
June 22	Madama Butterfly	R. Storchio *s.* E. Caronna *b.* E. Vitale *cond.*
June 25	Manon	R. Storchio *s.* E. Caronna *b.* G. Cirino *bs.* E. Vitale *cond.*

CORDOBA — TEATRO RIVERA INDARTE

June 28	Il barbiere di Siviglia	E. De Hidalgo *s.* M. Sammarco *b.* G. Cirino *bs.* G. Schottler *bs.* E. Vitale *cond.*
July	Madama Butterfly	R. Storchio *s.* E. Caronna *b.* E. Vitale *cond.*
July	Manon	R. Storchio *s.* E. Caronna *b.* G. Cirino *bs.* E. Vitale *cond.*

TUCUMÁN — TEATRO ODEON

July 9	Il barbiere di Siviglia	E. De Hidalgo *s.* M. Sammarco *b.* G. Cirino *bs.* G. Schottler *bs.* E. Vitale *cond.*

RIO DE JANEIRO — TEATRO MUNICIPAL

July 20	La traviata (1)	R. Storchio *s.* M. Sammarco *b.* E. Vitale *cond.*
July 22	Il barbiere di Siviglia (1)	E. De Hidalgo *s.* G. Danise *b.* G. Cirino *bs.* G. Schottler *bs.* E. Vitale *cond.*
July 23	Tosca (2)	H. I. Brugelman/M. De Lerma *s.* M. Sammarco/G. Danise *b.* E. Vitale *cond.*
July 26	Manon (2)	R. Storchio *s.* E. Caronna *b.* G. Cirino *bs.* E. Vitale *cond.*
July 28	La bohème (1)	G. Dalla Rizza *s.* A. Caterini *s.* E. Caronna *b.* T. Dentale *bs.* G. Cirino *bs.* E. Vitale *cond.*

SÃO PAULO — TEATRO MUNICIPAL

Aug 9	Manon	R. Storchio *s.* E. Caronna *b.* G. Cirino *bs.* E. Vitale *cond.*
Aug 10	Il barbiere di Siviglia	E. De Hidalgo *s.* M. Sammarco *b.* G. Cirino *bs.* G. Schottler *bs.* E. Vitale *cond.*
Aug 11	Tosca	M. De Lerma *s.* G. Danise *b.* E. Vitale *cond.*

SÃO PAULO — TEATRO POLITEAMA

Aug 16	La bohème (1)	G. Dalla Rizza *s.* A. Caterini *s.* E. Caronna *b.* T. Dentale *bs.* G. Cirino *bs.* T. De Angelis *cond.*

MONTEVIDEO — TEATRO SOLIS

Aug 20	Manon	R. Storchio *s.* E. Caronna *b.* G. Cirino *bs.* E. Vitale *cond.*
Aug 24	Il barbiere di Siviglia	E. De Hidalgo *s.* M. Sammarco *b.* G. Cirino *bs.* G. Schottler *bs.* E. Vitale *cond.*
Aug 25	La traviata	R. Storchio *s.* M. Sammarco *b.* E. Vitale *cond.*
Aug 29	Tosca	M. De Lerma *s.* M. Sammarco *b.* E. Vitale *cond.*
Sep 1	Don Pasquale	E. De Hidalgo *s.* G. Danise *b.* G. Schottler *bs.* E. Vitale *cond.*

GENOA — POLITEAMA GENOVESE
Oct 31   La sonnambula   G. Pareto *s.* A. Brondi *bs.* C. Castagnino *cond.*

BARI — TEATRO PICCINNI
Dec 8   Lucia di Lammermoor (8)   A. Galli-Curci/O. Morano *s.* E. Grandini/E. De Marco *b.* M. Fiore *bs.* P. La Rotella *cond.*
Dec 19   La traviata (7)   A. Galli-Curci/O. Morano *s.* E. Grandini *b.* P. La Rotella *cond.*

1915

NAPLES — TEATRO SAN CARLO
Jan 8   Manon (7)   E. Cervi Caroli/E. Boccolini Zacconi *s.* A. Gandolfi *b.* A. Masini-Pieralli *bs.* V. Gui *cond.*
Feb 2   Il barbiere di Siviglia (4)   E. De Hidalgo *s.* M. Sammarco *b.* A. Masini-Pieralli *bs.* G. De Vecchi *bs.* V. Gui *cond.*
Feb 11   La bohème (7)   G. Dalla Rizza/A. Fabiani/E. Boccolini Zacconi *s.* E. Boccolini Zacconi/O. Morano *s.* M. Sammarco/ A. Gandolfi *b.* G. De Vecchi *bs.* A. Masini-Pieralli/ P. Argentini *bs.* V. Gui/A. Morelli *cond.*
Mar 1   Rigoletto (9)   I. M. Ferraris *s.* T. Di Angelo *ms.* M. Sammarco/ A. Gandolfi *b.* O. Carozzi *bs.* V. Gui/B. Moltrasio *cond.*
Mar 25   Le donne curiose (10)   E. Boccolini Zacconi *s.* I. M. Ferraris *s.* N. Gontarouk *s.* T. Di Angelo *ms.* M. Govoni *b.* A. Gandolfi *b.* E. Vannuccini *bs.* O. Carozzi *bs.* V. Gui/B. Moltrasio *cond.*
Apr 10   La traviata (2)   E. Boccolini Zacconi *s.* G. Noto *b.* A. Morelli *cond.*

MILAN — TEATRO MANZONI
Oct 22   La bohème   M. Farneti *s.* E. Marchini *s.* L. Montesanto *b.* A. Guarnieri *cond.*

MILAN — TEATRO DAL VERME
Nov 6   Falstaff (7)   M. Farneti *s.* I. M. Ferraris *s.* V. Guerrini *ms.* T. Di Angelo *ms.* G. Rimini *b.* E. Badini *b.* V. Bettoni *bs.* A. Toscanini *cond.*
Nov 11   La traviata (3)   R. Storchio *s.* A. Rossi *b.* A. Toscanini *cond.*

MILAN — TEATRO ALLA SCALA
Dec 26   Prince Igor (6)   G. Dalla Rizza *s.* F. Anitua *ms.* G. Danise *b.* G. Cirino *bs.* L. Ferroni *bs.* G. Marinuzzi *cond.*

1916

MILAN — TEATRO ALLA SCALA (continued)
Feb 17   Manon (3)   R. Storchio *s.* A. Crabbé *b.* G. Cirino *bs.* G. Marinuzzi *cond.*

ROME — TEATRO COSTANZI
Mar 2   La bohème (6)   E. Cervi Caroli *s.* L. Lauri *s.* G. Rimini/A. Crabbé *b.* L. Paci *b.* C. Walter *bs.* E. Vitale/A. Martino *cond.*
Mar 9   Manon (6)   E. Cervi Caroli/R. Storchio *s.* A. Crabbé *b.* C. Walter *bs.* E. Vitale *cond.*

| Mar 16 | La traviata (5) | R. Storchio/G. Finzi Magrini *s.*
G. Rimini/A. Crabbé *b.* E. Vitale/T. De Angelis *cond.* |

ROME — SALA PALESTRINA
Mar 23   Concert

ROME — TEATRO COSTANZI

| Apr 7 | Il barbiere di Siviglia (5) | E. De Hidalgo *s.* R. Stracciari *b.* C. Walter *bs.*
G. De Vecchi *bs.* E. Vitale *cond.* |
| Apr 13 | Ivan (2) | G. Baldassarre Tedeschi *s.* L. Paci *b.*
E. Vitale *cond.* |

BUENOS AIRES — TEATRO COLÓN

June 28	La sonnambula (4)	M. Barrientos *s.* M. Journet *bs.* G. Baroni *cond.*
July 1	Manon (5)	N. Vallin Pardo *s.* A. Crabbé *b.* M. Journet *bs.* X. Leroux *cond.*
July 27	Falstaff (3)	R. Raisa *s.* N. Vallin Pardo *s.* E. Casazza/G. Bertazzoli *ms.* A. Roessinger *ms.* T. Ruffo *b.* A. Crabbé *b.* G. Mansueto *bs.* G. Baroni *cond.*
Aug 2	Il barbiere di Siviglia (3)	M. Barrientos *s.* T. Ruffo *b.* G. Mansueto *bs.* G. Niola *bs.* G. Baroni *cond.*

MONTEVIDEO — TEATRO SOLIS

Aug 15	La sonnambula	M. Barrientos *s.* M. Journet *bs.* G. Baroni *cond.*
Aug 18	Falstaff	R. Raisa *s.* N. Vallin Pardo *s.* E. Casazza *ms.* A. Roessinger *ms.* T. Ruffo *b.* A. Crabbé *b.* G. Mansueto *bs.* G. Baroni *cond.*
Aug 21	Il barbiere di Siviglia	M. Barrientos *s.* T. Ruffo *b.* G. Mansueto *bs.* G. Niola *bs.* G. Baroni *cond.*
Aug 24	Rigoletto	M. Barrientos *s.* G. Bertazzoli *ms.* T. Ruffo *b.* G. Mansueto *bs.* G. Baroni *cond.*
Aug 25	L'ultima gavotta	G. Dalla Rizza *s.* G. Rimini *b.* G. Papi *cond.*

RIO DE JANEIRO — TEATRO MUNICIPAL

Sep 6	La sonnambula (1)	M. Barrientos *s.* M. Journet *bs.* G. Baroni *cond.*
Sep 7	Manon (2)	N. Vallin Pardo *s.* A. Crabbé *b.* M. Journet *bs.* X. Leroux *cond.*
Sep 10	Rigoletto (2)	M. Barrientos *s.* G. Bertazzoli *ms.* A. Crabbé *b.* G. Mansueto *bs.* G. Baroni *cond.*
Sep 11	Falstaff (1)	R. Raisa *s.* N. Vallin Pardo *s.* G. Bertazzoli *ms.* A. Roessinger *ms.* G. Rimini *b.* A. Crabbé *b.* G. Mansueto *bs.* G. Baroni *cond.*
Sep 13	Il barbiere di Siviglia (2)	M. Barrientos *s.* A. Crabbé *b.* G. Mansueto *bs.* G. Niola *bs.* G. Baroni *cond.*

SÃO PAULO — TEATRO MUNICIPAL

Sep 21	La sonnambula (1)	M. Barrientos *s.* M. Journet *bs.* G. Baroni *cond.*
Sep 24	Rigoletto (2)	M. Barrientos *s.* G. Bertazzoli *ms.* A. Crabbé *b.* T. Dentale *bs.* G. Baroni *cond.*
Sep 25	Il barbiere di Siviglia (1)	M. Barrientos *s.* A. Crabbé *b.* G. Mansueto *bs.* G. Niola *bs.* G. Baroni *cond.*
Oct 3	Falstaff (1)	R. Raisa *s.* N. Vallin Pardo *s.* G. Bertazzoli *ms.* A. Roessinger *ms.* G. Rimini *b.* A. Crabbé *b.* G. Mansueto *bs.* G. Baroni *cond.*
Oct 5	Manon (1)	N. Vallin Pardo *s.* A. Crabbé *b.* M. Journet *bs.* G. Papi *cond.*
Oct 8	Tosca (1)	G. Dalla Rizza *s.* A. Crabbé *b.* G. Papi *cond.*

| Oct 10 | La traviata (1) | M. Barrientos *s*. A. Crabbé *b*. G. Baroni *cond*. |

RIO DE JANEIRO — TEATRO LIRICO

Oct 12	Il barbiere di Siviglia	M. Barrientos *s*. A. Crabbé *b*. G. Mansueto *bs*.
		G. Niola *bs*. G. Baroni *cond*.
Oct 14	La traviata	M. Barrientos *s*. A. Crabbé *b*. G. Baroni *cond*.
Oct 15	Tosca	G. Dalla Rizza *s*. A. Crabbé *b*. G. Papi *cond*.

BARCELONA — TEATRO DEL LICEO

Nov 23	Manon	G. Vix *s*. A. Crabbé *b*. A. Ricceri *bs*.
		A. Padovani *cond*.
Nov 25	Il barbiere di Siviglia	E. De Hidalgo *s*. A. Crabbé *b*. A. Masini-Pieralli
		bs. G. Pini Corsi *b*. A. Padovani *cond*.
Nov 27	Tosca (2)	A. Zeppilli *s*. M. Battistini *b*. A. Padovani *cond*.
Dec 14	L'elisir d'amore	E. De Hidalgo *s*. A. Crabbé *b*. G. Pini Corsi *b*.
		A. Padovani *cond*.

1917

BARCELONA — TEATRO DEL LICEO (continued)

Jan 1	Concert	
Jan 3	La sonnambula	M. Capsir *s*. A. Masini-Pieralli *bs*.
		A. Padovani *cond*.
Jan 6	Concert	
Jan 10	Manon	G. Vix *s*. A. Crabbé *b*. A. Ricceri *bs*.
		A. Padovani *cond*.

MADRID — TEATRO REAL

Jan 14	Manon (7)	C. Bonaplata Bau/B. Drymma/R. Storchio *s*.
		A. Crabbé *b*. J. Torres de Luna *bs*.
		A. Saco del Valle *cond*.
Jan 15	Il barbiere di Siviglia (6)	E. De Hidalgo *s*. A. Crabbé *b*. A. Masini-Pieralli
		bs. G. Pini Corsi *b*. T. Serafin *cond*.
Jan 27	Lakmé (3)	E. De Hidalgo *s*. C. Del Pozo *b*. J. Torres de Luna
		bs. A. Saco del Valle *cond*.
Feb 3	La bohème (1)	C. Bonaplata Bau/B. Drymma *s*. . . Delva *s*. J.
		Segura Tallien *b*. C. Del Pozo *b*. J. Torres de Luna
		bs. T. Serafin *cond*.

MADRID — PALAZZO DEL COMUNE

| Feb 7 | Concert |

MADRID — TEATRO REAL

| Feb 14 | Concert |

LISBON — TEATRO COLISEU

Feb 22	Manon (1)	M. Llacer *s*. M. Stabile *b*. G. Falconi *cond*.
Feb 24	Rigoletto (1)	A. Ottein *s*. M. Garcia Blanco *ms*. M. Stabile *b*.
		L. Rossato *bs*. G. Falconi *cond*.
Feb 26	a) La sonnambula (1)	A. Ottein *s*. L. Rossato *bs*. G. Falconi *cond*.
	b) Il barbiere di Siviglia,	A. Ottein *s*. M. Stabile *b*. G. Falconi *cond*.
	Act I	
Feb 28	Tosca (1)	C. Forni *s*. M. Stabile *b*. G. Falconi *cond*.
Mar 2	a) Manon, Act II-III	M. Llacer *s*. M. Stabile *b*. J. Martì *bs*.
		G. Falconi *cond*.

b) Rigoletto, Act IV   A. Ottein *s.* M. Garcia Blanco *ms.* M. Stabile *b.*
                        L. Rossato *bs.* G. Falconi *cond.*

MONTE CARLO — SALLE GARNIER

Mar 15   Tosca (1)   G. Dalla Rizza *s.* G. Petit *b.* G. Lauweryns *cond.*
Mar 27   La rondine (3)   G. Dalla Rizza *s.* I. M. Ferraris *s.* F. Dominici *t.*
                                     G. Huberdeau *bs.* G. Marinuzzi *cond.*
Apr 3   Rigoletto (1)   A. Zeppilli *s.* . . Rossi *ms.* M. Battistini *b.*
                                     M. Journet *bs.* G. Lauweryns *cond.*
Apr 5   La traviata (1)   F. Heldy *s.* A. Maguenat *b.* G. Lauweryns *cond.*

NAPLES — TEATRO SAN CARLO

Apr 12   La sonnambula (2)   G. Pareto *s.* L. Mugnoz *bs.* R. Ferrari *cond.*

BARCELONA — TEATRO DEL LICEO

Apr 24   Manon (3)   G. Vix *s.* C. Del Pozo *b.* C. Giralt *bs.*
                                     A. Padovani *cond.*

BARCELONA — TEATRO NOVEDADES

Apr 27   Concert

BARCELONA — TEATRO DEL LICEO

Apr 28   La traviata (1)   M. Farry *s.* J. Segura Tallien *b.* A. Padovani *cond.*
May 1   a) Rigoletto, Act IV   M. Farry *s.* G. Bertazzoli *ms.* J. Segura Tallien *b.*
                                     L. Nicoletti Korman *bs.* A. Padovani *cond.*
          b) Manon, Act III   G. Vix *s.* . . . Fernandez . . C. Giralt *bs.*
                                     A. Padovani *cond.*

LISBON — TEATRO COLISEU

May 12   Manon (1)   O. Nieto *s.* C. Del Pozo *b.* J. Martì *bs.*
                                     A. Padovani *cond.*
May 15   La favorita (1)   G. Gallanti *ms.* G. Del Chiaro *b.*
                                     L. Nicoletti Korman *bs.* A. Padovani *cond.*
May 17   Tosca (1)   O. Nieto *s.* M. Stabile *b.* A. Padovani *cond.*
May 19   Rigoletto (2)   M. Capsir *s.* L. Garcia Conde *ms.* M. Stabile *b.*
                                     J. Martì *bs.* A. Padovani *cond.*
May 26   Il barbiere di Siviglia (1) M. Capsir *s.* M. Stabile *b.* L. Nicoletti Korman *bs.*
                                     C. Del Pozo *b.* A. Padovani *cond.*
May 28   Mignon (1)   A. Baldi-Veltri *s.* M. Capsir *s.* L. Nicoletti Korman
                                     bs. A. Padovani *cond.*

LISBON — TEATRO SÃO CARLOS

May 29   Concert

LISBON — TEATRO COLISEU

May 31   a) Manon, Act II   O. Nieto *s.* C. Del Pozo *b.* A. Padovani *cond.*
          b) Mignon, Act III   A. Baldi-Veltri *s.* M. Capsir *s.*
                                     L. Nicoletti Korman *bs.* A. Padovani *cond.*
          c) Tosca, Act III   O. Nieto *s.* A. Padovani *cond.*

SAN SEBASTIAN — TEATRO VITTORIA EUGENIA

Aug 13   Manon   M. Llacer *s.* /G. Vix *s.* /A. Ottein *s.* F. Biancofiori *b.*
                                     M. Stabile *b.* G. Falconi *cond.*
Aug 14   Il barbiere di Siviglia   A. Ottein *s.* M. Stabile *b.* A. Masini-Pieralli *bs.* C.
                                     Del Pozo *b.* G. Falconi *cond.*
Aug 21   Mignon   A. Ottein *s.* A. Baldi-Veltri *s.* A. Masini-Pieralli *bs.*
                                     G. Falconi *cond.*
Aug 23   Rigoletto   A. Ottein *s.* M. Stabile *b.*

| Aug 25 | Tosca | M. Llacer *s.* M. Stabile *b.* |

BILBAO — COLISEO ALBIA

Sep 2	Manon	A. Baldi-Veltri *s.* C. Del Pozo *b.* A. Masini-Pieralli *bs.* G. Falconi *cond.*
Sep 3	Il barbiere di Siviglia	A. Ottein *s.* M. Stabile *b.* A. Masini-Pieralli *bs.* G. Falconi *cond.*
Sep 6	Rigoletto	A. Ottein *s.* E. Lucci I. M. Stabile *b.*
Sep 8	Tosca	M. Llacer *s.* M. Stabile *b.*

SANTANDER

BILBAO — COLISEO ALBIA

| Nov 9 | Rigoletto | A. Abasolo *s.* M. Stabile *b.* |

BARCELONA — TEATRO DEL LICEO

Nov 15	La sonnambula (2)	M. Barrientos *s.* A. Masini-Pieralli *bs.* G. Falconi *cond.*
Nov 22	Il barbiere di Siviglia (2)	M. Barrientos *s.* A. Crabbé *b.* G. Mansueto *bs.* G. Azzolini *bs.* G. Falconi *cond.*
Nov 27	Concert	

MADRID — TEATRO REAL

Dec 3	La sonnambula (2)	M. Barrientos *s.* A. Masini-Pieralli *bs.* G. Falconi *cond.*
Dec 6	Il barbiere di Siviglia (4)	M. Barrientos/A. Ottein *s.* A. Crabbé *b.* A. Masini-Pieralli *bs.* G. Azzolini *bs.* G. Falconi/A. Saco del Valle *cond.*
Dec 11	Rigoletto (4)	M. Barrientos/A. Ottein/Y. Gall *s.* G. Gallanti *ms.* A. Crabbé *b.* M. Journet *bs.* G. Falconi *cond.*

MADRID — PRESS ASSOCIATION

| Dec 19 | Concert | |

MADRID — TEATRO REAL

| Dec 25 | Manon (3) | N. Vallin Pardo *s.* C. Del Pozo *b.* A. Masini-Pieralli *bs.* G. Falconi *cond.* |

1918

MADRID — TEATRO REAL (continued)

| Jan 1 | Mignon (3) | N. Vallin Pardo *s.* A. Ottein *s.* A. Masini-Pieralli *bs.* A. Saco del Valle *cond.* |

BARCELONA — TEATRO DEL LICEO

Jan 12	Rigoletto	A. Ottein *s.* G. Zinetti *ms.* J. Segura Tallien *b.* G. Mansueto *bs.* G. Falconi *cond.*
Jan 18	Manon	N. Vallin Pardo *s.* M. Stabile *b.* G. Mansueto *bs.* G. Falconi *cond.*
Jan 24	Mignon	N. Vallin Pardo *s.* A. Ottein *s.* G. Mansueto *bs.* G. Falconi *cond.*
Feb 1	a) Mignon, Act III	N. Vallin Pardo *s.* A. Ottein *s.* G. Mansueto *bs.* G. Falconi *cond.*
	b) Manon, Act II	N. Vallin Pardo *s.* M. Stabile *b.* G. Falconi *cond.*
	c) Rigoletto, Act IV	A. Ottein *s.* G. Zinetti *ms.* M. Stabile *b.* G. Mansueto *bs.* G. Falconi *cond.*

MADRID — TEATRO REAL
Feb 15   Jugar con fuego (1)   E. Mazzoleni *s*. N. Vallin Pardo *s*. G. Besanzoni *ms*.
                                 M. Stabile *b*. A. Masini-Pieralli *bs*. . . Barrera *cond*.

MONTE CARLO — GRAND-THÉÂTRE
Feb 28   Rigoletto (2)   G. Pareto *s*. C. Mattei *ms*. M. Battistini *b*.
                                    M. Journet *bs*. G. Lauweryns *cond*.
Mar 3   Manon (3)   M. Bugg *s*. R. Couzinou *b*. M. Journet *bs*.
                                    L. Jehin *cond*.
Mar 5   La traviata (1)   G. Pareto *s*. M. Battistini *b*. G. Lauweryns *cond*.
Mar 14   Tosca (2)   G. Dalla Rizza *s*. M. Battistini *b*.
                                    V. De Sabata *cond*.
Mar 17   Manole (3)   G. Dumaine *s*. M. Journet *bs*. L. Jehin *cond*.
Mar 24   Lucia di Lammermoor (1)   G. Pareto *s*. A. Maguenat *b*. M. Journet *bs*.
                                    G. Lauweryns *cond*.
Mar 31   Il barbiere di Siviglia (1)   G. Pareto *s*. R. Couzinou *b*. M. Journet *bs*.
                                    . . Ceccarelli *bs*. V. De Sabata *cond*.

SEVILLE — TEATRO CERVANTES
Apr 10   Manon   B. Drymma *s*. M. Stabile *b*. J. Torres de Luna *bs*.
                                    J. Tolosa *cond*.
Apr 11   Il barbiere di Siviglia   A. Ottein *s*. M. Stabile *b*. J. Torres de Luna *bs*.
                                    C. Del Pozo *b*. J. Tolosa *cond*.
Apr 13   Rigoletto   A. Ottein *s*. J. Tolosa *cond*.
Apr 15   Lucia di Lammermoor   A. Ottein *s*. . . Jorda *b*. . . Tanci *bs*.
                                    J. Tolosa *cond*.

CADIZ — TEATRO PRINCIPAL
Apr 19?   Manon   B. Drymma *s*. C. Del Pozo *b*.
Apr 21   Rigoletto   . . Gilina *s*. A. Beinat *ms*. M. Stabile *b*.
Apr 24   Tosca   B. Drymma *s*. M. Stabile *b*.

JEREZ DE LA FRONTERA
Apr 26   Rigoletto

MALAGA
Apr 27   Manon   B. Drymma *s*.
Apr 29   Rigoletto   . . Gilina *s*. A. Beinat *ms*. M. Stabile *b*.
Apr 30   Il barbiere di Siviglia   A. Ottein *s*.
May 1   La sonnambula (?)   A. Ottein *s*.

LISBON — TEATRO COLISEU
May 6   Manon   C. Bonaplata Bau *s*. L. Brias *b*.
                                    A. Masini-Pieralli *bs*. A. Terragnolo *cond*.
May 9   Rigoletto (2)   A. Abazolo/C. Ortigas *s*. M. Valverde *ms*.
                                    L. Brias/A. Mascarenhas *b*. F. Font *bs*.
                                    F. Camalló/P. Blanch *cond*.
May 11   La sonnambula   C. Ortigas *s*. A. Masini-Pieralli *bs*.
                                    A. Terragnolo *cond*.

LISBON — SÃO CARLOS
May 12   Manon   C. Bonaplata Bau *s*. L. Brias *b*. A. Masini-Pieralli
                                    bs. A. Terragnolo *cond*.

LISBON — TEATRO COLISEU
May 15   Tosca   E. Mazzoleni *s*. L. Rossi-Morelli *b*. P. Blanch *cond*.
May 18   Lucia di Lammermoor   C. Ortigas *s*. L. Rossi-Morelli *b*. F. Font *bs*.
                                    P. Blanch *cond*.

May 22	Mignon	M. Capuana *ms.* A. Abasolo *s.* A. Masini-Pieralli *bs.* A. Terragnolo *cond.*
May 24	Il barbiere di Siviglia	C. Ortigas. *s.* F. De Andrade *b.* A. Masini-Pieralli *bs.* J. Hernandez *bs.* P. Blanch *cond.*
May 31	Werther	C. Bonaplata Bau *s.* C. Ortigas *s.* L. Brias *b.* P. Blanch *cond.*
June 3	a) Werther, Act III	C. Bonaplata Bau *s.* C. Ortigas *s.* L. Brias *b.* P. Blanch *cond.*
	b) Manon, Act II	C. Bonaplata Bau *s.* L. Brias *b.* A. Terragnolo *cond.*
	c) Rigoletto, Act IV	C. Ortigas *s.* M. Valverde *ms.* A. Mascarenhas *b.* F. Font *bs.* P. Blanch *cond.*

BILBAO — TEATRO COMPOS ELISEOS

Sep 2	Rigoletto	. . Alcaraz *s.*
Sep 4	Il barbiere di Siviglia	. . Alcaraz *s.* . . Jorda *b.* J. Torres de Luna *bs.* C. Del Pozo *b.*
Sep 8	Manon	O. Nieto *s.* C. Del Pozo *b.* J. Torres de Luna *bs.*

SAN SEBASTIAN — TEATRO VITTORIA EUGENIA

Sep 10	Manon	O. Nieto *s.* C. Del Pozo *b.* J. Torres de Luna *bs.*
Sep 12	Rigoletto	. . Alcaraz *s.*
Sep 15	Il barbiere di Siviglia	A. Abasolo *s.* J. Torres de Luna *bs.* C. Del Pozo *b.*

BILBAO — COLISEO ALBIA

Sep 18	Manon	G. Vix *s.*

BARCELONA — TEATRO DEL LICEO

Nov 25	Manon (2)	G. Vix *s.* G. Giardini *b.* A. Masini-Pieralli *bs.* E. Vitale *cond.*
Dec 9	Il barbiere di Siviglia	G. Pareto *s.* D. Viglione Borghese *b.* A. Masini-Pieralli *bs.* G. Rebonato *bs.* E. Vitale *cond.*
Dec 11	Werther	L. Pasini Vitale *s.* F. Surinach *s.* C. Maugeri *b.* E. Vitale *cond.*
Dec 20	Concert	

1919

BARCELONA — TEATRO DEL LICEO (continued)

Jan 1	Fra Diavolo (3)	F. Surinach *s.* A. Lahowska *ms.* C. Maugeri *b.* A. Masini-Pieralli *bs.* G. Rebonato *bs.* E. Vitale *cond.*
Jan 3	a) Manon, Act I	G. Vix *s.* G. Giardini *b.* E. Vitale *cond.*
	b) Il barbiere di Siviglia, Act I	G. Pareto *s.* D. Viglione Borghese *b.* G. Rebonato *bs.* E. Vitale *cond.*
	c) Werther, Act III	L. Pasini Vitale *s.* F. Surinach *s.* C. Maugeri *b.* E. Vitale *cond.*

MADRID — TEATRO REAL

Jan 15	Tosca	O. Nieto *s.* L. Rossi-Morelli *b.* G. Falconi *cond.*
Jan 24	a) Il barbiere di Siviglia, Act I	. . Alcaraz *s.* C. Galeffi *b.* V. Bettoni *bs.* G. Azzolini *bs.* G. Falconi *cond.*
	b) Rigoletto, Act IV	. . Alcaraz *s.* M. Capuana *ms.* C. Galeffi *b.* V. Bettoni *bs.* G. Falconi *cond.*
	c) Manon, Act II	O. Nieto *s.* L. Rossi-Morelli *b.* G. Falconi *cond.*
Jan 26	a) Il barbiere di Siviglia, Act I	. . Alcaraz *s.* C. Galeffi *b.* V. Bettoni *bs.* G. Azzolini *bs.* G. Falconi *cond.*

	b) Manon, Act II	O. Nieto *s*. L. Rossi-Morelli *b*. G. Falconi *cond*.
	c) Tosca, Act III	O. Nieto *s*. G. Falconi *cond*.
Jan 29	La bruja (1)	E. Mazzoleni *s*. O. Nieto *s*. M. Gay *ms*.
		B. De Muro *t*. L. Rossi-Morelli *b*.
		A. Saco del Valle *cond*.

ROME — TEATRO COSTANZI

Feb 12	Rigoletto (2)	E. Graziani/E. De Hidalgo *s*. M. Galeffi *ms*.
		C. Galeffi *b*. P. Argentini *bs*. G. Marinuzzi *cond*.
Feb 15	Il barbiere di Siviglia (2)	E. De Hidalgo *s*. C. Galeffi *b*. N. De Angelis *bs*.
		C. Di Cola *bs*. G. Marinuzzi *cond*.
Feb 20	Tosca (2)	M. Labia *s*. E. Molinari *b*. V. Bellezza *cond*.

MONTE CARLO — GRAND-THÉÂTRE

Mar 2	Rigoletto (3)	M. Raffaelli/A. Borghi Zerni *s*. T. Di Angelo *ms*.
		M. Battistini *b*. M. Journet *bs*. G. Lauweryns *cond*.
Mar 9	Lucia di Lammermoor (31)	A. Borghi Zerni *s*. L. Cérésole *b*. M. Journet *bs*.
		G. Lauweryns *cond*.
Mar 11	Il barbiere di Siviglia (2)	E. De Hidalgo *s*. M. Battistini *b*. M. Journet *bs*.
		G. Lauweryns *cond*.

NAPLES — TEATRO SAN CARLO

Mar 22	L'amico Fritz (7)	N. Marmora *s*. G. Lufrano *ms*. A. Granforte *b*.
		P. Mascagni *cond*.
Apr 2	Lodoletta, Act I	N. Marmora *s*. A. Granforte *b*. P. Mascagni *cond*.

MONTE CARLO — GRAND-THÉÂTRE

Apr 8	Tosca (2)	G. Dalla Rizza *s*. M. Journet *bs*. V. De Sabata *cond*.
Apr 12	La rondine (2)	G. Dalla Rizza *s*. E. Marchini *s*. C. Bonfanti *t*.
		. . Deleuze *bs*. V. De Sabata *cond*.

SEVILLE — TEATRO SAN FERNANDO

Apr 25	Manon	G. Vix *s*. . . Jorda *b*. J. Torres de Luna *bs*.
May 4	Tosca	G. Vix *s*. L. Rossi-Morelli *b*.
May 12	Il barbiere di Siviglia	. . Jorda *b*. A. Masini-Pieralli *bs*. C. Del Pozo *bs*.

BUENOS AIRES — TEATRO COLISEO

June 8	Rigoletto	A. Ottein *s*. A. Gramegna *ms*. L. Montesanto *b*.
		C. Walter *bs*. G. Falconi *cond*.
June 15	Il barbiere di Siviglia	A. Ottein *s*. A. Crabbé *b*. N. De Angelis *bs*.
		G. Azzolini *bs*. G. Falconi *cond*.
June 22	Manon	N. Vallin Pardo *s*. A. Crabbé/M. Stabile *b*.
		C. Walter *bs*. G. Falconi *cond*.
June 23	Concert	
July 12	Werther	G. Bertazzoli *ms*./N. Vallin Pardo *s*. A. Giacomucci
		s. M. Stabile *b*. G. Marinuzzi *cond*.
July 26	Tosca	G. Dalla Rizza *s*. L. Montesanto *b*. V. Bellezza *cond*.
Aug 5	Prince Igor	M. Carena *s*. G. Bertazzoli *ms*. L. Montesanto *b*.
		C. Walter *bs*. T. Dentale *bs*. G. Marinuzzi *cond*.
Aug 18	Mignon	N. Vallin Pardo *s*. A. Ottein *s*. C. Walter *bs*.
		G. Marinuzzi *cond*.

MONTEVIDEO — TEATRO URQUIZA

Aug 21	Manon	N. Vallin Pardo *s*. A. Crabbé *b*. C. Walter *bs*.
		G. Marinuzzi *cond*.
Aug 24	Il barbiere di Siviglia	A. Ottein *s*. A. Crabbé *b*. N. De Angelis *bs*.
		G. Azzolini *bs*. G. Marinuzzi *cond*.

Aug 27	Werther	N. Vallin Pardo s. A. Giacomucci s. V. Damiani b. G. Marinuzzi cond.
Aug 29	Rigoletto	A. Ottein s. M. Galeffi ms. L. Montesanto b. C. Walter bs. G. Marinuzzi cond.

RIO DE JANEIRO — TEATRO MUNICIPAL

Sep 7	Werther (3)	G. Bertazzoli ms. A. Giacomucci s. V. Damiani b. G. Marinuzzi cond.
Sep 10	Il barbiere di Siviglia (1)	A. Ottein s. A. Crabbé b. N. De Angelis bs. G. Azzolini bs. G. Marinuzzi cond.
Sep 13	Manon (3)	N. Vallin Pardo s. A. Crabbé b. C. Walter bs. G. Marinuzzi cond.
Sep 20	Tosca (1)	G. Dalla Rizza s. L. Montesanto b. V. Bellezza cond.
Sep 26	Prince Igor (1)	M. Carena s. G. Bertazzoli ms. L. Montesanto b. C. Walter bs. T. Dentale bs. G. Marinuzzi cond.
Sep 30	Rigoletto (1)	A. Ottein s. M. Galeffi ms. L. Montesanto b. C. Walter bs. G. Marinuzzi cond.

SÃO PAULO — TEATRO MUNICIPAL

Oct 3	Manon (1)	N. Vallin Pardo s. A. Crabbé b. C. Walter bs. G. Marinuzzi cond.
Oct 5	Tosca (1)	G. Dalla Rizza s. L. Montesanto b. V. Bellezza cond.
Oct 8	Il barbiere di Siviglia (1)	A. Ottein s. A. Crabbé b. N. De Angelis bs. G. Azzolini bs. V. Bellezza cond.

SÃO PAULO — TEATRO POLITEAMA

Oct 9	Rigoletto (1)	A. Ottein s. M. Galeffi ms. L. Montesanto b. C. Walter bs. G. Marinuzzi cond.

SÃO PAULO — TEATRO MUNICIPAL

Oct	Werther (1)	G. Bertazzoli ms. A. Giacomucci s. V. Damiani b. G. Marinuzzi cond.

CHICAGO — AUDITORIUM

Dec 4	Rigoletto (2)	A. Galli-Curci/F. Macbeth s. M. Claessens ms. C. Galeffi/T. Ruffo b. E. Cotreuil bs. G. Marinuzzi cond.
Dec 10	Tosca (1)	R. Raisa s. G. Rimini b. G. Marinuzzi cond.
Dec 11	Manon (1)	Y. Gall s. A. Maguenat b. G. Huberdeau bs. G. Marinuzzi cond.
Dec 13	Il barbiere di Siviglia (2)	A. Galli-Curci/F. Macbeth s. C. Galeffi b. E. Cotreuil bs. V. Trevisan bs. G. Marinuzzi cond.
Dec 17	La sonnambula (3)	A. Galli-Curci s. V. Lazzari bs. T. De Angelis cond.
Dec 27	Don Pasquale (1)	A. Galli-Curci s. G. Rimini b. V. Trevisan bs. G. Marinuzzi cond.

1920

NEW YORK CITY — LEXINGTON THEATER

Feb 5	La sonnambula	A. Galli-Curci s. V. Lazzari bs. G. Marinuzzi cond.
Feb 6	Falstaff	R. Raisa s. M. Maxwell s. M. Claessens ms. C. Pascova ms. G. Rimini b. D. Defrère b. V. Lazzari bs. G. Marinuzzi cond.
Feb 14	Don Pasquale	A. Galli-Curci s. G. Rimini b. V. Trevisan bs. G. Marinuzzi cond.

TITO SCHIPA

Feb 20	Rigoletto	A. Galli-Curci *s*. M. Claessens *ms*. T. Ruffo *b*.
		E. Cotreuil *bs*. G. Marinuzzi *cond*.
Feb 24	Il barbiere di Siviglia	A. Galli-Curci *s*. C. Galeffi *b*. V. Lazzari *bs*.
		V. Trevisan *bs*. G. Marinuzzi *cond*.
Feb 26	La traviata	A. Galli-Curci *s*. C. Galeffi *b*. G. Marinuzzi *cond*.

BOSTON — OPERA

Mar 10	Rigoletto	F. Macbeth *s*. M. Claessens *ms*. T. Ruffo *b*.
		E. Cotreuil *bs*. G. Marinuzzi *cond*.
Mar 12	La sonnambula	A. Galli-Curci *s*. V. Lazzari *bs*. G. Marinuzzi *cond*.

MADRID — TEATRO REAL

Apr 4	Manon	O. Nieto *s*. C. Del Pozo *b*. V. Bettoni *bs*.
		A. Saco del Valle *cond*.
Apr 8	Tosca	O. Nieto *s*. L. Montesanto *b*.
		A. Saco del Valle *cond*.
Apr 13	Tosca	O. Nieto *s*. A. Saco del Valle *cond*.
Apr 17	a) Manon, Act II	O. Nieto *s*. L. Montesanto *b*.
		A. Saco del Valle *cond*.
	b) Il barbiere di Siviglia,	O. Nieto *s*. L. Montesanto *b*.
	Act I	A. Saco del Valle *cond*.
Apr 18	Il barbiere di Siviglia,	O. Nieto *s*. L. Montesanto *b*.
	Act I	A. Saco del Valle *cond*.

BARCELONA — TEATRO DEL LICEO

| Apr 20 | Manon, Act III | G. Vix *s*. C. Patino *b*. M. Journet *bs*. |

VALENCIA — TEATRO PRINCIPAL

Apr 23	Manon	O. Nieto *s*. V. Bettoni *bs*.
Apr 26	Il barbiere di Siviglia	A. Ottein *s*. L. Montesanto *b*. V. Bettoni *bs*.
Apr 27	Rigoletto	A. Ottein *s*. L. Montesanto *b*.

MALAGA

May 9	Manon	O. Nieto *s*. C. Del Pozo *b*.
May 10	Il barbiere di Siviglia	A. Ottein *s*. L. Montesanto *b*. V. Bettoni *bs*.
May 13	Tosca	O. Nieto *s*.
May 15	La sonnambula	A. Ottein *s*. V. Bettoni *bs*.
May 17	Rigoletto	A. Ottein *s*. L. Montesanto *b*. V. Bettoni *bs*.
May 20	Gala Concert	

LECCE — DUOMO

| Aug 25 | Mass (Messa)(2) | . . De Biase t. A. Zuccarello *b*. |
| | | . . De Magistris *cond*. |

SUMMER-AUTUMN 1920 — CONCERT TOUR

Sep 5	Gallipoli	Teatro Schipa
Nov 10	Boston	Symphonic Hall
Nov 17	New York City	Carnegie Hall

CHICAGO — AUDITORIUM

Nov 27	La traviata (3)	M. Craft/A. Galli-Curci/R. Storchio *s*. C. Galeffi/
		G. Rimini *b*. A. Smallens *cond*.
Dec 1	Lucia di Lammermoor (1)	A. Galli-Curci *s*. G. Rimini *b*. C. Nicolay *bs*.
		P. Cimini *cond*.
Dec 4	La sonnambula (1)	A. Galli-Curci *s*. V. Lazzari *bs*. P. Cimini *cond*.
Dec 7	Il barbiere di Siviglia (2)	A. Galli-Curci/F. Macbeth *s*. C. Galeffi *b*.
		V. Lazzari *bs*. V. Trevisan *bs*.
		G. Marinuzzi/G. Santini *cond*.

232

| Dec 15 | Falstaff (1) | R. Raisa *s*. M. Maxwell *s*. M. Claessens *ms*. C. Pascova *ms*. G. Rimini *b*. D. Defrère *b*. V. Lazzari *bs*. G. Marinuzzi *cond*. |
| Dec 18 | Lakmé (3) | A. Galli-Curci/F. Macbeth *s*. D. Defrère *b*. G. Baklanov *b*. H. Morin *cond*. |

1921

CHICAGO — AUDITORIUM (continued)

| Jan 5 | Linda di Chamonix (1) | R. Storchio *s*. G. Besanzoni *ms*. G. Rimini *b*. V. Lazzari *bs*. V. Trevisan *bs*. P. Cimini *cond*. |
| Jan 21 | Mignon (1) | G. Besanzoni *ms*. F. Macbeth *s*. V. Lazzari *bs*. P. Cimini *cond*. |

NEW YORK CITY — LEXINGTON THEATER

Jan 29	Rigoletto (2)	F. Macbeth/A. Galli-Curci *s*. C. Pascova *ms*. T. Ruffo/C. Galeffi *b*. V. Lazzari *bs*. G. Marinuzzi/P. Cimini *cond*.
Feb 5	La sonnambula	A. Galli-Curci *s*. G. Rimini *b*. P. Cimini *cond*.
Feb 11	Il barbiere di Siviglia	A. Galli-Curci/F. Macbeth *s*. C. Galeffi/T. Ruffo *b*. V. Lazzari *bs*. V. Trevisan *bs*. G. Marinuzzi *cond*.
Feb 15	Lakmé	A. Galli-Curci *s*. D. Defrère *b*. G. Baklanov *b*.
Feb 19	La traviata	A. Galli-Curci *s*. C. Galeffi *b*. A. Smallens *cond*.

CHICAGO — ORCHESTRA HALL

| Apr 21 | Concert | |

HAVANA — TEATRO NACIONAL

May 6	Manon	R. Storchio *s*. C. Del Pozo *b*. V. Bettoni *bs*. A. Padovani *cond*.
May 18	La traviata	R. Storchio *s*. G. Danise *b*. A. Padovani *cond*.
May 26	La sonnambula	A. Ottein *s*. V. Bettoni *bs*. A. Padovani *cond*.
May 27	Tosca	O. Nieto *s*. G. Danise/E. Faticanti *b*. A. Padovani *cond*.
June 7	Il viandante	O. Nieto *s*. R. Toniolo *ms*. A. Padovani *cond*.
June 11	La bohème	R. Storchio *s*. E. Faticanti *b*. C. Del Pozo *b*. V. Bettoni *bs*. A. Padovani *cond*.

LIMA — TEATRO FORERO

July 9	Manon	R. Storchio *s*.
July 16	La traviata	R. Storchio *s*. E. Faticanti *b*.
July 23	Il barbiere di Siviglia	T. Paggi *s*. G. Danise *b*.
Aug 3	Tosca	A. Rossi-Oliver *s*. E. Faticanti *b*.
Aug 5	Rigoletto	T. Paggi *s*. E. Faticanti *b*.

PANAMA CITY

| | Concert | |

MEXICO CITY — TEATRO ARBEU

Sep 19	Manon (2)	O. Nieto *s*. M. Valle *b*. V. Lazzari *bs*. A. Jacchia *cond*.
Sep 21	La traviata (2)	G. Pareto *s*. A. Ordoñez *b*. A. Jacchia *cond*.
Sep 26	Il barbiere di Siviglia (1)	G. Pareto *s*. A. Ordoñez *b*. V. Lazzari *bs*. M. Santancana *bs*. G. Bavagnoli *cond*.
Oct 4	Rigoletto (2)	G. Pareto *s*. S. De Mette *ms*. C. Galeffi *b*. V. Lazzari *bs*. G. Bavagnoli *cond*.

MEXICO CITY — PLAZA EL TOREO
Oct 8   Manon (1)   O. Nieto s. M. Valle b. V. Lazzari bs.
                                            A. Jacchia cond.

MEXICO CITY — TEATRO ESPERANZA IRIS
Oct 10   Mignon (1)   O. Nieto s. G. Pareto s. V. Lazzari bs.
                                            A. Jacchia cond.
Oct 13   Tosca (3)   C. Muzio s. C. Galeffi b. A. Jacchia cond.
Oct 15   Il barbiere di Siviglia (2)   F. Anitua ms. C. Galeffi b. V. Lazzari bs. A. Didur
                                            bs. A. Jacchia cond.

CHICAGO — AUDITORIUM
Nov 21   Rigoletto (3)   E. Mason s. I. Pavloska/. . Paperte ms. J. Schwarz /
                                            G. Rimini b. V. Lazzari bs. G. Polacco cond.
Dec 20   La traviata (2)   A. Galli-Curci s. J. Schwarz b. G. Polacco cond.
Dec 24   Lucia di Lammermoor (1)   A. Galli-Curci s. G. Rimini b. V. Lazzari bs.
                                            P. Cimini cond.
Dec 29   Il barbiere di Siviglia (2)   A. Galli-Curci/M. Ivogün s. V. Ballester b.
                                            V. Lazzari bs. V. Trevisan bs. R. Ferrari cond.

1922

CHICAGO — AUDITORIUM (continued)
Jan 11   Lakmé (1)   A. Galli-Curci s. A. Maguenat b. G. Baklanov b.
                                            G. Grovlez cond.

NEW YORK CITY — LEXINGTON THEATER
Feb 15   La traviata   G. Pareto s. J. Schwarz b. G. Marinuzzi cond.
Feb 21   Manon   E. Mason s. A. Maguenat b. P. Payan bs.
                                            G. Grovlez cond.
Feb 26   Rigoletto   A. Galli-Curci s. C. Pascova ms. C. Galeffi b.
                                            V. Lazzari bs. G. Marinuzzi cond.

WINTER-AUTUMN 1922 — CONCERT TOUR
Feb   New York City   Hippodrome
Apr 25   New Orleans   Gipsy Smith Auditorium
May 5   Newark   Hippodrome
July 17   Rome   Palazzo del Campidoglio
Oct 12   New York City   Carnegie Hall
Oct 23   Auburn   Auditorium
Nov 8   Savannah   Auditorium
Nov 13   New Orleans   Jerusalem Temple
Nov 21   Denver   Memorial Hall
Nov 23   Colorado Springs
Nov 26   Pueblo   Memorial Hall
Dec 1   Havana   Teatro Nacional
Dec 3   Havana   Teatro Nacional
Dec 5   Havana   Teatro Nacional

CHICAGO — AUDITORIUM
Dec 15   Lucia di Lammermoor (1)   A. Galli-Curci s. G. Rimini b. V. Lazzari bs.
                                            P. Cimini cond.
Dec 24   La traviata (3)   A. Galli-Curci s. G. Rimini b. G. Polacco cond.
Dec 29   Manon (2)   A. Galli-Curci s. D. Defrère b. E. Cotreuil bs.
                                            R. Hageman cond.

1923

CHICAGO — AUDITORIUM

Jan 3	Il barbiere di Siviglia (1)	A. Galli-Curci *s.* G. Rimini *b.* V. Lazzari *bs.* V. Trevisan *bs.* P. Cimini *cond.*
Jan 7	Rigoletto (1)	A. Galli-Curci *s.* I. Bourskaya *ms.* C. Formichi *b.* V. Lazzari *bs.* E. Panizza *cond.*
Jan 11	Martha (2)	E. Mason *s.* I. Bourskaya *ms.* G. Rimini *b.* V. Trevisan *bs.* R. Hageman *cond.*

NEW YORK CITY — WALDORF ASTORIA HOTEL

Jan 23   Concert

BOSTON — OPERA

Jan 25	Rigoletto	F. Macbeth *s.* I. Pavloska *ms.* C. Formichi *b.* V. Lazzari *bs.* E. Panizza *cond.*

WINTER-SPRING 1923 — CONCERT TOUR

Feb 6	Little Rock	High School
Feb 15	Daytona Feb 28	Youngstown
Mar 4	Cleveland	Masonic Auditorium
Mar 19	Albany	Blecker Hall
Apr 4	Montgomery	

HAVANA — TEATRO NACIONAL

Apr 24	Il barbiere di Siviglia	J. Lucchese *s.* T. Ruffo *b.* P. Ludikar *bs.* N. Cervi *bs.* C. Peroni *cond.*
Apr 27	Lucia di Lammermoor	J. Lucchese *s.* M. Valle *b.* P. De Biasi *bs.* C. Peroni *cond.*

SPRING 1923 — CONCERT TOUR

May 7	Cedar Rapids	Sinclair Memorial Chapel
May 17	New York City	Madison Square Garden
May 25	Chicago	Auditorium
May 28	Buffalo	Statler Hotel
June 3	New York City	Carnegie Hall
June 10	Milwaukee	Pabst Theater

CHICAGO — RAVINIA PARK

June 23	La traviata (2)	G. Pareto *s.* G. Danise/V. Ballester *b.* G. Papi *cond.*
June 27	Lucia di Lammermoor (1)	G. Pareto *s.* G. Danise *b.* V. Lazzari *bs.* G. Papi *cond.*
June 30	Manon (2)	T. Sabanieeva *s.* D. Defrère *b.* L. Rothier *bs.* L. Hasselmans *cond.*
July 6	Il barbiere di Siviglia (2)	G. Pareto *s.* V. Ballester *b.* V. Lazzari *bs.* P. Ananian *bs.* G. Papi *cond.*
July 13	Lakmé (3)	G. Pareto *s.* D. Defrère *b.* L. Rothier *bs.* L. Hasselmans *cond.*
July 25	L'amico Fritz (2)	T. Sabanieeva *s.* M. Telva *ms.* G. Danise *b.* G. Papi *cond.*
Aug 3	Martha (2)	G. Pareto *s.* I. Bourskaya *ms.* V. Lazzari *bs.* V. Trevisan *bs.* L. Hasselmans *cond.*
Aug 8	a) L'elisir d'amore (2)	G. Pareto *s.* V. Ballester *b.* P. Ananian *bs.* G. Papi *cond.*
	b) Don Pasquale (2)	G. Pareto *s.* V. Ballester *b.* P. Ananian *bs.* G. Papi *cond.*

Aug 15   Romeo e Giulietta (2)   G. Pareto *s.* D. Defrère *b.* L. Rothier *bs.*
                                    L. D'Angelo *bs.* L. Hasselmans *cond.*

SUMMER-AUTUMN 1923 — CONCERT TOUR
Aug 16   Winona Lake   Tabernacle
Oct 1   New York City   Carnegie Hall
Oct 3   Huntington   City Hall
Oct 5   Grand Rapids   Regent Theater
Oct 8   Toronto   Massey Hall
Oct 10   Madison   Christ Presbyterian Church
Oct 12   Des Moines   Hoyt Sherman Theater
Oct 15   Detroit   Arcadia Auditorium
Oct 25   Tacoma   Tacoma Theater
Oct 27   Seattle   Ladies' Musical Club
Oct 31   Portland   Heilig Theater
Nov 4   San Francisco   Columbia Theater
Nov 5   Saginaw   Auditorium
Nov 6   Oakland   Auditorium
Nov 8   Sacramento   State Theater
Nov 11   San Francisco   Columbia Theater
Nov 12   Pomona   Bridges Hall
Nov 13   Los Angeles   Auditorium
Nov 19   Tucson   Safford Auditorium
Nov 22   Phoenix   High School Auditorium
Nov 24   Los Angeles   Trinity Auditorium

CHICAGO — AUDITORIUM
Dec 9   Martha (4)   E. Mason/G. Pareto/F. Macbeth *s.* I. Pavloska *ms.*
                                       G. Rimini *b.* V. Trevisan *bs.*
                                       E. Panizza/P. Cimini *cond.*
Dec 12   La traviata (? perf.)   A. Galli-Curci *s.* G. Rimini *b.* G. Polacco *cond.*
Dec 16   Lakmé (2)   A. Galli-Curci/G. Pareto *s.* D. Defrère *b.*
                                       G. Baklanov *b.* E. Panizza *cond.*
Dec 21   Il barbiere di Siviglia (2) A. Galli-Curci/G. Pareto *s.* G. Rimini *b.*
                                       V. Arimondi/F. Chaliapin *bs.* V. Trevisan *bs.*
                                       E. Panizza *cond.*
Dec 23   Lucia di Lammermoor (2)   A. Galli-Curci/T. Paggi *s.* A. Gandolfi *b.* V. Lazzari
                                       bs. P. Cimini *cond.*

1924

CHICAGO — AUDITORIUM
Jan 7   La sonnambula (2)   G. Pareto *s.* V. Lazzari *bs.* P. Cimini *cond.*

WINTER-SUMMER 1924 — CONCERT TOUR
Jan 28   Pittsburgh   Syria Mosque
Feb 1   Saginaw   Auditorium
Feb 3   Milwaukee   Pabst Theater
Feb 5   Akron   Auditorium
Feb 7   Cincinnati   Gibson Hotel
Feb 9   Chicago   Auditorium
Feb 11   Kenosha   Orpheum Theater
Feb 13   Louisville   Woman's Club
Feb 18   Reading   Strand Theater
Feb 20   Rochester   Eastman Theater
Feb 21   Buffalo   Statler Hotel
Feb 22   Huntington   City Hall

Feb 24	Boston	Opera
Mar 18	New Orleans	Auditorium
Mar 25	Kansas City	Schubert Theater
Apr 11	Springfield	Memorial Hall
Apr 13	Oakland	Auditorium
Apr 23	Houston	City Auditorium
Apr 25	Amarillo	Auditorium
May 2	Tulsa	Convention Hall
May 23	Ann Arbor	Auditorium
May 28	Ann Arbor	Auditorium
July 21	Naples	Teatro Politeama
Aug 15	Varese	Grand-Hotel
Aug 29	Sintra	Casino
Aug 31	Sintra	Casino

SAN FRANCISCO — OPERA

Sep 29	Manon (1)	T. Sabanieeva *s.* M. Picco *b.* P. Ananian *bs.* G. Merola *cond.*
Oct 2	L'amico Fritz (1)	T. Sabanieeva *s.* M. Picco *b.* P. Ananian *bs.* G. Merola *cond.*
Oct 4	La traviata (1)	C. Muzio *s.* G. De Luca *b.* G. Merola *cond.*

LOS ANGELES — AUDITORIUM

Oct 6	Manon (1)	T. Sabanieeva *s.* M. Picco *b.* P. Ananian *bs.* G. Merola *cond.*
Oct 8	L'amico Fritz (1)	T. Sabanieeva *s.* Q. Eybel *ms.* G. De Luca *b.* G. Merola *cond.*

AUTUMN 1924 — CONCERT TOUR

Oct 13	El Paso	Liberty Hall
Oct 17	Muncie	High School Auditorium
Oct 19	Chicago	Auditorium
Oct 22	Omaha	Brandeis Theater
Oct 24	Peoria	Amateur Musical Theater
Oct 28	Kansas City	Schubert Theater
Oct 31	Ames	State Gymnasium
Nov 3	Louisville	Woman's Club Auditorium
Nov 5	Springfield	Memorial Hall
Nov 7	Lynenburg	Academy
Nov 11	Washington	Poli's Theater
Nov 12	Baltimore	Lyric Theater
Nov 14	Philadelphia	Academy of Music
Nov 17	Lawrence	Winter Garden
Nov 21	Syracuse	Mizpah Auditorium
Nov 24	Sheboygan	High School Auditorium
Nov 26	Kenosha	Orpheum Theater
Nov 29	Muncie	High School Auditorium

CHICAGO — AUDITORIUM

Dec 2	La traviata (4)	C. Muzio *s.* G. Pareto *s.* J. Schwarz *b.* P. Cimini *cond.*
Dec 7	Il barbiere di Siviglia (3)	G. Pareto/E. De Hidalgo *s.* G. Rimini *b.* F. Chaliapin *bs.* V. Trevisan *bs.* P. Cimini *cond.*
Dec 11	Lakmé (3)	G. Pareto/E. De Hidalgo *s.* D. Defrère *b.* E. Cotreuil *bs.* G. Baklanov *b.* C. Lauwers *cond.*
Dec 19	Fra Diavolo (2)	E. Mason *s.* F. Perini *ms.* E. Cotreuil *bs.* V. Lazzari *bs.* V. Trevisan *bs.* P. Cimini *cond.*

1925

CHICAGO — AUDITORIUM

Jan 7   Lucia di Lammermoor (1)   F. Macbeth *s*. G. Rimini *b*. V. Lazzari *bs*.
                                    P. Cimini *cond*.

Jan 14   Martha (2)   E. Mason *s*. F. Perini *ms*. V. Lazzari *bs*. V. Trevisan
                        bs. R. Moranzoni *cond*.

WINTER-SPRING 1925 — CONCERT TOUR

Jan 25	Milwaukee	Pabst Theater
Jan 26	Racine	Orpheum Theater
Jan 28	Grand Rapids	Powers' Theater
Jan 30	Lansing	Auditorium
Feb 2	Flint	Philharmonic Hall
Feb 3	Galesburg	
Feb 4	Detroit	Orchestra hall
Feb 6	Toledo	High School Auditorium
Feb 9	New York City	Carnegie Hall
Feb 11	New York City	Metropolitan Opera House
Feb 16	Palm Beach	Society of Arts
Feb 24	St. Louis	Odeon Theater
Feb 26	Pittsburgh	Syria Mosque
Mar 1	Cleveland	Masonic Hall
Mar 2	Galesburg	
Mar 4	Akron	Waldorf Theater
Mar 5	Cleveland	Masonic Hall
Mar 8	Pueblo	Memorial Hall
Mar 10	Cedar Falls	Teachers College
Mar 11	Colorado Springs	Burns Theater
Mar 16	Denver	Municipal Auditorium
Mar 19	Chicago	Orchestra Hall
Mar 22	Topeka	Grand-Theater
Mar 25	Wichita	Forum
Mar 30	Fort Worth	Auditorium
Apr 1	San Antonio	Beethoven Hall
Apr 4	Bisbee	High School Auditorium
Apr 7	Los Angeles	Auditorium
Apr 8	Los Angeles	Gamut Club
Apr 9	San Diego	Spreckels Theater
Apr 12	Los Angeles	Del Rey Palisades Amphitheater
Apr 13	Oakland	Auditorium
Apr 16	Los Angeles	Auditorium
Apr 17	Pomona	High School Auditorium
Apr 19	San Francisco	Columbia Theater
Apr 21	San Jose	Auditorium
Apr 26	San Francisco	Columbia Theater
Apr 29	Vancouver	Orpheum Theater
May 5	Seattle	Presbyterian Church
May 6	Bellingham	
May 9	San Francisco	Seven Arts Club

CHICAGO — RAVINIA PARK

June 28   Martha (1)   F. Macbeth *s*. I. Bourskaya *ms*. V. Lazzari *bs*.
                        V. Trevisan *bs*. L. Hasselmans *cond*.

July 4   Manon (3)   L. Bori *s*. D. Defrère *b*. L. Rothier *bs*.
                      L. Hasselmans *cond*.

July 9	a) L'elisir d'amore (1)	E. De Hidalgo *s*. M. Basiola *b*. V. Trevisan *bs*. G. Papi *cond*.
	b) Don Pasquale (1)	E. De Hidalgo *s*. M. Basiola *b*. V. Trevisan *bs*. G. Papi *cond*.
July 11	Il barbiere di Siviglia (1)	E. De. Hidalgo *s*. G. Rimini *b*. L. Rothier *bs*. V. Trevisan *bs*. G. Papi *cond*.
July 17	La traviata (2)	L. Bori *s*. M. Basiola *b*. G. Papi *cond*.
Aug 7	Lakmé (2)	E. De Hidalgo *s*. D. Defrère *b*. L. Rothier *bs*. L. Hasselmans *cond*.
Aug 13	Lucia di Lammermoor (2)	F. Macbeth/E. De Hidalgo *s*. V. Lazzari *bs*. G. Rimini/M. Basiola *b*. G. Papi *cond*.

SAN FRANCISCO — OPERA

| Sep 19 | Manon (2) | R. Torri *s*. A. Nicolich *b*. M. Journet *bs*. G. Merola *cond*. |

OAKLAND — K.G.S. STUDIOS

| Sep 23 | Concert | |

SAN FRANCISCO — OPERA

Sep 24	Il barbiere di Siviglia (2)	E. De Hidalgo *s*. R. Stracciari *b*. M. Journet *bs*. V. Trevisan *bs*. P. Cimini *cond*.
Sep 28	La traviata (1)	E. De Hidalgo *s*. R. Stracciari *b*. G. Merola *cond*.
Sep 30	Martha (1)	E. De Hidalgo *s*. E. Marlo *ms*. M. Journet *bs*. V. Trevisan *bs*. P. Cimini *cond*.

LOS ANGELES — AUDITORIUM

| Oct 6 | Manon (1) | R. Torri *s*. A. Nicolich *b*. M. Journet *bs*. G. Merola *cond*. |
| Oct 9 | Il barbiere di Siviglia (1) | E. De Hidalgo *s*. R. Stracciari *b*. M. Journet *bs*. V. Trevisan *bs*. P. Cimini *cond*. |

AUTUMN 1925 — CONCERT TOUR

Oct 11	Los Angeles	KFI Studios
Oct 12	Globe	High School Auditorium
Oct 13	Buffalo	Music Hall
Oct 15	El Paso	High School Auditorium
Oct 18	Chicago	Auditorium
Oct 22	San Antonio	Auditorium
Oct 23	Atlanta	Auditorium
Oct 25	Fort Worth	Auditorium
Oct 28	New Orleans	Jerusalem Temple
Nov 1	New York City	Carnegie Hall
Nov 4	Washington	Poli's Theater
Nov 6	Baltimore	Lyric Theater

CHICAGO — AUDITORIUM

| Nov 9 | Martha (5) | E. Mason/F. Macbeth *s*. I. Pavloska *ms*. V. Lazzari *bs*. V. Trevisan *bs*. R. Moranzoni *cond*. |

AUTUMN 1925 — CONCERT TOUR

Nov 12	Rochester	Eastman Theater
Nov 13	Buffalo	Music Hall
Nov 15	Hartford	Capitol Theater
Nov 16	South Bend	Palais Royal
Nov 23	Philadelphia	Forum
Nov 27	Cleveland	Masonic Hall

CHICAGO — AUDITORIUM
Nov 30   Concert
Dec 8   Lucia di Lammermoor (1)   T. Dal Monte *s.* R. Bonelli *b.* V. Lazzari *bs.*
                                        F. St. Leger *cond.*
Dec 9   La traviata (2)   C. Muzio *s.* R. Bonelli *b.* R. Moranzoni *cond.*

1926

CHICAGO — AUDITORIUM
Jan 18   Il barbiere di Siviglia (2)   M. Garrison *s.* G. Rimini *b.* V. Lazzari *bs.*
                                           V. Trevisan *bs.* R. Moranzoni *cond.*

BOSTON — OPERA
Jan 27   La traviata (1)   C. Muzio *s.* R. Bonelli *b.* R. Moranzoni *cond.*

WINTER 1926 — CONCERT TOUR
Jan 31   New York City   Carnegie Hall
Feb 2   Pittsburgh   Syria Mosque
Feb 4   Philadelphia   Academy of Music
Feb 8   Tampa   Centro Asturiano
Feb 10   Tampa   Centro Asturiano
F' 5 11   Daytona   Auditorium
Feb 13   Jacksonville   Auditorium
Feb 15   Memphis   Auditorium

CLEVELAND — PALACE THEATER
Feb 17   Martha (1)   E. Mason *s.* I. Pavloska *ms.* V. Lazzari *bs.*
                                           V. Trevisan *bs.* R. Moranzoni *cond.*

WINTER-SPRING 1926 — CONCERT TOUR
Feb 19   Rockford   Shrine Temple
Feb 21   Milwaukee   Pabst Theater
Feb 23   St. Paul   People's Church
Feb 25   Fargo   State Theater
Mar 1   Joliet   High School Auditorium
Mar 5   Kansas City   Convention Hall
Mar 8   San Antonio   Beethoven Hall
Mar 15   Alexandria   Louisiana College
Mar 18   Cincinnati   Emery Auditorium
Mar 22   Birmingham   Auditorium
Mar 25   Lawrence   Colonial Theater
Mar 26   Troy   Music Hall
Mar 28   Brockton   City Theater
Mar 30   Brooklyn   Roosevelt Hotel
Apr 1   New York City   Bellevue Hospital
Apr 5   Montreal   Windsor Hall

LECCE — POLITEAMA GRECO
May 9   Lucia di Lammermoor   M. Gentile *s.* G. Viviani *b.* G. Falconi *cond.*
May 15   Il barbiere di Siviglia   T. Paggi *s.* R. Stracciari *b.* G. Falconi *cond.*

SAN FRANCISCO — OPERA
Sep 21   Martha (1)   F. Macbeth *s.* E. Marlo *ms.* M. Journet *bs.*
                                       V. Trevisan *bs.* P. Cimini *cond.*
Sep 25   Il barbiere di Siviglia (1)   F. Macbeth *s.* R. Bonelli *b.* M. Journet *bs.*
                                       V. Trevisan *bs.* P. Cimini *cond.*

Sep 29	Rigoletto (1)	L. Melius *s*. E. Marlo *ms*. R. Bonelli *b*. M. Journet *bs*. P. Cimini *cond*.
Oct 2	Fra Diavolo (1)	F. Macbeth. *s*. E. Marlo *ms*. C. Bulotti *t*. V. Lazzari *bs*. V. Trevisan *bs*. P. Cimini *cond*.
Oct 5	Lucia di Lammermoor (1)	L. Melius *s*. R. Bonelli *b*. A. Nicolich *b*. P. Cimini *cond*.

LOS ANGELES — SHRINE AUDITORIUM

Oct 8	Martha (1)	F. Macbeth *s*. K. Meisle *ms*. R. Bonelli *b*. V. Trevisan *bs*. R. Hageman *cond*.
Oct 9	Rigoletto (1)	L. Melius *s*. K. Meisle *ms*. R. Bonelli *b*. V. Lazzari *bs*. P. Cimini *cond*.
Oct 12	Il barbiere di Siviglia (1)	L. Melius *s*. G. Rimini *b*. V. Lazzari *bs*. V. Trevisan *bs*. R. Hageman *cond*.

AUTUMN 1926 — CONCERT TOUR

Oct 24	Chicago	Auditorium
Oct 28	Grand Rapids	Philharmonic Hall
Oct 31	New York City	Carnegie Hall
Nov 3	Bloomington	Coliseum Theater
Nov 6	Lansing	City Auditorium
Nov 10	Rockford	Shrine Temple
Nov 12	Columbus	Memorial Hall
Nov 20	Washington	Memorial Hall
Nov 22	Philadelphia	Academy of Music
Nov 25	Detroit	Orchestra Hall
Nov 30	Cleveland	Masonic Hall
Dec 2	Rochester	Eastman Theater
Dec 5	Milwaukee	Pabst Theater

CHICAGO — AUDITORIUM

Dec 7	La sonnambula (2)	T. Dal Monte/F. Macbeth *s*. V. Lazzari *bs*. R. Moranzoni *cond*.
Dec 12	Martha (2)	E. Mason/F. Macbeth *s*. I. Pavloska/ L. D. Jackson *ms*. V. Lazzari *bs*. V. Trevisan *bs*. R. Moranzoni *cond*.
Dec 18	L'elisir d'amore (2)	F. Macbeth *s*. G. Rimini *b*. V. Trevisan *bs*. R. Moranzoni *cond*.
Dec 26	La traviata (3)	C. Muzio *s*. R. Bonelli *b*. R. Moranzoni *cond*.
Dec 31	Don Giovanni (2)	R. Raisa *s*. L. Loring *s*. E. Mason *s*. V. Marcoux *b*. V. Lazzari *bs*. V. Trevisan *bs*. A. Kipnis *bs*. G. Polacco *cond*.

1927

WINTER-SPRING 1927 — CONCERT TOUR

Jan 31	Saginaw	Auditorium
Feb 2	Kalamazoo	Philharmonic Hall
Feb 6	Brockton	City Theater
Feb 12	Miami	White Temple
Feb 14	Tampa	Municipal Auditorium
Feb 16	Lakeland	Auditorium
Feb 17	Tampa	Gordon Keller Hospital
Feb 18	St. Petersburg	Congregational Church
Feb 24	Denver	Auditorium
Feb 28	San Francisco	Auditorium
Mar 1	Fresno	High School Auditorium

Mar 3	Los Angeles	Philharmonic Auditorium
Mar 7	Portland	Auditorium
Mar 9	Tacoma	Baptist Auditorium
Mar 11	Spokane	Masonic Temple
Mar 14	Seattle	Metropolitan Theater
Mar 20	Oakland	Auditorium
Mar 22	San Jose	San Jose College
Mar 27	Los Angeles	Philharmonic Auditorium
Apr 2	Sacramento	New Auditorium
Apr 16	El Paso	Liberty Hall
Apr 18	San Antonio	Auditorium
Apr 20	Houston	City Auditorium
Apr 27	Wichita	Forum
May 1	Indianapolis	Murat Theater
May 16	London	Queen's Hall
June 8	Madrid	Teatro de la Zarzuela
June 11	Rome	Augusteo

BUENOS AIRES — TEATRO COLÓN

July 7   L'elisir d'amore (4)   T. Dal Monte/L. Romelli s. G. Vanelli b. G. Azzolini bs. G. Marinuzzi cond.

July 10   Il barbiere di Siviglia (3)   T. Dal Monte s. B. Franci/C. Galeffi b. E. Pinza/T. Pasero bs. G. Azzolini bs. E. Panizza/A. Sabino cond.

July 24   La traviata (3)   C. Muzio s. C. Galeffi b. G. Marinuzzi cond.

July 29   Manon (1)   F. Heldy s. H. Girard b. M. Journet bs. E. Panizza cond.

MONTEVIDEO — TEATRO SOLIS

Aug 8   Concert

RIO DE JANEIRO — TEATRO MUNICIPAL

Aug 20   L'elisir d'amore (2)   T. Dal Monte s. G. Vanelli b. G. Azzolini bs. G. Marinuzzi cond.

Aug 22   Il barbiere di Siviglia (1)   T. Dal Monte s. C. Galeffi b. E. Pinza bs. G. Azzolini bs. E. Panizza cond.

Aug 27   Manon (1)   F. Heldy s. H. Girard b. M. Journet bs. E. Panizza cond.

Sep 2   La traviata (1)   C. Muzio s. B. Franci b. G. Marinuzzi cond.

SÃO PAULO — TEATRO MUNICIPAL

Sep 10   L'elisir d'amore (1)   T. Dal Monte s. G. Vanelli b. G. Azzolini bs. G. Marinuzzi cond.

Sep 13   Il barbiere di Siviglia (1)   T. Dal Monte s. C. Galeffi b. E. Pinza bs. G. Azzolini bs. E. Panizza cond.

Sep 15   La traviata (1)   C. Muzio s. B. Franci b. G. Marinuzzi cond.

CHICAGO — AUDITORIUM

Oct 23   Concert

MILWAUKEE — AUDITORIUM

Nov 1   Concert

CHICAGO — AUDITORIUM

Nov 3   La traviata (3)   C. Muzio s. R. Bonelli b. G. Polacco/H. Weber cond.

TULSA — CONVENTION HALL
Nov 7   Concert

VINCENNES — PANTHEON THEATER
Nov 10   Concert

CHICAGO — AUDITORIUM
Nov 12   Lucia di Lammermoor (1)   T. Dal Monte *s.* L. Montesanto *b.* V. Lazzari *bs.*
                                      G. Polacco *cond.*
Nov 15   Martha (2)   E. Mason *s.* I. Pavloska *ms.* V. Lazzari *bs.*
                                      V. Trevisan *bs.* R. Moranzoni *cond.*

AUTUMN 1927 — CONCERT TOUR
Nov 18   Memphis   Auditorium
Nov 21   New York City   Carnegie Hall
Nov 25   Toledo   Rivoli Theater
Nov 27   Boston   Symphony Hall
Dec 3   Indianapolis   Murat Theater

CHICAGO — AUDITORIUM
Dec 5   Il barbiere di Siviglia (2)   T. Dal Monte *s.* G. Rimini *b.* V. Lazzari *bs./V.*
                                         Marcoux *b.* V. Trevisan *bs.* R. Moranzoni *cond.*
Dec 13   Linda di Chamonix (2)   T. Dal Monte *s.* L. D. Jackson *ms.* L. Montesanto *b.*
                                         V. Lazzari *bs.* V. Trevisan *bs.* R. Moranzoni *cond.*

AUTUMN 1927-WINTER 1928 — CONCERT TOUR
Dec 15   Chicago   Blackstone Hotel

1928

CONCERT TOUR (continued)
Jan 22   Los Angeles   Philharmonic Auditorium
Jan 30   Detroit   Arcadia Auditorium
Feb 3   St. Louis   Odeon Theater
Feb 4   St. Louis   Odeon Theater
Feb 6   Pittsburgh   Syria Mosque
Feb 13   Minneapolis   University
Feb 22   Youngstown   Stambaugh Auditorium
Feb 24   Cleveland   Masonic Hall
Feb 27   New York City   Gallo's Theater
Mar 11   London   Albert Hall

ROME — TEATRO REALE DELL'OPERA
Mar 17   L'elisir d'amore (4)   L. Pasini *s.* V. Weinberg *b.* G. Azzolini/A. Pacini *bs.*
                                     G. Bavagnoli/G. Marinuzzi *cond.*
Mar 31   La sonnambula (3)   T. Dal Monte/L. Pasini *s.* A. Mongelli *bs.*
                                     G. Marinuzzi *cond.*
Apr 14   Lucia di Lammermoor (1)   L. Pasini *s.* B. Franci *b.* A. Mongelli *bs.*
                                     G. Marinuzzi *cond.*
Apr 19   La traviata (3)   C. Muzio *s.* R. Stracciari *b.* G. Marinuzzi *cond.*

FLORENCE — POLITEAMA FIORENTINO
Apr 24   L'elisir d'amore (3)   L. Pasini *s.* F. Ronchi *b.* G. Quinzi-Tapergi *bs.*
                                     F. Ghione *cond.*

SPRING 1928 — CONCERT TOUR

May 7	Bologna	Teatro Comunale
May 9	Turin	Teatro Regio
May 13	London	Albert Hall
May	Bari	Teatro Petruzzelli
May	Taranto	Teatro Orfeo
June 30	Turin	Teatro Regio

CHICAGO — RAVINIA PARK

Aug 4	L'elisir d'amore (2)	F. Macbeth *s*. M. Basiola *b*. V. Trevisan *bs*. G. Papi *cond*.
Aug 8	Martha (2)	F. Macbeth *s*. I. Bourskaya/G. Swarthout *ms*. V. Lazzari *bs*. V. Trevisan *bs*. L. Hasselmans *cond*.
Aug 11	Il barbiere di Siviglia (1)	F. Macbeth *s*. M. Basiola *b*. V. Lazzari *bs*. V. Trevisan *bs*. G. Papi *cond*.
Aug 15	Lucia di Lammermoor (2)	F. Macbeth *s*. M. Basiola *b*. V. Lazzari *bs*. G. Papi *cond*.
Aug 18	Manon (1)	Y. Gall *s*. D. Defrère *b*. L. Rothier *bs*. L. Hasselmans *cond*.
Aug 21	Don Pasquale (2)	F. Macbeth *s*. M. Basiola *b*. V. Trevisan *bs*. G. Papi *cond*.
Aug 25	La traviata (1)	Q. Mario *s*. G. Danise *b*. G. Papi *cond*.
Sep 3	a) Don Pasquale, Act II	F. Macbeth *s*. M. Basiola *b*. V. Trevisan *bs*. G. Papi *cond*.
	b) Martha, Act III	F. Macbeth *s*. G. Swarthout *ms*. V. Lazzari *bs*. V. Trevisan *bs*. L. Hasselmans *cond*.

AUTUMN 1928 — CONCERT TOUR

Oct 18	Los Angeles	Shrine Auditorium
Oct 24	Joplin	Memorial Hall
Oct 26	Cincinnati	Taft Auditorium
Oct 28	New Orleans	Auditorium
Nov 1	Detroit	Orchestra Hall
Nov 11	New York City	Carnegie Hall
Nov 18	Hartford	Capitol Theater
Nov 20	Rockford	Shrine Temple
Nov 22	Lexington	Woodland Auditorium
Nov 25	Boston	Symphony Hall
Nov 28	Toronto	Massey Hall

CHICAGO — AUDITORIUM

Dec 6	Il barbiere di Siviglia (3)	M. Salvi *s*. R. Bonelli *b*. V. Lazzari *bs*. V. Trevisan *bs*. R. Moranzoni *cond*.
Dec 9	Lakmé (2)	A. Mock *s*. D. Defrère *b*. E. Cotreuil *bs*. C. Lauwers *cond*.

MADISON — STOCK PAVILION

Dec 10	Concert

CHICAGO — AUDITORIUM

Dec 12	Don Giovanni (2)	F. Leider *s*. H. Burke *s*. E. Mason *s*. V. Marcoux *b*. A. Kipnis *bs*. V. Lazzari *bs*. C. Baromeo *bs*. G. Polacco *cond*.
Dec 22	L'elisir d'amore (3)	M. Salvi *s*. B. Hill *b*. V. Trevisan *bs*. R. Moranzoni *cond*.

1929

WINTER-SPRING 1929 — CONCERT TOUR

Feb 6	Tucson	Music Temple
Feb 12	Los Angeles	Philharmonic Auditorium
Feb 14	Oakland	Auditorium
Feb 19	San Francisco	Auditorium
Feb 21	Sacramento	Memorial Auditorium
Feb 25	Portland	Auditorium
Feb 27	Seattle	Meany Hall
Mar 1	Victoria	Dreamland Auditorium
Mar 6	Eugene	McArthur Court
Mar 9	Salt Lake City	City Tabernacle
Mar 11	Stockton	High School Auditorium
Mar 15	Long Beach	Municipal Auditorium
Mar 17	San Francisco	Auditorium
Mar 21	Pasadena	Junior College Auditorium
Mar 27	Edmonton	Music Hall
Mar 29	Calgary	Victoria Pavilion
Apr 1	Winnipeg	Central Church
Apr 4	Chicago	Orchestra Hall
Apr 7	Philadelphia	Academy of Music
Apr 12	Richmond	City Auditorium
Apr 15	Waterbury	Buckingham Hall
Apr 23	Havana	Teatro Nacional
Apr 26	Havana	Teatro Nacional

NAPLES — TEATRO SAN CARLO
May 16   L'elisir d'amore (6)   J. Novotna *s*. L. Paci *b*. G. Cirino *bs*.
E. Vitale *cond.*

FLORENCE — POLITEAMA FIORENTINO
May 31   Lucia di Lammermoor (2)   L. Pagliughi *s*. E. Molinari *b*. G. Vaghi *bs*.
D. Messina *cond.*

SAN FRANCISCO — OPERA
Sep 14   L'elisir d'amore (1)   N. Morgana *s*. M. Picco *b*. P. Malatesta *bs*.
P. Cimini *cond.*

Sep 18   Il barbiere di Siviglia (1)   N. Morgana *s*. G. De Luca *b*. L. Rothier *bs*.
P. Malatesta *bs*. P. Cimini *cond.*

Sep 23   Martha (1)   Q. Mario *s*. L. Ivey *ms*. G. De Luca *b*. P. Malatesta
bs. K. Riedel *cond.*

Sep 27   Don Pasquale (1)   N. Morgana *s*. G. De Luca *b*. P. Malatesta *bs*.
A. Dell'Orefice *cond.*

Sep 30   Manon (1)   Q. Mario *s*. G. De Luca *b*. L. Rothier *bs*.
G. Merola *cond.*

LOS ANGELES — SHRINE AUDITORIUM
Oct 4   L'elisir d'amore (1)   N. Morgana *s*. M. Picco *b*. P. Malatesta *bs*.
P. Cimini *cond.*

Oct 6   Martha (1)   Q. Mario *s*. L. Ivey *ms*. G. De Luca *b*.
P. Malatesta *bs*. P. Cimini *cond.*

Oct 10   Il barbiere di Siviglia (1)   N. Morgana *s*. G. De Luca *b*. L. Rothier *bs*.
P. Malatesta *bs*. P. Cimini *cond.*

Oct 12   Manon (1)   Q. Mario *s*. G. De Luca *b*. L. Rothier *bs*.
G. Merola *cond.*

BARCELONA — TEATRO DEL LICEO

Nov 20   L'elisir d'amore (3)   L. Pasini *s.* P. Lombardo b./*bs.* M. Fiore *bs.*
A. Padovani *cond.*

Nov 28   Concert

MILAN — TEATRO ALLA SCALA

Dec 11   L'elisir d'amore (4)   A. Saraceni *s.* G. Vanelli *b.* S. Baccaloni *bs.*
G. Del Campo *cond.*

Dec 19   Don Giovanni (2)   G. Arangi Lombardi *s.* G. Cigna *s.* M. Favero *s.*
M. Stabile *b.* F. Autori *bs.* S. Baccaloni *bs.*
A. Marone *bs.* A. Guarnieri *cond.*

NAPLES — TEATRO SAN CARLO

Dec 27   L'elisir d'amore (3)   A. Gargiulo *s.* L. Paci *b.* V. Bettoni *bs.*
E. Vitale *cond.*

1930

ROME — TEATRO REALE DELL'OPERA

Jan 2   L'elisir d'amore (3)   L. Pasini *s.* E. Ghirardini *b.* A. Pacini/G. Cirino *bs.*
G. Santini *cond.*

FLORENCE — TEATRO IMPERIALE

Jan 8   Concert

ROME — TEATRO REALE DELL'OPERA

Jan 10   Don Pasquale (2)   B. Sayão *s.* R. Stracciari *b.*
S. Baccaloni/U. Di Lelio *bs.* G. Marinuzzi *cond.*

CHICAGO — CIVIC THEATER

Jan 25   Il barbiere di Siviglia (1)   M. Salvi *s.* G. Rimini *b.* V. Lazzari *bs.* V. Trevisan
bs. R. Moranzoni *cond.*

Jan 26   Lucia di Lammermoor (1)   M. Salvi *s.* G. Rimini *b.* C. Baromeo *bs.* F. St.
Leger *cond.*

Jan 28   La traviata (2)   C. Muzio *s.* R. Bonelli *b.* R. Moranzoni *cond.*

Jan 30   Don Pasquale (1)   M. Salvi *s.* G. Rimini *b.* V. Trevisan *bs.*
R. Moranzoni *cond.*

ROCHESTER — EASTMAN THEATER

Feb 8   Concert

NEW YORK CITY — CARNEGIE HALL

Feb 10   Concert

DETROIT — CIVIC AUDITORIUM

Feb 18   Lucia di Lammermoor (1)   M. Salvi *s.* B. Hill *b.* V. Lazzari *bs.*
F. St. Leger *cond.*

Feb 22   Don Pasquale (1)   M. Salvi *s.* G. Rimini *b.* V. Trevisan *bs.*
F. St. Leger *cond.*

COLUMBUS — AUDITORIUM

Feb 24   Lucia di Lammermoor (1)   M. Salvi *s.* R. Bonelli *b.* V. Lazzari *bs.*
F. St. Leger *cond.*

LOUISVILLE — MEMORIAL AUDITORIUM

Feb 27   Lucia di Lammermoor (1)   M. Salvi *s.* G. Rimini *b.* V. Lazzari *bs.*
F. St. Leger *cond.*

JACKSON — CITY AUDITORIUM
Mar 2   Lucia di Lammermoor (1)   M. Salvi *s*. R. Bonelli *b*. V. Lazzari *bs*.
                                       F. St. Leger *cond*.

NEW ORLEANS — AUDITORIUM
Mar 5   Lucia di Lammermoor (1)   M. Salvi *s*. G. Rimini *b*. V. Lazzari *bs*.
                                       F. St. Leger *cond*.

MEMPHIS — AUDITORIUM
Mar 8   Lucia di Lammermoor (1)   M. Salvi *s*. R. Bonelli *b*. V. Lazzari *bs*.
                                       F. St. Leger *cond*.

DALLAS — STATE FAIR AUDITORIUM
Mar 12   Lucia di Lammermoor (1)   M. Salvi *s*. G. Rimini *b*. V. Lazzari *bs*.
                                       F. St. Leger *cond*.

SAN ANTONIO — MUNICIPAL AUDITORIUM
Mar 14   Lucia di Lammermoor (1)   M. Salvi *s*. G. Rimini *b*. V. Lazzari *bs*.
                                       F. St. Leger *cond*.

TULSA — CONVENTION HALL
Mar 18   Lucia di Lammermoor (1)   M. Salvi *s*. R. Bonelli *b*. V. Lazzari *bs*.
                                       F. St.Leger *cond*.

MINNEAPOLIS — AUDITORIUM
Mar 21   Lucia di Lammermoor (1)   M. Salvi *s*. R. Bonelli *b*. V. Lazzari *bs*.
                                       F. St. Leger *cond*.

OMAHA — COLISEUM THEATER
Mar 26   Lucia di Lammermoor (1)   M. Salvi *s*. R. Bonelli *b*. V. Lazzari *bs*.
                                       E. Cooper *cond*.

KANSAS CITY — CONVENTION HALL
Mar 28   Lucia di Lammermoor (1)   M. Salvi *s*. R. Bonelli *b*. V. Lazzari *bs*.
                                       E. Cooper *cond*.

SPRING 1930 — CONCERT TOUR
Apr 4   Los Angeles   Philharmonic Hall
Apr 7   Los Angeles   Shrine Auditorium
Apr 16   Cleveland   Singers Club
Apr 20   Chicago   Civic Theater
Apr 28   Philadelphia   Academy of Music
May 1   New York City   N.B.C. Studios
May 20   Paris   Palais Chaillot

BUENOS AIRES — TEATRO COLÓN
June 17   L'elisir d'amore (5)   L. Romelli *s*. E. Ghirardini *b*. S. Baccaloni *bs*.
                                        E. Panizza *cond*.
June 24   Don Pasquale (3)   I. Marengo *s*. E. Ghirardini *b*. S. Baccaloni *bs*.
                                        F. Calusio *cond*.
July 13   Concert
July 15   Manon (4)   M. Nespoulous *s*. E. Ghirardini *b*. C. Walter *bs*.
                                        F. Paolantonio *cond*.
July 18   Il barbiere di Siviglia (4) L. Romelli *s*. C. Galeffi *b*. F. Chaliapin *bs*.
                                        S. Baccaloni *bs*. F. Calusio *cond*.
Aug 1   Sadko (3)   M. Nespoulous *s*. A. Cravcenco *ms*. M. Falliani *ms*.
                                        G. Thill *t*. V. Damiani *b*. G. Lanskoy *bs*.
                                        E. Panizza *cond*.

247

Aug 3   Concert
Aug 10   Concert

MONTEVIDEO — TEATRO URQUIZA
Aug 23   Concert
Aug 25   Il barbiere di Siviglia   L. Romelli s. C. Galeffi b. F. Chaliapin bs.
                                       S. Baccaloni bs.

SANTIAGO — TEATRO MUNICIPAL
Sep 9   L'elisir d'amore (2)   M. Salvi s. L. Cérésole b. E. Faticanti b.
                                       A. Padovani cond.
Sep 16   Concert
Sep 20   Il barbiere di Siviglia (2) M. Salvi s. C. Morelli b. U. Di Lelio/G. Mansueto
                                       bs. M. Fiore bs. A. Padovani cond.
Sep 23   Manon (2)   M. Nespoulous s. L. Cérésole b. U. Di Lelio bs.
                                       A. D'Ayala cond.
Sep 26   Lucia di Lammermoor (2)   M. Salvi s. B. Franci b. P. Friggi bs.
                                       A. Padovani cond.

BUENOS AIRES — TEATRO COLÓN
Oct 5   Lucia di Lammermoor (2)   L. Romelli s. V. Damiani b. C. Walter bs.
                                       F. Paolantonio cond.
Oct 7   Il barbiere di Siviglia (1) L. Romelli s. C. Galeffi b. T. Pasero bs. A. Muzio
                                       bs. F. Paolantonio cond.
Oct 8   Concert

FLORENCE — POLITEAMA FIORENTINO
Dec 25   Concert

1931

CHICAGO — CIVIC THEATER
Jan 8   Don Giovanni (2)   F. Leider s. H. Burke s. M. Rajdl s.
                                       V. Marcoux b. V. Lazzari bs. S. Baccaloni bs.
                                       C. Baromeo bs. E. Cooper cond.
Jan 13   Mignon (12)   C. Glade ms. M. Salvi s. C. Baromeo bs.
                                       E. Cooper cond.
Jan 24   La traviata (1)   C. Muzio s. R. Bonelli b. R. Moranzoni cond.

PITTSBURGH — SYRIA MOSQUE
Jan 26   Concert

BOSTON — OPERA
Feb 1   La traviata (1)   C. Muzio s. R. Bonelli b. R. Moranzoni cond.

PITTSBURGH — SYRIA MOSQUE
Feb 9   Lucia di Lammermoor (1)   M. Salvi s. R. Bonelli b. V. Lazzari bs.
                                       F. St. Leger cond.

LOUISVILLE — MEMORIAL AUDITORIUM
Feb 11   Mignon (1)   C. Glade ms. M. Salvi s. C. Baromeo bs.
                                       E. Cooper cond.

MEMPHIS — AUDITORIUM
Feb 13   Mignon (1)   C. Glade ms. M. Salvi s. C. Baromeo bs.
                                       E. Cooper cond.

CHRONOLOGY

TULSA — CONVENTION HALL

Feb 16   Mignon (1)   C. Glade *ms*. M. Salvi *s*. C. Baromeo *bs*.
                                                E. Cooper *cond*.

DALLAS — FAIR PARK AUDITORIUM

Feb 18   Mignon (1)   C. Glade *ms*. M. Salvi *s*. C. Baromeo *bs*.
                                                E. Cooper *cond*.

LOS ANGELES — SHRINE AUDITORIUM

Feb 23   La traviata (1)   C. Muzio *s*. J. C. Thomas *b*. R. Moranzoni *cond*.

Feb 27   Lucia di Lammermoor (1)   M. Salvi *s*. R. Bonelli *b*. C. Baromeo *bs*.
                                                F. St. Leger *cond*.

SAN FRANCISCO — OPERA

Mar 1   La traviata (1)   C. Muzio *s*. J. C. Thomas *b*. R. Moranzoni *cond*.
Mar 5   Lucia di Lammermoor (1)   M. Salvi *s*. R. Bonelli *b*. V. Lazzari *bs*.
                                                F. St.Leger *cond*.

SEATTLE — CIVIC AUDITORIUM

Mar 9   La traviata (1)   C. Muzio *s*. J. C. Thomas *b*. R. Moranzoni *cond*.
Mar 12   Mignon (1)   C. Glade *ms*. M. Salvi *s*. C. Baromeo *bs*.
                                                E. Cooper *cond*.

PORTLAND — PUBLIC AUDITORIUM

Mar 14   Lucia di Lammermoor (1)   M. Salvi *s*. R. Bonelli *b*. V. Lazzari *bs*.
                                                F. St. Leger *cond*.
Mar 16   La traviata   C. Muzio *s*. J. C. Thomas *b*. R. Moranzoni *cond*.

SPRING 1931 — CONCERT TOUR

Mar 28   Chicago   Civic Theater
Apr 5   New York City   Carnegie Hall
Apr 10   Allentown   High School Auditorium
Apr 13   Montreal   Théâtre St. Denis
Apr 19   New York City   Metropolitan Opera House
Apr 21   Stapleton   Paramount Theater
May 8   Turin   Teatro Regio
May 12   Paris   Salle Pleyel

BUENOS AIRES — TEATRO COLÓN

July 9   Il barbiere di Siviglia (9)   L. Pons *s*. C. Galeffi *b*. E. Pinza *bs*.
                                                S. Baccaloni *bs*. F. Calusio *cond*.

July 12   Concert
July 19   Concert
July 26   Concert
July 31   L'elisir d'amore (3)   I. Marengo *s*. A. Gaudin *b*. S. Baccaloni *bs*.
                                                F. Calusio *cond*.

Aug 9   Concert

MONTEVIDEO — TEATRO SOLIS

Aug 26   Concert

CHICAGO — CIVIC THEATER

Dec 8   La traviata (3)   C. Muzio *s*. A. Beuf/V. Damiani *b*.
                                                R. Moranzoni *cond*.
Dec 15   Martha (3)   L. Turner *s*. C. Glade *ms*. V. Lazzari *bs*.
                                                S. Baccaloni *bs*. F. St. Leger *cond*.

MINNEAPOLIS — MEMORIAL AUDITORIUM
Dec 18   Concert

CHICAGO — CIVIC THEATER
Dec 24   Il barbiere di Siviglia (3)   M. Salvi *s*. V. Damiani/G. Rimini *b*.
                                        V. Marcoux *b*. S. Baccaloni *bs*. R. Moranzoni *cond*.
Dec 31   Mignon (2)   M. Salvi *s*. C. Glade *ms*. V. Marcoux *b*.
                                        E. Cooper *cond*.

1932

WINTER 1932 — CONCERT TOUR
Feb 6   Oakland   Auditorium
Feb 13   San Francisco   Civic Auditorium
Feb 19   Santa Barbara   Lobero Theater
Feb 23   Los Angeles   Philharmonic Auditorium
Feb 27   Chicago   Civic Theater
Mar 1   Lexington   Woodland Auditorium
Mar 4   Toronto   Massey Hall
Mar 9   Boston   Statler Hotel

ROME — TEATRO REALE DELL'OPERA
Mar 30   Don Pasquale (5)   M. Capsir/P. Giri *s*. G. Vanelli *b*. G. Cirino *bs*.
                              G. Santini *cond*.

MILAN — TEATRO ALLA SCALA
Apr 16   L'elisir d'amore (4)   I. Marengo *s*. P. Biasini *b*. S. Baccaloni *bs*.
                                  E. Panizza *cond*.

SPRING-AUTUMN 1932 — CONCERT TOUR
Apr 25   Turin   E.I.A.R. Studios
June 21   Paris   Salle Pleyel
June 24   Trieste   Teatro Verdi
Nov 3   Peoria   Shrine Temple
Nov 7   Greenwich   Pickwick Theater
Nov 9   Grand Rapids   Regent Theater
Nov 11   Detroit   Orchestra Hall
Nov 15   Providence   Loewe's Theater

NEW YORK CITY — METROPOLITAN OPERA HOUSE
Nov 23   L'elisir d'amore (2)   E. Fleischer/N. Morgana *s*. G. De Luca *b*.
                                    E. Pinza *bs*. T. Serafin *cond*.
Nov 26   Lucia di Lammermoor (2)   L. Pons *s*. G. De Luca *b*. L. Rothier/T. Pasero *bs*.
                                    V. Bellezza *cond*.

PHILADELPHIA — ACADEMY OF MUSIC
Nov 29   Il barbiere di Siviglia (1)   L. Pons *s*. R. Bonelli *b*. E. Pinza *bs*.
                                        P. Malatesta *bs*. V. Bellezza *cond*.

NEW YORK CITY — METROPOLITAN OPERA HOUSE
Dec 1   La traviata (2)   R. Ponselle/Q. Mario *s*. R. Bonelli/G. De Luca *b*.
                             T. Serafin *cond*.

BROOKLYN — AUDITORIUM
Dec 6   La traviata (1)   R. Ponselle *s*. L. Tibbett *b*. T. Serafin *cond*.

NEW YORK CITY — METROPOLITAN OPERA HOUSE
Dec 17   Don Giovanni (2)   R. Ponselle *s.* M. Müller *s.* E. Fleischer *s.*
                                      E. Pinza *bs.* T. Pasero *bs.* P. Malatesta *bs.*
                                      L. D'Angelo *bs.* T. Serafin *cond.*
Dec 18   Concert

PHILADELPHIA — ACADEMY OF MUSIC
Dec 27   La traviata (1)   L. Bori *s.* R. Bonelli *b.* T. Serafin *cond.*

1933

WINTER 1933 — CONCERT TOUR
Jan 1   New York City   N.B.C. Studios
Feb 21   New Haven   Woolsey Hall
Feb 25   San Francisco   Wiba Studios
Mar 6   Columbus   Memorial Hall
Mar 27   Turin   E.I.A.R. Studios

MILAN — TEATRO ALLA SCALA
Apr 6   Mignon (2)   G. Besanzoni *ms.* M. Carosio *s.*
                                      T. Pasero/J. Santiago Font *bs.* F. Ghione *cond.*
Apr 15   Don Pasquale (3)   T. Dal Monte/L. Grani *s.* G. Rimini *b.*
                                      E. Badini *b.* F. Ghione *cond.*
Apr 22   Il barbiere di Siviglia (1)   T. Dal Monte *s.* B. Franci *b.* F. Chaliapin *bs.*
                                      S. Baccaloni *bs.* F. Ghione *cond.*

PARMA — TEATRO REGIO
May 17   L'elisir d'amore (2)   M. Capsir/M. Carosio *s.* P. Biasini *b.*
                                      G. Cirino *bs.* G. Podestà *cond.*

FIDENZA — TEATRO MAGNANI
May   Lucia di Lammermoor

GENOA — POLITEAMA GENOVESE
June 20   L'elisir d'amore (3)   M. Carosio *s.* A. Pilotto *b.* U. Sartori *bs.*
                                      A. Padovani *cond.*

BERGAMO — TEATRO DONIZETTI
Oct 7   Don Pasquale (2)   M. Capsir *s.* M. Stabile *b.* S. Baccaloni *bs.*
                                      G. Del Campo *cond.*

AUTUMN 1933 — CONCERT TOUR
Nov 5   Hartford   Bushnell Memorial Hall
Nov 16   Detroit   Orchestra Hall
Nov 20   Montreal   Imperial Theater
Dec 11   Chicago   Civic Theater
Dec 13   Northrop   Auditorium

NEW YORK CITY — METROPOLITAN OPERA HOUSE
Dec 30   Mignon (1)   L. Bori *s.* L. Pons. *s.* L. Rothier *bs.*
                                      L. Hasselmans *cond.*

1934

NEW YORK CITY — METROPOLITAN OPERA HOUSE (continued)
Jan 1   La traviata (2)   C. Muzio/R. Ponselle *s.* R. Bonelli/J. C. Thomas *b.*
                                    T. Serafin *cond.*
Jan 3   Don Giovanni (3)   R. Ponselle *s.* M. Müller *s.* E. Fleischer *s.*
                                    E. Pinza *bs.* V. Lazzari *bs.* L. D'Angelo *bs.*
                                    T. Serafin *cond.*

PHILADELPHIA — ACADEMY OF MUSIC
Jan 9   Mignon (3)   L. Bori *s.* L. Pons *s.* L. Rothier *bs.*
                                    L. Hasselmans *cond.*

NEW YORK CITY — METROPOLITAN OPERA HOUSE
Jan 11   Manon (3)   L. Bori *s.* G. De Luca *b.* L. Rothier *bs.*
                                    L. Hasselmans *cond.*

NEW YORK CITY — N.B.C. STUDIOS
Jan 14   Concert

PHILADELPHIA — ACADEMY OF MUSIC
Jan 16   La traviata (1)   C. Muzio *s.* R. Bonelli *b.* T. Serafin *cond.*

CHICAGO — CIVIC THEATER
Jan 24   Martha (1)   E. Mason *s.* I. Pavloska *ms.* G. Interrante *b.*
                                    V. Trevisan *bs.* G. Papi *cond.*
Jan 27   Mignon (1)   C. Glade *ms.* L. Meusel *s.* C. Baromeo *bs.*
                                    H. Weber *cond.*

PHILADELPHIA — ACADEMY OF MUSIC
Jan 30   Manon (1)   L. Bori *s.* G. De Luca *b.* L. Rothier *bs.*
                                    L. Hasselmans *cond.*

WINTER 1934 — CONCERT TOUR
Feb 4   New York City   Metropolitan Opera House
Feb 14   Pittsburgh   Syria Mosque
Feb 19   Toledo   Museum Peristyle
Feb 21   Kansas City   Convention Hall
Feb 23   Boise   High School Auditorium
Feb 27   Los Angeles   Shrine Auditorium
Mar 2   Oakland   Auditorium
Mar 5   Claremont   Bridges Auditorium
Mar 9   San Francisco   Columbia Theater
Mar 14   New York City   Town Hall
Mar 20   Washington   Constitution Hall

MILAN — TEATRO ALLA SCALA
Apr 12   La traviata (6)   G. Cigna *s.* G. Danise/P. Biasini *b.*
                                    S. Failoni/E. Fornarini *cond.*
Apr 27   Werther (3)   G. Pederzini *ms.* M. Merlo *s.* P. Biasini *b.*
                                    F. Ghione *cond.*

TUNIS — THÉÂTRE MUNICIPAL
May   Concert
May   Concert

BUENOS AIRES — TEATRO COLÓN

July 3	L'elisir d'amore (4)	I. Marengo s. E. Dall'Argine/V. Damiani b. S. Baccaloni bs. E. Panizza cond.
July 9	Il barbiere di Siviglia (3)	L. Pons s. V. Damiani b. G. Vaghi bs. S. Baccaloni bs. E. Panizza cond.
July	Concert	
July	Concert	
July 26	La sonnambula (2)	L. Pons s. G. Vaghi/F. Romito bs. E. Panizza/F. Paolantonio cond.
Aug 7	Concert	

SÃO PAULO — TEATRO MUNICIPAL

Aug 17	L'elisir d'amore (1)	A. Archi s. V. Damiani b. S. Baccaloni bs. A. De Angelis cond.

RIO DE JANEIRO — TEATRO MUNICIPAL

Aug 22	L'elisir d'amore (2)	A. Archi s. V. Damiani b. S. Baccaloni bs. E. Panizza cond.
Aug 28	La sonnambula (1)	A. Archi s. J. Santiago Font bs. E. Panizza cond.
Aug 31	Concert	

BARI — TEATRO PETRUZZELLI

Sep 15	L'elisir d'amore (2)	L. Pasini s. G. Vanelli b. M. Fiore bs. V. Bellezza cond.
Sep 20	Lucia di Lammermoor (3)	M. Gentile s. G. Vanelli b. G. Tomei bs. V. Bellezza cond.

EASTERN EUROPE

Oct, Nov	Poland and the Baltic Countries, among others

LONDON — QUEEN'S HALL

Dec 14	Concert

AMSTERDAM — STADS SCHWAUBURG

Dec 21	L'elisir d'amore

1935

MILAN — TEATRO ALLA SCALA

Jan 1	La sonnambula (4)	T. Dal Monte s. T. Pasero bs. A. Guarnieri cond.

TURIN — TEATRO REGIO

Jan 15	Werther (3)	I. Adami Corradetti s. L. Grani s. C. Cavallini b. F. Ghione cond.

MILAN — TEATRO ALLA SCALA

Jan 22	Werther (3)	M. Caniglia s. M. Merlo s. P. Biasini b. A. Guarnieri cond.

NEW YORK CITY — METROPOLITAN OPERA HOUSE

Feb 9	Don Giovanni (1)	R. Ponselle s. M. Müller s. E. Fleischer s. E. Pinza bs. V. Lazzari bs. L. D'Angelo bs. E. Panizza cond.
Feb 11	Manon (1)	Q. Mario s. G. De Luca b. L. Rothier bs. L. Hasselmans cond.

Feb 15   La traviata (1)   R. Ponselle *s*. R. Bonelli *b*. E. Panizza *cond*.
Feb 23   Don Pasquale (3)   L. Bori *s*. G. De Luca *b*. E. Pinza *bs*.
                                            E. Panizza *cond*.

BROOKLYN — AUDITORIUM
Feb 26   Lucia di Lammermoor (1)   L. Pons *s*. G. De Luca *b*. V. Lazzari *bs*.
                                            V. Bellezza *cond*.

NEW YORK CITY — METROPOLITAN OPERA HOUSE
Mar 11   La sonnambula (1)   L. Pons *s*. V. Lazzari *bs*. E. Panizza *cond*.
Mar 15   Mignon (1)   L. Bori *s*. T. Sabanieeva *s*. L. Rothier *bs*.
                                            L. Hasselmans *cond*.

CHICAGO — CIVIC THEATER
Mar 31   Concert

MILAN — TEATRO LIRICO
May 1   La Principessa Liana (2)   G. Pederzini *ms*. G. Tess *ms*. T. Menotti *s*.
                                            G. Del Signore *t*. E. Badini *b*. T. Schipa *cond*.

LECCE — POLITEAMA GRECO
May   Werther   I. Adami Corradetti *s*. M. Merlo *s*. P. Biasini *b*.
                                            P. Fabbroni *cond*.
May 31   Mignon   E. Stignani *ms*. M. Carosio *s*. D. Baronti *bs*.
                                            P. Fabbroni *cond*.
June 6   La Principessa Liana   I. Adami Corradetti *s*. M. Carosio *s*.
                                            E. Parmeggiani *t*. E. Badini *b*. T. Schipa *cond*.

ROME — E.I.A.R. STUDIOS
June   La Principessa Liana   I. Adami Corradetti *s*. A. Dubbini *ms*. L. Maguet *s*.
                                            G. Del Signore t. E. Badini *b*. T. Schipa *cond*.

PRAGUE — DEUTSCHES OPER
June   Manon   M. Favero *s*. A. Votto *cond*.

CATANIA — GIARDINI BELLINI
July 9   La sonnambula   M. Gentile *s*. J. Santiago Font *bs*.
                                            G. Del Campo *cond*.

ROME — BASILICA DI MASSENZIO
July 23   Concert

BERGAMO — TEATRO DONIZETTI
Sep 19   Werther (2)   G. Pederzini *ms*. R. Villani *s*. L. Borgonovo *b*.
                                            G. Del Campo *cond*.

AUTUMN 1935 — CONCERT TOUR
Oct 4   Detroit   Orchestra Hall
Oct 8   Seattle   Moore Theater
Oct 11   Portland   Public Auditorium
Oct 18   Sacramento   Memorial Auditorium
Oct 29   Los Angeles   Philharmonic Auditorium
Nov 11   Los Angeles   N.B.C. Studios

SAN FRANCISCO — WAR MEMORIAL OPERA HOUSE
Nov 16   Martha (2)   H. Jepson *s*. C. Glade/E. Gruninger *ms*. H. Shefoff
                                            b. L. D'Angelo *bs*. R. Lert *cond*.

Nov 22	Werther (1)	C. Glade *ms*. A. Young *s*. A. Gandolfi *b*. G. Merola *cond*.
Nov 25	Il barbiere di Siviglia (1)	J. Tuminia *s*. R. Bonelli *b*. E. Pinza *bs*. L. D'Angelo *bs*. G. Merola *cond*.
Nov 29	Rigoletto (1)	E. Hardy *s*. E. Gruninger *ms*. R. Bonelli *b*. E. Pinza *bs*. G. Merola *cond*.

OAKLAND — AUDITORIUM
Dec 3   Concert

SAN FRANCISCO —WAR MEMORIAL OPERA HOUSE
Dec 6   Concert

1936

MILAN — TEATRO ALLA SCALA

| Jan 1 | Il matrimonio segreto (5) | M. Favero *s*. I. Adami Corradetti *s*. G. Tess *ms*. F. Autori *bs*. S. Baccaloni *bs*. G. Marinuzzi *cond*. |
| Jan 22 | Lucia di Lammermoor (6) | T. Dal Monte *s*. C. Tagliabue/A. Borgioli *b*. D. Baronti *bs*. G. Antonicelli *cond*. |

FLORENCE — TEATRO COMUNALE
Feb 8   Concert

GENOA — TEATRO CARLO FELICE

| Feb 11 | L'elisir d'amore (4) | E. Alberti/L. Grani *s*. G. Vanelli *b*. E. Badini *b*./U. Sartori *bs*. F. Previtali *cond*. |

NAPLES — TEATRO SAN CARLO

| Feb 23 | L'elisir d'amore (3) | H. Reggiani *s*. I. Del Chiaro *b*. M. Luise *bs*. F. Capuana *cond*. |

TURIN — TEATRO VITTORIO EMANUELE

| Mar 1 | L'elisir d'amore (2) | L. Grani *s*. A. Poli *b*. E. Badini *b*. F. Ghione *cond*. |
| Mar 7 | Il barbiere di Siviglia (2) | A. Ottein *s*. G. De Luca *b*. F. Autori *bs*. E. Badini *b*. F. Ghione *cond*. |

ROME — TEATRO REALE DELL'OPERA

| Mar 24 | Werther (4) | G. Pederzini *ms*. L. Albanese/M. Esposito *s*. G. Manacchini *b*. T. Serafin *cond*. |
| Apr 2 | Mignon (2) | G. Pederzini *ms*. G. Perea Labia *s*. G. Vaghi *bs*. V. Bellezza *cond*. |

MILAN — TEATRO ALLA SCALA

| Apr 11 | L'Arlesiana (3) | G. Pederzini *ms*. M. Laurenti/M. Carosio *s*. M. Basiola *b*. L. Paci *b*. G. Antonicelli *cond*. |
| Apr 16 | Don Pasquale (3) | M. Carosio *s*. G. De Luca *b*. E. Badini *b*. G. Marinuzzi *cond*. |

MILAN — TEATRO LIRICO
Apr 18   Concert

TURIN — TEATRO VITTORIO EMANUELE

| May 4 | La Principessa Liana (1) | G. Pederzini *ms*. G. Tess *ms*. T. Menotti *s*. G. Del Signore *t*. E. Badini *b*. T. Schipa *cond*. |

TITO SCHIPA

SPRING 1936 — CONCERT TOUR

May 17	Buffalo	Consistory Auditorium
May 24	Chicago	Civic Theater
June 5	Mexico City	Teatro Alameda
June 14	Mexico City	Plaza el Toreo
June 18	Mexico City	Palacio de Bellas Artes
June 21	New York City	N.B.C. Studios
June 23	New York City	City School Stadium

VERONA — ARENA

Aug 2   L'elisir d'amore (3)   M. Carosio *s*. E. Ghirardini *b*. E. Faticanti *b*. T. Serafin *cond*.

WASHINGTON — CONSTITUTION HALL

Oct 25   Concert

BROOKLYN — AUDITORIUM

Oct 27   Concert

CHICAGO — CIVIC THEATER

Nov 4   Martha (2)   H. Jepson *s*. M. Barova *ms*. G. Rimini *b*. V. Trevisan *bs*. R. Moranzoni *cond*.

Nov 9   Mignon (2)   C. Glade *ms*. J. Antoine *s*. C. Baromeo/N. Ruisi *bs*. L. Hasselmans *cond*.

Nov 18   L'elisir d'amore (1)   V. Della Chiesa *s*. G. Rimini *b*. V. Trevisan *bs*. R. Moranzoni *cond*.

Nov 23   Il barbiere di Siviglia (1)   J. Antoine *s*. R. Bonelli *b*. N. Ruisi *bs*. V. Trevisan *bs*. S. Samossoud *cond*.

OKLAHOMA CITY — AUDITORIUM

Dec 2   Concert

CLEVELAND — SINGERS CLUB

Dec 9   Concert

MILAN — TEATRO ALLA SCALA

Dec 27   Mignon (5)   G. Pederzini *ms*. M. Carosio *s*. T. Pasero/D. Baronti *bs*. A. Guarnieri *cond*.

1937

MILAN — TEATRO ALLA SCALA (continued)

Jan 14   L'amico Fritz (2)   M. Favero *s*. V. Palombini *ms*. P. Biasini *b*. G. Antonicelli *cond*.

TURIN — E.I.A.R. STUDIOS

Jan 18   Concert

GENOA — TEATRO CARLO FELICE

Jan 29   Lucia di Lammermoor (1)   L. Pagliughi *s*. G. Vanelli *b*. G. Neri *bs*. A. Costaguta *cond*.

Jan 31   L'amico Fritz (3)   L. Albanese *s*. C. Elmo *ms*. G. Vanelli *b*. V. Gui *cond*.

NAPLES — TEATRO SAN CARLO

Feb 11   Werther (4)   I. Adami Corradetti *s*. /G. Pederzini *ms*. P. Giri *s*. G. Vanelli/G. Manacchini *b*. A. Sabino *cond*.

ROME — TEATRO REALE DELL'OPERA
Feb 20   L'Arlesiana (5)   G. Pederzini *ms*. L. Albanese *s*. E. Ghirardini *b*.
                                 S. Meletti *b*. O. De Fabritiis *cond*.
Mar 9   L'elisir d'amore (4)   M. Carosio *s*. E. Ghirardini *b*. S. Baccaloni *bs*.
                                 V. Bellezza *cond*.
Mar 16   The Magic Flute (3)   L. Albanese/A. Sielska *s*. E. Sack *s*. A. Conte *s*.
                                 E. Ghirardini *b*. T. Pasero *bs*. B. Sbalchiero *bs*.
                                 T. Serafin *cond*.

PALERMO — TEATRO MASSIMO
Apr 2   L'elisir d'amore (3)   L. Falconieri *s*. G. Vanelli *b*. M. Luise *bs*.
                                 F. Capuana *cond*.

MILAN — TEATRO ALLA SCALA
Apr 16   L'elisir d'amore (5)   M. Carosio/T. Menotti *s*. G. De Luca *b*.
                                 S. Baccaloni *bs*. G. Del Campo *cond*.

SPRING-SUMMER 1937 AUSTRALIA — CONCERT TOUR
May, June, July

HONOLULU — PRINCESS THEATER
Aug 4   Concert

CHICAGO — GRANT PARK
Aug 16   Concert

BOLOGNA — TEATRO COMUNALE
Oct 18   L'elisir d'amore (1)   M. Capsir *s*. G. De Luca *b*. V. Bettoni *bs*.
                                 A. Guarnieri *cond*.

BOSTON — SYMPHONY HALL
Dec 5   Concert

JAMESTOWN — AUDITORIUM
Dec 7   Concert

CHICAGO — CIVIC THEATER
Dec 10   Martha (2)   E. Mason/H. Jepson *s*. C. Glade/ . . Barrow *ms*.
                                 G. Rimini *b*. V. Trevisan *bs*. D. Bigalli *cond*.

AUTUMN 1937-WINTER 1938 — CONCERT TOUR
Dec 14   San Francisco   Shrine Auditorium

1938

CONCERT TOUR (continued)
Jan 29   Hollywood   Auditorium
Feb 16   Milwaukee   Pabst Theater
Feb 20   Chicago   Civic Theater
Feb 22   Detroit   Orchestra Hall

ROME — TEATRO REALE DELL'OPERA
Mar 16   Werther (4)   P. Tassinari *s*. L. Cortini *s*. G. Manacchini *b*.
                                 T. Serafin *cond*.
Mar 22   Il barbiere di Siviglia (3) M. Carosio *s*. C. Galeffi *b*. G. Vaghi *bs*.
                                 F. Romito *bs*. V. Bellezza *cond*.

257

NAPLES — TEATRO SAN CARLO
Mar 29   L'Arlesiana (3)   G. Pederzini *ms.* M. Laurenti *s.* M. Basiola *b.*
                                   M. Cavallo *b.* A. Questa *cond.*

MILAN — TEATRO ALLA SCALA
Apr 10   Il barbiere di Siviglia (6)   M. Carosio *s.* C. Galeffi *b.* V. Bettoni *bs.*
                                         S. Baccaloni *bs.* F. Capuana *cond.*
Apr 23   Marcella (2)   M. Olivero *s.* G. Manacchini *b.* F. Capuana *cond.*

VENICE — TEATRO LA FENICE
May 8   L'elisir d'amore (3)   M. Carosio *s.* G. Vanelli *b.* U. Di Lelio *bs.*
                                   A. Guarnieri *cond.*

CESENA — TEATRO COMUNALE
May 22   Werther (2)   R. Corsi *ms.* V. Massari *s.* L. Paci *b.*
                                   G. Podestà *cond.*

ROME — E.I.A.R. STUDIOS
July 18   Linda di Chamonix (2)   A. Archi *s.* A. Cravcenco *ms.* G. Manacchini *b.*
                                   A. Beuf *b.* S. Baccaloni *bs.* A. Sabino *cond.*

SUMMER 1938 BRITISH ISLES — CONCERT TOUR
Sep

AUTUMN 1938 EASTERN EUROPE — CONCERT TOUR
Oct, Nov

AUTUMN 1938 ROME — TEATRO REALE DELL'OPERA
Dec 11   L'Arlesiana (4)   G. Pederzini *ms.* L. Albanese *s.* G. Bechi *b.*
                                   T. Gobbi *b.* O. De Fabritiis *cond.*

MILAN — TEATRO ALLA SCALA
Dec 27   Werther (5)   G. Pederzini *ms.* T. Menotti/D. Micelli *s.*
                                   F. Valentino *b.* F. Capuana *cond.*

1939

TRIESTE — TEATRO VERDI
Jan 11   L'Arlesiana (3)   I. Minghini Cattaneo *ms.* J. Cirillo *s.* A. Reali *b.*
                                   O. Serpo *b.* G. Santini *cond.*

ROME — TEATRO REALE DELL'OPERA
Jan 21   La sonnambula (4)   M. Carosio *s.* G. Vaghi *bs.* T. Serafin *cond.*

SAN REMO — TEATRO DEL CASINO
Feb 4   Werther (2)   R. Corsi *ms.* V. Massari *s.* G. De Surra *b.*
                                   P. Fabbroni *cond.*

GENOA — TEATRO CARLO FELICE
Feb 9   L'Arlesiana (2)   G. Pederzini *ms.* M. Laurenti *s.* A. Granforte *b.*
                                   C. Cavallini *b.* F. Capuana *cond.*

BERLIN — CONCERT SERIES
June

BUENOS AIRES — TEATRO COLÓN
Aug   Concert
Aug   Concert
Aug   Concert

SÃO PAULO — TEATRO MUNICIPAL
Aug 20   L'Arlesiana (1)   N. Giani *ms*. T. Ferreira *s*. C. Ramirez *b*.
                                       M. Brunati *b*. A. De Angelis *cond*.
Aug 23   L'elisir d'amore (1)   J. Azevedo *s*. C. Ramirez *b*. M. Girotti *bs*.
                                       G. Papi *cond*.
Aug 28   La traviata (1)   B. Sayão *s*. G. Danise *b*. G. Papi *cond*.
Aug 30   Werther (1)   N. Giani *ms*. M. Arbuffo *s*. S. Vieira *b*.
                                       A. De Angelis *cond*.

SAN FRANCISCO — WAR MEMORIAL OPERA HOUSE
Oct 13   Manon (1)   B. Sayão *s*. R. Bonelli *b*. N. Cordon *bs*.
                                       G. Merola *cond*.

Oct 25   Lucia di Lammermoor (1)   L. Pons *s*. S. Ballarini *b*. N. Cordon *bs*.
                                       G. Papi *cond*.

CHICAGO — CIVIC THEATER
Nov 1   La traviata (1)   H. Jepson *s*. J. C. Thomas *b*. H. Weber *cond*.
Nov 3   Il barbiere di Siviglia (2) H. Reggiani *s*. J. C. Thomas/C. Morelli *b*.
                                       V. Lazzari *bs*. P. Malatesta *bs*. A. Canarutto *cond*.
Nov 6   Mignon (2)   G. Swarthout *ms*. . . Haskins *s*. E. Pinza *bs*.
                                       L. Hasselmans *cond*.
Nov 25   Lucia di Lammermoor (1)   L. Pons *s*. C. Morelli *b*. V. Lazzari *bs*.
                                       . . Kopp *cond*.

1940

BUENOS AIRES — TEATRO COLÓN
July 16   L'elisir d'amore (1)   I. Marengo *s*. V. Damiani *b*. S. Baccaloni *bs*.
                                       F. Calusio *cond*.

RIO DE JANEIRO — TEATRO MUNICIPAL
Aug 16   Concert
Aug 24   La traviata (2)   B. Sayão *s*. A. Borgioli *b*. F. Ghione *cond*.

SÃO PAULO — TEATRO MUNICIPAL
Aug 28   L'elisir d'amore (1)   M. Sà Earp *s*. J. Villa *b*. S. Baccaloni *bs*.
                                       A. De Angelis *cond*.
Sep 3   La traviata (1)   B. Sayão *s*. J. Villa *b*. G. Papi *cond*.

RIO DE JANEIRO — TEATRO MUNICIPAL
Sep 13   L'elisir d'amore (1)   M. Sà Earp *s*. V. Damiani *b*. S. Baccaloni *bs*.
                                       E. De Guarnieri *cond*.

SAN FRANCISCO — OPERA
Nov 1   Manon (1)   B. Sayão *s*. J. Brownlee *b*. L. Alvary *bs*.
                                       G. Merola *cond*.

CHICAGO — CIVIC THEATER
Nov 16   Don Giovanni (2)   R. Bampton *s*. . . Witwer *s*. M. Bokor *s*.
                                       E. Pinza *bs*. V. Lazzari *bs*. L. Alvary *bs*. F. Destal
                                       bs. P. Breisach *cond*.

| Nov 18 | La traviata (1) | J. Novotna *s*. S. Sved *b*. M. Abravanel *cond*. |
| Nov 23 | Manon (2) | H. Jepson/G. Moore *s*. G. Czaplicki *b*. L. Rothier *bs*. M. Abravanel/ . . Kopp *cond*. |

1941

NEW YORK CITY — METROPOLITAN OPERA HOUSE
Mar 7   Don Giovanni (2)   Z. Milanov *s*. J. Novotna *s*. B. Sayão *s*. E. Pinza *bs*.
S. Baccaloni *bs*. A. Kent *bs*. N. Cordon *bs*.
B. Walter *cond*.

PHILADELPHIA — ACADEMY OF MUSIC
Mar 18   Don Giovanni (1)   Z. Milanov *s*. J. Novotna *s*. B. Sayão *s*. E. Pinza *bs*.
S. Baccaloni *bs*. A. Kent *bs*. N. Cordon *bs*.
B. Walter *cond*.

BOSTON — OPERA
Mar 31   Don Giovanni (2)   Z. Milanov *s*. J. Novotna *s*. M. Farell *s*. E. Pinza
bs. S. Baccaloni *bs*. A. Kent *bs*. N. Cordon *bs*.
B. Walter *cond*.
Apr 5   Il barbiere di Siviglia (1)   J. Tuminia *s*. J. C. Thomas *b*. E. Pinza *bs*.
S. Baccaloni *bs*. G. Papi *cond*.

CLEVELAND — PUBLIC HALL
Apr 18   Il barbiere di Siviglia (1)   B. Sayão *s*. J. Brownlee *b*. N. Cordon *bs*.
S. Baccaloni *bs*. G. Papi *cond*.

RIO DE JANEIRO — TEATRO MUNICIPAL
Aug 19   Lucia di Lammermoor (3)   J. Tuminia/T. Ferreira *s*. G. Manacchini *b*.
D. Baronti/L. Sergenti *bs*. G. Papi/S. Guerra *cond*.
Aug 30   Concert
Sep 9   Il barbiere di Siviglia (1)   M. Sà Earp *s*. A. Borgioli *b*. G. Vaghi *bs*.
S. Baccaloni *bs*. G. Papi *cond*.
Sep 11   La traviata (3)   N. Greco/A. Briani *s*. A. Borgioli/R. Galeno *b*.
G. Papi/S. Guerra *cond*.

SÃO PAULO — TEATRO MUNICIPAL
Sep 17   Lucia di Lammermoor (1)   J. Tuminia *s*. P. Ansaldi *bs*. A. De Lucchi *bs*.
A. Belardi *cond*.
Sep   La traviata (1)   N. Greco *s*. A. Borgioli *b*. A. Belardi *cond*.
Sep   Il barbiere di Siviglia (1)   M. Sà Earp *s*. A. Borgioli *b*. G. Vaghi *bs*.
M. Girotti *bs*. A. Belardi *cond*.

RIO DE JANEIRO — TEATRO MUNICIPAL
Oct 26   Concert

1942

BOLOGNA — TEATRO COMUNALE
Jan 18   Concert

ROME — TEATRO REALE DELL'OPERA
Jan 24   Lucia di Lammermoor (2)   M. Carosio *s*. E. Mascherini *b*. G. Neri *bs*.
V. Bellezza *cond*.

CHRONOLOGY

BRESCIA — TEATRO GRANDE
Feb L'elisir d'amore (2) M. Piccarolo *s*. E. De Franceschi *b*. L. Siravo *bs*. G. Podestà *cond*.

FLORENCE — TEATRO COMUNALE
Feb 12 L'elisir d'amore (2) E. Ribetti *s*. V. Polotto *b*. C. Maugeri *b./V*. De Taranto *bs*. U. Berrettoni *cond*.

GENOA — TEATRO PAGANINI
Feb 20 L'elisir d'amore L. Cortini *s*. P. Guelfi *b*. U. Sartori *bs*. C. Moresco *cond*.

PISA — TEATRO VERDI
Mar 10 L'elisir d'amore (3) L. Aimaro *s*. A. Poli *b*. A. Gelli *bs*. G. Podestà *cond*.

GENOA — TEATRO CARLO FELICE
Mar 21 Don Giovanni (3) C. Ebers *s*. S. Danco *s*. T. Menotti *s*. M. Stabile *b*. I. Tajo *bs*. E. Molinari *b*. G. Melnik *bs*. A. Erede *cond*.

TURIN — TEATRO VITTORIO EMANUELE
Apr 5 L'elisir d'amore (3) L. Grani *s*. P. Biasini *b*. I. Tajo/V. De Taranto *bs*. G. Santini *cond*.

REGGIO EMILIA — TEATRO MUNICIPALE
Apr 21 L'elisir d'amore (2) D. Montano *s*. G. Vanelli *b*. G. Noto *b*. A. Narducci *cond*.

MILAN — TEATRO ALLA SCALA
Apr 26 L'elisir d'amore (1) M. Favero *s*. T. Gobbi *b*. M. Stabile *b*. G. Marinuzzi *cond*.

MILAN — CONSERVATORIO GIUSEPPE VERDI
May 9 Concert

FLORENCE — TEATRO COMUNALE
May 14 La sonnambula (3) M. Carosio *s*. T. Pasero *bs*. G. Marinuzzi *cond*.

FOGGIA — TEATRO FLAGELLA
June 1 L'elisir d'amore (2) L. Grani *s*. M. Gubiani *b*. M. Luise *bs*. F. Del Cupolo *cond*.

BOLOGNA — ARENA PUCCINI
July 14 L'elisir d'amore (3) L. Aimaro *s*. C. Togliani *b*. M. Luise *bs*. R. Zamboni *cond*.

FORLÌ — TEATRO COMUNALE
Sep 6 Concert

PADUA — TEATRO VERDI
Sep L'elisir d'amore

RAVENNA — TEATRO ALIGHIERI
Nov 7 Concert

BOLOGNA — TEATRO COMUNALE
Nov 16   L'Arlesiana (2)   G. Pederzini *ms.* C. Togliani *b.* A. Baracchi *b.*
                                              O. De Fabritiis *cond.*

ROME — TEATRO REALE DELL'OPERA
Dec 30   Werther (4)   G. Pederzini/R. Corsi *ms.* M. Bertozzini *s.* G.
                                              Manacchini/M. Borriello *b.* O. De Fabritiis *cond.*

1943

TRIESTE — TEATRO VERDI
Jan 9   Werther (3)   G. Pederzini *ms.* T. Viezzoli Gasperini *s.*
                                              G. Vanelli *b.* F. Capuana *cond.*

MILAN — TEATRO ALLA SCALA
Mar 10   L'Arlesiana (3)   E. Stignani *ms.* A. Perris *s.* T. Gobbi/A. Poli *b.*
                                              A. Salsedo *b.* A. Questa *cond.*

TURIN — E.I.A.R. STUDIOS
Mar 15   Concert

VENICE — TEATRO LA FENICE
Mar 24   Manon (2)   M. Favero *s.* G. Vanelli *b.* A. Cassinelli *bs.*
                                              G. Del Campo *cond.*

TURIN — E.I.A.R. STUDIOS
Mar 29   Concert

LISBON — TEATRO COLISEU
May 20   Werther (2)   R. Corsi *ms.* A. Luba *s.* L. Piccioli *b.*
                                              N. Annovazzi *cond.*
May 22   L'elisir d'amore   C. Gracia *s.* L. Piccioli *b.* P. Lombardo *bs.*
                                              N. Annovazzi *cond.*
May 27   Manon (2)   R. Corsi *ms.* L. Piccioli *b.* G. Flamini *bs.*
                                              P. De Freitas Branco *cond.*

OPORTO — TEATRO COLISEU
June 3   L'elisir d'amore   C. Gracia *s.* L. Piccioli *b.* P. Lombardo *bs.*
                                              N. Annovazzi *cond.*
June 6   Manon   R. Corsi *ms.* L. Piccioli *b.* F. Flamini *bs.*
                                              N. Annovazzi *cond.*
June 8   Werther   R. Corsi *ms.* N. Corradi *s.* L. Piccioli *b.*
                                              N. Annovazzi *cond.*

LISBON — TEATRO SÃO CARLOS
June 13   Concert

ROME — TEATRO DELL'OPERA
Dec 18   Werther (3)   R. Corsi *ms.* M. Bertozzini *s.* S. Meletti *b.*
                                              F. Capuana *cond.*
Dec 26   La traviata (1)   R. Gigli *s.* R. De Falchi *b.* O. De Fabritiis *cond.*

COMO — TEATRO SOCIALE
Dec 28   Werther (3)   G. Pederzini *ms.* C. Bergamini *s.* A. Poli *b.*
                                              G. Marinuzzi *cond.*

1944

FLORENCE — TEATRO COMUNALE
Jan 1   L'elisir d'amore (1)   M. Carosio *s*. S. Marchi *b*. M. Luise *bs*.
                                        M. Rossi *cond*.

COMO — TEATRO SOCIALE
Jan 9   Don Pasquale (3)   M. Carosio *s*. M. Stabile *b*. V. Bettoni *bs*.
                                        G. Marinuzzi *cond*.

BOLOGNA — TEATRO COMUNALE
Jan 16   Concert

BERGAMO — TEATRO DONIZETTI
Feb 4   Werther (3)   G. Pederzini *ms*. C. Bergamini *s*. A. Poli *b*.
                                        G. Marinuzzi *cond*.

BRESCIA — TEATRO GRANDE
Feb   Werther (2)   G. Pederzini *ms*. E. Vaiani *s*. G. Vanelli *b*.
                                        M. Cordone *cond*.

BERGAMO — TEATRO DONIZETTI
Feb 23   Il matrimonio segreto (2) R. De Ferrari *s*. D. Ottani *s*. F. Barbieri *ms*.
                                        A. Poli *b*. V. Bettoni *bs*. G. Marinuzzi *cond*.

MANTUA — TEATRO SOCIALE
Mar 5   Werther (2)   C. Elmo *ms*. C. Lodetti *s*. G. Vanelli *b*.
                                        A. Sabino *cond*.

MILAN — TEATRO LIRICO
Mar 12   Il matrimonio segreto (2) M. Carosio *s*. D. Ottani *s*. F. Barbieri *ms*.
                                        A. Poli *b*. V. Bettoni *bs*. G. Marinuzzi *cond*.

SALO — TEATRO COMUNALE
Mar   Werther (1)   G. Pederzini *ms*. C. Bergamini *s*. A. Poli *b*.
                                        G. Marinuzzi *cond*.

MILAN — TEATRO LIRICO
Mar 25   Werther (3)   G. Pederzini *ms*. C. Bergamini *s*. A. Poli *b*.
                                        G. Marinuzzi *cond*.

FLORENCE — TEATRO COMUNALE
Apr 9   Lucia di Lammermoor (13)   M. Carosio *s*. G. Bechi *b*. G. Neri *bs*.
                                        M. Rossi *cond*.

TURIN — TEATRO CARIGNANO
Apr 17   Don Pasquale   M. Carosio *s*. A. Poli *b*. V. Bettoni *bs*.
                                        G. Marinuzzi *cond*.

MILAN — TEATRO OLIMPIA
May 7   Concert

BERGAMO — TEATRO DONIZETTI
Oct 14   L'Arlesiana (2)   C. Elmo *ms*. C. Petrella *s*. A. Poli *b*. A. Baracchi *b*.
                                        G. Podestà *cond*.

263

Oct 31   Concert

PIACENZA — TEATRO MUNICIPALE
Dec   Werther   I. Colasanti *ms*. D. De Stefani *s*. L. Piccioli *b*.
                                     G. Podestà *cond*.

TURIN — TEATRO DEL POPOLO
Dec 30   L'elisir d'amore   C. Bergamini *s*. A. Poli *b*. A. Gelli *bs*.
                                     C. Castagnino *cond*.

1945

WINTER 1945 — CONCERT TOUR
Jan 9   Milan   E.I.A.R. Studios
Jan 14   Milan   Teatro Ars
Mar 1   Milan   E.I.A.R. Studios
Mar 8   Monza   Teatro Ponti
Mar 22   Bergamo   Teatro Rubini
Mar 24   Bergamo   Oratorio di Bergamo Palazzo
Mar 25   Milan

MILAN — TEATRO LIRICO
Mar 31   Mignon (2)   G. Pederzini *ms*. L. Aimaro *s*. T. Pasero *bs*.
                                     A. Guarnieri *cond*.

GENOA — TEATRO GRATTACIELO
Apr 7   Werther (3)   I. Colasanti *ms*. D. De Stefani *s*. P. Campolonghi *b*.
                                     M. Cordone *cond*.

PAVIA
Apr 19   L'elisir d'amore

MILAN — TEATRO LIRICO
Apr 21   Don Giovanni (2)   C. Castellani *s*. S. Scuderi *s*. M. Favero *s*.
                                     M. Stabile *b*. T. Pasero *bs*. E. Coda *bs*. C. Forti *bs*.
                                     G. Marinuzzi *cond*.

BERGAMO — HOTEL STAZIONE
May 9   Concert

BERGAMO
July 15   Concert

BOLOGNA — ARENA BARRACANO
July 31   L'elisir d'amore (3)   M. Gentile *s*.

SUMMER-AUTUMN 1945 — CONCERT TOUR
Aug 6   Bologna
Aug 22   Ravenna   Teatro Alighieri
Aug 29   Solignano
Sep 8   Bagnara
Sep 9   Sesto Imolese
Sep 13   Imola
Sep 16   Lugo
Sep 28   Rapallo
Sep 30   Faenza

Oct 2   Parma
Oct 4   Castelvetro

ROME — TEATRO REALE DELL'OPERA
Oct 12   L'elisir d'amore (3)   A. Noni *s*. M. Borriello *b*. V. De Taranto *bs*.
                                         A. Questa *cond*.
Oct 18   Lucia di Lammermoor (1)   A. Noni *s*. E. Mascherini *b*. G. Neri *bs*.
                                         G. Mucci *cond*.
Oct 24   L'Arlesiana (3)   G. Alfano *ms*. A. Anzellotti *s*. A. Dadò *b*.
                                         E. Titta *b*. R. Santarelli *cond*.
Oct 26   Il barbiere di Siviglia (2)   A. Tuccari *s*. A. Dadò *b*. G. Neri *bs*. G. Tomei *bs*.
                                         F. Salfi *cond*.
Nov 1   Don Pasquale (3)   A. Noni *s*. G. De Luca *b*. I. Tajo *bs*.
                                         G. Santini *cond*.
Nov 13   Werther (3)   R. Corsi *ms*. N. Corradi *s*. S. Meletti/M. Borriello
                                         b. O. De Fabritiis *cond*.

ROME — TEATRO ADRIANO
Nov 30   Don Giovanni (2)   C. Castellani *s*. S. Danco *s*. A. Noni *s*. M. Stabile
                                         b. I. Tajo *bs*. C. Dalamangas *bs*. C. Platania *bs*.
                                         J. Perlea *cond*.

NAPLES — TEATRO SAN CARLO
Dec 5   Lucia di Lammermoor (2)   M. Carosio/M. Bertozzini *s*. C. Tagliabue/P.
                                         Silveri *b*. A. Romani *bs*. F. Capuana *cond*.
Dec 7   L'elisir d'amore (4)   M. Carosio/R. Mariosa *s*. S. Meletti *b*. M. Luise *bs*.
                                         F. Capuana *cond*.

NAPLES — CHIESA DI SAN DOMENICO
Dec 22   Concert

SALERNO — TEATRO VERDI
Dec 29   L'elisir d'amore

1946

LISBON — TEATRO COLISEU
Jan 25   Werther   G. Alfano *ms*. M. Huder *s*. S. Meletti *b*.
                                         A. Questa *cond*.
Jan 29   Manon   O. Fineschi *s*. S. Meletti *b*. M. Stefanoni *bs*.
                                         P. De Freitas Branco *cond*.
Feb 1   Lucia di Lammermoor   M. Del Pozo *s*. S. Meletti *b*. M. Stefanoni *bs*.
                                         A. Questa *cond*.
Feb 4   L'elisir d'amore   A. Archi *s*. S. Meletti *b*. I. Santafè *b*. A.
                                         Questa *cond*.
Feb 6   a) Manon, Act II   O. Fineschi *s*. S. Meletti *b*. M. Stefanoni *bs*.
                                         P. De Freitas Branco *cond*.

         b) Werther, Act III   G. Alfano *ms*. M. Huder *s*. S. Meletti *b*.
                                         P. De Freitas Branco *cond*.

         c) L'elisir d'amore, Act III A. Archi *s*. S. Meletti *b*. I. Santafè *b*.
                                         G. Mucci *cond*.

OPORTO — TEATRO COLISEU
Feb 10   Manon   O. Fineschi *s*. S. Meletti *b*. M. Stefanoni *bs*.
                                         A. Questa *cond*.
Feb 16   L'elisir d'amore   A. Archi *s*. S. Meletti *b*. M. Stefanoni *bs*.
                                         A.Questa *cond*.

265

Feb 20   Lucia di Lammermoor   M. Del Pozo *s.* S. Meletti *b.* M. Stefanoni *bs.*
A. Questa *cond.*

LISBON — TEATRO COLISEU
Mar 20   La traviata   M. Del Pozo *s.* P. Vidal *b.* A. Questa *cond.*
Mar 22   Manon   M. Lisson/C. Castellani *s.* P. Vidal *b.*
M. Stefanoni *bs.* P. De Freitas Branco *cond.*

LISBON — ISTITUTO DON BOSCO
Mar 23   Concert

LISBON — TEATRO COLISEU
Mar 31   Manon, Acts II - III   C. Castellani *s.* P. Vidal *b.* M. Stefanoni *bs.*
P. De Freitas Branco *cond.*

LISBON — AMBASCIATA U.S.A.
Apr 12   Concert

SARAGOSSA — TEATRO PRINCIPAL
May 18   Werther
May 20   Manon

MADRID — TEATRO ALBENIZ
May 26   Don Giovanni (1)   L. Rodriguez Aragon *s.* R. Ravina *s.* L. De
Miranda *s.* R. Torres *b.* C. Gonzalo *bs.*
N. Annovazzi *cond.*
May 30   Werther (1)   L. Cabrera *s.* C. Langa *s.* E. Lisboa *b.*
J. M. Franco *cond.*
June 7   Don Pasquale (1)   L. Rodriguez Aragon *s.* A. Poli *b.* M. Luise *bs.*
N. Annovazzi *cond.*

BRUSSELS — PALAIS DES BEAUX ARTS
June 12   Concert

PARIS — THÉÂTRE SARAH BERNHARDT
June 14   Manon

PARIS — SALLE PLEYEL
June 17   Concert
June 21   Concert

MONTE CARLO — PALAIS DE LA MÉDITERRANÉE
June 25   Concert

PARIS — THÉÂTRE SARAH BERNHARDT
July 2   Don Pasquale

CAPE VERDE ISLAND
July 18   Concert

SUMMER 1946 SÃO PAULO — CONCERT SERIES
July 31   Radio Gazeta
Aug 2   Radio Gazeta
Aug 5   Radio Gazeta
Aug 6   Radio Gazeta
Aug 9   Radio Gazeta
Aug 10   Boîte Clipper
Aug 11   Boîte Clipper

Aug 12	Boîte Clipper	
Aug 13	Boîte Clipper	
Aug 14	Boîte Clipper	
Aug 15	Boîte Clipper	
Aug 16	Boîte Clipper	
Aug 17	Boîte Clipper	
Aug 18	Boîte Clipper	
Aug 19	Radio Gazeta	
Aug 20	Boîte Clipper	
Aug 21	Boîte Clipper	
Aug 23	Cinema Piratininca	
Aug 24	Boîte Clipper	
Aug 25	Boîte Clipper	

SUMMER-AUTUMN 1946 — CONCERT TOUR

Aug 29	Campinas	Teatro Municipal
Sep 1	São Paulo	Chiesa Madonna della Pace
Sep 3	São Paulo	Chiesa di San Andrea
Sep 22	Buenos Aires	Radio Studio
Sep 24	Buenos Aires	Teatro Colon
Sep 25	Buenos Aires	Teatro Politeama
Oct 20	Hartford	Capitol Theater
Oct 22	Troy	Auditorium
Oct 23	Troy	Auditorium
Oct 25	Auburn	Auditorium
Oct 27	Chicago	Orchestra Hall
Oct 28	Chicago	Orchestra Hall
Oct 29	Saginaw	
Oct 30	Chicago	Orchestra Hall
Nov 5	Boston	Auditorium
Nov 10	Pensacola	City Hall

PHILADELPHIA — ACADEMY OF MUSIC

Nov 14	Il barbiere di Siviglia	E. Mascherini b.

AUTUMN 1946-WINTER 1947 — CONCERT TOUR

Nov 23	San Francisco	Shrine Auditorium
Dec 11	Los Angeles	Philharmonic Auditorium
Dec 14	Salt Lake City	Auditorium
Dec 16	Logan	Auditorium

1947

CONCERT TOUR (continued)

Jan 7	Pasadena	Auditorium
Jan 16	Vancouver (B.C.)	Auditorium
Jan 17	Victoria (B.C.)	Empress Hotel
Jan 23	Detroit	Auditorium
Jan 25	Detroit	Auditorium
Jan 26	Detroit	Auditorium

PHILADELPHIA — ACADEMY OF MUSIC

Feb 5	Lucia di Lammermoor

NEW YORK CITY

Feb 9	Il Progresso Italo-Americano

TITO SCHIPA

POUGHKEEPSIE — NELSON HOUSE
Feb 19   Concert

NEW PALTZ
Feb 19   Concert

MIAMI BEACH
Mar 1   Il barbiere di Siviglia

ORLANDO
Mar 7   Il barbiere di Siviglia

WINTER-AUTUMN 1947 — CONCERT TOUR

Mar 12	Palm Beach	
Mar 29	Pasco	
Mar 31	Tacoma	Tacoma Theater
Apr 14	Pasadena	Auditorium
Apr 22	Joliette (Quebec)	
Apr 24	Quebec	City Hall
Apr 28	Quebec	City Hall
May 2	Cedar Rapids	
May 6	Havana	Teatro Nacional
May 9	Havana	Teatro Nacional
May 18	New York City	Carnegie Hall
June 16	Montevideo	Radio Nacional
June 17	Montevideo	Teatro 18 Julio
June 19	Montevideo	Radio Nacional
June 20	Montevideo	Teatro 18 Julio
June 22	Montevideo	Scuola Italiana
June 23	Montevideo	Teatro 18 Julio
June 25	Montevideo	Radio Nacional
July 1	Buenos Aires	Radio el Mundo
July 4	Buenos Aires	Radio el Mundo
July 5	La Plata	Politeama Argentino
July 8	Buenos Aires	Radio el Mundo
July 11	Buenos Aires	Radio el Mundo
July 13	La Plata	Politeama Argentino
July 15	Buenos Aires	Radio el Mundo
July 17	San Fernando	
July 18	Buenos Aires	Radio el Mundo
July 20	Rosario	Teatro Odeon
July 22	Buenos Aires	Radio el Mundo
July 25	Buenos Aires	Radio el Mundo
July 29	Buenos Aires	Radio el Mundo
Aug 13	Mendoza	Teatro Condor
Aug 16	Santiago	S.N.A. Radio
Aug 18	Santiago	Teatro Municipal
Aug 19	Santiago	S.N.A. Radio
Aug 21	Santiago	Teatro Municipal
Aug 23	Santiago	S.N.A. Radio
Aug 25	Valparaiso	Teatro Municipal
Aug 26	Santiago	Ministry of Education
Aug 28	Santiago	Teatro Municipal
Sep 5	Montevideo	Teatro 18 Julio
Sep 8	Montevideo	Teatro 18 Julio
Sep 9	Rivera (Uruguay)	Hotel du Casino
Sep 18	Rio de Janeiro	Teatro Municipal
Sep 20	Rio de Janeiro	Teatro Municipal

Oct 23	Brussels	Palais des Beaux Arts
Oct 27	Leeds	Town Hall
Nov 2	Manchester	Houldsworth Hall
Nov 3	Bristol	Central Hall
Nov 5	London	Central Hall
Nov 9	Zürich	Tonhalle
Nov 11	Geneva	Salle de la Reformation
Nov 14	Amsterdam	Concertgebouw
Nov 17	Oslo	Forum
Nov 20	Oslo	Forum
Nov 23	Stockholm	Centro Sportivo

STOCKHOLM — TEATRO REALE
| Nov 25 | L'elisir d'amore | |

AUTUMN 1947 — CONCERT TOUR
Nov 27	Stockholm	City Hall
Nov 29	Goteborg	Concerthouse
Dec 1	Copenhagen	K.B. Allen
Dec 6	The Hague	Gebouw Voor Kunsten en Vetenschappen
Dec 7	Hilversum	Radio Studio
Dec 9	Brussels	Palais des Beaux Arts
Dec 11	Paris	Salle Pleyel
Dec 14	Brussels	Palais des Beaux Arts

MILAN — TEATRO ALLA SCALA
Dec 27	L'elisir d'amore (5)	M. Carosio/L. Cortini *s.* P. Guelfi *b.*
		V. De Taranto *bs.* A. Guarnieri/A. Quadri *cond.*

1948

ROME — TEATRO DELL'OPERA
Jan 15	L'elisir d'amore (5)	A. Noni/M. Bertozzini *s.* M. Borriello *b.*
		L. Neroni *bs.*/L. Paci *b.* A. Questa *cond.*
Jan 23	Werther (4)	G. Pederzini *ms.* N. Corradi *s.* S. Meletti *b.*
		O. De. Fabritiis/R. Santarelli *cond.*

WINTER-SPRING 1948 — CONCERT TOUR
Jan 31	Rome	Teatro Quirino
Feb 12	Nice	Palais de la Méditerranée
Feb 29	London	Albert Hall
Mar 10	Barcelona	Teatro del Liceo
Mar 11	Barcelona	Teatro del Liceo
Mar 14	Barcelona	Teatro del Liceo
Mar 16	Barcelona	Teatro del Liceo
Mar 21	Valencia	Teatro Principal
Mar 28	Seville	Teatro Lope de Vega
Mar 30	Jerez	Teatro Villamarta
Apr 7	Madrid	Teatro de la Zarzuela
Apr 9	San Sebastian	Kursaal
Apr 11	Bilbao	Teatro Ayala
Apr 14	San Sebastian	Kursaal
May 2	Amsterdam	Concertgebouw
May 5	Nimega	
May 9	Utrecht	Teatro Tivoli
May 12	Rotterdam	
May 14	The Hague	Gebouw Voor Kunsten en Vetenschappen

June 10   Rome   R.A.I Studios

ROME — TEATRO VALLE
June 17   L'elisir d'amore (2)   L. Pagliughi *s.* M. Borriello *b.* L. Neroni *bs.* F. Previtali *cond.*

PARIS — SALLE PLEYEL
June 24   Concert

PARIS — TOUR EIFFEL
June 30   Concert

GENOA — TEATRO COLOSSEO
July 12   L'elisir d'amore (1)   G. Mazzoleni *s.* C. Togliani *b.* U. Sartori *bs.* R. Zamboni *cond.*

CERTOSA — TEATRO LIGURE
July 18   L'elisir d'amore (1)   G. Mazzoleni *s.* C. Togliani *b.* U. Sartori *bs.* R. Zamboni *cond.*

ROME — TERME DI CARACALLA
July 23   L'elisir d'amore (3)   A. Noni *s.* A. Poli *b.* L. Neroni *bs.* A. Questa *cond.*

ROME — TERME DI CARACALLA
July 27   Lucia di Lammermoor (1)   A. Noni *s.* A. Dadò *b.* L. Neroni *bs.* V. Bellezza *cond.*

SUMMER 1948-WINTER 1949 — CONCERT TOUR

Aug 20	Caracas	Teatro Municipal
Aug 23	Caracas	Teatro Municipal
Sep 1	Caracas	Radio Nacional
Sep 2	Caracas	Radio Nacional
Sep 3	Caracas	Radio Nacional
Sep 6	Barquisimento	Teatro Rialto
Sep 8	Barquisimento	Teatro Rialto
Sep 9	Maracaibo	Cinema Baralt
Sep 11	Maracaibo	Cinema Baralt
Oct 2	Trois Rivieres	Capitol Theater
Oct 4	Quebec	Palais Montecalm
Oct 25	Winnipeg	Auditorium
Nov 1	Columbus	Auditorium
Nov 6	Chicago	Orchestra Hall
Nov 9	Wolfville (N.S.)	
Nov 11	San Juan (P.R.)	
Nov 22	Austin	
Nov 26	New York City	Hunter College
Nov 29	Pittsburgh	Auditorium
Dec 10	Los Angeles	The Examiner

1949

CONCERT TOUR (continued)

Jan 25	London	Albert Hall
Feb 1	Paris	Théâtre des Champs Elysées
Feb 4	Strasbourg	

| Feb 7 | Geneva | Victoria Hall |
| Feb 9 | Bern | Stadttheater |

CREMONA — TEATRO PONCHIELLI
| Feb 13 | L'elisir d'amore (2) | C. Frediani *s*. C. Bergonzi *b*. A. Gelli *bs*. |
| | | A. Strano *cond*. |

WINTER 1949 — CONCERT TOUR
Feb 22	Antwerp	Hippodrome
Feb 25	Zürich	Tonhalle
Feb 28	Vienna	Konzerthaus
Mar 3	Budapest	Liszt Academy

BUDAPEST — OPERAHÁS
| Mar 5 | Lucia di Lammermoor |

BUDAPEST — LISZT ACADEMY
| Mar 6 | Concert |

VIENNA — KONZERTHAUS
| Mar 9 | Concert |

MILAN — TEATRO ALLA SCALA
| Mar 22 | Il matrimonio segreto (4) | A. Noni *s*. H. Güden *s*. F. Barbieri *ms*. |
| | | B. Christoff *bs*. S. Bruscantini *bs*. M. Rossi *cond*. |

PRATO — TEATRO METASTASIO
| Apr 5 | L'elisir d'amore (1) | V. Chiericati *s*. C. Togliani *b*. A. Gelli *bs*. |
| | | R. Zamboni *cond*. |

CAGLIARI — TEATRO MASSIMO
| Apr 11 | Werther (3) | R. Corsi *ms*. G. Calaresu *s*. A. Poli *b*. |
| | | F. Molinari Pradelli *cond*. |

SPRING 1949 — CONCERT TOUR
May 12	Johannesburg	City Hall
May 15	Johannesburg	Plaza Theater
May 18	Johannesburg	City Hall
May 20	Pretoria	City Hall
May 22	Pretoria	City Hall
May 24	Durban	City Hall
May 29	Johannesburg	Plaza Theater
June 1	Cape Town	City Hall
June 3	Cape Town	City Hall
June 7	Cape Town	City Hall
June 16	Port Elisabeth	City Hall
June 19	Johannesburg	Radio Studio
June 21	Johannesburg	Selborne House

ROME — TERME DI CARACALLA
| Aug 6 | La traviata (3) | M. Caniglia *s*. T. Gobbi/A. Poli *b*. |
| | | A.Questa *cond*. |

BUDAPEST — OPERAHÁS
| Aug 30 | Don Giovanni |
| Sep 1 | Lucia di Lammermoor |

BUDAPEST — MARGHERITA ISLAND
Sep 3   Concert

BUDAPEST — OPERAHÁS
Sep 6   Don Pasquale
Sep 9   Il barbiere di Siviglia
Sep 10   La traviata

LECCE — TEATRO ARISTON
Sep 21   Concert
Sep 22   Concert

PARIS — SALLE PLEYEL
Oct 5   Concert
Oct 8   Concert

TURIN — TEATRO NUOVO
Oct 11   Werther (2)   G. Pederzini *ms*. M. Erato *s*. A. Poli *b*.
                                      G. Gavazzeni *cond*.

AUTUMN 1949 — CONCERT TOUR
Oct 20   Novi Ligure   Teatro Italia
Nov 25   Cairo   Royal Theater
Dec 2   Cairo   Royal Theater
Dec 6   Alexandria, Egypt   Mohamed Aly Theater
Dec 8   Alexandria, Egypt   Mohamed Aly Theater

SAVONA — TEATRO CHIABRERA
Dec 17   L'elisir d'amore (2)   M. Erato *s*. M. Rossi *b*. U. Sartori *bs*.
                                      I. Savini *cond*.

GENOA — TEATRO AUGUSTUS
Dec 26   L'elisir d'amore (2)   M. Erato *s*. M. Rossi *b*. U. Sartori *bs*.
                                      I. Savini *cond*.

1950

ROME — TEATRO DELL'OPERA
Jan 4   Il barbiere di Siviglia (5)   G. Arnaldi/H. Marino *s*. T. Gobbi/P. Silveri *b*.
                                            G. Neri *bs*. V. De Taranto *bs*.
                                            O. De Fabritiis/G. Morelli *cond*.

LECCE — POLITEAMA GRECO
Jan 16   Werther (2)   A. Oltrabella *s*. C. Piccini *s*. C. Togliani *b*.
                                      G. Mucci *cond*.

BIELLA — TEATRO SOCIALE
Jan 31   L'elisir d'amore (1)   M. Cucchio *s*. C. Bergonzi *b*. V. Baldo *bs*.
                                      R. Martini *cond*.

CASALE MONFERRATO — TEATRO POLITEAMA
Feb 2   L'elisir d'amore (1)   M. Cucchio *s*. C. Bergonzi *b*. V. Baldo *bs*.
                                      R. Martini *cond*.

PAVIA — TEATRO FRASCHINI
Feb 4   L'elisir d'amore (1)   M. Cucchio *s*. C. Bergonzi *b*. V. Baldo *bs*.
                                      R. Martini *cond*.

PARMA — TEATRO REGIO
Feb 7   L'elisir d'amore (3)   L. Grani *s.* L. Borgonovo *b.* V. Bettoni *bs.*
                                     F. Molinari Pradelli *cond.*

WINTER 1950 — CONCERT TOUR
Feb 14   San Remo   Teatro Astra
Feb 16   Genoa   Cinema Sampierdarena
Feb 26   Genoa   Cinema Splendor

ROME — TEATRO DELL'OPERA
Mar 9   Werther (4)   C. Petrella *s.* N. Corradi/R. Zerbini *s.*
                                    S. Meletti/M. Cortis *b.* O. De Fabritiis *cond.*

VALLETTA (MALTA) — RADIO CITY
Mar 25   Concert
Mar 26   Concert

PALERMO — TEATRO MASSIMO
Mar 28   L'elisir d'amore (3)   A. Noni *s.* R. Cesari *b.* A. Mongelli *bs.*
                                    O. Ziino *cond.*

SPRING-SUMMER 1950 — CONCERT TOUR
May 17   Brisbane   Town Hall
May 19   Brisbane   Town Hall
May 23   Melbourne   Town Hall
May 26   Melbourne   Town Hall
May 30   Melbourne   Town Hall
June 1   Sidney   Town Hall
June 3   Sidney   Town Hall
June 6   Sidney   Town Hall
June 9   Sidney   Town Hall
June 13   Melbourne   Town Hall
June 22   Christchurch
June 24   Christchurch
June 28   Napier   Auditorium
June 30   Auckland   Town Hall
July 4   Auckland   Town Hall
July 6   Auckland   Town Hall
July 9   Rotarna   Town Hall
July 11   Hamilton   Town Hall
July 13   New Plymouth   Auditorium
July 15   North Palmiston   City Hall
July 17   Wellington   Town Hall
July 19   Wellington   Town Hall
July 24   Wellington   Town Hall
Aug 9   Djakarta   Radio Studio
Aug 11   Singapore   Radio Studio

AUTUMN 1950 SOUTH AMERICA — CONCERT TOUR
Oct, Nov, Dec

1951

COMO — TEATRO SOCIALE
Jan 21   L'Arlesiana (2)   A. Oltrabella *s.* M. L. Wanner/J. Torriani *s.*
                                    L. Borgonovo *b.* E. Cecchetelli *b.* F. Patanè *cond.*

LUCCA — TEATRO DEL GIGLIO
Feb 15   L'elisir d'amore (1)   E. Ribetti *s.* G. Buttironi *b.* C. Gasperini *bs.*
G. Fratini *cond.*

PISA — TEATRO VERDI
Feb 17   L'elisir d'amore (2)   E. Ribetti *s.* G. Buttironi *b.* C. Gasperini *bs.*
G. Fratini *cond.*

BERGAMO — TEATRO RUBINI
Feb 22   L'elisir d'amore (1)   E. Ribetti *s.* G. Buttironi *b.* C. Gasperini *bs.*
S. Tagliapietra *cond.*

CODOGNO — TEATRO SOCIALE
Feb 24   L'elisir d'amore (1)   E. Ribetti *s.* G. Buttironi *b.* C. Gasperini *bs.*
S. Tagliapietra *cond.*

GARLASCO — TEATRO SOCIALE
Feb 26   L'elisir d'amore (1)   E. Ribetti *s.* G. Buttironi *b.* C. Gasperini *bs.*
S. Tagliapietra *cond.*

CARRARA — TEATRO VERDI
Feb 28   L'elisir d'amore (1)   E. Ribetti *s.* G. Buttironi *b.* C. Gasperini *bs.*
E. Zanoni *cond.*

WINTER-SPRING 1951 — CONCERT TOUR
Mar 8	Lyon	Théâtre de l'Opéra
Mar 11	Paris	Théâtre des Champs Elysées
Mar 19	Montpellier	Théâtre de l'Opéra
Mar 20	Marseilles	Grand-Théâtre
Mar 22	Nice	Palais de la Méditerranée
Mar 26	Adria	Teatro Comunale
Apr 2	Turin	R.A.I. Studios

CATANIA — TEATRO BELLINI
Apr 9   L'Arlesiana (3)   W. Madonna *ms.* M. L. Gavioli *s.* E. Serini *b.*
O. Ziino *cond.*

SPRING 1951-WINTER 1952 — CONCERT TOUR
Apr 21	Trieste	Teatro Verdi
Apr 30	Tel Aviv	Rama Hall
May 10	Paris	Radio Luxembourg
May 22	Piombino	Teatro Odeon
June 24	The Hague	Kursaal
June 27	Paris	Palais Chaillot
June 28	Vichy	Teatro du Casino
Aug 3	Biarritz	
Aug 5	Nice	Palais de la Méditerranée
Aug 11	Rovereto	Teatro Comunale
Aug 26	Lecce	Cathedral
Sep 1	Gallipoli	Arena
Sep 3	Campi Salentina	
Sep 6	Brindisi	Palazzo Comunale
Sep 9	Lecce	Politeama Greco
Sep 11	Lecce	Arena
Sep 12	Ostuni	Ospedale
Sep 13	Bari	Teatro Petruzzelli
Sep 16	Bari	Teatro Petruzzelli
Oct 11	Tel Aviv	Rama Hall

Oct 18	Jerusalem	Sala Edison
Oct 24	Jerusalem	Ester Theater
Oct 25	Haifa	Sala Majo
Oct 29	Tel Aviv	Sala Dante Alighieri
Oct 30	Ramadjan	Rama Hall
Nov 1	Tel Aviv	Rama Hall
Nov 2	Haifa	Sala Majo
Nov 3	Haifa	Sala Majo
Nov 16	Glasgow	St. Andrew's Hall
Nov 19	London	Festival Hall
Nov 28	Zürich	Town Hall
Dec 1	Geneva	Victoria Hall
Dec 28	Belgrade	National Theater
Dec 30	Belgrade	National Radio

1952

CONCERT TOUR (continued)

Jan 3	Sarajevo	Army Hall
Jan 6	Zagreb	
Jan 28	Milan	Teatro Manzoni
Mar 3	Lisbon	Teatro Coliseu
Mar 6	Lisbon	Teatro Coliseu
Mar 11	Busto Arsizio	Quartet Society
Mar 15	Rome	Pius VI Hall

TERNI — TEATRO VERDI
Mar 18   L'elisir d'amore

RIETI — TEATRO VESPASIANO
Mar 22   L'elisir d'amore

TORRE ANNUNZIATA
Mar 24   L'elisir d'amore

ROME — TEATRO ELISEO
Mar 29   Concert

CASSINO — TEATRO METROPOL
Mar 31   Concert

TORRE DEL GRECO
Apr 5   L'elisir d'amore

SPRING 1952 — CONCERT TOUR

Apr 16	Pordenone	Teatro Cristallo
Apr 18	Portogruaro	Teatro Sociale
Apr 22	Udine	Teatro Puccini
Apr 24	Treviso	Teatro Comunale

CIVITAVECCHIA — TEATRO TRAIANO
May 3   Lucia di Lammermoor   I. Varni s.

BOLOGNA — TEATRO DUSE
May 7   Concert

FERRARA — TEATRO VERDI
May 12   Lucia di Lammermoor   G. De Marco *cond.*

QUISTELLO — TEATRO COMUNALE
May 22   Lucia di Lammermoor   V. Chiericati *s.* A. Alvisi *cond.*

FLORENCE — TEATRO COMUNALE
May 26   Concert

REGGIO EMILIA — TEATRO ARIOSTO
May 29   Concert

BOLOGNA — TEATRO DUSE
June 3   Werther

ROME — TEATRO SISTINA
June 10   Werther (2)   N. De Rosa *s.* N. De Robertis *s.* G. Vanelli *b.*
G. Mucci *cond.*

PADUA
June 18   Concert

SAPRI
June 28   Lucia di Lammermoor

SIENA
June 30   Concert

PARIS
July 18   Concert

MONTECATINI — GIARDINI VERDI
July 28   Lucia di Lammermoor   O. Rech *s.* A. Gilardoni *b.* G. Calò *bs.*
M. Braggio *cond.*

SALSOMAGGIORE — TEATRO NUOVO
Sep 12   L'elisir d'amore   V. Chiericati *s.* G. Buttironi *b.* P. Lombardo *bs.*
R. Castagnino *cond.*

VARESE — TEATRO IMPERO
Oct 21   Lucia di Lammermoor   O. Rech *s.* A. Gilardoni *b.* G. Calò *bs.*
M. Braggio *cond.*

TURIN — TEATRO ALFIERI
Oct 26   Lucia di Lammermoor (1)   O. Rech *s.* A. Gilardoni *b.* G. Calò *bs.*
M. Braggio *cond.*

ASTI — TEATRO ALFIERI
Oct 28   Lucia di Lammermoor (1)   O. Rech *s.* A. Gilardoni *b.* G. Calò *bs.*
M. Braggio *cond.*

AUTUMN 1952-WINTER 1953 — CONCERT TOUR
Oct 31   Milan   Teatro Lirico
Nov 19   Zürich   Tonhalle
Nov 23   Arnhem
Nov 28   The Hague
Nov 30   Utrecht

Dec 4   Brussels   Théâtre de la Monnaie
Dec 30   Schio   Teatro Astra

1953

CONCERT TOUR (continued)
Jan 3   Schio   Teatro Astra

VIGEVANO — TEATRO CAGNONI
Jan 8   L'elisir d'amore   V. Chiericati *s*. O. Borgonovo *b*. P. Lombardo *bs*.
                               E. Pessina *cond*.

ONEGLIA — TEATRO ROSSINI
Jan 13   Concert

SAVONA — TEATRO CHIABRERA
Jan 16   Concert

NICE — PALAIS DE LA MÉDITERRANÉE
Jan 29   Werther
Feb 1   Don Pasquale   A. De Angeli *s*. L. Piccioli *b*. M. Luise *bs*.
                               M. Pasquariello *cond*.

WINTER-SPRING 1953 — CONCERT TOUR
Feb 4   Nervi   Teatro Ambra
Feb 5   Sampierdarena   Teatro Mameli
Feb 10   Santa Margherita Ligure
Feb 12   Chiavari
Feb 19   Savona   Teatro Chiabrera
Feb 26   Albenga
Mar 8   Verona   Teatro Nuovo
Mar 10   Turin   Teatro Alfieri
Mar 24   Fossano   Teatro Astra
Apr 13   Turin   Conservatorio Giuseppe Verdi
Apr 22   Reggio Emilia   Teatro Ariosto
May 2   Nottingham   Albert Hall
May 9   Bournemouth   Winter Garden
May 14   Leeds   Town Hall

PAVIA — CASTELLO
Aug 1   Lucia di Lammermoor   V. Chiericati *s*. G. Diani *b*. G. Foiani *bs*.
                                   G. Mucci *cond*.

SUMMER 1953 — CONCERT TOUR
Aug 29   Lecce   Politeama Greco
Sep 10   Venice   Conservatorio
Sep 17   London   Festival Hall

MONZA — TEATRO PONTI
Oct 20   Lucia di Lammermoor (1) M. Rogers *s*. S. Lo Capo *b*. . . Zini . .
                                    G. Sansoni Savini *cond*.

LECCO — TEATRO IMPERO
Oct 22   Lucia di Lammermoor (1) M. Rogers *s*. F. Sordi *b*. . . Zini . .
                                    G. Sansoni Savini *cond*.

ROME — CASTEL SAN ANGELO
Oct 25   Concert

LECCE — POLITEAMA GRECO
Oct 29   Lucia di Lammermoor (2) M. Ingrosso *s*. F. Mieli *b*. G. Amodeo *bs*.
          V. Marini *cond*.

NAPLES — TEATRO MERCADANTE
Nov 28   Lucia di Lammermoor (1) C. Scarangella *s*. M. Cavallo *b*. G. Amodeo *bs*. G.
          Ruisi *cond*.
Dec 1   La traviata (2)   M. Masseroni *s*. M. Cavallo *b*. G. Ruisi *cond*.

1954

BUENOS AIRES — TEATRO COLÓN
Jan 20   Lucia di Lammermoor (2) B. R. Baigorri *s*. A. Mattiello/D. De Matthaeis *b*.
          J. Zanin *bs*. R. Zamboni *cond*.
Jan 24   L'elisir d'amore (2)   B. R. Baigorri *s*. A. Mattiello *b*. V. Bacciato *b*.
          R. Zamboni *cond*.
Jan 29   La traviata (2)   B. R. Baigorri *s*. A. Mattiello *b*.
          J. E. Martini *cond*.

WINTER-SPRING 1954 — CONCERT TOUR
Feb 13	Buenos Aires	Carceri Giudiziarie
Feb 18	Buenos Aires	
Feb 23	Mendoza	Teatro Condor
Feb 25	San Juan	
Feb 27	San Rafael	
Mar 3	Mendoza	Teatro Condor
Mar 13	Mar de la Plata	
Mar 24	Tucumán	Teatro Alberdi
Mar 27	Tucumán	Teatro Alberdi
Apr 5	Montevideo	Teatro 18 Julio
Apr 9	Porto Alegre	Teatro San Pedro
Apr 13	Ponta Grosa	Teatro Cineopera
Apr 14	Curitiba	Club Concordia
Apr 20	Londrina	Teatro Oroverde
Apr 27	Campinas	Teatro Municipal
Apr 29	Rio de Janeiro	Teatro Municipal
May 3	Belo Horizonte	Teatro Brasil
May 5	Rio de Janeiro	Teatro Municipal
May 8	São Paulo	Teatro Cultura Artistica
May 11	Ourinhos	
May 16	São Paulo	
May 18	Rio de Janeiro	Radio Tupi
May 20	Juiz de Fora	
May 22	Rio de Janeiro	Teatro Republica
May 25	Rio de Janeiro	Teatro Republica
May 27	São Paulo	Radio Tupi
May 30	Nuova Trieste	Chiesa
June 1	Piracicaba	
June	Lavras	
June	Pernambuco	
June	Bahia	

SPRING-SUMMER 1954 SOUTH AMERICA — CONCERT TOUR
June-Aug   Peru and Colombia, among other countries

LUCCA
Oct 19   Concert

LECCE — POLITEAMA GRECO
Oct 28   L'elisir d'amore   F. C. Forti *s.*

AUTUMN 1954-WINTER 1955 — CONCERT TOUR
Nov 12   Squinzano
Nov 14   Squinzano   Caserma Trussi
Nov 17   Taranto   Prefettura
Nov 20   Rome   Teatro Sistina
Dec 4   Prato   Teatro Metastasio

1955

CONCERT TOUR (continued)
Jan 12   Naples   Teatro San Carlo
Jan 27   Savigliano   Teatro Iride

ROME — R.A.I. STUDIOS
Feb 9   Participant in the program "Il mio personaggio"

WINTER 1955 — CONCERT TOUR
Feb 12   Ostenda   Kursaal
Feb 13   Antwerp   Hippodrome
Feb 14   Gand   Théâtre Royal
Feb 15   Brussels   Club Royal
Feb 16   Brussels   Club Royal
Feb 17   La Louvière (Belgium)
Feb 18   Namur (Belgium) Théâtre Royal
Feb 19   Charleroi (Belgium) Théâtre Royal
Feb 20   Liège   Conservatorio
Feb 21   Heisden

MILAN — R.A.I. STUDIOS
Feb 24   Participant in the Program "Una risposta per voi"

MARSEILLES — TEATRO ALCAZAR
Mar 25   Concert
Mar 27   Concert
Mar 28   Concert

BARI — TEATRO PETRUZZELLI
Apr 14   L'elisir d'amore (2)   S. Baruffi *s.* A. Manelli *b.* C. Romano *bs.*
                                  C. Vitale *cond.*

SPRING-AUTUMN 1955 — CONCERT TOUR
June 4   Munich
June 5   Munich
June 11   Bozzolo   Teatro Comunale
July 1   Montreux

279

July 9	Venice	Casino Municipale
July 31	Lugano	
Aug 3	Alassio	
Aug 4	Varazze	Teatro Eden
Aug 23	Acqui Terme	Nuovo Hotel delle Terme
Sep 17	Lanciano	Teatro Fenaroli
Oct 20	Milan	Carcere di San Vittore

1957

SPRING-AUTUMN 1957 — CONCERT TOUR

May 18	Madrid	Teatro Calderon
May 19	Madrid	Radio Studio
May 23	Barcelona	Teatro Principal
May 25	Madrid	Teatro Calderon
May 28	Valencia	Teatro Principal
May 31	Saragossa	Teatro Principal
June 2	Bilbao	Teatro Ayala
June 4	San Sebastian	Teatro Principal
June 6	Santander	Teatro Cervantes
June 8	Oviedo	Teatro Campoamor
June 10	Gijon	Teatro Javellanos
June 14	Leon	Teatro Principal
June 16	La Coruna	Teatro Joffre
June 20	Vigo	Teatro Garcia Barbon
June 22	Orense	Teatro Coliseo
June 25	Valladolid	Teatro Lope de Vega
July 1	Irun	Teatro Principal
Aug 11	Imperia	Teatro Cavour
Aug 16	Moscow	Conservatory
Aug 18	Moscow	Tchaikovsky Theater
Aug 20	Leningrad	
Aug 22	Leningrad	
Aug 25	Riga	
Aug 27	Riga	
Dec 5	Arpino	
Dec 24	Castiglione dei Pepoli	

1958

FROSINONE — TEATRO DELLE VITTORIE
Jan 25   Concert

1959

SPRING-SUMMER 1959 — CONCERT TOUR
May 5   Frascati
June 28   Nocera Umbra
Aug 2   Vienna

SUMMER-AUTUMN 1959 POLAND — CONCERT TOUR
Sep-Oct

AUTUMN 1959 — CONCERT TOUR
Oct 27   Tirana (Albania)
Oct 31   Volendam
Dec 27   Rome   Chiesa di San Luigi dei Francesci

1962

NEW YORK CITY — TOWN HALL
Oct 3   Concert

PROVIDENCE — COLUMBUS THEATER
Nov 1   Concert

1963

WINTER-SUMMER 1963 — CONCERT TOUR
Jan 24   Auckland   Auditorium
Feb 8   Los Angeles   Philharmonic Hall
Aug   Viareggio   Teatro Margherita
Sep 4   Cascais (Portugal)   Teatro Gil Vicente
Sep 24   Lisbon   Teatro da Trindade

ACKNOWLEDGMENTS

In updating the chronology, Thomas Kaufman would like to thank Mr. Umberto Ponce and Mr. Anibal Corvetto of Lima (Peru); Dr. Andrés Moreno of Seville (Spain); and Mr. Nino Dentici of Bilbao (Spain).

Index of Artists

282

INDEX OF ARTISTS

283

Dalamangas, Cristiano *bs.* 1945
Dall'Argine, Eugenio *b.* 1934
Dalla Rizza, Gilda *s.* 1914-1919
Dal Monte, Toti *s.* 1925-1928, 1933, 1935-1936
Damiani, Victor *b.* 1919, 1930-1931, 1934, 1940
Damiano, Guilhermo *b.* 1940
Danco, Suzanne *s.* 1942, 1945
D'Angelo, Louis *bs.* 1923, 1932, 1934-1935
Danise, Giuseppe *b.* 1914-1915, 1921, 1923, 1928, 1934, 1939
D'Arsago, Lydia *s.* 1912
D'Ayala, Antonio *cond.* 1930
De Andrade, Francisco *b.* 1918
De Angeli, Adriana *s.* 1953
De Angelis, Arturo *cond.* 1934, 1939-1940
De Angelis, Nazzareno *bs.* 1919
De Angelis, Teofilo *cond.* 1914, 1916, 1919
De Bernardi, Giuseppe *bs.* 1912
De Biase *t.* 1920
De Biasi, Pietro *bs.* 1923
De Fabritiis, Oliviero *cond.* 1937-1938, 1942-1943, 1945, 1948, 1950
De Falchi, Raffaele *b.* 1943
De Ferran, Raffaele *b.* 1911
De Ferrari, Rina *s.* 1944
De Franceschi, Enrico *b.* 1942
De Frate, Isabella *s.* 1911-1912
De Freitas Branco, Pedro *cond.* 1943, 1946
Defrère, Désiré *b.* 1920-1925, 1928
De Guarnieri, Edoardo *cond.* 1940
De Hidalgo, Elvira *s.* 1914-1917, 1919, 1924-1925
Del Campo, Giuseppe *cond.* 1929, 1933, 1935, 1937, 1943
Del Chiaro, Giuseppe *b.* 1917
Del Chiaro, Ilio *b.* 1936
Del Cupolo, Federico *cond.* 1942
De Lerma, Matilde *s.* 1914
Deleuze *bs.* 1919
De Lieto Sammartino, Anna *s.* 1914
Della Chiesa, Vivien *s.* 1936
Dell'Orefice, Antonio *cond.* 1929
Del Pozo, Carlos *b.* 1917-1921
Del Pozo, Marimì *s.* 1946
Del Signore, Gino *t.* 1935-1936
De Luca, Giuseppe *b.* 1914, 1924, 1929, 1932, 1934-1937, 1945
De Lucchi, Alexandro *bs.* 1941
Delva *s.* 1917
De Magistris *cond.* 1920
De Marco, Edgardo *b.* 1914
De Marco, Giannella *cond.* 1952
De Matthaeis, Duilio *b.* 1954

De Mette, Stella *ms.* 1921
De Miranda, Leontina *s.* 1946
De Muro, Bernardo *t.* 1919
Dentale, Teofilo *bs.* 1914, 1916, 1919
De Robertis, Nietta *s.* 1952
De Rosa, Nora *s.* 1952
De Sabata, Victor *cond.* 1918-1919
Destal, Fred *bs.* 1940
De Stefani, Dora *s.* 1944-1945
De Surra, Giovanni *b.* 1939
De Taranto, Vito *bs.* 1942, 1945, 1947, 1950
De Vecchi, Gino *bs.* 1915-1916
Di Angelo, Tina *ms.* 1913, 1915, 1919
Diani, Giovanni *b.* 1953
Di Cola, Cesare *bs.* 1919
Didur, Adam *bs.* 1921
Di Lelio, Umberto *bs.* 1930, 1938
Dominici, Francesco *t.* 1917
Donatello, Maria *s.* 1912, 1914
Drymma, Bianca *s.* 1917-1918
Dubbini, Agnese *ms.* 1935
Dumaine, Graziella *s.* 1918

Ebers, Clara *s.* 1942
Elmo, Cloe *ms.* 1937, 1944
Enenkel, Toinon *s.* 1912
Erato, Maria *s.* 1949
Erede, Alberto *cond.* 1942
Esposito, Maria *s.* 1936
Eybel, Querita *ms.* 1924

Fabiani, Adele *s.* 1915
Fabbroni, Piero *cond.* 1935, 1939
Failoni, Sergio *cond.* 1934
Falconi, Giulio *cond.* 1917-1919, 1926
Falconieri, Lia *s.* 1937
Falliani, Marù *ms.* 1930
Farell, Marita *s.* 1941
Farneti, Maria *s.* 1915
Farry, Mercedes *s.* 1917
Faticanti, Edoardo *b.* 1921, 1930, 1936
Favaron, P. *b.* 1911
Favero, Mafalda *s.* 1929, 1935-1937, 1942-1943, 1945
Fernandez 1917
Ferraioli, Luigi *bs.* 1911
Ferrari, Rodolfo *cond.* 1917, 1921
Ferraris, Ines Maria *s.* 1913, 1915, 1917
Ferreira, Tita *s.* 1939, 1941
Ferroni, Luigi *bs.* 1915
Fineschi, Onelia *s.* 1946
Finzi Magrini, Giuseppina *s.* 1913, 1916
Fiore, Michele *bs.* 1914, 1929-1930, 1934
Fitziu, Anna *s.* 1914
Flamini, Giuseppe *bs.* 1943
Fleischer, Editha *s.* 1932, 1934-1935

Lanskoy, George *bs.* 1930
La Rotella, Pasquale *cond.* 1914
Laurenti, Maria *s.* 1936, 1938-1939
Lauri, Laura *s.* 1916
Lauwers, Charles *cond.* 1924, 1928
Lauweryns, Georges *cond.* 1917-1919
Lazzari, Virgilio *bs.* 1919-1928, 1930-1931, 1934-1935, 1939-1940
Leider, Frida *s.* 1928, 1931
Leroux, Xavier *cond.* 1916
Lert, Richard *cond.* 1935
Lisboa, Enrico *b.* 1946
Lisson, Maria *s.* 1946
Llacer, Maria *s.* 1917
Lo Capo, Salvatore *b.* 1953
Lodetti, Carla *s.* 1944
Lombardo, Pasquale *b./bs.* 1929, 1943, 1952-1953
Longari, Maria *ms.* 1910
Loring, Louise *s.* 1926
Luba, Antonia *s.* 1943
Lucchese, Josephine *s.* 1923
Lucci, E. *ms.* 1917
Ludikar, Pavel *bs.* 1913, 1923
Lufrano, Giuseppina *ms.* 1919
Luise, Melchiorre *bs.* 1936-1937, 1942, 1944-1946, 1953

Macbeth, Florence *s.* 1919-1921, 1923, 1925-1926, 1928
Madonna, Wanda *ms.* 1951
Magliulo, Elvira *s.* 1914
Maguenat, Alfred *b.* 1917-1919, 1922
Maguet, Lydia *s.* 1935
Malatesta, Pompilio *bs.* 1929, 1932, 1939
Manacchini, Giuseppe *b.* 1936-1938, 1941-1942
Manelli, Armando *b.* 1955
Mansueto, Gaudio *bs.* 1916-1918, 1930
Marchi, Spartaco *b.* 1944
Marchini, Elisa *s.* 1915, 1919
Marcoux, Vanni *b.* 1926-1928, 1931
Marengo, Isabel *s.* 1930-1932, 1934, 1940
Marini, Vincenzo *cond.* 1953
Marino, Hedda *s.* 1950
Marinuzzi, Gino *cond.* 1915-1917, 1919-1922, 1927-1928, 1930, 1936, 1942-1945
Mario, Queena *s.* 1928-1929, 1932, 1935
Mariosa, Rina *s.* 1945
Marlo, Elinor *ms.* 1925-1926
Marmora, Nera *s.* 1919
Marone, Albino *bs.* 1929
Marrone, Giuseppe *cond.* 1910
Martellato, Alessandro *b.* 1912
Martì, José *bs.* 1917
Martini, Juan Emilio *cond.* 1954

Martini, Renzo *cond.* 1950
Martino, Alfredo *cond.* 1916
Mascagni, Pietro *cond.* 1919
Mascarenhas, Alfredo *b.* 1918
Mascherini, Enzo *b.* 1942, 1945-1946
Masini-Pieralli, Angelo *bs.* 1915-1919
Mason, Edith *s.* 1921-1928, 1934, 1937
Massari, Vanna *s.* 1938-1939
Masseroni, Maria *s.* 1953
Massucci, Tina *ms.* 1912
Mattei, Charlotte *ms.* 1918
Mattiello, Angel *b.* 1954
Maugeri, Carmelo *b.* 1918-1919, 1942
Maxwell, Margery *s.* 1920
Mazzoleni, Ester *s.* 1918-1919
Mazzoleni, Giuditta *s.* 1948
Meisle, Kathryn *ms.* 1926
Meletti, Saturno *b.* 1937, 1943, 1945-1946, 1948, 1950
Melius, Luella *s.* 1926
Melnik, Gregorj *bs.* 1942
Melocchi, Carlo *bs.* 1912
Mengaldo, Lina *ms.* 1913
Menotti, Tatiana *s.* 1935-1938, 1942
Merlo, Marisa *s.* 1934-1935
Merola, Gaetano *cond.* 1924-1925, 1929, 1935, 1939, 1940
Meroni, Renato *b.* 1912
Messina, Domenico *cond.* 1929
Meusel, Lucille *s.* 1934
Micelli, Diana *s.* 1938
Micucci, Linda *s.* 1912
Mieli, Franco *b.* 1953
Milanov, Zinka *s.* 1941
Minghini Cattaneo, Irene *ms.* 1939
Mock, Alice *s.* 1928
Molinari, Enrico *b.* 1919, 1929, 1942
Molinari Pradelli, Francesco *cond.* 1949-1950
Moltrasio, Beniamino *cond.* 1915
Mongelli, Andrea *bs.* 1928, 1950
Montano, Dedy *s.* 1942
Montesanto, Luigi *b.* 1910, 1915, 1919-1920, 1927
Montico, Teobaldo *bs.* 1910
Moore, Grace *s.* 1940
Morano, Olga *s.* 1914-1915
Moranzoni, Roberto *cond.* 1925-1928, 1930-1931, 1936
Morelli, Alfredo *cond.* 1914-1915
Morelli, Carlo *b.* 1930, 1939
Morelli, Giuseppe *cond.* 1950
Moresco, Carlo *cond.* 1942
Morgana, Nina *s.* 1929, 1932
Morin, Henri *cond.* 1920
Mucci, Graziano *cond.* 1946, 1950, 1952-1953

Ricceri, Angelo *bs.* 1916-1917
Riedel, Karl *cond.* 1929
Rimediotti, Brunetto *bs.* 1913
Rimini, Giacomo *b.* 1915-1916, 1919-1927, 1930-1931, 1933, 1936-1937
Rizzini, Adelina *s.* 1910
Rizzo, Arturo *bs.* 1911
Rodriguez Aragon, Lola *s.* 1946
Roessinger, Adele *ms.* 1916
Rogers, Maria *s.* 1953
Romani, Augusto *bs.* 1945
Romano, Carlo *bs.* 1955
Romelli, Lina *s.* 1927, 1930
Romito, Felipe *bs.* 1934, 1938
Ronchi, Fabio *b.* 1928
Rossato, Luigi *bs.* 1917
Rossi *ms.* 1917
Rossi, Anafesto *b.* 1915
Rossi, Carlo *bs.* 1911-1912
Rossi de Castelnuovo *b.* 1911
Rossi, Marcello *b.* 1949
Rossi, Mario *cond.* 1944, 1949
Rossi-Morelli, Luigi *b.* 1918-1919
Rossini *bs.* 1911
Rossi-Oliver, Angela *s.* 1921
Rothier, Léon *bs.* 1923, 1925, 1928-1929, 1932-1935, 1940
Rubini, Clotilde *s.* 1911
Rubino, Giuseppe *cond.* 1911
Ruffo, Titta *b.* 1916, 1919-1921, 1923
Ruisi, Giuseppe *cond.* 1953
Ruisi, Nino *bs.* 1936

Sabanieeva, Thalia *s.* 1923-1924, 1935
Sabater, José *cond.* 1920
Sabino, Antonio *cond.* 1927, 1937-1938, 1944
Sack, Erna *s.* 1937
Saco del Valle, Arturo *cond.* 1917-1920
Sà Earp, Maria *s.* 1940-1941
Salfi, Francesco *cond.* 1945
Salsedo, Antonio *b.* 1943
Salvi, Margarita *s.* 1928, 1930-31
Sammarco, Mario *b.* 1913-1915
Samossoud, Samuel *cond.* 1936
Sansoni Savini, Giacomo *cond.* 1953
Santancana, Miguel *bs.* 1921
Santafè, Ildebrando *b.* 1946
Santarelli, Riccardo *cond.* 1945, 1948
Santiago Font, José *bs.* 1933-1935
Santini, Gabriele *cond.* 1920, 1930, 1932, 1939, 1942, 1945
Saraceni, Adelaide *s.* 1929
Sartori, Umberto *bs.* 1933, 1936, 1942, 1948-1949
Savini, Ino *cond.* 1949
Sayão, Bidù *s.* 1930, 1939-1941

Sbalchiero, Bruno *bs.* 1937
Scarangella, Clara *s.* 1953
Scattola, Carlo *bs.* 1913
Schottler, Giorgio *bs.* 1914
Schwarz, Josef *b.* 1921-1922, 1924
Scialiapin, Fedor *bs.* 1923-1924, 1930, 1933
Scuderi, Sara *s.* 1945
Segura Tallien, José *b.* 1917-1918
Serafin, Tullio *cond.* 1917, 1932, 1934, 1936-1939
Sergenti, Lisandro *bs.* 1941
Serini, Enzo *b.* 1951
Serpo, Ottavio *b.* 1939
Shefoff, Henri *b.* 1935
Sielska, Ariana *s.* 1937
Sigismondo, Arturo *cond.* 1909-1911
Silveri, Paolo *b.* 1945, 1950
Silvetti, Luigi *b.* 1909
Simeoli, Lina *s.* 1909, 1911
Siravo, Luigi *bs.* 1942
Smallens, Alexander *cond.* 1920-1921
Sordi, Franco *b.* 1953
Stabile, Mariano *b.* 1911, 1917-1919, 1929, 1933, 1942, 1944-1945
Stefanoni, Marco *bs.* 1946
Stignani, Ebe *ms.* 1935, 1943
St. Leger, Frank *cond.* 1925, 1930-1931
Storchio, Rosina *s.* 1914-1917, 1920-1921
Stracciari, Riccardo *b.* 1913, 1916, 1925-1926, 1928, 1930
Strano, Alfredo *cond.* 1949
Surinach, Filomena *s.* 1918-1919
Sved, Sándor *b.* 1940
Swarthout, Gladys *ms.* 1928, 1939

Tagliabue, Carlo *b.* 1936, 1945
Tagliapietra, Silvio *cond.* 1951
Tajo, Italo *bs.* 1942, 1945
Tanci *bs.* 1918
Tassinari, Pia *s.* 1938
Tegani, Riccardo *b.* 1913-1914
Telva, Marion *ms.* 1923
Tensini-Peretti, Maria *s.* 1909-1910
Terragnolo, Alfredo *cond.* 1918
Tess, Giulia *s.* /*ms.* 1914, 1935-1936
Thill, Georges *t.* 1930
Thomas, John Charles *b.* 1931, 1934, 1939, 1941
Tibbett, Lawrence *b.* 1932
Titta, Enzo *b.* 1945
Togliani, Carlo *b.* 1942, 1948-1950
Tolosa, J. *cond.* 1918
Tomei, Giulio *bs.* 1934, 1945
Toniolo, Rhea *ms.* 1921
Torres, Raimundo *b.* 1946
Torres de Luna, José *bs.* 1917-1919

288

The Recordings of Tito Schipa

A Discography

by William Shaman with William R. Moran and Alan Kelly

Between November, 1913, and October, 1957, Tito Schipa made just over three-hundred recordings for five commercial firms: the Gramophone Company, Ltd. (principally for its Italian affiliate, the Società Nazionale del Grammofono, Milan); Pathé Frères, Milan and New York; the Victor Talking Machine Company (later RCA Victor), Camden, New Jersey, and its South American affiliate; Durium, Milan; and CCCP, Moscow. Supplementing the studio recordings are a number of extant, non-commercial items spanning the thirty years from 1934 to 1964. These consist of broadcasts, transcribed either off-the-air ("air checks") or over network lines prior to broadcast ("line checks"), in-house recordings of live performances, and private recordings. Schipa also appeared in thirteen films between 1929 and 1951, eleven of them features.

This discography was compiled using the registers and recording sheets of the Gramophone Company, Ltd. (EMI) and the Victor Talking Machine Company/ RCA Victor, making it possible to document for the first time Schipa's many unpublished records and the precise dates of most of the later European issues. Listed are all known studio recordings, published and unpublished, non-commercial recordings, regardless of their reissue status, and the films of both Tito and Carlo Schipa. The layout is chronological—by matrix number or date, depending upon the medium, with allowances made for any overlap between proper *groups* of recordings. Indices of titles (musical works and films) and assisting artists are included, along with notes for individual recordings and a selective list of long-playing Schipa reissues.

ABBREVIATIONS

Language *or Dialect*

(I) = Italian
(F) = French
(La) = Latin
(G) = German
(E) = English

(Le) = Leccese
(N) = Neapolitan
(S) = Spanish
(V) = Venetian

Accompaniment

orch/ = orchestra, conductor as noted
pf/ = piano, pianist as noted
vln/ = violin, violinist as noted

"Orch" designates an unnamed studio orchestra. The majority of the South American Victors (nos. 151-160 and 163-164) are labeled "con orquesta tipica." Note that for many of the HMVs (1929-1953), a distinction is made on the recording sheets between a full orchestra and "orchestrina," the latter designated as "(small orch/)" in the discography. The orchestra of Teatro alla Scala, Milano, designated "(Scala Orch/)" in the discography, was most often labeled as members of that ensemble. A few of the items so attributed seem a bit unlikely (especially those conducted by Semprini, most labeled simply as "Orchestra"), but the description has been verified in company documents. Several of the later, popular tunes recorded for HMV are accompanied by a small "jazz" orchestra, but in only one case (no. 189) is this actually distinguished as such.

General

( ) = Catalog numbers in parentheses were assigned but not issued.
[ ] = HMV *face* numbers: a continuation of single-sided catalog numbers for discs issued only in the double-sided format.
s/s = single-sided or single-face disc
d/s = double-sided or double-face disc
tk = (recording) take

Italian Radio:
EIAR = Ente Italiano Audizioni Radiofoniche (pre-war)
RAI = Radio[television] Audizioni Italiana (post-war)

The Gramophone Company, Ltd.

For the 1913 recordings, Schipa's first, matrix suffix "ah" designates ten-inch (25 cm), "aj" twelve-inch (30 cm). 7-52000 and 7-54000 (ten-inch) and 052000 and 2-052000 (twelve-inch) catalog numbers are red label; 252000 and 254060 are green-label. Single-sided catalog numbers were used for red-label issues until 1924, when they were relegated to "face" numbers for double-sided issues. These face numbers were finally discontinued on Italian issues in 1934, with the introduction of the 0BA/2BA matrix prefixes. "DA-" and "DB-" prefixes are double-sided, red-label "celebrity," ten- and twelve-inch, respectively. DA 100-4000 and DB 100-4049 are international issues; DA 4432 is German; DA 4831 and 4916 French; DB 5350-5351 Italian. "IR" and "IRX" catalog numbers are ten- and twelve-inch Irish pressings. "HMB"-prefix reissues are vinyl repressings from Historic Masters, Ltd. (U.K.).

The complete 1932 *Don Pasquale* was issued as "C"-prefix plum-label in Britain, "S"-prefix green-label in Italy, and "EH"-prefix plum-label in Germany. Electrical Gramophone Company matrix prefixes BM-, 0M-, 0W-, and 0BA are ten-inch; CM-, 2M-, 2W-, and 2BA are twelve-inch, all recorded in Milan except 0W 1928-1 (no. 200), a Naples recording. The 1932 0PG-prefix matrices are ten-inch, recorded in Paris.

Pathé Frères

Schipa's first two sessions for Pathé were recorded in Milan in 1916 and 1919, respectively. A third, smaller group was recorded in New York in 1921. All were paper-label issues. Catalog numbers indicate place of origin but not size: the majority of the Schipa Pathés were 11-inch pressings, issued both single- and double-sided in the U.S. Pathé 3282 (nos. 32 and 49) was a solitary Belgian vertical-cut issue. Lateral-cut Pathé-Actuelle and Actuelle reissues are either European ("X"-prefix and 15000 series) or American (025000 series); the 10000 and 11000 series are American Perfect; the 6000 series of laterals could not be traced. CRS-47 is a ten-inch (lateral) rerecording issued by Jack Caidin's Collectors Record Shop, New York City, in 1948.

American Pathé matrix numbers—really master cylinder numbers—were prefixed with an upper-case "E" (for "États" perhaps), while lateral-cut pressings on

Actuelle and Perfect almost invariably carried the same numbers, prefixed "N" to designate "needle-cut." That the suffixes may indicate take numbers has not been confirmed with any certainty: see the endnote for no. 48.

Victor Talking Machine Company / RCA Victor / RCA Victor, Argentina

"B"- and "C"-prefix Victor matrix numbers designate acoustical recordings, "BVE" and "CVE" electrical recordings, all made in New York or Camden. "BAVE" and "CAVE" are South American electricals, recorded in Buenos Aires. For all three, the "B" indicates ten-inch, the "C" twelve-inch; the intervening "A" in the South American prefixes was used by the Gramophone Company to designate American recordings.

66000 and 74000 catalog numbers are single-sided, Red Seal, ten- and twelve-inch, respectively. The double-sided Schipa Red Seals began in the 800s (ten-inch) and the 6000s (twelve-inch). 10- and 11-prefix Victors are late ten- and twelve-inch Red Seal issues and reissues (commenced June, 1942): the Schipa block of ten-inch issues (10-0021/10-0033) were listed in August, 1948. 26650 (nos. 134-135) is a black-label reissue from circa 1940-1941; the 25-7000s are purple-label exports (Italian). 423- and 425-prefixes are ten-inch South American, 766- ten-inch Argentinean, and 886 (nos. 161-162) ten-inch dubbings used in Uruguay.

ACKNOWLEDGMENTS

Acknowledgment is made to the previous Schipa discographies of Winstanley and Hutchinson (1960) and Maurizio Tiberi (in the 1993 Italian edition of the Schipa, Jr. biography). Additional thanks to Messrs. Juan E. Dzazópulos, Santiago, Chile; Robert Fazio, Long Island; Herbert Glass, Champaign, Illinois, and James B. McPherson, Rexdale, Ontario.

William Shaman, Bemidji, Minnesota
W. R. Moran, La Cañada, California
Alan Kelly, Sheffield, England
July, 1996

COMMERCIAL RECORDINGS

I THE GRAMOPHONE COMPANY, LTD. / SOCIETÀ NAZIONALE DEL GRAMMOFONO, Milano, 1913

	s/s HMV	d/s HMV	s/s Victor	d/s Victor	Reissue
*1. Manon, Act III: Ah! dispar vision [Ah! fuyez, douce image] (Massenet) (I) (orch/?Sabajno)					
10 Nov 1913	052421	DB 969	74629	----	HMB 21
	2-052150				
722aj NOT BY SCHIPA					
723aj - 730aj					
*2. La bohème, Act I: Che gelida manina (Puccini) (I) (orch/?Sabajno)					
14 Nov 1913	052422	DB 969	----		HMB 21
731aj NOT BY SCHIPA					
732aj - 734aj					
*3. w. GARELLI and Chorus: La traviata, Act II: Scena della Borsa [sic] (Verdi) (I) (orch/?Sabajno)					
15 Nov 1913	unpublished				
735aj NOT BY SCHIPA					
736aj - 749aj					
*4. w. GARELLI, BETTONI, and Chorus: Mefistofele, Act IV: Forma ideal purissima (Boito) (I) (orch/?Sabajno)					
750aj	unpublished				
*5. w. GARELLI, BETTONI, and Chorus: Mefistofele, Act IV: Forma ideal purissima (Boito) (I) (orch/?Sabajno)					
751aj	unpublished				
752aj - NOT BY SCHIPA					
*6. La Gioconda, Act II: Cielo e mar! (Ponchielli) (I) (orch/?Sabajno)					
12 Nov 1913	252130	----	----	----	----
2893ah					
*7. Lucia di Lammermoor, Act III: Tu che a Dio spiegasti l'ali (Donizetti) (I) (orch/?Sabajno)					
12 Nov 1913	252142	DA 365	64806	----	----
	7-52123				
2894ah					
*8. Tosca, Act I: Recondita armonia (Puccini) (I) (orch/?Sabajno)					
12 Nov 1913	252133	----	----	----	----
2895ah					
*9. Tosca, Act III: E lucevan le stelle (Puccini) (I) (orch/?Sabajno)					
12 Nov 1913	252134	----	----	----	----
2896ah					
2897ah - 2899ah NOT BY SCHIPA					
*10. w. GARELLI: La traviata, Act I: Un dì felice, eterea (Verdi) (I) (orch/?Sabajno)					
14 Nov 1913	254060	----	----	----	----
	7-54020				
2900ah					

	s/s HMV	d/s HMV	s/s Victor	d/s Victor	Reissue
*11. Rigoletto, Act II: Ella mi fu rapita! (Verdi) (I) (orch/?Sabajno) 2901ah 14 Nov 1913	252143 7-52125	DA 366	64804	925	----
*12. Rigoletto, Act II: Parmi veder le lagrime (Verdi) (I) (orch/?Sabajno) 2902ah 14 Nov 1913	252144 7-52124	DA 366	64805	925	----
*13. Cavalleria rusticana: O Lola ch'ai di latti la cammisa ["Siciliana"] (Mascagni) (I) (orch/?Sabajno) 2903ah 14 Nov 1913	252127 7-52205	DA 364	----	----	----
*14. w. GARELLI and Chorus: La traviata, Act I: Libiamo, libiamo ["Brindisi"] (Verdi) (I) (orch/?Sabajno) 2904ah 15 Nov 1913 2905ah - 2906ah NOT BY SCHIPA	254059	----	----	----	----
*15. w. Chorus: Cavalleria rusticana: Intanto, amici, quà ... Viva il vino ["Brindisi"] (Mascagni) (I) (orch/?Sabajno) 2907ah 21 Nov 1913 2908ah - 2915ah NOT BY SCHIPA	252128 7-52204	DA 364	----	----	----
*16. Faust, Act III: Salve dimora [Salut! demeure chaste et pure] (Gounod) (I) (orch/?Sabajno) 2916ah 26 Nov 1913	252147 7-52122	DA 365	67661	----	----

II PATHÉ FRÈRES, Milan and New York, 1916-1921

PATHÉ, Milano

	Vertical Italy	Vertical U.S.A.	Vertical France	Vertical U.K.	Lateral Reissue	78 rpm Rerecording
17. Tosca, Act III: O dolci mani (Puccini) (I) (orch/?) 86557 1916	10242	59009	0386	---- 6122	15146 X-32	----
18. Zazà, Act II: Ed ora io mi domando (Leoncavallo) (I) (orch/?) 86559 1916	10241	59052	----	----	15127	CRS-47(rr)

19. *L'Arlesiana*, Act II: [È la solita storia del pastore] ... C'è nel sonno l'oblio ["Lamento di Federico"] (Cilea) (I) (orch/?)
    86561   1916   10243   59007   5214 ... 15129 X-48 ||----

20. *Il barbiere di Siviglia*, Act I: Ecco ridente in cielo [part 1] (Rossini) (I) (orch/?)
    86562   1916   10244   59057   ---- ... 5215 ... 15111 15191 X-69 ||----

21. w. BALDASSARE-TEDESCHI: *Tosca*, Act III: Amaro sol per te (Puccini) (I) (orch/?)
    86563   1916   12554   59052   ---- ... 15109 15198 X-50 X-54   CRS-47(rr)

22. *Il barbiere di Siviglia*, Act I: Ecco ridente in cielo [part 2] (Rossini) (I) (orch/?)
    86564   1916   10244   59057   5215 ... 15111 15191 X-69 ||----

23. w. BALDASSARE-TEDESCHI: *Tosca*, Act III: E non giungono ... Trionfal di nuova speme (Puccini) (I) (orch/?)
    86565   1916   12554   59072   ---- ... 5216 ... 15109 15198 X-50 ||----

24. *I pagliacci*, Act II: O Colombina ["Harlequin's Serenade"] (Leoncavallo) (I) (orch/?)
    86566   1916   10241   59009   0386 ... 15127 15223 X-29 ||----

25. *Manon*, Act II: Chiudo gli occhi [Enfermant les yeux] ["Le Rêve"] (Massenet) (I) (orch/?)
    86567   1916   10243   59007   ---- ... 5214 ... ---- ||----

26. *Rigoletto*, Act I: Questa o quella (Verdi) (I) (orch/?)
    86568   1916   10242   59072   0826 ... 5216
                  10316 ... 15100 15146 15186 X-48 ||----

*27. *La bohème*: Act I: Che gelida manina (Puccini) (I) (orch/?)
    80841   1919   10314   54033   ---- ... ---- ||----

28. *Tosca*, Act I: Recondita armonia (Puccini) (I) (orch/?)
    80842   1919   10315   54035   ---- ... 15108 15228 X-28 ||----

	Vertical Italy	Vertical U.S.A.	Vertical France	Vertical U.K.	Lateral Reissue	78 rpm Rerecording
29. Tosca, Act III: E lucevan le stelle (Puccini) (I) (orch/?)	80843 1919 10315	54032	-----	-----	15108 15228 X-29	
30. Rigoletto, Act III: La donna è mobile (Verdi) (I) (orch/?)	80845 1919 10316	54040	0862	5544 15186	15100 X-28	
31. Cavalleria rusticana: O Lola ch'ai di latti la cammisa ["Siciliana"] (Mascagni) (I) (orch/?)	80846 1919 10314	54034	-----	-----	15129 15223 X-32 6122	
32. Guyana: Ay, ay, ay [A sóma te a la ventana] [Creole Song] (arr. Perez-Freire) (S) (?orch/?)	80847 1919 13090	54037	3284 3282	-----	15100 X-3003 10925	
33. Emigrantes: Granadinas (Calleja y Barrera) (S) (pf/?)	80848 1919 -----	54041	-----	-----	-----	
34. "Pesca d'ammore" (Bracco; Barthélemy) (N) (pf/?)	80851 1919 13081	54073	-----	-----	15139 X-3002 10925	
35. "Chi se nne scorda 'cchiù" (Marvasi; Berthélemy) (N) (?pf/?)	80852 1919 13081	-----	-----	-----	15139 X-3002	
36. "Amarilli mia bella" (Guarini; G. Caccini) (I) (pf/?)	80853 1919 13082	-----	-----	-----	X-3003	
37. "Panis Angelicus" (Franck) (La) (pf/?)	80854 1919 13083	-----	-----	-----	-----	
38. "Agnus Dei" (Bizet) (La) (pf/?)	80855 1919 13082	-----	-----	-----	X-3003	

	Vertical U.S.A.	Vertical Italy	Vertical France	Vertical U.K.	Lateral Reissue
39. "Ave Maria" (Schipa) (La) (pf/?)					
80856 1919	13083			----	----
40. "La bruja" (Chapí) (S) (?pf/?)					
80859 1919	13080			----	10438
*41. *La corte del amor:* La de ojos azules ["Princesita"/"Mariposa"] [(Palomero; Padilla) (S) (?pf/?)					
?80960 1919	13080			----	10438

PATHÉ, New York

	Vertical U.S.A.	Vertical Italy	Vertical France	Vertical U.K.	Lateral Reissue
42. *La traviata,* Act II: Lunge da lei per me ... De' miei bollenti spiriti (Verdi) (I) (orch/?)					
E-68256-2 1921	54045	----	----	5544	----
*43. "Cuando ti Lia la facce" ["Cuando te aai la faace"] ["Canto popolare leccese"] (trad.; arr. Schipa) (Le) (?orch/?)					
E-68356-? 1921	?unpublished				
**44. "Bella ragazza delle trecce bionde" ["Canto popolare"] (?trad.; ?arr. Schipa) (I) (?orch/?)					
E-68357-? 1921	?unpublished				
45. "Somewhere A Voice is Calling" (Newton; Tate) (E) (orch/?)					
E-68381-2 1921	54047	----	----	----	025090 11524
46. *La sonnambula,* Act I: Prendi, l'anel ti dono (Bellini) (I) (orch/?)					
E-68382-1 1921	54052	----	0334	5579	025083 10389 11505
47. *Don Pasquale,* Act II: Povero Ernesto! ... Cercherò lontana terra (Donizetti) (I) (orch/?)					
E-68383-1 1921	54046	10407	0441	5579	025090 11524
*48. *Falstaff,* Act II: Dal labbro il canto estasiato (Verdi) (I)					
E-68384 1921	54060	10438	0334 0386	----	025083 10389 11505

	Vertical Italy	Vertical U.S.A.	Vertical France	Vertical U.K.	Lateral Reissue
49. "Santa Lucia" (Cossovich; Cottrau) (I) (orch/?)					
E-68385-1 1921	54049	10368 13090	3284	5591 3282	025063 10622 11512
50. "Marechiare" (di Giacomo; Tosti) (I) (orch/?)					
?E-68386-1 1921	54051	10407	0441	5591	025063 10622 11512
***51. La corte del amor: Mariposa ["Princesita"/"La de ojos azules"] (Palomero; Padilla) (S) (pf/?)**					
? 1921	54075	-----	-----		-----

III VICTOR TALKING MACHINE COMPANY / RCA VICTOR, New York and Camden, 1921-1941

	s/s Victor	d/s Victor	s/s HMV	d/s HMV	Other
52. w. BORI, soprano: La bohème, Act IV: Sono andati? (Puccini) (I) (orch/Pasternack)					
C-25143-1, 2, 3 6 Apr 1921	unpublished				
53. w. BORI, soprano: La bohème, Act IV: O! Dio, Mimì! (Puccini) (I) (orch/Pasternack)					
C-25144-1, 2, 3 6 Apr 1921	unpublished				
***54. La corte del amor: Princesita ["Mariposa"/"La de ojos azules"] (Palomero; Padilla) (S) (orch/Pasternack)**					
B-26107-1, -2, -3 2 Feb 1922	-----	-----			-----
-4, -5, -6 3 Feb 1922		-----			-----
-7, -8, -9 2 Mar 1922					-----
-10, -11, -12 9 Mar 1922	66067	827		7-62051	DA 362
BVE-26107-13, -14 7 Sep 1926	-----	1182		7-62146	DA 834
-15, -16 9 Sep 1926		10-0029			
55. Emigrantes: Granadinas (Calleja y Barrera) (S) (orch/Pasternack)					
B-26108-1, -2, -3 2 Feb 1922	-----	-----			-----
-4, -5, -6 3 Feb 1922	66039	827		7-62035	DA 362
BVE-26108-7, -8 7 Sep 1926	-----	1182		7-62147	DA 834
		10-0029			

56. I pagliacci, Act II O Colombina ["Harlequin's Serenade"] (Leoncavallo) (I) (orch/Pasternack)

B-26109-1, -2	2 Feb 1922	----	828	7-52216	DA 363	----
-3, -4	3 Feb 1922	66045	1183	7-52364	DA 875	----
BVE-26109-5, -6, -7	8 Sep 1927	----	----	----	----	----

57. Guayana: Ay, ay, ay [A sóma te a la ventana] [Creole Song] (arr. Pérez-Freire) (S) (orch/Pasternack)

B-26110-1, -2, -3	3 Feb 1922	----	----	----	----	----
-4, -5, -6	2 Mar 1922	----	----	----	----	----
-7, -8, -9	9 Mar 1922	----	----	----	----	----
C-26110-1, -2, -3	10 Mar 1922	74753	6423	2-062010	DB 694	----
-4, -5, -6, -7	28 Mar 1922	----	6601	----	----	----
CVE-26110-8	7 Sep 1926	----	11-0028	----	----	----

58. Manon, Act II: Chiudo gli occhi [En fermant les yeux] ["Le Rêve"] (take 4 in French; all others in Italian) (Massenet) (orch/Pasternack)

B-26140-1, -2, -3, -4	2 Mar 1922	----	828	7-52217	DA 363	----
-5, -6, -7	9 Mar 1922	----	1183	7-52365	DA 875	----
-8, -9, -10, -11	28 Mar 1922	----	----	----	----	----
-12, -13, -14, -15	2 May 1922	----	----	----	----	----
-16, -17, -18, -19	3 May 1922	66077	----	----	----	----
BVE-26140-20, -21, -22	8 Sep 1926	----	----	----	----	----

59. w. GALLI-CURCI: Don Pasquale, Act III: Tornami a dir che m'ami (Donizetti) (I) (orch/Bourdon)

B-26890-1, -2, -3	22 Sep 1922	----	----	----	----	----
-4, -5, -6	1 Jun 1923	----	----	----	----	----
-7, -8	18 Sep 1924	----	3034	7-54031	DA 646	----
BVE-26890-9, -10, 11	6 Sep 1928	----	3056	40-2899	DA 1161	----
			1755			
			10-0026			

60. w. BORI: "¡Ay Chiquita!" (Yradier) (S) (w. vln, pf, guitar, mandolin/Shilkret)

B-26954-1, -2, -3	13 Oct 1922	unpublished

61. "Chi se nne scorda 'cchiù" (Marvasi; Berthélemy) (N) (w. vln, pf, guitar, mandolin/Shilkret)

B-27115-1, -2, -3, 4	3 Nov 1922	66117	952	7-52228	DA 1054	----
BVE-27115-5, -6, 7	10 Sep 1928	----	1415	----	----	----

62. "Napulitanata" (di Giacomo; Costa) (N) (small orch/Shilkret)

B-27116-1, -2, -3	3 Nov 1922	66121	952	7-52272	----	DA 1054
BVE-27116-4, -5	10 Sep 1928	----	1415	----	----	----

		s/s Victor	d/s Victor	s/s HMV	d/s HMV	Other
63. "Quiéreme mucho" (Roig) (S) (orch/Bourdon)						
B-27598-1, -2, -3, -4	12 Mar 1923	66142	929	7-62055	DA 431	----
BVE-27598-5, -6	9 Sep 1926	----	1181	7-62156	DA 876	----
			423-0065			
*64. "A la orilla de un palmar" (Ponce) (S) (orch/Bourdon)						
B-27599-1, -2, -3, -4	12 Mar 1923	66143	929	7-62056	DA 431	----
BVE-27599-5, -6	9 Sep 1926	----	1181	7-62157	DA 876	----
			423-0056			
65. "A Granada--Canción Andaluza" (Palacios) (S) (orch/Shilkret)						
C-27992-1, -2, -3	31 May 1923	(74839)	6423	2-062012	DB 964	----
CVE-27992-4, -5	7 Sep 1926	----	6601	----	DB 1051	----
			11-0028			
66. Il barbiere di Siviglia, Act I: Ecco ridente in cielo (Rossini) (I) (orch/Shilkret)						
B-27993-1, -2, -3, -4	31 May 1923	(66192)	965	7-52254	DA 594	----
BVE-27993-5, -6, -7	10 Sep 1926	----	1180	7-52362	DA 874	----
			10-0021			
67. w. GALLI-CURCI: La sonnambula, Act I: Son geloso del zefiro (Bellini) (I) (orch/Bourdon)						
C-27994-1, -2, -3	1 Jun 1923	----	8067	2-054151	DB 811	----
					DB 2397	
68. Il barbiere di Siviglia, Act I: Se il mio nome saper (Rossini) (I) (guitar/Schipa; pf/?)						
B-28050-1, -2, -3	5 Jun 1923	(66193)	965	7-52255	----	----
-4, -5, -6	22 Sep 1923	----	1180	7-52363	DA 594	----
BVE-28050-7, -8, -9	10 Sep 1926	----	10-0021		DA 874	----
69. Rigoletto, Act III: La donna è mobile (Verdi) (I) (orch/Bourdon)						
B-28492-1, -2, -3	21 Sep 1923	----		7-52300	DA 739	----
BVE-28492-4, -5, -6	16 Jun 1925	----	1099			----
70. "Pesca d'ammore" (Bracco; Barthélemy) (N) (orch/Bourdon)						
B-28493-1, -2, -3	21 Sep 1923	----				----
-4, -5, -6	28 Sep 1923					----
-7, -8, -9	15 May 1924					----
-10, -11, -12	18 Sep 1924		1063	7-52285	DA 705	----
BVE-28493-13, -14, -15	23 Dec 1926		1438	7-52374	DA 1110	----

71. *Lakmé*, Act I: Fantaisie aux divins mensonges (Delibes) (F) (orch/Bourdon)

B-28494-1, -2, -3, -4	21 Sep 1923	----	----	----
-5, -6, -7	28 Sep 1923	----	----	----
BVE-28494-8, -9, -10	25 Nov 1925	1187	7-32109	DA 870

72. *Mignon*, Act III: Ah! non credevi tu [Elle ne croyait pas] (Thomas) (I) (orch/Bourdon)

C-30079-1, -2, -3	14 May 1924	6465	2-052282	DB 843

73. *Mignon*, Act II: Addio, Mignon! fa core [Adieu, Mignon, courage] (Thomas) (I) (orch/Bourdon)

C-30080-1, -2, -3	14 May 1924	6465	2-052281	DB 843

74. "Mi viejo amor" (Esparza Oteo) (S) (orch/Bourdon)

B-30081-1, -2, -3	14 May 1924	1030	----	----
BVE-30081-4, -5	17 Oct 1927	----	----	DA 667
-6, -7	19 Oct 1927	1299	7-62181	DA 957

75. "Serenata medioevale" (Cimmino; Silvestri) (I) (orch/Bourdon)

B-30082-1 -2, -3	14 May 1924	1063	7-52284	DA 705
BVE-30082-4, -5, -6	17 Oct 1927	----	----	----

76. "Rosalinda" (Sanchez de Fuentes) (S) (orch/Bourdon)

B-30083-1, -2	14 May 1924	1030	7-62180	DA 667
BVE-30083-3, -4	17 Oct 1927	1299	----	DA 957

77. "Ave Maria" (Schipa) (La) (orch/Bourdon)

C-30085-1, -2, -3	15 May 1924	6543	2-052292	DB 873
CVE-30085-4, -5, -6	16 May 1925	11-0027	----	----

*78. *Siete Canciónes Populares Españoles*, no. 4: Jota ["Dicen que nos queremos"] (Sierra; Falla) (S) (harp/Lapitino; orch/Mr. Prince)

B-30086-1-2, 3	15 May 1924	1031	----	----
-4, -5	16 May 1924	1153	----	----
BVE-30086-6, -7, -8	16 Jun 1925	10-0025	7-62086	DA 751

79. "Liebestraum" (Liszt, Op. 62/3; arr. Schipa) (I) (pf/Longás [1924]; pf/Echániz [1925])

C-30087-1, -2, -3	16 May 1924	----	----	----
-4, -5, -6	22 Sep 1924	----	----	----
-7, -8, -9	14 Nov 1924	----	----	----
CVE-30087-10 -11	15 Jun 1925	6543	2-052293	DB 873
-12, -13, -14	19 Jun 1925	11-0027	----	----

*80. Suzanne: Comme un petit oiseau (Paladilhe) (F) (orch/Bourdon)

	s/s Victor	d/s Victor	s/s HMV	d/s HMV	Other
B-30088-1 -2, -3 16 May 1924	-----				[CD]

*81. "Á Cuba" (Schipa) (S) (orch/Mr. Prince [1924]/Bourdon [1925])

	s/s Victor	d/s Victor	s/s HMV	d/s HMV	Other
B-30093-1 -2 16 May 1924	-----	1031			-----
BVE-30093-3, -4, -5 15 Jun 1925	-----	-----			-----
-6, -7 16 Jun 1925	-----	-----			-----
-8, 9, 10 19 Jun 1925	-----	1153 / 10-0025 / 423-0046		DA 1091	-----

82. w. GALLI-CURCI: La traviata, Act I: Un dì felice, eterea (Verdi) (I) (orch/Bourdon)

	s/s Victor	d/s Victor	s/s HMV	d/s HMV	Other
B-30907-1, -2, 3 17 Sep 1924	-----	3038	7-54034	DA 711	-----
BVE-30907-4, -5, -6, Z 6 Sep 1928	-----	3054 / 1754	40-2395	DA 1133	-----

83. w. GALLI-CURCI: La traviata, Act III: Parigi, o cara (Verdi) (I) (orch/Bourdon)

	s/s Victor	d/s Victor	s/s HMV	d/s HMV	Other
B-30908-1, -2, 3 17 Sep 1924	-----	3038	7-54035	DA 711	-----
BVE-30908-4, -5, -6 6 Sep 1928	-----	3054 / 1754	-----	DA 1133	-----
-7, -8, -9 7 Sep 1928			40-2396		

84. w. GALLI-CURCI: Rigoletto, Act I: È il sol dell'anima (Verdi) (I) (orch/Bourdon)

	s/s Victor	d/s Victor	s/s HMV	d/s HMV	Other
B-30909-1, -2 17 Sep 1924	-----	3034	7-54032	DA 646	-----
BVE-30909-3, -4, -6 6 Sep 1928	-----	3056 / 1755 / 10-0026	-----	DA 1161	-----
-7, -8 7 Sep 1928			40-2900		

*85. w. GALLI-CURCI: Lucia di Lammermoor, Act I: Verrano a tè (Donizetti) (I) (orch/Bourdon)

	s/s Victor	d/s Victor	s/s HMV	d/s HMV	Other
C-30910-1 17 Sep 1924	-----	8067	2-054152	DB 811	-----
-2, -3, -4 18 Sep 1924	-----	-----	-----	-----	-----
CVE-30910-5, -6, -7 7 Sep 1928	-----	-----			

86. "Ce steva 'na vota" (de Cescenzo) (N) (orch/Bourdon)

	s/s Victor	d/s Victor	s/s HMV	d/s HMV	Other
B-30911-1, -2, 3 18 Sep 1924	-----	1438 / 25-7279 / 425-7003	7-52305	DA 739	[CD]
BVE-30911-4, -5, -6 15 Jun 1925	-----				-----

87. "Madrigal español" (Campero; Huerta) (S) (orch/Bourdon)
BVE-32897-1, -2, -3   15 Jun 1925   ----   1126   7-62087   DA 751

88. "Ave Maria" (Schipa) (La) (pf/Echániz)
CVE-33000-1, -2   15 Jun 1925   unpublished   ----   ----   ----

89. "'O sole mio" (Capurro; di Capua) (I) (orch/Bourdon)
BVE-33001-1, -2   15 Jun 1925   ----   1099   7-52301   DA 729
-3, -4   16 Jun 1925   25-7278
                       425-7278

*90. a) "La Farfalletta" (trad.; arr. Schipa) (I) ; b) "La Girometta" (?Sibella) (I) (pf/Echániz)
BVE-33002-1, -2   16 Jun 1925   ----   ----   ----   DA 729
-3, -4, 5   19 Jun 1925   1126   7-52302

91. "La niña querida" (Buzzi-Peccia) (S) (orch/Bourdon)
BVE-33937-1, -2, 3   24 Nov 1925   ----   1186   7-62158   DA 877

92. "Mal d'amore" (Buzzi-Peccia) (I) (orch/Bourdon)
BVE-33938-1, -2, 3   24 Nov 1925   ----   1186   7-52359   DA 877

*93. Martha, Act III: M'appari [Ach, so fromm] (Flotow) (I) (orch/Bourdon)
CVE-33939-1, -2, 3   24 Nov 1925   ----   6570   2-052298   DB 1064

94. L'elisir d'amore, Act II: Una furtiva lagrima (Rossini) (I) (orch/Bourdon)
CVE-33940-1, -2, 3   24 Nov 1925   ----   6570   (2-052299)   (DB 1064)

95. w. BORI: La bohème, Act IV: Sono andati? (Puccini) (I) (orch/Bourdon)
CVE-33943-1, -2, 3   24 Nov 1925   ----   8068   2-054155   DB 911

96. w. BORI: La bohème, Act IV: O! Dio, Mimì! (Puccini) (I) (orch/Bourdon)
CVE-33944-1, -2, 3   24 Nov 1925   ----   8068   2-054156   DB 911

*97. Werther, Act III: Pourquoi me réveiller? (Massenet) (F) (orch/Bourdon)
BVE-33945-1, -2, 3   25 Nov 1925   ----   1187   7-32110   DA 870

*98. "Piscatore 'e Pusilleco" (Murolo; Tagliaferri) (N) (orch/Bourdon)
BVE-35855-1, -2   7 Sep 1926   ----   1236   7-52368   DA 882

99. "Santa Lucia" (Cossovich; Cottrau) (I) (orch/Bourdon)
BVE-35856-1, -2   7 Sep 1926   ----   1204   7-52347   DA 841

100. "Guapparia" (Bovio; Falvo) (N) (orch/Bourdon)
BVE-35857-1, -2   8 Sep 1926   ----   1236   7-52369   DA 882

	s/s Victor	d/s Victor	s/s HMV	d/s HMV	Other
101. "La Campana di San Giusto" (Drovetti; Arona) (I) (orch/Bourdon)					
CVE-35858-1, -2, -3 8 Sep 1926	------	6629	2-052324	DB 1038	------
102. "Vieni sul mar!" (trad.; ?arr. Vergine) (I) (orch/Bourdon)					
BVE-35859-1, -2, -3 8 Sep 1926	------	1204 10-0033	7-52348	DA 841	------
103. *Rigoletto*, Act I: Questa o quella (Verdi) (I) (orch/Bourdon)					
BVE-35860-1, -2, -3 8 Sep 1926	------	1282 10-0027	7-52370	DA 885 IR 380	------
104. "Amapola" (Lacalle) (S) (orch/Pasternack)					
BVE-35861-1, -2, -3 9 Sep 1926	------	1177 10-0023	7-62124	DA 821	------
105. *Don Pasquale*, Act I: Sogno soave e casto (Donizetti) (I) (orch/Pasternack)					
BVE-35862-1, -2, -3 9 Sep 1926	------	1282 10-0027	7-52371	DB 885 IR 380	------
106. "Mamma mia, che vò'sape" (Russo; Nutile) (N) (orch/Pasternack)					
CVE-35863-1, -2, -3 9 Sep 1926	------	6629	2-052325	DB 1038	------
107. "Valencia" (Boyer; Charles; Padilla; arr. Bourdon) (S) (orch/Pasternack)					
BVE-35864-1, -2, -3 9 Sep 1926	------	1177 10-0023	7-62123	DA 821	------
108. "La Partida" (Blasco; Alvarez) (S) (orch/Bourdon)					
CVE-37324-1, -2 23 Dec 1926	------	6632	------	DB 1079	------
109. "Alma de Dios" ["Canción del Vagabundo"] (Serrano) (S) (orch/Bourdon)					
CVE-37325-1, -2, -3 23 Dec 1926	------	6632	------	DB 1079	------
110. "Himno Nacional de Colombia," part 1 (Nuñez; Sindici) (S) (orch/Bourdon)					
BVE-37326-1, -2, -3 23 Dec 1926	------	1217	------	------	------
111. "Himno Nacional de Colombia," part 2 (Nuñez; Sindici) (S) (orch/Bourdon)					
BVE-37327-1, -2, -3 23 Dec 1926	------	1217	------	------	------
112. *Serse*, Act I: Ombra mai fu ["Largo"] (Handel) (I) (harp/Lapitino; orch/Bourdon)					
CVE-37328-1, -2, -3 23 Dec 1926	------	6753 11-0026	2-052339	DB 1064	------

113. w. DE GOGORZA: "A la luz de la luna" (Anton y Michelena) (S) (orch/Bourdon)
BVE-38379-1, -2, -3   3 May 1927
-4, -5, -6   17 Feb 1928   3049 / 1751 / 10-0022   7-64033   DA 976   ----

114. w. DE GOGORZA: "Los Rumberos" (Guaracha) (S) (orch/Bourdon)
BVE-38380-1, -2,-3,-4   3 May 1927
-5, -6, -Z, -8   17 Feb 1928   3049 / 1751 / 10-0022   7-64034   DA 976   ----

115. L'Arlesiana, Act II: È la solita storia ["Lamento di Federico"] (Cilea) (I) (orch/Bourdon)
BVE-38381-1, -2   3 May 1927
CVE-38381-1, -2   11 Sep 1928   7583   42-1191   DB 1610 / DB 3461   ----

116. La favorita, Act I: Una vergine [Une ange, une femme inconnue] (Donizetti) (I) (orch/Bourdon)
BVE-38382-1, -2   3 May 1927
-3, -4   17 Oct 1927   ----   ----   ----   ----

117. Don Giovanni, K. 527, Act II: Il mio tesoro (Mozart) (I) (orch/Bourdon)
BVE-39897-1, -2   17 Oct 1927   1362   7-52417   DA 1016   ----

118. Don Giovanni, K. 527, Act I: Dalla sua pace (Mozart) (I) (orch/Bourdon)
BVE-39898-1, -2   17 Oct 1927   1308 / 1308, 10-0024   7-52398 / 7-52397   DA 963 / DA 963   ----

119. "'A vucchella" (d'Annunzio; Tosti) (N) (Tosti) (orch/Bourdon)
BVE-39899-1, -2   17 Oct 1927   1317 / 10-0030   7-52399   DA 974   ----

120. "Ave Maria" [adapted from the Cavalleria rusticana "Intermezzo"] (Mascagni) (La) (orch/Bourdon)
CVE-40700-1, -2   19 Oct 1927   6753 / 11-0026   2-052371   DA 1387   ----

121. "Nina" ["Tre giorni son che Nina"] (Ciampi; formerly attr. Pergolesi) (I) (orch/Bourdon)
BVE-40701-1, -2   19 Oct 1927   1317 / 10-0030   7-52400   DA 974   ----

*122. "Angela Mia" (Schipa; Rapee; Pollack) (I) (orch/Bourdon)
BVE-42936-1, -2, 3   10 Sep 1928   1347   7-52413   DA 1001   ----

	s/s Victor	d/s Victor	s/s HMV	d/s HMV	Other
123. "Femmena 'ngannatora" (Cutillo; Schipa) (N) (orch/Bourdon)					
BVE-42937-1, -2, 3 10 Sep 1928	——	1347	7-52414	DA 1001	——
124. "I Shall Return" (Cross; Schipa) (E) (orch/Bourdon)					
BVE-42938-1, -2, -3 10 Sep 1928	——	——	——	——	——
-4, -5 13 Feb 1930	——	1479	40-2531	DA 1147	
125. "When You're in Love" (Donaldson; Blaufuss) (E) (Orch/Bourdon)					
BVE-42939-1, -2 11 Sep 1928	——	——	——	——	——
-3, -4 13 Feb 1930	——	1479	40-2532	DA 1147	
*126. "El Gaucho" (Schipa) (S) (orch/Bourdon)					
BVE-42940-1, -2, -3 11 Sep 1928	——	1372 / 10-0028	7-62286	DA 1042	DA 1486
127. "Luna castellana" (Schipa; Rose; Longás) (S) (orch/Bourdon)					
BVE-42941-1, -2 11 Sep 1928	——	1372 / 10-0028	7-62287	DA 1042	——
*128. Rigoletto, Act II: Ella mi fu rapita! ... Parmi veder le lagrime (Verdi) (I) (orch/Bourdon)					
CVE-42942-1, -2 11 Sep 1928	——	7145	42-679	DB 1372	——
129. Luisa Miller, Act II: Quando le sere al placido (Verdi) (I) (orch/Bourdon)					
CVE-42943-1, -2, 3 11 Sep 1928	——	7145	42-709	DB 1372	——
130. L'elisir d'amore, Act I: Adina, credimi (Donizetti) (I) (orch/Bourdon)					
BVE-47430-1, -2, 3 6 Sep 1928	——	1362	7-52419	DB 1016	——
131. "Prece" ["Preghiera"] (Schipa) (I) (organ/Mark Andrews; orch/Bourdon)					
BVE-47431-1, -2, 3 7 Sep 1928	——	7583	42-1192	DB 1610	——
132. "Sevillana" (Ochoa; Longás) (S) (pf/Longás)					
BVE-47432-1, -2 7 Sep 1928	——	1421	40-1213	DA 1132	——
133. Spanish Dance, no. 5: "Playera" ["Playera-Andaluza"] (Granados; arr. Schipa) (I) (pf/Longás)					
BVE-47433-1, -2 7 Sep 1928	——	1421	40-1212	DA 1132	——
134. "Ideale" (Errico; Tosti) (I) (orch/Bourdon)					
BVE-58655-1, -2 13 Feb 1930	——	1461 / 26650	40-1837	DA 1114	——
135. "Marechiare" (di Giacomo; Tosti) (I) (orch/Bourdon)					
BVE-58656-1, -2, -3 14 Feb 1930	——	1461 / 26650	40-1838	DA 1114	——

*136. "Tu sonrisa del cristal" ["The Sunshine of Your Smile"] (Cooke; Ray) (S) (orch/Bourdon)

| BVE-58657-1, -2, -3 | 14 Feb 1930 | 1451 | 40-2099 | DA 1117 | ----- |

*137. Naughty Marietta: Oh! dulce misterio de la vida [Ah! Sweet Mystery of Life] (Young; Herbert; trans. Lopez Serna) (S) (orch/Bourdon)

| BVE-58663-1, -2, -3 | 17 Feb 1930 | 1451 | 40-2034 | DA 1117 | ----- |

*138. L'elisir d'amore, Act II: Una furtiva lagrima (Donizetti) (I) (pf/Huarte)

| CS-81053-1, -1A | 15 Jan 1934 | ----- | ----- | ----- |

*139. "Chi se nne scorda 'cchiù" (Marvasi; Barthélemy) (N) (pf/Huarte)

| BS-81054-1, -1A | 15 Jan 1934 | ----- | ----- | [CD] |

*140. "Comme facette mammeta?" (Capaldo; Gambardella) (N) (pf/Sciarretti)

| BS-063716-1, -2, -3 | 3 Apr 1941 | ----- | ----- | [LP] |

*141. "Napoli che nun more" ["Napule ca nun more"] (Bonavolontà; Manlio) (N) (pf/Sciarretti)

| BS-063717-1, -2 | 3 Apr 1941 | ----- | ----- | ?[LP] |
| -3 | 8 Apr 1941 | ----- | ----- | ?[LP] |

*142. "Sincerita" (Murolo; Schipa) (N) (pf/Sciarretti)

| BS-063335-1, -2 | 8 Apr 1941 | ----- | ----- | [LP] |

*143. "Passione" (Bovio; Tagliaferri; Valente) (N) (pf/Sciarretti)

| BS-063336-1, -2 | 8 Apr 1941 | ----- | ----- | [LP] |

*144. Il Pompeo: O cessate di piagarmi (A. Scarlatti) (I) (pf/Sciarretti)

| BS-063337-1, -2, -3 | 8 Apr 1941 | ----- | ----- | [LP] |

*[145]. [TITLE UNKNOWN]

| BS-063338-? | ?8 Apr 1941 | unpublished |

*146. "Querer con la guitarra (Yo canto para ti)" (Grever) (S) (pf/Sciarretti)

| BS-063339-1, -2 | 10 Apr 1941 | ----- | ----- | [LP] |

*147. "Fragancia de amor" (Bavino; Grever) (S) (pf/Sciarretti)

| BS-063340-1, -2, 3 | 10 Apr 1941 | ----- | ----- | [LP] |

148. "Liebestraum" (Liszt, Op. 62/3; arr. Schipa) (I) (pf/Sciarretti)

| CS-063341-1, -2, -3, -4 | 10 Apr 1941 | ----- | ----- | --- |
| -5, -6 | 11 Apr 1941 | 18068 | ----- | --- |

149. "Separate pur spirate" (Donaudy) (I) (pf/Sciarretti)

| BS-063342-1, -2, -3 | 10 Apr 1941 | unpublished |

150. "In a Persian Palace" (Harbach; Sevino) (E) (pf/Sciarretti)

| BS-063343-1, -2, -3 | 10 Apr 1941 | unpublished |

IV RCA VICTOR, ARGENTINA, *Buenos Aires, 1930-1934*

		dls *Victor*	*HMV face* *numbers*	*dls* *HMV*	*Other*
151. "La Cumparsita" (Rodriguez) (S) (orch/?)					
BAVE-60449-1, -2, -3	6 Oct 1930	1488 1633 766-009	----	-----	----
152. "Ammore canta" (Murolo; Tagliaferri) (N) (orch/?)					
BAVE-60450-1, -2, -3	6 Oct 1930	1488	----	-----	----
153. "Confesión" (Discépolo; Amadori) (S) (orch/?)					
BAVE-60884-1, -2	6 Aug 1931	1533 1633 10-0024	40-4302	DA 1262	----
154. "¿Dónde estás, corazón?" (Serrano; Berto) (S) (orch/?)					
BAVE-60885-1, -2	6 Aug 1931	1535	----	-----	----
155. "Tinieblas" (Velich; Valdaro) (S) (orch/?)					
BAVE-60886-1, -2	6 Aug 1931	1536 766-009	----	-----	----
BAVE-60886A-T1	[6 Aug 1931]	----	40-4437	DA 1300	----
156. "Ojos lindos y mentirosos" (Schipa) (S) (orch/?)					
BAVE-60887-1, -2	6 Aug 1931	1534	40-4425	DA 1262	----
157. "O surdato 'nnammurato" (Calfano; Cannio) (N) (orch/?)					
BAVE-60888-1, -2	6 Aug 1931	1536	40-4438	DA 1247	----
158. "Fenesta ascura" (Bracco; Pizzaroni) (N) (orch/?)					
BAVE-60889-1, -2	6 Aug 1931	1535	----	-----	----
159. "Napule" (Schipa; Hinton) (N) (orch/?)					
BAVE-60890-1, -2	6 Aug 1931	1533	40-4344	DA 1247	----
160. "Mariá, marí" (Russo; di Capua) (N) (orch/?)					
BAVE-60891-1, -2	6 Aug 1931	1534	----	-----	[LP]
161. El matrero, Act I: Pontezuela; mi vigüela sabe que viene a llorar ["Canto di Pedro"] (Boero) (S) (orch/?)					
BAVE-60904-1, -2	Aug 1931	1543	----	886-0033	----

*162. *Sadko*, Scene iv: Chant hindou (Rimsky-Korsakov) (F) (orch/?)
      BAVE-60905-1, -2   Aug 1931   1543   -----

*163. "Dimelo al oido" (Lomuto) (S) (Lomuto Orquesta Tipica/Lomuto)
      BAVE-86551-1, -2, -3 Oct 1934 1680   886-0033   -----

*164. "¡Vida mia!" (Fresedo) (S) (Fresedo Orquesta Tipica/Fresedo)
      BAVE-86552-1, -2, -3 Oct 1934 1680   -----

*165. "Gesu, noi adoriamo" (Padre Antonio da Monterosso, cappuccino) (I) (organ/Prof. R. Moreau)
      CAVE-86565-1, -2   Oct 1934   36128   -----

*166. w. DE PAMPHILIS: "Christus vincit" ["Canto Liturgico"] (?) (La) (organ/?Prof. R. Moreau)
      CAVE-86566-1, -2   Oct 1934   36128   -----

V THE GRAMOPHONE COMPANY, LTD. / SOCIETÀ NAZIONALE DEL GRAMMOFONO, *Milano*, 1930-1953

	HMV	Victor
167. *L'elisir d'amore*, Act II: Una furtiva lagrima (Donizetti) (I) (Scala Orch/Sabajno) CM 1335-1, 2 13 Dec 1929	DB 1387 [32-1153] DB 3461	-----
*168. "Ninna-nanna" (Sandro Benelli) (I) (small orch/Sabajno) BM 1336-1, 2 16 Dec 1929	DA 1088 [30-2530]	1532
*169. "Luntananza amara" ["Melodia napoletana"] (Cutillo; Schipa) (N) (orch/Sabajno) BM 1337-1, 2 16 Dec 1929	DA 1089 [30-2531]	1546
*170. "Gitana" (Ochoa; Longás) (S) (Scala Orch/Sabajno) BM 1341-1, 2 17 Dec 1929	DA 1091 [30-2532]	1532
*171. "Scrivenno a mammena" ["Melodia napoletana"] (Cutillo; Schipa) (N) (Scala Orch.Sabajno) BM 1342-1, 2 17 Dec 1929	DA 1089 [30-2533]	1547
172. "Fa la nana bambin" ["Fa la nanna mio piccino"] (Geni Sadero) (V) (small orch/Sabajno) BM 1346-1, 2 18 Dec 1929	DA 1088 [30-2534]	1546
*173. "Nun è carmela mia!" ["Canzone napoletana"] (Fiore; Valente) (N) (small orch/Sabajno) BM 1347-1, 2 18 Dec 1929	DA 1110 [30-2535]	1547
174. "Mandulinata a Napule" ["Serenata"] (Murolo; Tagliaferri) (N) (small orch/Sabajno) BM 1358-1, 2 20 Dec 1929	DA 1090 [30-2536]	1545

	d/s Victor	HMV face numbers	d/s HMV	Other
175. "'A Canzone d''e stelle" ["Barcarola all'antica"] (Murolo; Tagliaferri) (N) (small orch/Sabajno)	BM 1359-1, 2	20 Dec 1929	DA 1090 [30-2537]	1545
*176. Sento nel core certo dolore: Sento nel core (Alessandro Scarlatti) (I) (small orch/Sabajno)	2M 481-1, 2	20 Apr 1932	DB 1723 [32-2894]	——
	-3	9 May 1932	----	——
*177. Orfeo ed Euridice, Act II: Che farò senza Euridice (Gluck) (I) (orch/Sabajno)	2M 482-1, 2	20 Apr 1932	----	——
	-3	9 May 1932	DB 1723 [32-2895]	——
178. "Sei tu" (D'Andrea; Schipa) (I) (small orch/Sabajno)	0M 483-1, 2	20 Apr 1932	DA 1275 [30-8771]	——
*179. "Catina" (Trevisan; Schipa) (V) (small orch/Sabajno)	0M 484-1, 2	20 Apr 1932	DA 1275 [30-8772]	——
*180. "Plaisir d'amour" (Martini) (F) (small orch/Sabajno)	2M 485-1, 2	20 Apr 1932	DB 2131 [32-2914]	——
181. "Aimant la rose, le rossignol," Op. 2/2 ["Plenivshis' rozoy, solovey"] (Koltzov; Rimsky-Korsakov) (F) (small orch/Sabajno)	0M 492-1, 2	22 Apr 1932	DA 1323 [30-8773]	——
*182. "Senza nisciuno" (Barbieri; de Curtis) (N) (small orch/Sabajno)	0M 493-1, 2	22 Apr 1932	DA 1271 [30-8774] / DA 1323	1970
183. "Torna!" ["Canzone napoletana"] (Vento; Valente) (N) (small orch/Sabajno)	0M 502-1, 2	27 Apr 1932	DA 1271 [30-8802]	1970
184. "Dicitencello vuje" ["Canzone napoletana"] (Fusco; Falvo) (N) (orch/Sabajno)	0M 523-1, 2, 3	9 May 1932	DA 1272 [30-8775]	1657
185. "'Te vurria vasà'" ["Canzone napoletana"] (Russo; di Capua) (N) (orch/Sabajno)	0M 524-1, 2	9 May 1932	DA 1272 [30-8776]	1657
186. "Andaluza" (Ochoa; Schipa) (S) (orch/Sabajno)	0M 525-1, 2	10 May 1932	DA 1273 [30-8777]	1621
187. "El Manicero" ["Rumba"] (Simons Moises) (S) (orch/Sabajno)	0M 531-1, 2 11 May 1932 DA 1273 [30-8803] 1621			

Don Pasquale (Donizetti) (I) Complete opera in 3 acts
Members of the Chorus and Orchestra of Teatro alla Scala, Milano/Carlo Sabajno; Vittore Veneziani, chorus master
CAST: Ernesto Badini (*Don Pasquale*); Afro Poli (*Doctor Malatesta*); Adelaide Saraceni (*Norina*); Tito Schipa (*Ernesto*); Giordano Callegari (*Notary*).
Recorded Milan, 26 September–12 October, 1932, with retakes in November. Issued as Gramophone Company Record Library set 177 (manual: C.2519–2533; automatic C.7247–7261); Italian *La Voce del Padrone* S10410-10424; Victor set 187 (manual M187: 11563-11577; automatic AM187: 11578-11592; and drop DM187: 13330-13344). In addition to the original HMV matrix numbers in the wax, Victor pressings bear domestic matrices CVE-73691-73700 and CVE 77700-77719, with matching take prefixes.

		HMV [International]	Italy	HMV Germany	HMV Victor
*188 [1]. Overture (pt. 1) 2M 815-1, 2	September, 1932	C.2519 [32-3457] C.7247	S10410	EH1160	11563 11578 13330
[2]. Overture (pt. 2) 2M 816-1, 2	September, 1932	C.2519 [32-3217] C.7248	S10410	EH1160	11563 11579 13331
[3]. BADINI and POLI: Act I: Son nov'ore 2M 812-1, 2	September, 1932	C.2520 [32-3214] C.7249	S10411	EH1161	11564 11580 13332
[4]. POLI and BADINI: Act I: Bella siccome un angelo 2M 813-1, 2	September, 1932	C.2520 [32-3215] C.7250	S10411	EH1161	11564 11581 13333
[5]. BADINI and SCHIPA: Act I: Ah! Ah! un foco insolito 2M 868-1, 2	October, 1932	C.2521 [32-3437] C.7251	S10412	EH1162	11565 11582 13334
[6]. SCHIPA and BADINI: Act I: Prender moglie! 2M 869-1, 2	October, 1932	C.2521 [32-3446] C.7252	S10412	EH1162	11565 11583 13335

(*188 continued)	HMV [International]	Italy	HMV Germany	HMV Victor
[7]. SCHIPA and BADINI: Act I: Due parole ancor di volo 2M 870-1, 2 October, 1932	C.2522 [32-3438] C.7253	S10413	EH1163	11566 11584 13336
[8]. SARACENI: Act I: Quel guardo il cavaliere 2M 902-1, 2 October, 1932	C.2522 [32-3454] C.7254	S10413	EH1163	11566 11585 13337
[9]. SARACENI and POLI: Act I: E il Dottor non si vede! 2M 828-1, 2 September, 1932	C.2523 [32-3316] C.7255	S10414	EH1164	11567 11586 13338
[10]. SARACENI and POLI: Act I: Pronto io son 2M 900-1, 2 October, 1932	C.2523 [32-3445]	S10414 C.7256	EH1164	11567 11587 13339
[11]. POLI and SARACENI: Act I: Collo torto 2M 901-1, 2 October, 1932	C.2524 [32-3453] C.7257	S10415	EH1165	11568 11588 13340
[12]. SCHIPA: Act II: Prelude; Povero Ernesto! 2M 871-1, 2 ?6 Oct 1932	C.2524 [32-3439] C.7258	S10415	EH1165	11568 11589 13341
[13]. SCHIPA and BADINI: Act II: Cercherò lontana terra 2M 872-1, 2 ?6 Oct 1932	C.2525 [32-3440] C.7259	S10416	EH1166	11569 11590 13342
[14]. POLI, SARACENI, and BADINI: Act II: Via, da brava 2M 818-1, 2 September, 1932 -3, 4 November, 1932	---- C.2525 [32-3455] C.7260	---- S10416	---- EH1166	11569 11591 13343

Entry	Matrix / Date	C.	S	EH	
[15]. BADINI and SARACENI: Act II: Non abbiate paura	2M 829-1, 2 September, 1932 -3, ?November, 1932	C.2526 [32-3317] C.7261	---- S10417	---- EH1167	---- 11570 11592 13344
[16]. POLI, CALLEGARI, BADINI, SCHIPA, and SARACENI: Act II: Fra da'una parte et cetera	2M 879-1, 2 October, 1932	C.2526 [32-3447] C.7261	S10417	EH1167	11570 11592 13330
[17]. BADINI, SCHIPA, POLI, SARACENI, and CALLEGARI: Act II: S'era in faccende, giunto	2M 880-1, 2 October, 1932	C.2527 [32-3448] C.7260	S10418	EH1168	11571 11591 13331
[18]. SARACENI, POLI, BADINI, and SCHIPA: Act II: Provato ho a prenderti	2M 881-1, 2 October, 1932	C.2527 [32-3441] C.7259	S10418	EH1168	11571 11590 13332
[19]. SARACENI, BADINI, POLI, and SCHIPA: Act II: Riunita immantinente la servitù qui voglio	2M 882-1, 2 October, 1932	C.2528 [32-3442] C.7258	S10419	EH1169	11572 11589 13333
[20]. a) Orchestra: Act III: Prelude; b) BADINI, Act III: I diamanti, presto, presto	2M 899-1, 2 October, 1932 C.7257	C.2528 [32-3452]	S10419	EH1169	11572 11588 13334
[21]. BADINI and SARACENI: Act III: Vediamo: alla modista, cento scudi	2M 819-1, 2 September, 1932	C.2529 [32-3315] C.7256	S10420	EH1170	11573 11587 13335
[22]. BADINI and SARACENI: Act III: È finita, Don Pasquale	2M 820-1, 2 September, 1932 -3, 4 November, 1932	C.2529 [32-3456] C.7255	---- S10420	---- EH1170	---- 11573 11586 13336
[23]. BADINI, POLI, and SCHIPA: Act III: Qualche nota di cuffie e di merletti	2M 887-1, 2 8 Oct 1932	C.2530 [32-3449] C.7254	S10421	EH1171	11574 11585 13337

(*188 continued)	HMV [International]	Italy	HMV Germany	HMV Victor	Victor
[24]. POLI and BADINI: Act III: Questa repentina chiamata					
September, 1932					
2M 831-1, 2	C.2530 [32-3318]	S10421	EH1171	11574	
	C.7253			11584	
				13338	
[25]. BADINI and POLI: Act III: Cheti, cheti immantinente nel giardino discendiamo					
September, 1932					
2M 814-1, 2	C.2531 [32-3216]	S10422	EH1172	11575	
	C.7252			11583	
				13339	
[26]. BADINI and POLI: Act III: Aspetta, aspetta, cara sposina					
September, 1932					
2M 817-1, 2	C.2531 [32-3314]	S10422	EH1172	11575	
	C.7251			11582	
				13340	
[27]. SCHIPA: Act III: Com'è gentil					
2M 888-1, 2 8 Oct 1932	C.2532 [32-3450]	S10423	EH1173	11576	
	C.7250			11581	
				13341	
[28]. SARACENI and SCHIPA: Act III: Tornami a dir che m'ami					
2M 891-1, 2 8 Oct 1932	C.2532 [32-3451]	S10423	EH1173	11576	
	C.7249			11580	
				13342	
[29]. BADINI, POLI, SARACENI, and SCHIPA: Act III: Eccoli; attenti ben					
2M 890-1, 2 8 Oct 1932	C.2533 [32-3444]	S10424	EH1174	11577	
	C.7248			11579	
				13343	
[30]. POLI, BADINI, SARACENI, and SCHIPA: Act III: Senz'andar lungi					
2M 889-1, 2 8 Oct 1932	C.2533 [32-3443]	S10424	EH1174	11577	
	C.7247			11578	
				13344	

	HMV				Victor
*189. "Mu! Mu!" (de Angelis; R. Bellini) (I) ("jazz" orch/Sabajno)					
0M 873-1, 2	6 Oct 1932				unpublished

*190. Minnie: Caravana nella notte (de Angelis; R. Bellini) (I) (Scala Orch/Sabajno)
 0M 883-1, 2   7 Oct 1932   DA 1300 [30-10181]   -----

*191. "Esperanza" (Mancini; Galdieri; Schipa) (S) ("tango" orch/Sabajno)
 0M 884-1, 2   7 Oct 1932   DA 1297 [30-10182]   1641

*192. "Sérénade à la lune" (Mancini; Galdieri; Schipa) (F) (w. banjo/? and guitar/?)
 0M 885-1, 2   7 Oct 1932   unpublished

*193. "Serenata alla luna" (Mancini; Galdieri; Schipa) (I) (w. banjo/? and guitar/?)
 0M 886-1, 2   7 Oct 1932   DA 1297 [30-10129]   1641

*194. "Canto per te" (Mancini; Galdieri; Caslar) (I) (orch/Bervily)
 0PG 122-1   11 Oct 1932   DA 1293 [30-10077]   1996

*195. "Je chante pour toi" (Mancini; Galdieri; Caslar) (F) (orch/Bervily)
 0PG 123-1, 2   11 Oct 1932   DA 4831 [50-?]   -----

*196. "Quand?" (Galdieri; Caslar) (F) (orch/Bervily)
 0PG 124-1, 2   11 Oct 1932   DA 4831 [50-?]   -----

*197. "Quando?" (Galdieri; Caslar) (I) (orch/Bervily)
 0PG 125-1, 2   11 Oct 1932   DA 1293 [30-10083]   1996

*198. Minnie: Caravana nella notte (de Angelis; R. Bellini) (I) (Scala Orch/Semprini)
 0M 1280-1, 2   14 Mar 1933   DA 1300 [30-10181]   -----

*199. "Mu! Mu!" (de Angelis; R. Bellini) (I) (Scala Orch/Semprini)
 0M 1281-1, 2   14 Mar 1933   DA 1323 [30-10772]   -----

*200. "Serenata matutina" (Murolo; Schipa) (N) (orch/Tagliaferri)
 0W 1928-1   31 Aug 1933   DA 1361 [30-11368]   1668

*201. "En effeuillant la marguérite" (de Badet; Longàs) (F) (Scala Orch/Semprini)
 0W 2034-1, 2   3 Oct 1933   DA 1350 [30-11367]   -----

*202. Piedigrotta, 1933: "Che bene voglio 'a tte!" (Murolo; Tagliaferri) (N) (Scala Orch/Semprini)
 0W 2035-1, 2   ?3 Oct 1933   unpublished
 -3, 4   3 Oct 1933 DA 1361 [30-11697]   1668

203. w. DAL MONTE: Don Pasquale, Act III: Tornami a dir che m'ami (Donizetti) (I) (Scala Orch/Ghione)
 0W 2038-1, 2   4 Oct 1933   DA-1351 [30-11369]   2057 / IR 367

204. w. DAL MONTE: La sonnambula, Act I: Prendi, l'anel ti dono (Bellini) (I) (Scala Orch and Chorus/Ghione)
 0W 2039-1, 2   4 Oct 1933   DA 1351 [30-11370]   2057 / IR 367

	HMV	Victor
205. "O del mio amato ben" (Donaudy) (I) (Scala Orch/Semprini) 2W 2072-1, 2 12 Oct 1933	DB 2131 [32-4301]	-----
206. "Le plus beau moment du jour" (de Badet; Richepin) (F) (Scala Orch/Semprini) 0W 2073-1, 2 12 Oct 1933	DA 1350 [30-11417]	-----
*207. La canzone di ognuno: M'hai detto di no! ["Canzone fox lento"] (Galdieri; Caslar) (I) (Scala Orch/Semprini) 0W 2108-1, 2 22 Oct 1933	DA 1352 [30-11470]	-----
208. "Il mio biricchino" (Giubra; Meroff; King; Hirsch) (I) (Scala Orch/Semprini) 0W 2109-1, 2 22 Oct 1933	DA 1352 [30-11471]	-----
*209. "That Little Boy of Mine" (Meroff; King; Hersch) (E) (Scala Orch/Semprini) 0W 2110-1, 2 22 Oct 1933	unpublished	
210. "Dans les jardins du Luxembourg--Rêverie" ["In the Luxembourg Gardens"] (Kathleen Lockhart Manning) (F) (Scala Orch/Semprini) 0W 2111-1, 2 22 Oct 1933	unpublished	
211. Manon, Act III: Ah! dispar vision [Ah! fuyez, douce image] (Massenet) (I) (Scala Orch/Ghione) 2W 2481-1, 2 4 May 1934	DB 2237 [32-4590]	8422 11-0030
212. Werther, Act III: Ah, non mi ridestar [Pourquoi me réveiller?] (Massenet) (I) (Scala Orch/Ghione) 2W 2482-1, 2 4 May 1934	DB 2237 [32-4591] DB 5351	8422 11-0030
213. "O marenariello" (Ottaviano; Gambardella) (N) (Scala Orch and chorus/Olivieri) 0W 2483-1, 2, 3 4 May 1934	DA 1379 [30-12108]	1717 10-0032 25-7240
*214. "En effeuillant la marguérite" (de Badet; Longás) (F) (Scala Orch/Olivieri) 0W 2484-1, 2 4 May 1934	DA 1350 [30-11367]	---
215. "Torna a Surriento" ["Canzone napoletana"] (de Curtis; de Curtis) (N) (Scala Orch/Olivieri) 0W 2485-1, 2 4 May 1934	DA 1379 [30-12109]	1717 10-0032 25-7240
216. "Canzone d'abbrile" (Murolo; Schipa) (N) (Scala Orch/Olivieri) 0BA 256-1, 2 9 Nov 1934	DA 1407	-----

217. "'O balcone 'e Napule" (Murolo; de Curtis) (N) (Scala Orch/Olivieri)
OBA 257-1, 2 — 9 Nov 1934 — DA 1407

*218. Ellens Dritter Gesang, D. 839, no. 6: Ave Maria ["Ave Maria! Jungfrau mild!"] (Scott; Ottolini; Perego; Schubert) (I) (Scala Orch/Olivieri)
OBA 258-1, 2 — 9 Nov 1934 — DA 1408 — 1903

*219. Schwanengesang, D. 957, no. 4: La serenata [Ständchen: "Leise flehen"] (Rellstab; Ottolini; Perego; Schubert) (I) (takes 1-2: Scala Orch/Olivieri; takes 3-4: small orch/Olivieri)
OBA 259-1,2 — 9 Nov 1934 — unpublished
OBA 259-3, 4 — 25 Jan 1935 — DA 1408 — 1903

220. "Girotondo" ["Canzoncina infantile"] (de Flavius; R. Bellini) (I) (Scala Orch/Olivieri)
OBA 401-1, 2 — 25 Jan 1935 — DA 1421

221. "Ninna-nanna a Liana" ["Canzoncina infantile"] (de Flavius; R. Bellini) (I) (Scala Orch/Olivieri)
OBA 402-1, 2 — 25 Jan 1935 — DA 1421

*222. "L'Anguria" ["Barcarola veneziana popolare"] (Rocca; Liberati) (V) (Scala Orch and chorus/Olivieri)
OBA 1312-1, 2 — 2 May 1936 — DA 1484

*223. "Cuandu te aai la faace" ["Canto popolare leccese"] (trad.; arr. Schipa) (Le) (Scala Orch and chorus/Olivieri)
OBA 1313-1 — 2 May 1936 — DA 1485

*224. La Principessa Liana: La Principessa Liana ["Barcarola veneziana"] (Rocca; Schipa) (V) (Scala Orch/Olivieri)
OBA 1314-1 — 2 May 1936 — DA 1484 / DA 1486

225. "Beddha e trista" ["Bella e cattiva"] (Schipa; Preite) (Le) (Scala Orch/Olivieri)
OBA 1315-1, 2 — 2 May 1936 — DA 1485

*226. "Vivere!" ["Canzone fox trot"] (Bixio) (I) (orch and chorus/Olivieri)
OBA 1563-1, 2 — 3 Oct 1936 — DA 1530 / DA 1558 — 1880, 1900, 2023, 10-0031

*227. "Nostalgia" ["Canzone slow fox"] (Fusco; Giannini; Gema) (I) (orch/Olivieri)
OBA 1564-1, 2 — 3 Oct 1936 — DA 1530 — 10-0031

*228. "Romantico Slow" ["Romanticismo"] ["Canzone fox lento"] (Cortopassi) (I) (orch/Olivieri)
OBA 1565-1, 2 — 3 Oct 1936 — DA 1531

*229. "Torna, piccina!" ["Canzone slow tango"] (Bixio) (I) (orch/Olivieri)
OBA 1566-1, 2 — 3 Oct 1936 — DA 1531 / DA 1558 — 1880, 1900, 2023

	Date	HMV	Victor
*230. "Torna la serenata" (Cherubini; Bixio) (I) (orch/Olivieri) 0BA 1567-1, 2	3 Oct 1936	DA 1549	----
*231. "Eternamente mia" ["Canzone fox trot"] (Cantelmo) (I) (orch/Olivieri) 0BA 1696-1, 2	4 Jan 1937	DA 1549	----
232. w. MAFALDA FAVERO: L'amico Fritz, Act II: Suzel buon di ["Cherry Duet," pt. 1] (Mascagni) (I) (Scala Orch/Antonicelli) 2BA 1700-1, 2	January, 1937	DB 3067 IRX 20	15837 11-0029
233. w. MAFALDA FAVERO: L'amico Fritz, Act II: Tutto tace ["Cherry Duet," pt. 2] (Mascagni) (I) (Scala Orch/Antonicelli) 2BA 1701-1, 2	January, 1937	DB 3067 IRX 20	15837 11-0029
*234. "Era de maggio" ["Mattinata"] (di Giacomo; Costa) (N) (orch/Avitabile) 0BA 1904-1, 2	27 Apr 1937	unpublished	
*235. "Tu, ca nun chiagne!" (Bovio; de Curtis) (N) (orch/Avitabile) 0BA 1905-1, 2	27 Apr 1937	unpublished	
236. "Core miu!" ["Nostalgia leccese"] (Preite; Casarano) (Le) (Scala Orch/Preite) 0BA 1909-1	29 Apr 1937	DA 1564	----
237. "Lecce mia!" ["Stornello leccese"] (Pizzi; Preite) (Le) (Scala Orch/Preite) 0BA 1910-1, 2	29 Apr 1937	DA 1564	----
*238. "Voce 'e notte" (Nicolardi; de Curtis) (N) (orch/Avitabile) 0BA 1911-1, 2	29 Apr 1937	unpublished	
*239. "El Pampero" (Schipa; Barthélemy) (S) (orch/Avitabile) 0BA 1912, 1, 2	29 Apr 1937	unpublished	
*240. "Chi è più felice di me?" (Bixio) (I) (orch/Olivieri) 0BA 2179-1, 2	October, 1937	DA 1595	1898
*241. "Io e la luna" (Cherubini; Bixio) (I) (orch/Olivieri) 0BA 2180-1, 2	October, 1937	DA 1595	1898
242. "Se tu mi parli d'amore" (Galdieri; Schipa) (I) (orch/Olivieri) 0BA 2181-1, 2	October, 1937	DA 1596 DA 5356	----
*243. "Bimbo mio" (Adonni; Bianchini) (I) (orch/Olivieri) 0BA 2182-1, 2	October, 1937	DA 1596	----
*244. "El Pampero" (Schipa; Barthélemy) (S) (orch/Olivieri) 0BA 2183-1, 2	November, 1937	DA 1565	----

No. / Title	Matrix	Date	Issue	Reissue
*245. "Era de maggio" ["Mattinata"] (di Giacomo; Costa) (N) (orch/Olivieri)	0BA 2184-1, 2	November, 1937	DA 1592	---
*246. "Voce 'e notte" (Nicolardi; de Curtis) (N) (orch/Olivieri)	0BA 2185-1, 2	November, 1937	DA 1592	---
*247. "Tu, ca nun chiagne!" (Bovio; de Curtis) (N) (orch/Olivieri)	0BA 2186-1, 2	November, 1937	DA 1565	---
*248. "Wo ist mein kleines Mädel?" ["Torna, piccina!"] (Bixio) (G) (orch/?)	0BA 2458-1, 2	12 Apr 1938	DA 4432	---
*249. "Sans Toi" ["Torna, piccina!"] (Bixio) (F) (orch/?)	0BA 2459-1, 2	12 Apr 1938	DA 4916	---
*250. "Vivre!" ["Vivere!"] ["Fox Trot"] (Bixio) (F) (orch/?)	0BA 2460-1, 2	12 Apr 1938	DA 4916	---
251. Marcella, Episode 3: Dolce notte misteriosa (Giordano) (I) (orch/Capuana)	0BA 2465-1, 2	15 Apr 1938	DA 5352	---
252. Andrea Chénier, Act IV: Come un bel dì di maggio (Giordano) (I) (orch/Capuana)	0BA 2466-1, 2	15 Apr 1938	DA 5352	---
253. "Surdate" (Bovio; Nardella) (N) (orch/Olivieri)	0BA 2471-1, 2	27 Apr 1938	DA 5353	2056
254. "Comme facette mammeta?" (Capaldo; Gambardella) (N) (orch/Olivieri)	0BA 2472-1, 2	27 Apr 1938	DA 5354	---
*255. "Serenata a Surriento" (Califano; Gambardella) (N) (?orch/Olivieri)	0BA 2473-1 [2]	27 Apr 1938	DA 5353	2056
256. "Canzone appassiunata" (Mario) (N) (orch/Olivieri)	0BA 2474-1, 2	27 Apr 1938	DA 5354	---
*257. "Femmene belle" (Scotto; Koger; Rodor; Nisa) (N) (orch/Olivieri)	0BA 2729-1, 2 -3	?	unpublished DA 5356	---
*258a.	0BA 2730	14 Sep 1938	NO INFORMATION	
*258b. "Se canta il mare" (Panzeri; Rastelli; Scotto) (I) (orch/Olivieri)	0BA 2731-1, 2	14 Sep 1938	DA 5357	1974
*259a.	0BA 2732	14 Sep 1938	NO INFORMATION	
*259b. "Mariù" (Panzeri; Rastelli; Scotto) (I) (orch/Olivieri)	0BA 2733-1	14 Sep 1938	DA 5357	1974
*260. "Ave Maria" (Schipa) (La) (organ/?; bells/?)	0BA 2740-?	15 Sep 1938	unpublished	---

			HMV	Victor
261. "Malia" (Pagliara; Tosti) (I) (orch/Olivieri)				
0BA 2741-1	15 Sep 1938		DA 5358	——
262. "L'alba separa dalla luce l'ombra" (D'Annunzio; Tosti) (I) (orch/Olivieri)				
0BA 2742-1, 2	15 Sep 1938		DA 5358	——
*263. "Ave Maria" (Schipa) (La) (organ/?; bells/?)				
2BA 2814-1	[21 Oct 1938]		DB 5351	18068
264. "Tu!" (Galdieri; Schipa) (I) (orch/Olivieri)				
0BA 2909-1, 2	5 Jan 1939		DA 5361	2097
265. "Amavi tanto le mie rose" (Galdieri; Schipa) (I) (?orch/Olivieri)				
0BA 2910-1, 2	5 Jan 1939		DA 5361	2097
*266. Il Pirro e Demetrio: Rugiadose, odorose, violette graziose ["Le violette"] (Alessandro Scarlatti) (I) (orch/Olivieri)				
0BA 2911-1, 2	7 Jan 1939		DA 5362	2062
*267. La donna ancora è fedele: Son tutta duolo (Alessandro Scarlatti) (I) (orch/Olivieri)				
0BA 2912-1, 2	7 Jan 1939		DA 5362	2062 10-0033
*268. "Napoli che nun more" ["Napule ca nun more"] (Bonavolontà; Manlio) (N) (mandolins and orch/Olivieri)				
0BA 2975-1, 2	11 Feb 1939		DA 5363	——
*269. "Marinaresca" (Murolo; Valente) (N) (mandolins, orch, and chorus/Olivieri)				
0BA 2976-1	11 Feb 1939		DA 5363	——
*270. "Villa triste" (Ruccione; de Torres; Simeoni) (I) (orch/Olivieri)				
0BA 5010-?	1942		DA 5421	——
*271. "Luna marinara" (Bonagura; Simionini) (I) (orch/Olivieri)				
0BA 5011-?	1942		DA 5421	——
*272. "Core 'ngrato" (Cordiferro; Cardillo) (N) (orch/Olivieri)				
0BA 5012-1, 2	1942		DA 5422	——
*273. "Varca napulitana" (Scala; Frustaci) (N) (orch/Olivieri)				
0BA 5013-?	1942		DA 5422	——
*274. "Desesperadamente" (Mendez; Ruiz) (S) (orch/Olivieri)				
0BA 5014-1	1942		DA 5423	——

*275. "Oracion caribe" (Lara) (S) (orch/Olivieri)	0BA 5015-1, 2	1942	DA 5423	---
*276. *Werther*, Act I: O natura [O nature], pt. 1 (Massenet) (I) (orch/Cordone)	0BA 5022-1, 2	1942	DA 5420	---
*277. *Werther*, Act I: O natura [O nature], pt. 2 (Massenet) (I) (orch/Cordone)	0BA 5023-1, 2	1942	DA 5420	---
*278. "'O vico" (de Mura; Oliviero) (N) (?orch/Olivieri)	0BA 7336-1	3 Apr 1950	DA 11319	---
*279. "Rondini del Gesù" (Manlio; Concina) (N) (?orch/Olivieri)	0BA 7337-1	3 Apr 1950	DA 11323	---
*280. "Musso 'e musso" (Manlio; Schipa) (N) (orch/Olivieri)	0BA 7338-1	3 Apr 1950	DA 11318	---
*281. "Povero ammore mio" (Manlio; Oliviero) (N) (?orch/Olivieri)	0BA 7339-?	3 Apr 1950	DA 11321	---
*282. "Non ti scordar di Napoli" (Manlio; Panzuti) (L) (?orch/Olivieri)	0BA 7340-?	3 Apr 1950	DA 11323	---
*283. "Tutt'e tre" (Manlio; Schipa) (N) (?orch/Olivieri)	0BA 7341-?	3 Apr 1950	DA 11319	---
*284. "Bello 'e papà" (Manlio; Oliviero) (N) (orch/Olivieri)	0BA 7342-?	3 Apr 1950	DA 11318	---
*285. "Me so 'mbriacato 'e sole" (Manlio; D'Esposito) (N) (orch/Olivieri)	0BA 7343-?	3 Apr 1950	DA 11320	---
*286. "Prima matina" (de Mura; Oliviero) (N) (?orch/Olivieri)	0BA 7344-?	3 Apr 1950	DA 11321	---
*287. "Addio mia bella Napoli" (Manlio; Valente) (I) (orch/Olivieri)	0BA 7345-?	3 Apr 1950	DA 11322	---
*288. "Mandulinata a sera" (Manlio; Panzuti) (N) (orch/Olivieri)	0BA 7346-?	3 Apr 1950	DA 11322	---
*289. "Anima e core" (Manlio; D'Esposito) (N) (orch/Olivieri)	0BA 7347-?	3 Apr 1950	DA 11320	---
*290. "Manolita" (Scarpelli; Schipa) (I) (?orch/Guarino)	0BA 8295-?	16 Mar 1953	DA 11342	---
*291. "Fiammata" (Rende; Schipa) (N) (orch/Guarino)	0BA 8296-?	16 Mar 1953	DA 11343	---

*292. "Surriento" (Schipa) (N) (?orch/Guarino)
0BA 8297-? 16 Mar 1953 DA 11342 -----

*293. "Ma che sarrà?" (Rende) (N) (orch/Guarino)
0BA 8298-? 16 Mar 1953 DA 11343 -----

VI DURIUM, MILANO

British and Italian 78 rpm and long-playing issues (33.3 and 45 rpm) of these eight monaural, high-fidelity recordings appeared on the Durium label. A1.6023 and A1.6024 are Italian 45 rpm. A1.547 and DLU. 96020 are ten-inch LPs. The American and Canadian LP issue (matrix ASH 1337T1/1338T1) appeared on the Richmond label, a subsidiary of London Records.

	78 rpm Italy	78 rpm U.K.	LP Italy	LP U.K.	LP U.S./Canada

*294. "Passione" (Bovio; Tagliaferri; Valente) (N) (w. Orchestra Napoletana della Canzone/Campanio)

| 1D-4661 Milan, circa Oct 1955 | A1.10638 | ------ | A1.6023 / A1.547 / B1.7040 | DLU.96020 | B-20111 |

*295. "'Na sera 'è maggio" (Cioffi; Pisano) (N) (w. Orchestra Napoletana della Canzone/Campanio)

| Milan, circa Oct 1955 | A1.10638 | ------ | A1.547 / B1.7040 | DLU.96020 | B-20111 |

*296. "Funiculì, funiculà" (Turco; Denza) (N) (w. Orchestra Napoletana della Canzone/Campanio)

| 1D-4661 Milan, circa Oct 1955 | A1.10639 | DC.16583 | A1.6023 / A1.547 / B1.7040 | DLU.96020 | B-20111 |

*297. "Chi se nne scorda 'cchiù" (Marvasi; Barthélemy) (N) (w. Orchestra Napoletana della Canzone/Campanio)

| 1D-4660 Milan, circa Oct 1955 | A1.10639 | DC.16583 | A1.547 / B1.7040 | DLU.96020 | B-20111 |

*298. "Te sto' aspettanno" (Manlio; Caslar) (N) (w. Orchestra Napoletana della Canzone/Campanio)

| 1D-4674 Milan, circa Oct 1955 | A1.10640 | DC.16584 | A1.6024 / A1.547 / B1.7040 | DLU.96020 | B-20111 |

*299. "Desiderio 'è sole" (Manlio; Gigante) (N) (w. Orchestra Napoletana della Canzone/Campanio)

| 1D-4675 Milan, circa Oct 1955 | A1.10640 | DC.16584 | A1.6024 / A1.547 / B1.7040 | DLU.96020 | B-20111 |

	78 rpm Italy	78 rpm U.K.	LP Italy	LP U.K.	LP U.S./Canada
*300. "'O ciucciariello" (Murolo; Oliviero) (N) (w. Orchestra Napoletana della Canzone/Campanio) Milan, circa Oct 1955	A1.10641	DC.16584	A1.547	DLU.96020 B1.7040	B-20111
*301. "Pianefforte 'è notte" (di Giacomo; Schipa) (N) (w. Orchestra Napoletana della Canzone/Campanio) Milan, circa Oct 1955	A1.10641	DC.16584	A1.547 B1.7040	DLU.96020	B-20111

VII CCCP [USSR], MOSCOW, circa October, 1957

	U.S.S.R. 78 rpm	U.S.S.R. LP	LP Reissues
*302. "Torna a Surriento" (de Curtis; de Curtis) (N) (pf/A. Erochin) Moscow, ?1957 30018/2-1 [D004169/4-1]	CCCP-5289-56	Melodiya D004168	EJS 469 Pearl GEMM CD 9988
*303. "Marechiare" (di Giacomo; Tosti) (I) (pf/A. Erochin) Moscow, ?1957 30019/2-1 [D004168/4-1]	CCCP-5289-56	Melodiya D004168	EJS 469 Pearl GEMM CD 9988
*304. "Chi se nne scorda 'cchiù" (Marvasi; Barthélemy) (N) (pf/A. Erochin) Moscow, ?1957 [D004168/4-1]	-----	Melodiya D004168	EJS 469 Pearl GEMM CD 9988
*305. "Manolita" (Scarpelli; Schipa) (I) (pf/A. Erochin) Moscow, ?1957 [D004168/4-1]	-----	Melodiya D004168	Pearl GEMM CD 9988
*306. "A Granada--Canción Andaluza" (Palacios) (S) (pf/A. Erochin) Moscow, ?1957 [D004169/4-1]	-----	Melodiya D004168	EJS 469 Pearl GEMM CD 9988
*307. "'O ciucciariello" (Murolo; Oliviero) (N) (pf/A. Erochin) Moscow, ?1957 [D004169/4-1]	-----	Melodiya D004168	EJS 469 Pearl GEMM CD 9988

PUBLISHED BROADCASTS, LIVE, AND PRIVATE RECORDINGS

This listing includes all known broadcast transcriptions, live concert, and private recordings rumored to exist (nos. 318 and 320q) or published in some form. EJS ("The Golden Age of Opera"), UORC ("Unique Opera Records Corporation"), and ANNA ("A.N.N.A. Record Company") were private LPs produced and issued by the late Edward J. Smith between 1956 and 1982; MDP ("Collectors Limited Editions"), issued by Michael D. Polimeni, and HOPE ("Historical Operatic Performances Edition)" were also private American labels. The Timaclub ("Edizione Timaclub SIAE"), Cetra ("Documents" series), and Eklipse ("Eklipse Records, Ltd.) LPs and CDs are listed among the LONG-PLAYING REISSUES OF THE COMMERCIAL RECORDINGS. With the exception of EJS 288 and EJS 469, both tenor recitals, EJS 558 (the 1941 St. Louis *Don Giovanni* excerpts coupled with a Mercadante recital), EJS 563 (a potpourri of singers "Sixty-Two and Over", UORC 254 (a potpourri), and ANNA 1036 (a Rosa Ponselle recital), all of the long-playing issues listed were either devoted to the individual performances cited (nos. 308-324) or solely to Schipa.

*308. *Don Giovanni*, K. 527 (Mozart) (I) Opera in 2 acts (excerpts)
Metropolitan Opera House Orchestra and Chorus/Tullio Serafin. Metropolitan Opera broadcast, WJZ and WEAF [NBC], NYC, 20 Jan 1934
CAST: Ezio Pinza (*Don Giovanni*); Rosa Ponselle (*Donna Anna*); Editha Fleischer (*Zerlina*); Maria Müller (*Donna Elvira*); Tito Schipa (*Don Ottavio*); Virgilio Lazzari (*Leporello*); Louis D'Angelo (*Masetto*); Emanuel List (*Commandant*).
Act I: a) PONSELLE, PINZA, LAZZARI, LIST, SCHIPA, and MÜLLER: Overture ... ogni borgo, ogni paese è testimon di sue donne che imprese (recitative to "Madamina!")
         b) MÜLLER, SCHIPA, PONSELLE, and PINZA: [Non ti fidar, o misera] ... Te vuol tradir ancor! Cieli! Che aspetto nobile! ... Che mi fan determinar
         c) SCHIPA: Act I: Come mai creder deggio ... Dalla sua pace
         d) SCHIPA: Act II: Il mio tesoro
            LP: UORC 216; ANNA 1036 (Act I duet with Ponselle)

*309. *Werther* (Massenet) (I) Opera in 4 acts (excerpts)
Orchestra of Teatro alla Scala, Milano/Franco Ghione. Broadcast, Teatro alla Scala, EIAR, Rome, 27 April, 1934
CAST: Tito Schipa (*Werther*); Gianna Pederzini (*Charlotte*); Marina da Merlo (*Sophie*); Carlo Scattola (*Schmidt*); Piero Biasini (*Alberto*).
Act I: a) SCHIPA: Io non so se son desto... O natura [Je ne sais si je veille... O nature]
            LP: EJS 371; MDP 024; Timaclub TIMA 41
            CD: Tima CLAMA CD-14
         b) SCHIPA and PEDERZINI: Ah! perché m'han guardato [Ah! pourvu que je vois... C'est que l'image]
            LP: EJS 371; MDP 024; UORC 221; Timaclub TIMA 41
            CD: Tima CLAMA CD-14
Act III: c) SCHIPA and PEDERZINI: Ah non mi ridestar [Pourquoi me réveiller?]
            LP: EJS 371; MDP 024; UORC 221; Timaclub TIMA 41
            CD: Tima CLAMA CD-14
Act IV: d) SCHIPA and PEDERZINI: No! Io muoio... to the end of the opera [Non, Charlotte, je meurs ... to the end of the opera] (Massenet) (I)

LP: EJS 371; UORC 221; MDP 024; Timaclub TIMA 41

    CD: Tima CLAMA CD-14

*310. *Manon* (Massenet) (F) Opera in 5 Acts (Act II: excerpts)

San Francisco Opera House Orchestra and Chorus/Gaetano Merola

San Francisco Opera Broadcast, War Memorial Opera House, KGO [NBC], San Francisco, 13 Oct 1939

CAST: Bidú Sayão (*Manon*); Tito Schipa (*Des Grieux*); Richard Bonelli (*Lescaut*); André Ferrier (*Guillot*); George Cehanovsky (*De Brétigny*); Margaret Ritter (*Maid*); Norman Cordon (*Count Des Grieux*); Stanley Noonan (*Guard*); Max Edwards (*Guard*).

Act II: a) SAYÃO, SCHIPA, BONELLI, and CEHANOVSKY: Beginning … En fermant les yeux ["Le rêve"]

        LP: EJS 227; MDP 024

    b) Selected excerpt(s)

        CD: Eklipse EKR CD41

*311. ?Broadcast, Concert, Berlin, ?June or November, 1939

    a) *Il Pompeo:* O cessate di piagarmi (Alessandro Scarlatti) (I) (pf/Michael Raucheisen)

        LP: ?Melodiya M10-43189-90

    b) "Marechiare" (di Giacomo; Tosti) (I) (pf/Michael Raucheisen)

        LP: UORC 221; Melodiya M10-43189-90

        CD: Eklipse EKR CD10

    c) "Ideale" (Errico; Tosti) (I) (pf/Michael Raucheisen)

        LP: UORC 221; ?Melodiya M10-43189-90

        CD: Eklipse EKR CD10

    d) *La donna ancora è fedele:* Se Florindo è fedele (A. Scarlatti) (I) (pf/Michael Raucheisen)

        LP: UORC 221

        CD: ?Pearl GEMM CD 9988; Eklipse EKR CD10

    e) "Fa la nanna bambin" ["Fa la nanna mio piccino"] (Geni Sadero) (V) (pf/Michael Raucheisen)

        LP: UORC 221; ?Melodiya M10-43189-90

        CD: Eklipse EKR CD10

    f) "Nina" ["Tre giorni son che Nina"] (Ciampi; formerly attr. Pergolesi) (I) (pf/Michael Raucheisen)

        LP: UORC 221; ?Melodiya M10-43189-90

        CD: Eklipse EKR CD10

    g) "Torna a Surriento" (de Curtis; de Curtis) (N) (pf/Michael Raucheisen)

        LP: UORC 221; Melodiya M10-43189-90

        CD: Eklipse EKR CD10

    h) "Chi se nne scorda 'cchiù" (Marvasi; Barthélemy) (N) (pf/Michael Raucheisen)

        LP: UORC 221

        CD: Eklipse EKR CD10

*312. ?Broadcast, Concert, Berlin, ?June or November, 1939
    a) *Il Pompeo*: O cessate di piagarmi (Alessandro Scarlatti) (I) (pf/Michael Raucheisen)
        LP: ?Melodiya M10-43189-90
    b) "Ideale" (Errico; Tosti) (I) (pf/Michael Raucheisen)
        LP: UORC 221; ?Melodiya M10-43189-90
        CD: Eklipse EKR CD10
    c) "'A vucchella" (d'Annunzio; Tosti) (N) (pf/Michael Raucheisen)
        LP: UORC 221; Melodiya M10-43189-90
        CD: Eklipse EKR CD10
    d) *La donna ancora è fedele*: Se Florindo è fedele (A. Scarlatti) (I) (pf/Michael Raucheisen)
        LP: UORC 221
        CD: ?Pearl GEMM CD 9988; Eklipse EKR CD10
    e) "Fa la nanna bambin" ["Fa la nanna mio piccino"] (Geni Sadero) (V) (pf/Michael Raucheisen)
        LP: UORC 221; ?Melodiya M10-43189-90
        CD: Eklipse EKR CD10
    f) "Nina" ["Tre giorni son che Nina"] (Ciampi; formerly attr. Pergolesi) (I) (pf/Michael Raucheisen)
        LP: UORC 221; ?Melodiya M10-43189-90
        CD: Eklipse EKR CD10
    g) "Se tu m'ami" (Parisotti; formerly attr. Pergolesi) (I) (pf/Michael Raucheisen)
        LP: UORC 221; Melodiya M10-43189-90
        CD: Pearl GEMM CD 9988; Eklipse EKR CD10

*313. ?Broadcast, Concert, Berlin, circa 1939-1942
    a) "Comme facette, mammeta?" (Capaldo; Gambardelli) (N) (pf/Hans Priegnitz)
        LP: Melodiya M10-43189-90

*314. *Don Giovanni*, K. 527 (Mozart) (I) Opera in 2 acts (Act II: abridged)
    Orchestra and Chorus of the St. Louis Opera/Laszlo Halasz
    Broadcast, St. Louis Grand Opera, Municipal Opera House, KMOX [CBS], St. Louis, 16 Apr 1941
    CAST: Ezio Pinza (*Don Giovanni*); Tito Schipa (*Don Ottavio*); Anne Roselle (*Donna Anna*); Vivian Della Chiesa (*Donna Elvira*); Margit Bokor (*Zerlina*); Lorenzo Alvary (*Leporello*); Carlos Alexander (*Masetto*); Nicola Moscona (*The Commandant*).
Act II:
    a) CAST: Beginning .... Il mio tesoro
        LP: EJS 558; HOPE 208
    b) Selected excerpt(s)
        CD: Eklipse EKR CD41

*315. Broadcast, Reichssender, Berlin, 1942

    a) *L'Arlesiana*, Act II: È la solita storia ["Lamento di Federico"] (Cilèa) (I) (Berlin Reichssender Orchester/Franz Marszalek)

        LP: UORC 221

        CD: Eklipse EKR CD10

    b) *Rigoletto*, Act II: Ella mi fu rapita ... Parmi veder le lagrime (Verdi) (I) (Berlin Reichssender Orchester/Franz Marszalek)

        LP: UORC 221; Melodiya M10-43189-90

        CD: Eklipse EKR CD10

*316. *Werther* (Massenet) (I) Opera in 4 acts (excerpts)

    Orchestra of Teatro dell'Opera, Roma/Oliviero de Fabritiis or Riccardo Santarelli. Broadcast, Teatro dell'Opera, RAI, Rome, 3 Feb 1948

    CAST: Tito Schipa (*Werther*); Gianna Pederzini (*Charlotte*); Nelly Corradi (*Sophie*); Saturno Meletti (*Schmidt*); ? (*Alberto*).

    a) Excerpt(s)

        LP: Cetra DOC 16

*317. *Il matrimonio segreto* (Cimarosa) (I) Opera in 2 acts (excerpts)

    Orchestra and Chorus of Teatro alla Scala, Milano/Mario Rossi. Broadcast, Teatro alla Scala, RAI, Milan, 22 Mar 1949

    CAST: Tito Schipa (*Paolino*); Boris Christoff (*Count Robinson*); Alda Noni (*Carolina*); Hilde Güden (*Elisetta*); Fedora Barbieri (*Fidalma*); Sesto Bruscantini (*Geronimo*).

    Act I: a) SCHIPA and NONI: Cara, non dubitar ["Cara! cara!"]

          b) SCHIPA and NONI: Io ti lascio, perché uniti

             LP: EJS 331; MDP 024

          c) CAST: Sì, coraggio mi faccio ... to the end of the act

             LP: EJS 371

    Act III: d) SCHIPA: Pria che spunti il ciel (Cimarosa) (I)

             LP: UORC 221

*318. Recital or Broadcast, Volendam, Holland, 31 Oct 1959

    pf/Franz Beeldsnijder

    [Program unknown]

        TAPE/LP/CD: Publication unknown

*319. Broadcast, Volendam, Holland, 3 Nov 1959

    a) *Il Pirro e Demetrio*: Rugiadose, odorose, violette graziose ["Le violette"] (A. Scarlatti) (I) (pf/?Franz Beeldsnijder)

        LP: EJS 469

        CD: Eklipse EKR CD10

b) "Desesperadamente" (Mendez; Ruiz) (S) (pf/?Franz Beeldsnijder)
   LP: EJS 469
   CD: Eklipse EKR CD10
c) "Canzone Napoletana" (?) (N) (pf/?Franz Beeldsnijder)
   CD: Eklipse EKR CD10

*320. In-house recording, Town Hall recital, New York City, 3 Oct 1962

a) *Ellens Dritter Gesang*, D. 839, no. 6: Ave Maria ["Ave Maria! Jungfrau mild!"] (Scott; Schubert) (I) (pf/Albert Carlo Amato)
   LP: National Music Theater LP 100
b) *Schwanengesang*, D. 957, no. 4: La Serenata [Ständchen: "Leise flehen"] (Rellstab; Schubert) (I) (pf/Albert Carlo Amato)
   LP: National Music Theater LP 100
c) *Il Pirro e Demetrio*: Rugiadose, odorose, violette graziose ["Le violette"] (Alessandro Scarlatti) (I) (pf/Albert Carlo Amato)
   LP: National Music Theater LP 100
d) *Semele*: Where'er you walk (Handel) (E) (pf/Albert Carlo Amato)
   LP: National Music Theater LP 100
e) *L'elisir d'amore*, Act II: Una furtiva lagrima (Donizetti) (I) (pf/Albert Carlo Amato)
   LP: National Music Theater LP 100
f) *Don Pasquale*, Act II: Povero Ernesto! ... Cercherò lontana terra (Donizetti) (I) (pf/Albert Carlo Amato)
   LP: National Music Theater LP 100
g) *Martha*, Act III: M'appari [Ach, so fromm] (Flotow) (I) (pf/Albert Carlo Amato)
   LP: National Music Theater LP 100; EJS 563
h) "Torna, piccina!" (Bixio) (I) (pf/Albert Carlo Amato)
   LP: National Music Theater LP 100
i) "Desesperadamente" (Mendez; Ruiz) (S) (pf/Albert Carlo Amato)
   LP: National Music Theater LP 100
j) "Tte vurria vasa'" (Russo; di Capua) (N) (pf/Albert Carlo Amato)
   LP: National Music Theater LP 100
k) "Manolita" (Scarpelli; Schipa) (I) (pf/Albert Carlo Amato)
   LP: National Music Theater LP 100
l) "Marechiare" (di Giacomo; Tosti) (I) (pf/Albert Carlo Amato)
   LP: National Music Theater LP 100
m) "Chi se nne scorda 'cchiù" (Marvasi; Barthélemy) (N) (pf/Albert Carlo Amato)
   LP: National Music Theater LP 100
n) "Vivere!" (Bixio) (I) (pf/Albert Carlo Amato)
   LP: National Music Theater LP 100
o) *L'Arlesiana*, Act II: È la solita storia del pastore ["Lamento di Federico"] (Cilea) (I) (pf/Albert Carlo Amato)
   LP: National Music Theater LP 100

p) *Werther*, Act III: Pourquoi me réveiller? (Massenet) (F) (pf/Albert Carlo Amato)
   LP: National Music Theater LP 100; Rubini GV 29

q) [Spoken] Interview (E)
   TAPE/LP/CD: Publication unconfirmed

*321. In-house recording, recital, 1962 (?Columbus Theater, Providence, 1 November) or 1963 (?Philharmonic Auditorium, Los Angeles, 8 February)

a) *Ellens Dritter Gesang*, D. 839, no. 6: Ave Maria! Jungfrau mild!"] (Scott; Schubert) (I) (pf/Albert Carlo Amato)
   PRIVATE TAPE ONLY

b) *Schwanengesang*, D. 957, no. 4: La Serenata [Ständchen: "Leise flehen"] (Rellstab; Schubert) (I) (pf/Albert Carlo Amato)
   PRIVATE TAPE ONLY

c) *Il Pirro e Demetrio*: Rugiadose, odorose, violette graziose ["Le violette"] (Alessandro Scarlatti) (I) (pf/Albert Carlo Amato)
   PRIVATE TAPE ONLY

d) *Semele*: Where 'er you walk (Handel) (E) (pf/Albert Carlo Amato)
   PRIVATE TAPE ONLY

e) *L'elisir d'amore*, Act II: Una furtiva lagrima (Donizetti) (I) (pf/Albert Carlo Amato)
   PRIVATE TAPE ONLY

f) *Don Pasquale*, Act II: Povero Ernesto! ... Cercherò lontana terra (Donizetti) (I) (pf/Albert Carlo Amato)
   PRIVATE TAPE ONLY

g) *Martha*, Act III: M'apparì [Ach, so fromm] (Flotow) (I) (pf/Albert Carlo Amato)
   PRIVATE TAPE ONLY

h) "Torna, piccina!" (Bixio) (I) (pf/Albert Carlo Amato)
   PRIVATE TAPE ONLY

i) "A Granada--Canción Andaluza" (Palacios) (S) (pf/Albert Carlo Amato)
   PRIVATE TAPE ONLY

j) "Desesperadamente" (Mendez; Ruiz) (S) (pf/Albert Carlo Amato)
   PRIVATE TAPE ONLY

k) "I'te vurria vasa'" (Russo; di Capua) (N) (pf/Albert Carlo Amato)
   PRIVATE TAPE ONLY

l) "Manolita" (Scarpelli; Schipa) (I) (pf/Albert Carlo Amato)
   PRIVATE TAPE ONLY

m) "Marechiare" (di Giacomo; Tosti) (I) (pf/Albert Carlo Amato)
   PRIVATE TAPE ONLY

n) ENCORE: "Chi se nne scorda 'cchiù" (Marvasi; Barthélemy) (N) (pf/Albert Carlo Amato)
   PRIVATE TAPE ONLY

o) ENCORE: "Vivere!" (Bixio) (I) (pf/Albert Carlo Amato)
   PRIVATE TAPE ONLY

*322.

p) ENCORE: "Torna a Surriento" (de Curtis; de Curtis) (N) (pf/Albert Carlo Amato)
PRIVATE TAPE ONLY

a) w. FRANCIS ROBINSON (introduced by MILTON CROSS): [Spoken] Interview (E)
Broadcast, *Biographies in Music, Third Intermission Feature,* Metropolitan Opera broadcast, WOR, New York City, 15 Dec 1962
TAPE: Opera Dubs ODA-3168
LP: Rubini GV 29 (Schipa excerpts *only*)

b)   1. SCHIPA: Pre-recorded opening statement for programming (Howard Rhines)
2. HOWARD RHINES: Introduction to prepartory session with Schipa, Mme. Curci, and Carl Princi
3. SCHIPA, MME. CURCI [-CACCIA], and CARL PRINCI: Open-mike preparatory session with Schipa
4. SCHIPA and CARL PRINCI: Final interview pre-recording
5. HOWARD RHINES: After-interview summary
Recorded at station KFAC, Los Angeles, 30 Jan 1963
Broadcast [excerpts] date unknown
TAPE ONLY: La Cañada Memorial Library/Stanford University Archive of Recorded Sound

c) w. WILLIAM H. WELLS: [Spoken] Interview (E) Broadcast, *Opera for You,* WRFM, New York City, 6 March, 1963
TAPE ONLY: Opera Dubs ODA-3168

*323. Private recordings, source unknown, ?New York, 2 September, 1964
a) *La rondine,* Act III: Dimmi che vuoi (Puccini) (I) (pf/?)
b) *La rondine,* Act III: No! non lasciarmi solo! (Puccini) (I) (pf/?)
c) "Inno a Diana" (Abeniacar [Salvatori]; Puccini) (I) (pf/?)
d) *Iris,* Act I: Apri la tua finestra (Mascagni) (I) (pf/?)
e) *Fedora,* Act II: Amor ti vieta (Giordano) (I) (pf/?)
f) *Il Pompeo:* O cessate di piagarmi (Scarlatti) (I) (pf/?)
g) *Paride ed Elena,* Act I: O del mio dolce ardor (Gluck) (I) (pf/?)
LP: EJS 331

*324. Vocal Exercises, source and date unknown (pf/?)
PRIVATE TAPE ONLY

FILMOGRAPHY

The following are all sound films, feature-length except for the first two. [CT] designates a copyright title.

*F1. *Tito Schipa* [CT]
Paramount Famous Lasky Corporation (1929)
One-reel
Director: Joseph Santley
MP 505 c25 July 1929
Cast: Tito Schipa with unknown pianist and conductor

*F2. *Tito Schipa: World Premiere Lyric Tenor*
aka *Tito Schipa No. 2* and *Tito Schipa Concert No. 2* [CT]
Paramount Lasky/Publix Corporation (1929)
One-reel
Presented by Adolph Zukor
Director: Joseph Santley
LP 1327 c22 May 1930
Cast: Tito Schipa with unknown pianist and conductor

*F3. *Tre uomini in frac* [*Trois Hommes en Habit; Three Lucky Fools*]
aka *I Sing for You Alone*
Caesar Film, Roma (1932)
Director: Mario Bonnard
No copyright information
Cast: Tito Schipa, Assia Noris, Milly, Peppino de Filippo, ?Eduardo de Filippo

*F4. *Vivere!* [U.S.: *To Live*]
Appia-Safa / Metro-Goldwyn-Mayer S.A.I. (1937)
Director Guido Brignone
No copyright information
Cast: Tito Schipa, Caterina Boratto, Nino Besozzi, Doris Duranti, Paola Borboni

*F5. *Chi è più felice di me?* [U.S.: *Who is Happier Than I?*]
Safa (1938)
Director: Guido Brignone
No copyright information
Cast: Tito Schipa, Caterina Boratto

F6. *Terra di fuoco*
Manenti / Metro-Goldwyn-Mayer S.A.I. / Scalzaferri (1938)
Directors: Marcel L'Herbier and Giorgio Ferroni
No copyright information
Cast: Tito Schipa, Mirelle Balin, Marie Glory, Louise Carletti, André Lefaur

F7. *In cerca di felicità*
Fono Roma / Lux (1943)
Director: Giacomo Gentilomo
No copyright information
Cast: Elena Luber, Alberto Rabagliati, Tito Schipa, Lauro Gazzolo

F8. *Rosalba*
Scalera (1944)
Director: ?
No copyright information
Cast: Tito Schipa, Doris Duranti, Luigi Tosi

F9. *Vivere ancora*
Nord Italia Film (1944)
Director: Nino Giannini
No copyright information
Cast: Tito Schipa, Nuto Navarrini, Fausto Tommei

*F10. *Il cavalieri del sogno* [U.S.: *The Life of Donizetti*]
aka *L'inferno degli amanti*
Seyta-Radici / Titanus / Lupa Film (1946)
Director: Camillo Mastrocinque
No copyright information
Cast: Amedeo Nazzari, Mariella Lotti, Mario Ferrari, Dina Sassoli, Giulio Tomassini, Tito Schipa

*F11. *Follie per l'opera* [U.S.: *Mad About Opera*]
Scalera (1948)
Director: Mario Costa
Musical director and conductor: Giuseppe Morelli (Orchestra of Teatro dell'Opera, Roma)
No copyright information
Cast: Carlo Campanini, Gina Lollobrigida, Aroldo Tieri, Constance Dowling; Aldo Silvani; Gino Bechi, Maria Caniglia, Beniamino Gigli, Tito Gobbi, Tito Schipa; Franco Mannino, pianist; Nives Poli, ballerina.

F12. *I misteri di Venezia*
aka *Il faro della laguna* and *Il faro abbandonato*
Industriafilm (1950)
Director: Ignazio Ferronetti
No copyright information
Cast: Virginia Belmont, Renato Valente, Tito Schipa, Diana Prandi

*F13. *Soho Conspiracy*
Do-U-Know Films (Britain) (1951)
Producer: Edwin J. Fancey
Director: Cecil H. Williamson
[Conductor: Giuseppe Morelli (Orchestra of Teatro dell'Opera, Roma)]
No copyright information
Cast: Jacques Labreque, Zena Marshall, John Witty, Peter Gawthorne, Syd Harrison, Max Harrison; Gino Bechi, Beniamino Gigli, Tito Gobbi, Tito Schipa.

AMERICAN FEATURE FILMS FEATURING CARLO SCHIPA

Little Annie Rooney (Pickford-United Artists, 1925); *Sally* (First National, 1925); *The Fighting Hombre* (Bob Custer Productions, 1927); *Strictly Dishonorable* (Universal, 1931); *Whom the Gods Destroy* (Columbia, 1934); *Love Me Forever* (Columbia, 1935); *Don't Gamble with Love* (Columbia, 1936); *Appointment with Murder* (Falcon, 1948); *Federal Man* (Eagle-Lion, 1950).

SOUNDTRACK EXCERPTS PUBLISHED ON LONG-PLAYING DISCS

From the soundtrack of *Tre uomini in frac* (1932), issued on the EJS "Golden Age of Opera" (LP) label:

S1. "Luna piangente" (Galdieri; Caslar) (I) (pf/?)
    EJS 331

S2. "Ti voglio bene" (Galdieri; Caslar) (I) (orch/?)
    EJS 331

S3. "Io son un immenso tenore" (Galdieri; Caslar) (I) (orch/?)
    EJS 331

S4. "Melancolia de mi alma" (Galdieri; Caslar) (S) (orch/?)
    EJS 331
S5. "Quando?" (Galdieri; Caslar) (I) (orch/?)
    EJS 331
S6. "Nina" ["Tre giorni son che Nina"] (Ciampi; formerly attr. Pergolesi) (I) (orch/?)
    EJS 288
    EJS 331
S7. "Marechiare" (di Giacomo; Tosti) (I) (orch/?)
    EJS 331

NOTES TO THE DISCOGRAPHY

I COMMERCIAL RECORDINGS, PUBLISHED BROADCASTS, LIVE, AND PRIVATE RECORDINGS

1-16: Sabajno is assumed to have conducted these first sessions, but he is not cited on the recording sheets. In addition to the three unpublished titles (nos. 3-5), the majority of missing matrix numbers correspond to recordings of Nina Garelli, Vincenzo Bettoni, Gino Lussardi, Orazio Cosentino, and others. Note that nos. 2 and 16 are sung a half-step below score pitch.

27: Sung a half-step below score pitch.

41: This song, long associated with Schipa, appeared originally in *La corte del amor*, a zarzuela. Italian Pathé 13080 is labeled "La de ojos azules," from the second phrase of the lyric; American Pathé 54075 (no. 51) is labeled "Mariposa," from the third phrase.

43 and 44: Only master cylinder numbers were reported for these two items, neither verified, so it is assumed that they were not published in any form.

48: Lateral-cut pressings (Actuelle) are found as master cylinder (matrix) number N-68384-1, while vertical-cut pressings (Pathé) are found as both E-68384-2 and -3, though all appear to be the same performance.

51: The master cylinder number is unreadable on pressings of this disc. See also no. 41.

54: See no. 41.

64: RCA Victor LPT 3010 cites the date 10 September, 1926 for published take -5.

78: Conductor as noted in the Victor ledgers. This is almost certainly *not* Charles A. Prince (1869-1937), for many years the studio director of the Columbia Graphophone (later *Phonograph*) Company, Bridgeport, Connecticut.

80: A test pressing of B-30088-1 exists, as issued on BMG/RCA CD 7969-2-RG.

81: See endnote for no. 78.

85: Transposed down a half-step. Extant test pressings, all bearing the same performance, have been reported variously as CVE-30910-3, -5, and -6. A Seward Galli-Curci LP (DPA-1041) and Voce-88 show take -5, while BMG/RCA compact disc 7969-2-RG shows take -6. A forthcoming Romophone Galli-Curci CD insists that the pressing used was marked take -3.

90: HMV DA 729 cites booh songs as traditional; the Winstanley and Tiberi discographies show Sibella as the composer of "La Girometta."

93 and 97: Both sung a half-step below score pitch.

98: Song from the Italian feature film *La città canora*.

122: Labeled "Cinematografia 'Angela della Strada.'" The song was written by Schipa for the 1928 Fox feature film, *Street Angel*, with Janet Gaynor and Charles Farrell.

126: Schipa wrote this song for the film *The Gaucho*, a 1927 Douglas Fairbanks feature produced by the Elton Corp. and released through United Artists.

128: A test pressing of CVE-42942-2 exists.

136-137: Assigned the domestic catalog number 1451, the record appeared only in dealer's catalogs as "Records in domestic series. Listed in U.S. Foreign catalogs only."

138-139: Both CS-81053 and BS-81054 are listed as "personal recordings" in the company register. Judging from the dim piano accompaniment of the "Chi se nne scorda 'cchiù" (of which a test pressing exists, take unknown), the records were obviously made for some special purpose. "Music Notes," in the *New York Times* (31 January, 1934, p. 21:1), reported that Schipa was to supervise the rehearsal of a marionette show that morning, "when two of Podrecca's puppets costumed by Mme. Pangoni of the Metropolitan [Opera] will 'impersonate' the tenor as Nemorino in 'Elisir d'Amore' and in full dress in a Neapolitan song." The show, *The Piccoli of Podrecca*, was playing at the Ambassador Theater in New York City. "Unaccompanied phonograph records of these airs made by Schipa for the purposes" (sic), the article continued, "will be used with the puppets in a public performance on Friday evening ..." Considering the date they were recorded (15 January, 1934) and their designated status as "personal recordings," CS-81053 and BS-81054 appear to be the two records in question. More than likely, the dim piano backing was meant to accommodate the live accompaniment of the show.

140-143: Issued on RCA Victor LPS LPT 3009 and LM 20088; no. 140 was also included on Italian HMV QBLP 5030. The takes used have not been determined.

144: A test pressing exists, take unknown. Issued on UORC LP 254, dated 1926. Pearl GEMM CD 9988 gives the correct date, take unidentified.

145: Matrix B-063338 has been reported as an unpublished Schipa recording, title unknown, based probably on the obvious gap between nos. 144 and 146, but in fact, the number was not assigned in the company register. If it

was used, it was probably recorded during the 8 April session.

146-147: Issued on RCA Victor LP LPT 3008, takes as noted.

151-162: The studio conductor of the 1930-1931 titles is unknown; the exact date of what appears to have been a second August session (nos. 161-162) has not been documented. No. 161 is labeled only "Cantodi Pedro" from Felipe Boero's *El matrero*, a three-act grand opera, libretto by Yamandú Rodríguez (Teatro Colón, Buenos Aires, 12 July, 1929).

163-166: The exact dates of these October, 1934 sessions are not known. The issued takes -3 of nos. 163 and 164 were dubbings, but it is not known which of the original recordings (takes -1 or -2) were used for the transfers. Nos. 165 and 166 were labeled as recorded in the Basilica del SS. Sacramento during the "XXXII Congreso Eucarístico Internacional" in Buenos Aires. The "Gesù, noi adoriamo" is labeled "Dedicado a Su Santidad Pio XI," while the "Christus vincit," composer unknown, was dedicated to the Vatican's official delegate to the Congress, "S. Em. El Card. E. Pacelli, Delgado" (Eugenio Maria Giuseppe Giovanni Pacelli, later Pope Pius XII, 1939-1958). Both records are announced by Schipa; Francesco de Pamphilis, possibly a cleric, provides the responses in the "Christus vincit," which include salutations to Augustín Pedro Justo, president of the Republic of Argentina from 1932 to 1938, Vittorio Emanuele III, the King of Italy, and Italian dictator Benito Mussolini. Schipa's announcement of "Christus vincit" concludes with the place and date of this Eucharistic Congress: Buenos Aires, 10-14 October, 1934. Twelve-inch Argentine Victor 36128 was issued with a special, decorative red label, although the 36000 series was generally black-label.

168: Marked "Dedicato alla figlia del tenore Schipa" on the recording sheet.

169: Marked "Dedicato a Federico Longás" on the recording sheet.

170: Listed elsewhere as matrix BM 1341-2. Marked "Dedicato a P. Casals" on the recording sheet. Coupled on DA 1091 with no. 81.

171: Marked "Dedicato alla madre del tenore Schipa" on the recording sheet.

173: Coupled on DA 1110 with no. 70.

176: The recording date for take -2 is provisional.

177: Both takes -2 and -3 have been reported as published. The recording sheet shows take -3 as issued on DB 1723.

179: Take -1 shown as "broken."

180: The recording sheet show 2M 485-2 as a twelve-inch transfer from an unlisted ten-inch "OM"-prefix master.

182: Take -1 shown as "broken."

188: Precise dates could not be assigned to all of the individual parts of the *Don Pasquale*. Matrices 2M 812-2, 2M 815-1, 2M 816-1, 2M 818-1, 2M 828-2, and 2M 829-1 are marked "broken" on the recording sheet; 2M 831-2 is marked "damaged." The exact date of recording (6 October, 1932) is uncertain for 2M871-2 and 2M 872-1. 2M 829-3, the take used by Victor, is not shown on the recording sheet.

189: 0M-873-1 rejected; -2 "spoiled in bath." See the issued rerecording of this title, no. 199.

190: 0M 883-2 marked "spoiled in bath." Take -1 was replaced by 0M 1280-2 on DA 1300: see no. 198.

191-197: Studio recordings (not soundtrack transfers) from the 1932 feature film *Tre uomini in frac*. For the four Paris recordings, nos. 194-197, Pearl GEMM CD 9988 incorrectly cites "Bertily" as the conductor: M. E. Bervily made a number of recordings for French HMV in 1929 with the orchestra of the Théâtre des Bouffes-Parisiens, with which he was apparently associated. No. 192 is an unpublished French version of no. 193: 0M 885-1 is marked "rejected." 0M 884-2, and 885-2 are marked "spoiled in bath." The (French) face-numbers for nos. 195 and 196 have not been traced.

198: 0M 1280-2 replaced the original (issued) 0M 883-1 on DA 1300: see no. 190.

199: The accompaniment of the published master, OM 1281-2, is noted on the recording sheet as members of the Scala Orchestra, but in fact Schipa is backed here by a small "jazz" orchestra. A group of Scala musicians may have been selected for the occasion, however. See also no. 189. 200: Recorded in Naples.

201: Matrix 0W 2034-2 was issued on DA 1350 in February, 1934 and replaced later that year by 0W 2484-1 (no. 214).

202: Two masters, probably takes -3 and -4, are marked as having been sent to Hayes. The *Piedigrotta* was an annual Neapolitan song festival to which songs were submitted as competitive entries.

207: *La canzone di ognuno* was a review ("revista"). The song title is given in the company register as "M'hai detto di no!," but has made its way into print variously as "M'ha detto: 'No!'" and "M'ha detto di 'No!'" Caslar was the pseudonym of Casolaro Donato (1888-1959).

209: 0W 2110-1 and -2 were rejected English-language versions of no. 208.

214: See also no. 201. Both takes of OW 2484 have been reported as issued on DA 1350, but the recording sheet shows only one take recorded.

218-219: Songs used in the Italian feature film *Angeli senza paradiso*.

222: The composer may be Ermete Liberati (1902-1960).

223: Probably labeled "Cuandu te llai la faace." Tiberi gives the title as "Cuando te llai la facce." Pearl GEMM CD 9988 cites take -2, but according to the recording sheet, only a single take was recorded and issued.

224: *La Principessa Liana* was Schipa's own operetta, to a Venetian libretto by G. Rocca. The work apparently premiered at the Teatro Lirico on 1 May, 1935 (2 performances) and was heard again at the Teatro Greco, Lecce, on 6 June, 1935 and Teatro Vittorio Emanuele, Torino on 4 May, 1936. An EIAR broadcast from June, 1936 could not be verified in Gualerzi and Roscioni's *50 Anni di opera lirica alla RAI, 1931-1980*(Torino: ERI/RAI, 1980). All of the stage performances have been documented as conducted by the composer–Schipa reaffirmed this in a 1963 interview (see no. 322b). A "Barcarola veneziana" is noted on the recording sheet as 0BA 1316-1, issued as DA 1486 (coupled with no. 126), but that matrix does not belong to Schipa and simply confuses 0BA 1316 for 0BA 1314.

226-229: Studio recordings (not soundtrack transfers) from the 1937 feature film *Vivere!* Matrix 0BA 1564-1 is also noted in the company register as having been issued on DA 1530.

230: Song from the Italian feature film *Re di denari*.

231: Studio recording (not a soundtrack transfer) from the 1937 feature film *Vivere!* The entry following matrix 0BA 1696 reads "W252ST repeat" on the recording sheet, its meaning unclear.

234-235 and 238-239: Issued versions of these four songs appeared on HMV DA 1565 and DA 1592 (nos. 244-247). Conductor Avitabile, first name unknown, directed a number of popular music recordings for Italian HMV as early as 1929.

240-241: Studio recordings (not soundtrack transfers) from the 1938 feature film *Chi è più felice di me?*

243: Studio recording (not a soundtrack transfer) from the 1938 feature film *Chi è più felice di me?*

244-247: See nos. 234-235 and 238-239.

248-250: Studio recordings (not soundtrack transfers) from the feature film 1937 *Vivere!* These are alternate German and French versions of nos. 229 and 226, respectively. Contrary to published sources and the recording sheet, "Wo ist mein kleines Mädel?" has also been reported as "Wo ist mein kleines Mädchen?"

255: Take -2 is not noted on the recording sheet.

257: A studio recording (not a soundtrack transfer) from the 1938 feature film *Terra di fuoco.* OBA 2729 is noted on the recording sheet as "5-1-39 (27-10-38 transf.)"

258-259: Studio recordings (not soundtrack transfers) from the 1938 feature film *Terra di fuoco.* No information is given for matrices OBA 2730 and 2732 (14 September, 1938) in the company register, but both are likely to have been unpublished Schipa titles.

260 and 263: Studio recording (not a soundtrack transfer) from the 1938 feature film *Terra di fuoco.* 2BA 2814-1 is a transfer, dated 21 October, 1938, from the original ten-inch OBA 2740-?, recorded 15 September, 1938, and is labeled "Ave Maria #2 from *Terra di Fuoco.*"

266-267: Both labeled by aria title only and "Aria Antica." Takes -1 and -2 of OBA 2912 have been reported as published, but the recording sheet notes only take -1 as issued on DA 5362.

268-269: Songs from the Italian feature film *Napoli che non muore.* Tito Manlio was the pseudonym of Domenico Titomaglio.

270-277: Few of the 1942 recordings carry (issued) take numbers on the recording sheet; none is dated there more precisely. Only a few commercial pressings have been examined.

278-293: Of the 1950 and 1953 recordings, only nos. 278-280 have been verified as first takes in the recording sheet. After the introduction of magnetic tape mastering at EMI, circa October, 1948, takes -1 and -1A (thought in this case to designate *tape transfers* of the same performances) seem to

predominate. No. 287 is a song from the Italian feature film *Addio mia bella Napoli.*

294-301: In the compilers' opinion, the American and Canadian LP issues of these songs, as issued on the Richmond label, have been transferred from tape nearly a half-step high, perhaps unwittingly.

302-307: Melodiya D004168 is an eight-inch LP. The bracketed numbers are the LP matrix numbers. Tiberi lists "'Na sera 'è maggio" among the Melodiya recordings, confusing this for the "Marechiare." Schipa's 1957 tour of the Soviet Union found him concertizing in Moscow (Conservatory, 16 August, and Tchaikovsky Theater, 18 August), Leningrad (20 and 22 August, theaters unknown), and Riga (25 and 27 August, theaters unknown). In a 1963 interview (no. 322c) he explained that the trip had been sponsored by both the Italian and Soviet governments. It is thought that these seven selections may actually derive from Moscow broadcasts, but it has been assumed, owing to their commercial release on Melodiya, that they were in fact studio recordings, possibly intended for broadcast.

308: This extraordinary performance was reportedly recorded complete, but with many more or less "traditional" (pre-Bruno Walter) Met performance cuts in the recitatives. Sixteen excerpts (about 110 minutes), including the first two scenes of Act I virtually complete, were included on UORC 216, the fragmentary nature of which was the result of missing acetates. ANNA 1036 was a Ponselle recital and included only the first-act duet with Schipa. *Don Ottavio's* "Il mio tesoro," with the orchestral introduction intact, is all that has survived from Act II/ii.

309: This was the first of three performances of this *Werther* production. The label of UORC 221 credits the San Francisco Opera, 22 November, 1935, with Coe Glade as *Charlotte,* Gaetano Merola conducting. Arthur Bloomfield's *The San Francisco Opera: 1922-1978* (Sausalito, CA: Comstock, 1978), p. 66, noted that, except for Schipa, the San Francisco cast sang the opera in French: *Charlotte* is clearly being sung here in Italian. *Werther's* entrance is completed on EJS 371 with Schipa's 1942 studio recording of the aria (no. 277), patched in at the wrong speed. Pederzini's Act III "Letter Scene" was included on MDP 024 and on both Timaclub issues. See also the endnote for no. 316.

matrimonio segreto. The Act I excerpts were not given in score order on EJS 331. The "Sì, coraggio mi faccio" is complete as performed except for minor lapses in the continuity resulting from acetate breaks. Together, the two EJS LPS contain nearly 90 percent of the first act as broadcast.

318: A 31 October, 1959 Volendam recital has been documented, but whether any excerpts from it were recorded or published in any form, or if any of the three items attributed to 3 November, 1959 (no. 319) were actually taken from the 31 October recital, remains uncertain.

319: The Eklipse CD recital cites "Frank" Beeldsnijder as Schipa's pianist for the 31 October, 1959 concert in Volendam, Holland: it is likely, therefore, that Beeldsnijder also accompanied the 3 November, 1959 Dutch broadcast excerpted here. The unidentified "Canzone napoletana" may be from 31 October (no. 318).

320: This 3 October, 1962 recital was Schipa's first American concert appearance in almost fourteen years (his last had been in Los Angeles on 10 December, 1948). The concert was advertised in the *New York Times* as standing room only and the hall was indeed packed to the aisles. The National Music Theater LP (LP-100) claims that the Town Hall material was drawn from at least two recitals, recorded "during October and November 1962," but Schipa gave only a single farewell recital in New York. The reviews quoted in the liner notes are all dated 4 October, 1962. See also the endnote for no. 321.

Note that the National Music Theater LP was pressed by American Columbia (matrices XTV 86900-1B/86901-1B) in excellent sound.

The *Werther* aria (no. 320p) is listed as November, 1962 on Rubini GV 129. Both the Rubini and National Music Theater LPS list the aria as sung in Italian (as "Ah, non mi ridestar") but this is not the case.

The interview (no. 320q) is mentioned by Francis Robinson (see the endnote for no. 322a), but is not known to have been recorded or published in any form.

The *L'elisir d'amore* (e), *Don Pasquale* (f), and *L'Arlesiana* (o) arias were sung a half-step below score pitch, while the *Martha* (g) and *Werther* (p) were transposed down a whole-step.

310: Only the second act of this season premiere *Manon* was broadcast. The source of EJS 227 was the official NBC acetates (two sixteen-inch sides, numbered ENG. 183 9-37, broadcast no. 9-263), which coupled the excerpt with installments of *Pepper Young's Family* and *David Harum.*

311-312: Source and date unverified. Dated 1942, this German material appeared on Melodiya M10-43189-90, a 1981 Schipa LP recital, crediting Raucheisen as accompanist. The notes to the Eklipse CD are quite emphatic about dates (1939) and personnel, as reflected in the listing above. The Melodiya LP, moreover, contains single performances of the Scarlatti aria, Tosti's "Ideale," Sadero's "Fa la nanna bambin," and Ciampi's "Nina," so it is not clear from which of the two sets these derive. See also nos. 313 and 315.

313: Source and date unverified. Melodiya M10-43189-90 includes this song, undated, with Priegnitz given as the accompanist. Whether it was performed during Schipa's 1939 Berlin tour or slightly later (circa 1942) has not been determined. See also nos. 311-312 and 315.

314: This *Don Giovanni* appeared on EJS 558 complete as broadcast (about 40 minutes). Act II of this season-opener was scheduled to air nationally over CBS, but the last verse and coda of Schipa's "Il mio tesoro" are heard in the background of network announcements and the final sign-off. This was the first in a series of four live Municipal Opera House broadcasts during the 1941 St. Louis Grand Opera Association spring season—the company's fourth. Critic Herbert W. Cost of *Musical America* is heard in commentary alongside an unnamed CBS announcer.

315: Source and date unverified. Melodiya M10-43189-90 assigns the date 1942 and credits Marszalek (*Marschalek*) as conductor: see also the endnotes for nos. 311-312 and 313.

316: There were four performances of this production, conducted variously by de Fabritiis and Santarelli, the first on 23 January, 1948. The excerpts featured on Cetra DOC 16 are unknown. See David Hamilton's "Discoveries" in the *ARSC Journal,* 18/1-3 (1986), pp. 249-250 for details of this and the 1934 *Werther* (no. 309) long-playing issues.

317: This was the first of four performances of this La Scala production of *Il*

321: The private tape on which this concert performance has circulated claims only that it is a November, 1962 *Chicago* concert, Amato accompanying. It was poorly recorded from the audience and is clearly one of the 1962-1963 farewell tour recitals. Schipa's itinerary for 1962 included only the Town Hall recital in New York City and a 1 November, 1962 recital at the Columbus Theater, Providence, Rhode Island; his last appearance in Chicago was in concert at Orchestra Hall on 6 November, 1948. The latter may be the true source: note that the performances on the private tape and the National Music Theater LP are *not* from the same concert. Schipa's last recitals took place in 1963, in New Zealand (Auckland, 24 January), the U.S. (Los Angeles, 8 February), Italy (Viareggio, sometime in August), and Portugal (Cascais on 4 September, Lisbon on 24 September), but it is not known if any of these concerts were transcribed in any form. Considering the efforts to interview Schipa prior to the Los Angeles recital (see no. 322b), the 8 February Philharmonic Auditorium concert seems the likeliest choice. See also the endnote for No. 320.

The *L'elisir d'amore* (e) and *Don Pasquale* arias were sung a half-step below score pitch, while the *Martha* (g) was transposed down a whole-step.

322a: In the eighteen-minute program from 1962, introduced by Milton Cross and conducted by Francis Robinson, then assistant manager of the Metropolitan Opera, Schipa discusses, among other things, the link between repertory and vocal longevity, Toscanini, *Tosca*, the premiere of *La rondine*, and sings, unaccompanied, the first phrases of the *Werther* "Ah, non mi ridestar" (perfectly in pitch, lowered his customary half-step!). The excerpt on Rubini GV 29 is labeled "Short interview with Schipa [in] 1962," but in fact, contains all of Schipa's comments. Probably prerecorded, the interview itself was embedded in one of Robinson's series of Met *Intermission Features*, *Biographies in Music*, this one broadcast during an *Aida* matinee. Excerpts from Schipa's recordings were featured throughout, along with a summary of his life and career and Robinson's usual flights of critical appraisal. The *New York Times* radio log for 9 December, 1962 described the program only as Robinson "commenting and playing recordings of Tito Schipa." One statement by Schipa, "I never forced my voice. I never sang what I could not sing. That is my only secret," is introduced by Robinson as *spoken* in an interview granted prior to the Town Hall recital (see no. 320q), but appears to be *recreated* here for the benefit of Robinson's audience (it was also paraphrased by Schipa in his 1963 interviews, nos. 322b-c). It is very doubtful that this snippet was taken from the actual Town Hall interview, which is not known to exist in any form. The detached quote was also included in the Rubini GV 29 excerpt.

322b: The January, 1963 interview was undertaken to publicize Schipa's 8 February, 1963 recital at the Los Angeles Philharmonic Auditorium, one of several stops in what would prove to be his international "farewell tour." The material was prerecorded for broadcast on two regularly-scheduled KFAC programs, *Italian Holiday* (3 February, 1963) and *World of Opera* (date unknown). Contact with Schipa was made through Mme. Elvira Curci-Caccia, the widow of deceased singing teacher Gennaro Mario Curci, the brother-in-law and self-proclaimed teacher of soprano Amelita Galli-Curci.

In the brief, 40-second opening statement written for him by Howard Rhines, Schipa mentions his own sense of professional satisfaction and acknowledges the singer's debt to recording. "I assure you," he observes in a reference to his own legacy, "I am proud of my contribution to the literature of recorded music."

Rhines' introduction (1:44) to the informal, open-microphone preparatory session reviews the circumstances of Schipa's visit to the KFAC studios. Also noted is the fact that one spot in the session has been edited: "In his answers to the first question," Rhines tells us, "Mr. Schipa was both repetitive and hesitant," so it was assumed that "he would display himself better if we eliminated that pause and the repetition."

The seventeen-minute preparatory session, in both English and Italian, is a somewhat chaotic rehearsal for the recording of the interview that would eventually air over KFAC prior to Schipa's Los Angeles appearance. Schipa talks about *Bel Canto*, breathing, the kinship of singing to speech, projection, voice placement, resonance, diction, "natural" singing, and the singer's obligation to leave an audience with some understanding of that which has been sung. Schipa's stated preference for the concert stage, where a singer can better convey "intentions and feelings," is tempered by

Mme. Curci, who is worried that opera fans may be offended! Schipa also addresses a few more straightforward matters: his fidelity to the musical text, his own compositions—two masses, the operetta *La Principessa Liana* (see no. 224), and many songs—conducting, and his program for the 8 February concert (see also no. 321). Finally, his opening statement is recorded, after Princi records his own introduction to the **Italian Holiday** program. There is much discussion about whether to record the statement in English, Italian, or both (Schipa's English was poor and required scripting). Several phrases and sections prompted rerecording.

The final recording of the interview was brief (4:55), with a few retakes. In addition to the topics rehearsed at length in the preparatory session, Schipa mentions his farewell tours, his plans never to retire(!), and his surprisingly varied musical education. To young singers he offers familiar advice: don't force the voice and sing only the repertory appropriate to it (see also no. 322a).

Rhines' after-interview summary reveals that, as a singer, Schipa's favorite composers were Donizetti and Massenet and that his favorite Dulcamara (*L'elisir d'amore*) was bass Salvatore Baccaloni.

The Schipa material was recorded at the KFAC studios on Wednesday, 30 January, 1963, beginning at about 10:20 a.m., while Rhines' material was obviously recorded slightly later.

322c: The thirty-minute March 1963 broadcast was built around the tenor's recordings and the comments of "host and annotator" Wells. The interview with Schipa is fifteen minutes long and was clearly prerecorded in another location—complete with traffic noise. Schipa discusses his career, concert versus operatic singing, a debilitating fall in Milan a few years before, his 1910 (sic) debut and early career in Italy, the chore of singing *Cavaradossi*, performing under Toscanini's baton, his nineteen seasons in the U.S., Mozart, his favorite leading ladies, the 1957 tour of the Soviet Union, and teaching in Rome, as well as his (unrealized) plans to mount an eight-city tour of the U.S. in 1963-1964, to open a studio for teaching (also discussed in John Ardoin's 1964 interview with the singer, "Quote-Unquote [Tito Schipa]"), and to eventually tour Asia. Without so much as a pause, he names *Werther* as his favorite stage role (see also no. 322b).

There are undoubtedly other extant, privately-published (and perhaps unpublished) interviews with Schipa not listed here.

323: EJS 331 cites the date 2 September, 1964 for these recordings, but their source has not been verified. According to Renzo D'Andrea's *Tito Schipa nella vita, nell'arte, nel suo tempo*, Schipa was in Lecce during the winter of 1963-1964 and arrived back in New York on 4 February, 1964. He took up residence at 70/71 Groton Street in Forest Hills, Long Island, the same New York suburb to which Edward J. Smith, the producer of the "Golden Age of Opera" (GAO) series, would move in November, 1964 (68/34 Fleet Street). Schipa remained in Long Island through December, 1964 at which point he went to Italy for Christmas, returning to the United States sometime in late December, 1964 or early January, 1965 to meet his final illness. It is entirely possible, given his friendship with Smith and the latter's residence in September, 1964 (84/25 Elmhurst Avenue, Elmhurst, Long Island), that these 2 September, 1964 recordings were made by Smith somewhere in the New York area. Schipa's accompanist has not been identified.

It has been suggested that the two *La rondine* arias were made at Smith's suggestion precisely because Schipa created the role of *Ruggero* in Monte Carlo on 27 March, 1917. John Ardoin, in "Quote-Unquote," quotes Schipa as saying "This is an important year for me, the 50th anniversary of my first recordings (sic). I hope to celebrate this fall by making a new record, perhaps including arias from Puccini's *La rondine*, which I sang in at its world premiere." This description fits EJS GAO 331 closely, down to the probable date of the recordings.

The *Rondine* (a-b), *Iris* (d), *Fedora* (e), and *Paride ed Elena* (g) arias were all sung a whole-step below score pitch.

324: Vocal exercises performed by Schipa, probably to his own (piano) accompaniment. Announcements, in Italian, have been added between exercises by an unknown speaker. This may have been a prerecorded broadcast, though the private tapes have clearly been transferred from a vinyl pressing. It is difficult to date the scales and arpeggios from Schipa's voice, which had retained much of its youthful sound and had been exceptionally well-recorded for the occasion.

LONG-PLAYING REISSUES OF THE COMMERCIAL RECORDINGS

A selective list of long-playing reissues either currently available on compact disc or worth pursuing on vinyl. Everything listed is or was available internationally. However, only collections offering essential or unique repertory, and only those bearing acceptable transfers, have been included. LPs and CDs which include only live, broadcast, or private materials are given in that section of the discography (nos. 308-324).

For a detailed account of the many early long-playing Schipa issues released by RCA Victor in North and South America, the Gramophone Company, Ltd. in Italy and Germany, Scala, Famous Records of the Past (Jack L. Caidin), Eterna, TAP (Edward J. Smith), and other minor labels, all long out of print, see the Winstanley & Hutchinson Schipa discography in *The Record Collector*, pp. 100-102.

LPs

"Tito Schipa, Tenor" ["The World's Leading Interpreters of Music-Vocalists"]
Melodiya M10-43189-90 [U.S.S.R.]
Contents: 7; 16; 69; 72; 93; 117; 128; 130; 213; 215; 311a-c; 311e-g; 312a-c; 312e-g; 313; 315b.

"Tito Schipa at Town Hall"
National Music Theater LP 100 [U.S.A.]
Contents: 320a-p.

"Tito Schipa"
Preiser "Lebendige Vergangenheit" LV 185 [Austria]
Contents: 1; 56 (tk 6); 66 (tk 7); 68 (tk 8); 71; (tk 10); 72-73; 84 (tk 8); 95-97; 103; 105; 116; 128 (tk 1); 129-130.

"Tito Schipa II"
Preiser "Lebendige Vergangenheit" LV 219 [Austria]
Contents: 58 (tk 20); 67; 69; 77; 79; 82 (tk 7); 83 (tk 8); 85 (tk 1); 93-94; 112; 115; 117-118.

II FILMOGRAPHY

F1-F2: The first of the two Paramount shorts—incorrectly referred to as "Vitaphone" shorts in several published sources—features Schipa singing "Una furtiva lagrima" from Donizetti's *L'elisir d'amore*, Barthélemy's "Chi se nne scorda 'cchiù," and Schipa's own "I Shall Return." The second short (later distributed for American television by National Telefilm Associates, Inc. [NTA]), features "M'appari" from Flotow's *Martha* and Padilla's "Princesita" from *La corte del amor*.

F3: *Tre uomini in frac* was shot in three different versions: in Italian (*Tre uomini in frac*), French (*Trois Hommes en Habit*), and English (*Three Lucky Fools*, aka *I Sing for You Alone*). Excerpts from the soundtrack were issued on two Edward J. Smith LPS: EJS 288 and EJS 331.

F4: Released in the U.S. as *To Live* (Cine Roma, New York City, 14 November, 1938).

F5: Released in the U.S. as *Who is Happier than I?* (Cine Roma, New York City, 5 February, 1940).

F10: Released in the U.S. as *The Life of Donizetti* (Cinema Verdi, New York City, 25 April, 1952). The screenplay was written by Novarese Mastrocinque.

F11: Released in the U.S. as *Mad About Opera* (Little Cine Met, New York City, 5 April, 1950). Clips of the singers, all playing themselves, were later incorporated into the 1951 British remake, Soho Conspiracy (no. F13). Schipa sings the "Serenata" from Rossini's *Il barbiere di Siviglia*. The screenplay, after a story by Mario Monicelli and Steno, was written by Steno, Giovanna Sorie, and director Costa.

F13: The clips of Bechi, Gigli, Gobbi, and Schipa used in this film were taken from the original Italian version of the film, *Follie per l'opera* (no. F11).

"Tito Schipa III"
Preiser "Lebendige Vergangenheit" LV 247 [Austria]
Contents: 61 (tk 6); 62 (tk 5); 132-137; 168-172; 174-175.

"Tito Schipa IV"
Preiser "Lebendige Vergangenheit" LV 277 [Austria]
Contents: 54 (tk 16); 55 (tk 8); 57; 63 (tk 6); 64 (tk 5); 65 (tk 5); 70 (tk 14); 98-102; 104; 106-107.

"Tito Schipa V"
Preiser "Lebendige Vergangenheit" LV 1305 [Austria]
Contents: 74; 76; 108-111; 113-114; 119-127.

"Tito Schipa VI"
Preiser "Lebendige Vergangenheit" LV 1337 [Austria]
Contents: 178-179; 181-187; 191; 193-194; 197-198; 199; 207; 214.

"Around the World in Music - Tito Schipa: Spain Vol. 2"
RCA Victor LPT 3008 (10-inch LP); EPBT 3008 (45 rpm) [U.S.A.]
Contents: 55 (tk 8); 65 (tk 5); 78 (tk 7); 107-108; 132; 146 (tk 2); 147 (tk 2).

"Around the World in Music - Tito Schipa: Italy Vol. 2"
RCA Victor LPT 3009 (10-inch LP); EPBT 3009 (45 rpm) [U.S.A.]
Contents: 62 (tk 5); 102; 119; 135; 140 (tk ?); 141 (tk ?); 142 (tk ?); 143 (tk ?).

"Around the World in Music - Tito Schipa: Latin America Vol. 2"
RCA Victor LPT 3010 (10-inch LP); EPBT 3010 (45 rpm) [U.S.A.]
Contents: 54 (tk 16); 57 (tk 8); 63 (tk 6); 64 (tk 5); 74 (tk 6); 91; 104; 133.

"Tito Schipa [The Milan Recordings of 1913-14]"
Rubini GV 29 [U.K.]
Contents: 1-2, 6-16; 320p; 322a.

"Tito Schipa (Volume Two)"
Rubini GV 564 [U.K.]
Contents: 17; 19-21; 24-31; 33; 37.

"Great Singers"
Voce VOCE-88 [U.S.A.]
Contents: 85 (tk 5).

COMPACT DISCS

"Tito Schipa, Tenor"
Baskerville "Great Voices, Volume 3" [U.S.A.]
Contents: 1; 2; 23; 26; 48; 68 (tk 5); 71; 72; 83 (tk 8); 84 (tk 2); 93; 97; 124; 130; 188 [6-7]; 199; 232-233; 269; 295; 308.

"Tito Schipa: Mozart - Massenet - Donizetti - Handel" [RCA Victor Vocal Series]
BMG/RCA 7969-2-RG [U.S.A.]
Contents: 54 (tk 16); 56 (tk 6); 57 (tk 8); 58 (tk 20); 66 (tk 7); 67; 80 (tk 1); 82 (tk 7); 85 (tk 6?); 94; 97; 104; 112; 115 (CVE-38381-1); 117-119; 128 (tk 1); 135; 139; 301.

"Tito Schipa in Opera, 1939-1941"
Eklipse EKR CD41 [U.K.]
Contents: 1; 25; 310b; 314b.

Tito Schipa - Opera Arias
EMI CDH 7632002 [U.K.]
Contents: 2; 6-7; 11-13; 48; 167; 176-177; 203-204; 211-212; 232-233; 266.

[Tito Schipa]
EMI CDM 7692382 [Italy]
Contents: 174-175; 183; 214-215; 217; 245-246; 253; 272-273; 285.

"Don Pasquale, 1932 - Tito Schipa"
Music Memoria 30231 [France]
Contents: 188 [other material unconfirmed]

[Tito Schipa]
Nuova Era 2327-9 [Italy: 3 CDS]
Contents: 2; 6; 8-9; 13-16; 57 (tk 8); 58 (tk 20); 66 (tk 7); 68 (tk 8); 72; 82 (tk 7); 83 (tk 8); 85 (tk 1); 89; 93; 98; 102-104; 107; 112; 115-119; 122; 126; 128-130; 134-135; 154; 157; 164; 167; 172-173; 176; 181; 184-185; 188 (excerpts); 204-206; 213; 215; 232-233; 244; 251-252; 262.

"Tito Schipa [I]: Operatic Arias and Encores"
Pearl GEMM CD 9322 [U.K.]
Contents: 54 (tk 16); 56 (tk 6); 61 (tk 6); 66 (tk 7); 68 (tk 8); 71; 73; 79; 82 (tk 7); 83 (tk 8); 93; 97; 101; 107; 112; 128 (tk 1); 130; 167; 178.

"Tito Schipa Vol. II"
Pearl GEMM CD 9364 [U.K]
Contents: 62 (tk 5); 67; 69; 72-73; 84 (tk 2); 85 (tk 1); 87; 95-96; 99; 102-103; 105-106; 116-119; 121; 205-206; 213.

"Tito Schipa [III]: Rare [Little-Known] Recordings (1918-1957)"
Pearl GEMM CD 9988 [U.K.: 2 CDS]
Contents: 34; 75; 90; 98; 100; 113-114; 121; 144; 174-179; 181; 191; 193; 195-196; 198; 199; 206-208; 214; 220-221; 222-225; 236-237; 248-250; 254; 261; 265-266; 268-269; 302; 303-307; ?311d; ?312; 312g.

"Tito Schipa IV: Operatic Recordings 1913-1942"
Pearl GEMM CD 9017 [U.K.]
Contents: unknown

"Tito Schipa"
Pearl GEMM CD 9183 [U.K.: forthcoming]
Contents: 52 (tk 16); 53 (tk 8); 55 (tk 8); 61 (tk 6); 62 (tk 5); 63 (tk 5); 72 (tk 6); 74 (tk 4); 76 (tk 7); 79 (tk 9); 85; 89; 106; 107; 111; 112; 124; 125; 134; 135; 148; 152 (tk 2); 153; 167; 272

[Tito Schipa]
Ricordi CDOR-9055 [Italy]
Contents: 66 (tk 7); 72; 82 (tk 7); 83 (tk 8); 93; 115; 128-129; 167; 183; 188 (excerpts); 205; 212-215; 247; 272.

"Amelita Galli-Curci: The Complete Acoustic Recordings, Volume 2, 1920-1924"
Romophone 81004-2 [U.K.]
Contents: 59 (tk 8); 67; 82 (tk 2); 83 (tk 2); 84 (tk 2); 85 (tk 1).

"Lucrezia Bori: The Victor Recordings (1914-25)"
Romophone 81016-2 [U.K.]
Contents: 95-96.

"Tito Schipa - Recordings, Film Sound Tracks, and Live, 1920-47"
Timaclub CLAMA CD-14 [Italy]
Contents: excerpts from 311-313; 315; F2; F3; F5; F6; and F7; other material unknown.

INDEXES TO THE DISCOGRAPHY

Reference is made in the indexes to discography numbers. "S"-prefixed discography numbers designate soundtrack excerpts from *Tre uomini in frac*, issued on EJS 288 and EJS 331.

Index of Recorded Titles

'A Canzone d' 'e stelle (Murolo; Tagliaferri) 175.

'A vucchella (d'Annunzio; Tosti) 119, 312.

Á Cuba (Schipa) 81.

A Granada–Canción Andaluza (Palacios) 65, 306, 321.

A la luz de la luna (Anton y Michelena) 113.

A la orilla de un palmar (Ponce) 64.

Addio mia bella Napoli (Manlio; Valente) 287.

Agnus Dei (Bizet) 38.

Ah! Sweet Mystery of Life (see *Naughty Marietta*).

Aimant la rose, le rossignol, Op. 2/2 (Rimsky-Korsakov) 181.

L'Alba separa dalla luce l'ombra (D'Annunzio; Tosti) 262.

Alma de Dios ["Canción del Vagabundo"] (Serrano) 109.

Amapola (Lacalle) 104.

Amarilli mia bella (Guarini; G. Caccini) 36.

Amavi tanto le mie rose (Galdieri; Schipa) 265.

L'amico Fritz (Mascagni)
Act II: Suzel buon dì ["Cherry Duet," pt. 1] 232.
Act II: Tutto tace ["Cherry Duet," pt. 2] 233.

Ammore canta (Murolo; Tagliaferri) 152.

Andaluza (Ochoa; Schipa) 186.

Andrea Chénier, Act IV: Come un bel dì di maggio (Giordano) 252.

Angela Mia (Schipa; Rapee; Pollack) 122.

L'Anguria (Liberati; Rocca) 222.

Anima e core (Manlio; D'Esposito) 289.

L'Arlesiana, Act II: [E la solita storia] … C'è nel sonno l'oblio ["Lamento di Federico"] (Cilea) 19, 115, 315, 320.

Ave Maria [adapted from the *Cavalleria rusticana* "Intermezzo"] (Mascagni) 120.

Ave Maria (Schipa) 39, 77, 88, 260, 263.

Ave Maria (Scott; Schubert) (see *Ellens Dritter Gesang*).

Ay, ay, ay (see Guyana).

¡Ay Chiquita! (Yradier) 60.

Il barbiere di Siviglia (Rossini)
Act I: Ecco ridente in cielo (Rossini) 20, 22, 66.
Act I: Se il mio nome saper (Rossini) 68.

Beddha e trista ["Bella e cattiva"] (Schipa; Preite) 225.

Bella ragazza delle trecce bionde ["Canto popolare"] 44.

Bello 'e papà (Manlio; Oliviero) 284.

Bimbo mio (Adonni; Bianchini) 243.

La bohème (Puccini)
Act I: Che gelida manina 2, 27.
Act IV: Sono andati? 52, 95.
Act IV: O! Dio, Mimì! 53, 96.

La bruja (Chapí) 40.

La Campana di San Giusto (Drovetti; Arona) 101.

Canción del Vagabundo (see "Alma de Dios").

Canto di Pedro (see *El matrero*)

Canto per te (Mancini; Galdieri; Caslar) 194.

Canzone appassiunata (Mario) 256.

Canzone d'abbrile (Murolo; Schipa) 216.

La canzone di ognuno: M'hai detto di no! (Galdieri; Caslar) 207.

Canzone Napoletana (?) 319.

Catina (Trevisan; Schipa) 179.

Cavalleria rusticana (Mascagni):
O Lola ch'ai di latti la cammisa ["Siciliana"] 13, 31
Intanto, amici, quà … Viva il vino ["Brindisi"] (Mascagni) 15.

Ce steva 'na vota (De Cescenzo) 86.

Che bene voglio 'a tte! (see *Piedigrotta*, 1933).

Index of Film Titles

Index of Conductors and Accompanists

Repertory

AUBER, Daniel	FRA' DIAVOLO
BARBIERI, Francisco	JUGAR CON FUEGO
BELLINI, Vincenzo	LA SONNAMBULA
BOITO, Arrigo	MEFISTOFELE
BORODIN, Aleksandr	PRINCE IGOR
CASALAINA, Riccardo	ANTONY
CHAPÍ, Ruperto	LA BRUJA
CILEA, Francisco	ADRIANA LECOUVREUR
	L'ARLESIANA
CIMAROSA, Domenico	IL MATRIMONIO SEGRETO
CORTINAS, César	L'ULTIMA GAVOTTA
DELIBES, Léo	LAKMÉ
DONIZETTI, Gaetano	DON PASQUALE
	L'ELISIR D'AMORE
	LA FAVORITA
	LINDA DI CHAMONIX
	LUCIA DI LAMMERMOOR
FLOTOW, Friedrich von	MARTHA
GARCIA MANSILLA, Eduardo	IVAN
GIORDANO, Umberto	FEDORA
	MARCELLA
GOUNOD, Charles	FAUST
	ROMEO AND JULIET

GUNSBOURG, Raoul	MANOLE
LEONCAVALLO, Ruggiero	ZAZÀ
MASCAGNI, Pietro	L'AMICO FRITZ CAVALLERIA RUSTICANA LODOLETTA
MASSENET, Jules	MANON WERTHER
MOZART, Wolfgang Amadeus	DON GIOVANNI THE MAGIC FLUTE
PAER, Ferdinando	IL MAESTRO DI CAPPELLA
PAISIELLO, Giovanni	IL BARBIERE DI SIVIGLIA
PUCCINI, Giacomo	LA BOHÈME MADAMA BUTTERFLY LA RONDINE TOSCA
RIMSKY-KORSAKOV, Nikolai	SADKO
ROSSINI, Gioacchino	IL BARBIERE DI SIVIGLIA
SANCHEZ DE FUENTES, Eduardo	IL VIANDANTE
SCHIPA, Tito	MESSA LA PRINCIPESSA LIANA
THOMAS, Ambroise	MIGNON
VERDI, Giuseppe	FALSTAFF RIGOLETTO LA TRAVIATA
WOLF-FERRARI, Ermanno	LE DONNE CURIOSE

Repertory in Chronological Order

1909	LA TRAVIATA	(G. Verdi)
1910	ZAZÀ	(R. Leoncavallo)
	ADRIANA LECOUVREUR	(F. Cilea)
	MIGNON	(A. Thomas)
	MEFISTOFELE	(A. Boito)
	RIGOLETTO	(G. Verdi)
	FAUST	(C. Gounod)
1911	LA BOHÈME	(G. Puccini)
	IL BARBIERE DI SIVIGLIA	(G. Rossini)
	DON PASQUALE	(G. Donizetti)
	IL MAESTRO DI CAPPELLA	(F. Paer)
	WERTHER	(J. Massenet)
	FEDORA	(U. Giordano)
	LA SONNAMBULA	(V. Bellini)
	CAVALLERIA RUSTICANA	(P. Mascagni)
	FRA' DIAVOLO	(D. Auber)
1912	LUCIA DI LAMMERMOOR	(G. Donizetti)
	LA FAVORITA	(G. Donizetti)
	ANTONY	(R. Casalaina)
	TOSCA	(G. Puccini)
1913	FALSTAFF	(G. Verdi)
1914	MADAMA BUTTERFLY	(G. Puccini)
	MARCELLA	(U. Giordano)
	MANON	(J. Massenet)
1915	LE DONNE CURIOSE	(E. Wolf-Ferrari)

1916	IVAN	(E. Garcia Mansilla)
	L'ULTIMA GAVOTTA	(C. Cortinas)
	L'ELISIR D'AMORE	(G. Donizetti)
1917	LAKMÉ	(L. Delibes)
	LA RONDINE	(G. Puccini)
1918	JUGAR CON FUEGO	(F. Barbieri)
	MANOLE	(R. Gunsbourg)
	IL BARBIERE DI SIVIGLIA	(G. Paisiello)
1919	LA BRUJA	(R. Chapí)
	L'AMICO FRITZ	(P. Mascagni)
	LODOLETTA	(P. Mascagni)
1921	LINDA DI CHAMONIX	(G. Donizetti)
	IL VIANDANTE	(E. Sanchez de Fuentes)
1923	MARTHA	(F. Flotow)
	ROMEO ET JULIETTE	(C. Gounod)
1930	SADKO	(N. Rimsky-Korsakov)
1935	LA PRINCIPESSA LIANA	(T. Shipa)
1936	IL MATRIMONIO SEGRETO	(D. Cimarosa)
	L'ARLESIANA	(F. Cilea)
1937	THE MAGIC FLUTE	(W. A. Mozart)

Selective Bibliography

Ardoin, John. "Quote-Unquote [Tito Schipa]," *Musical America*, 84/7 (September, 1964), p. 32.

Cantophone Institute, New York. *Great Masters School of Voice: Beginners' Bel Canto*. New York. Cantophone Institute, 1958.

Celletti, Rodolfo. "Schipa, Tito," in Celletti, Rodolfo, compiler. *Le Grandi Voci: Dizionario Critico-Biografico dei Cantanti con Discografia Operistica*. Roma: Istituto per la Collaborazione Culturale,1964, pp. 727-734.

_____. *Tito Schipa: A Biographical and Critical Sketch*. London: The Gramophone Co., Ltd., n.d. [1961].

D'Andrea, Renzo. *Tito Schipa nella vita, nell'arte, nel suo tempo*. Fasano di Puglia: Schena, 1981 (discography by Daniele Rubboli).

Douglas, Nigel. *Legendary Voices*. London: André Deutsch, 1992.

Ewen, David. *Living Musicians*. New York: H. W. Wilson, 1940.

_____. *Musicians Since 1900: Performers in Concert and Opera*. New York: H. W. Wilson, 1978.

Hutchinson, Tom. "An Outline of the Career of Tito Schipa," *The Record Collector*, 13/4-5 (June-July, 1960), pp. 77-89.

Kaufman, Helen L. and Eva vB. Hansl. *Artists in Music Today*. New York: Grossett & Dunlap, 1933.

Lauri-Volpi, Giacomo. *Voci parallele*. Milano: Aldo Garzanti, 1955; 2nd. rev. and enlarged ed. Roma: Aldo Garzanti, 1960.

Monaldi, Gino. *Cantanti celebri (1829-1929)*. Roma: Tiber, 1929.

Natan, Alex. *Primo Uomo: grosse Sänger der Oper*. Basil: Basilius Presse, 1963.

Sánchez-Torres, Enrique. *Fleta, Lázaro, Schipa, Anselmi: crítica y versos con opiniones importantes*. Madrid: B. Izaguirre, 1924.

Schipa, Tito. *Tito Schipa si confessa*. Roma: Pubblimusica, 1961 (introduction by Giacomo Lauri-Volpi; preface and biographical summary by Rodolfo Celletti; discography by Raffaele Vegeto).

Schipa, Tito Jr. *Tita Schipa*. Firenze: Nuova Grafica Fiorentina, 1993 (discography by Maurizio Tiberi).

Scott, Michael. *The Record of Singing, Volume Two: 1914-1925*. London: Duckworth, 1979/R: Boston: Northeastern University Press, 1993.

Sguerzi, Angelo. *Le stirpi canore*. Bologna: Bongiovanni, 1978.

Steane, J. B. *The Grand Tradition: Seventy Years of Singing on Record [1900-1970]*. London: Duckworth/New York: Scribner's Sons, 1974; 2nd ed., Portland, Oregon: Amadeus Press, 1993.

_____. *Voices, Singers & Critics*. London: Duckworth, 1992.

Winstanley, Sydney, and Tom Hutchinson. "Schipa Recordings," *The Record Collector*, 13/4-5 (June-July, 1960), pp. 90-109.

Index

(of persons, roles, operas, films)

INDEX

Photo Sources

Tito Schipa, Jr.: 1-12, 14, 16-28, 30, 31, 33-38, 64, 65; Metropolitan Opera Archives: 13, 43-45, 48, 49, 54, 57; Bill Ecker: 15, 32, 40, 46, 50, 55; Bill Park: cover, 29, 66; Lt. Col. James Alfonte: 39; Morton Photographs for San Francisco Opera: 41, 42, 51, 53, 56, 58, 60-63; Joseph Tomaselli: 47, 52, 59.

Index of Film Titles